Russia's Security Policy und

This book examines the evolution of Russia's security policy under Putin in the twenty-first century, using a critical security studies approach.

Drawing on critical approaches to security the book investigates the interrelationship between the internal-external nexus and the politics of (in)security and regime-building in Putin's Russia. In so doing, it evaluates the way that this evolving relationship between state identities and security discourses framed the construction of individual security policies, and how, in turn, individual issues can impact on the meta-discourses of state and security agendas. To this end, the (de)securitization discourses and practices towards the issue of Chechnya are examined as a case study.

In so doing, this study has wider implications for how we read Russia as a security actor through an approach that emphasizes the importance of taking into account its security culture, the interconnection between internal/external security priorities and the dramatic changes that have taken place in Russia's conceptions of itself, national and security priorities and conceptualization of key contemporary security issues. These aspects of Russia's security agenda remain somewhat of a neglected area of research, but, as argued in this book, offer structuring and framing implications for how we understand Russia's position towards security issues, and perhaps those of rising powers more broadly.

This book will be of much interest to students of Russian security, critical security studies and IR.

Aglaya Snetkov is senior researcher at the Center for Security Studies (CSS), ETH Zurich, Switzerland and has a PhD in Russian and East European studies from the University of Birmingham.

CSS Studies in Security and International Relations
Series Editor: Andreas Wenger
Center for Security Studies, Swiss Federal Institute of Technology (ETH), Zurich

The *CSS Studies in Security and International Relations* series examines historical and contemporary aspects of security and conflict. The series provides a forum for new research based upon an expanded conception of security and will include monographs by the Center's research staff and associated academic partners.

War Plans and Alliances in the Cold War
Threat perceptions in the East and West
Edited by Vojtech Mastny, Sven Holtsmark and Andreas Wenger

Transforming NATO in the Cold War
Challenges beyond deterrence in the 1960s
Edited by Andreas Wenger, Christian Nuenlist and Anna Locher

US Foreign Policy and the War on Drugs
Displacing the cocaine and heroin industry
Cornelius Friesendorf

Cyber-Security and Threat Politics
US efforts to secure the Information Age
Myriam Dunn Cavelty

Securing 'the Homeland'
Critical infrastructure, risk and (in)security
Edited by Myriam Dunn Cavelty and Kristian Søby Kristensen

Origins of the European Security System
The Helsinki Process revisited
Edited by Andreas Wenger, Vojtech Mastny and Christian Nuenlist

Russian Energy Power and Foreign Relations
Edited by Jeronim Perovic, Robert W. Orttung and Andreas Wenger

European-American Relations and the Middle East
From Suez to Iraq
Edited by Daniel Möckli and Victor Mauer

EU Foreign Policymaking and the Middle East Conflict
The Europeanization of national foreign policy
Patrick Müller

The Politics of Nuclear Non-Proliferation
A pragmatist framework for analysis
Ursula Jasper

Regional Organisations and Security
Conceptions and practices
Edited by Stephen Aris and Andreas Wenger

Peacekeeping in Africa
The evolving security architecture
Edited by Thierry Tardy and Marco Wyss

Russia's Security Policy under Putin
A critical perspective
Aglaya Snetkov

Russia's Security Policy under Putin

A critical perspective

Aglaya Snetkov

LONDON AND NEW YORK

First published 2015
by Routledge

2 Park Square, Milton Park, Abingdon, Oxon OX14 4RN
711 Third Avenue, New York, NY 10017,USA

Routledge is an imprint of the Taylor & Francis Group, an informa business

First issued in paperback 2016

Copyright © 2015 Aglaya Snetkov

The right of Aglaya Snetkov to be identified as author of this work has been asserted by her in accordance with sections 77 and 78 of the Copyright, Designs and Patents Act 1988.

All rights reserved. No part of this book may be reprinted or reproduced or utilised in any form or by any electronic, mechanical, or other means, now known or hereafter invented, including photocopying and recording, or in any information storage or retrieval system, without permission in writing from the publishers.

Notice:
Product or corporate names may be trademarks or registered trademarks, and are used only for identification and explanation without intent to infringe.

British Library Cataloguing-in-Publication Data
A catalogue record for this book is available from the British Library

Library of Congress Cataloging-in-Publication Data
Snetkov, Aglaya.
Russia's security policy under Putin : a critical perspective / Aglaya Snetkov.
  pages cm – (Css studies in security and international relations)
  Includes bibliographical references and index.
  ISBN 978-0-415-82143-8 (hardback) – ISBN 978-0-203-55939-0 (ebook) 1. National security–Russia (Federation) 2. Russia (Federation)–Foreign relations–21st century. 3. Putin, Aleksandr, 1953–
  I. Title.
  UA770.S527 2014
  355'.033047–dc23   2014020621

ISBN: 978-0-415-82143-8 (hbk)
ISBN: 978-1-138-20079-1 (pbk)

Typeset in Times New Roman
by Wearset Ltd, Boldon, Tyne and Wear

Contents

Acknowledgements	ix
List of abbreviations	x
1 Introduction	1
2 Analysing security in a non-Western context	14

PART I
1999–2000   29

3 Russia in crisis 1999/2000	31
4 Russia's number one threat: the securitization of Chechnya	46

PART II
2000–2004   63

5 The rebuilding of Russia	65
6 The 'normalization' of Chechnya	79

PART III
2004–2008   99

7 Russia as a strong state and a great power?	101
8 A 'rebuilt' Chechnya in a securitized North Caucasus?	114

PART IV
2008 — 135

9 Modernization, resecuritization and patriotic fervour: Medvedev and Putin — 137

10 Russia's policy towards the North Caucasus and Chechnya — 173

11 Conclusion — 188

Bibliography — 208
Index — 247

Acknowledgements

I would like to thank Dr David White, for his unwavering support and help throughout the process of writing my PhD thesis that forms the basis of this book, and especially for reading through copious drafts and ideas, even at the last minute. The administrative support of Marea Arries, Tricia Carr and Veta Douglas at the University of Birmingham was also essential, and was offered however late in the day I requested it. In addition, I acknowledge the ESRC for the provision of a scholarship in order to undertake this research. I would also like to thank Dr Galina Yemelianova for her help and assistance.

Special mention is deserved for Elena Golubinskaya in Moscow, for helping me to arrange my fieldwork trips and for offering advice and assistance with numerous administrative matters, and for everyone else I met along the way who have contributed to the writing of this book. There are too many people to mention individually, but I would like to thank you all for helping me along this long and often arduous journey. Additionally, I am very grateful to Andreas Wenger, and everyone else at the Centre for Security Studies, ETH Zurich for providing me with lots of support, advice and laughs over the last few years. Special thanks must also go to Professors Richard J. Overy and John Russell for championing me on and for making me feel like I could do this no matter what – thank you very much!

Finally, I would like to thank my family for always being there, and for supporting me along the way. I am also very grateful to my friends, Daniel Stunell, Jennifer Simon and Abigail Ratcliffe for their support and encouragement, and for very graciously agreeing to proofread my PhD thesis that forms the basis of this book, and for everyone else for cheering me on when I was turning this book into a manuscript. This book would not have been possible without the support of Stephen Aris, to whom I am forever grateful, thank you!

Abbreviations

APEC	Asia-Pacific Economic Cooperation
CIS	Commonwealth of Independent States
CS	Copenhagen School of Security
CSTO	Collective Security Treaty Organization
EU	European Union
IMF	International Monetary Fund
NATO	North Atlantic Treaty Organization
NRC	Norwegian Refugee Council
OIC	Organization of the Islamic Conference
OSCE	Organization for Security and Cooperation in Europe
PACE	Parliamentary Assembly of the Council of Europe
SCO	Shanghai Cooperation Organization
UN	United Nations
WMD	Weapons of Mass Destruction
WTO	World Trade Organization
YUKOS	Yuganskneftegaz Kuybyshevnefteorgsintez

1 Introduction

Although losing its superpower status with the end of the Cold War, Russia continues to be seen as a central player within international security. In recent years, for example, it has played a high-profile role in a number of pertinent security events, crises and developments. These include making use of its status as a Permanent Member of the UN Security Council to, alongside China, veto a number of UN resolutions on the Syrian civil war, the signing of the 'new' START agreement on nuclear arms reductions with the US in 2010, an armed conflict with Georgia over the independence of Abkhazia and South Ossetia in 2008, and most recently its role and actions during the 2014 Ukraine crisis, which saw the annexation of Crimea, and have led to the re-emergence of high-level tensions in its relationship with Europe and NATO.

In light of its continued, and often somewhat unpredictable and antagonistic, role within international security, understanding Russia as a security actor continues to attract attention. Indeed, the increasingly conscious effort by the Putin-led regime to take a more assertive line in its foreign security policy, and to reassert its 'great power status' in general, has been followed closely by both Russia-watchers and those interested in international security writ large (Mankoff 2012; Kanet 2011). In parallel, the internal political situation in Russia has also been a source of interest to the some of the same audiences, who have sought to understand the rise of the Putin regime, its political project and the extent of its control over all aspects of Russian life. In this way, the nature, and future trajectory, of Russia as both a domestic polity and a foreign policy actor remains a pertinent question for scholars, analysts and policymakers alike.

However, due to the divisions between academic disciplines, these two realms of interest – Russian foreign security policy and Russian domestic politics – have largely been treated separately from one another, creating an artificial divide between two facets of what this book sees as connected whole. The consideration of domestic and foreign policy as independent from one another is a trend that is noticeable – and increasingly recognized as problematic – with regard to scholarship on and the analysis of many state actors within the international system. It, however, seems particularly self-limiting for understanding and interpreting Putin's Russia, in which the interconnections between the regime's state-building project and both its domestic and foreign security policy have been publically asserted within official discourse, from the regime's first day in office through to its reactions to the mass-protests against the return of Putin to the Presidency in 2012.

Making Russia strong again – both domestically and internationally – was and, to a large extent, remains the stated prime objective of the Putin regime. The regime's efforts to this end have encompassed a domestic state-building project, efforts to both consolidate and expand the regime's power domestically, and regain the prestige of a 'great power' within the international system. And, as the Putin regime's policies, perceptions and reactions have evolved since 2000, there have been various shifts in its state-building macro-discourse, which, in turn, has both shaped, and been shaped by, changes in the self-identification and prioritizations of Russia as a security actor.

Taking this into account, this book sets out to investigate and account for the evolution of Russia's security policy since 2000, under the presidency of both Putin and Medvedev. It seeks to shed light on this subject by dispensing with the artificial separation of domestic and foreign policy. This study, rather, focuses on tracing the mutually-constituted relationship between Russian state identity and security discourses – both foreign and domestic – since Putin came to power. Not only does this study avoid the pitfalls of 'black boxing' the domestic from the foreign, and vice versa, by considering security policy in relation to the regime's wider state building political project, it also analyses domestic and foreign security policy as a coherent and interdependent whole around the internal-external security nexus.

To examine the mutually-constituted interrelationship between state identity and security prioritization discourses in Putin's Russia, this study traces its impact on a single security policy: Chechnya. And how, in turn, this single policy issue impacted on these macro-level discourses. By analysing this particular single-policy, this study aims to gain insight not only into this specific policy issue, but also how the interrelationship between state identity and security discourses impacted on, and was impacted by, the evolution of individual policy decisions and discourse. In this way, the ebbs and flows of Russia's discourses and policies towards Chechnya can be seen as illustrative of concurrent shifts in Russia's national state identity and security discourses and priorities.

On coming to power, the Putin regime depicted Chechnya as a major threat to the fundamentals of the modern Russia nation-state – its territorial integrity and national sovereignty, with the regime making direct connections between the 'Chechnya issue' and wider state identity and their political project to rebuild Russia from a 'weak' to a 'strong' state. Whilst no longer considered a pre-eminent security concern by the Putin regime, a strong emphasis on the wider regional instability and terrorism in the North Caucasus, of which Chechnya is an important part, remains evident in both state and security discourses. Taking this into account, this book seeks to explain how Chechnya's symbolic importance within Russian state identity and security discourses altered from representing an existential threat in the early 2000s to being held up as an example of a wider trend of successful state-building by the end of the decade. In other words, it seeks to account for how the image of Chechnya changed from that of a *state-breaker* to *state-maker* in official Russian discourse under Putin and Medvedev.

Furthermore, this study's longitudinal approach will enable the changes and continuity within the nature of Russia as security actor since 2000 to be assessed. It will trace the interrelationships between all these discourses – state identity, internal security, external security and single policy issue – across this period. And thus provide a contextualized account of how they came together to shape Russia as a security actor at a particular time, and hence how changes in these discourses influenced one another, and ultimately impacted on Russian security policy. Therefore, rather than presenting Russia or the Putin regime as a more or less fixed entity as is often the case, this longitudinal approach reveals that the nature of Russia as a security actor has evolved in a much more dynamic manner than is usually suggested.

Moving beyond the exernal-internal divide in analysing Russian security policy

There is an extensive body of literature on the directions, interests and priorities of Russian security policy under both Putin and Medvedev. Most of these studies are situated within the International Relations (IR) literature, and apply theories and concepts from this field to an empirical examination of Russian foreign and security policy. Such studies have focused on Russia's relations with the West in general (de Haas 2010; Kanet 2005), and its external relations with the US, NATO or the EU in particular (Hallenberg and Karlsson 2006; Trenin *et al.* 2008; Averre 2005; Kaveshnikov 2010; Pouliot 2010). Others are based on Russia's approach and role with regard to particular international security issue areas, such as the proliferation and reduction of nuclear weapons (den Dekker 2010; Cimbala 2009; Shoumikhin 2002), the international arms trade and arms control agreements (Lahille 2008), weapons of mass destruction (Tsypkin 2009) or energy security (Dellecker and Gomart 2011; Wood 2009; Hadfield 2008; Proedrou 2007). In response to Russia's renewed interest in what it considers as its region, a number of works have examined Russia's external relations with other post-Soviet states in general (Freire and Kanet 2012; Pirchner 2005), and more specifically with regard to Central Asia (Paramonov, Strokov and Stolpovski 2009), the increasingly problematic relations with its Western neighbours of Ukraine and Belarus (Nygren 2005), and growing tensions with states in the South Caucasus, and Georgia in particular (Nygren 2007a). Within this body of works, there is an implicit assumption that Russian security policy is largely the product of the external, or the international, rather than the internal, or Russia's domestic, context.

While fewer in numbers, a series of studies on Russia's internal security context have appeared in recent years. These cover a wider-range of topics, including the nature and dynamics of the Russian military and its reform (Vendil 2009; de Haas 2004), the power and the influence of the *siloviki* in Russia (Renz

4 *Introduction*

2006; Soldatov and Borogan 2010; Taylor 2007), the politics of security (Galeotti 2010) and questions of food and environmental security (Sedik *et al.* 2003; Funke 2005; Stuvøy 2010; Wegren 2011). Such works have highlighted the impact of corruption, elite politics, the inefficiency of Russian bureaucracy, the misuse of resources and structural constraints on internal security problems in Russia. They, however, largely considered the Russian domestic security context as distinct to the international context of Russian foreign security policy (Hedenskog *et al.* 2005).

Whilst both sets of work provide valuable insights into Russian security policy, they proceed from a self-imposed and artificial separation between the internal/domestic or the external/international spheres of the Russian policymaking context, resulting in assessments exclusively focused on one or the other. As such, the interconnections and interrelationship between the domestic and foreign contexts of Russian security policy remain under-analysed. This book seeks to contribute to this gap in understanding, by approaching its analysis of the evolution of Russian security policy since 2000 from a perspective that considers the domestic and foreign security policy contexts as interrelated around an internal-external security nexus, whereby the internal and external spheres impacts on, and are impacted by, one another. In this way, it seeks to make a contribution to the existent literature by providing a comprehensive account of the evolution of Russian security policy from 2000 to 2014.

A post-positivist account of the internal-external nexus in Russian security policy

In large part, the self-governing and largely artificial separation between the internal and the external context within the analysis of Russian security policy stems from the fact that most studies take their theoretical lead from the realist perspective in IR. In contemporary IR, a structural realist perspective remains the default approach to analysis. Within such perspectives, states are treated as 'black boxed' units within an international system defined by anarchy, whereby the behaviour of and interaction between these units becomes the sole focus of analysis, with this being determined by the shifting balance-of-power or order within the system. In other words, developments inside state units are excluded from the analysis, and deemed irrelevant to the task in hand: analysis of the structural determinants governing state's behaviour towards each other (e.g. Waltz 1979). Against this background, many studies of Russian security policy – either explicitly, or implicitly by virtue of the fact that they underlie many proclaimed a-theoretical works – take their lead from such assumptions, and thus focus on the external dimension and exclude the internal.

In recent years, and in large part seeking to escape this 'black boxing' of domestic factors, a number of studies have sought to provide a post-positivist reading of Russian security policy (Neumann 2005; Hopf 2005; Morozov 2008; Tsygankov 2005, 2007, 2013; Clunan 2009). Thus, rather than focusing on examining objective structural determinants of Russian security behaviour and relationships with other actors, these works have sought to address post-positivist inspired research questions relating to how Russia interprets itself, others and the contexts in which its functions, and how this came to impact on certain policy decisions and actions. An illustrative example of how this approach to the analysis of Russian security policy switches the focus of investigation from 'why' to 'how' questions is that such studies are not interested in whether Russia is objectively a 'Great Power' within the international system, but rather in 'how' Russia has sought to construct its identity as based on being a 'Great Power', and, in turn, how this impacts on its security policy. Hence, the focus is on the nature and interrelationship between state identity and security, and the key principles, norms, discourses and parameters within this relationship (Lomagin 2007; Kassianova 2001; Hopf 2005; Williams and Neumann 2000). These studies demonstrate the way in which particular identity constructions – such as the example above of Russia as a 'Great Power' – enable, but also constrain, foreign and security policy options and outcomes (Clunan 2009; Tsygankov 2013).

However, as with positivist research on Russian security, most of these studies focus primarily on Russia's external security policy (Blum 2008; Neumann 2005; Morozov 2008; Tsygankov 2005, 2007, 2013; Clunan 2009), with the analysis approached from a foreign policy perspective. Hence, while the adoption of a post-positivist perspective opens up the possibility of extending the focus of investigation to include how domestic dynamics influence on foreign policy, and vice versa, the majority of these studies have taken a unidirectional focus: how domestic state identity shapes foreign policy. Therefore, there is a lack of post-positivist research on Russia's internal security policy in relation to its wider state and security agendas, and which traces the interrelationship between the internal and external security context in a bidirectional perspective around an internal-external security nexus. This book sets out to address this gap in post-positivist analysis of Russian security policy. To do so, it draws on insights from the Critical Security Studies research agenda that has emerged in recent decades, and in particular securitization theory.

Critical security studies in non-Western contexts

Since the end of the Cold War, the Critical Security Studies research agenda has sought to introduce a greater range of issues, theoretical perspectives and methodological approaches to the study of security within IR (see Browning and McDonald 2011; Peoples and Vaughan-Williams 2010). Of particular relevance to this study, many of these works have focused on investigating the nature of domestic insecurities. Indeed, with a focus on issues such as terrorism (Jackson 2005: Closs Stephens and Vaughan-Williams 2009), modes of governance (Bigo 2002; Dillon and Reid 2001), biopolitics (Epstein 2007; Bell 2006; Elbe 2006), borders and migration (Hysmans 2006; Doty 2007; Salter 2006) and risk and resilience (Beck 2002; Aradau and Van Munster 2007), these studies have sought to challenge the traditional 'black boxing' of security as based exclusively on external threats to states. Instead, these scholars ground their analysis within processes that take place within the domestic domains of states.

Until recently, this research agenda has only, by and large, been applied to European, North American and other 'Western' contexts. However, in recent years, there have been increasingly calls from within the Critical Security Studies community for a greater engagement with non-Western contexts and experiences (see Bilgin 2010; Vuori 2008, 2010; Wilkinson 2007). Indeed, reflecting the widespread academic focus on global order change and the growing role played by non-Western actors within this new order during the last decade, it is increasingly acknowledged that it is no longer sufficient to examine questions of global security primarily, or exclusively, through the experience of West (see Agathangelou and Ling 2009; Bilgin 2008; Hobson 2007; Barkawi and Laffey 2006). This realization is leading to a shift in the focus within IR, whereby the study of non-Western contexts and the position of non-Western powers is no longer deemed as 'alternative' or considered secondary to our reading and understanding of global security, but is now seen as at the very heart of it (see Zakaria 2011; Kupchan 2012; Murray and Brown 2012). Against this background, it is being increasingly suggested that Western theoretical models and labels designed for study of security should also take into account the positions, views and interests towards questions of security held within these non-Western contexts (Bilgin 2010; Vuori 2008, 2010; Wilkinson 2007; Acharya and Buzan 2007; Tickner and Wæver 2009; Shilliam 2010, Shani 2008; Barkawi and Laffey 2006; Agathangelou and Ling 2009).

More specifically, this book seeks to build on the securitization model of security, as put forward by Buzan and Wæver in their foundational text: *Security: A New Framework for Analysis* (1998). According to the theory of securitization, all issues in official state discourse are either non-politicized (the state does not deal with it, and it is not an issue in the public debate), politicized (an issue that is part of public debate and policy) or securitized (an issue that is presented as an existential threat, and can be dealt with using measures outside normal politics), and 'any issue can end up on any part of the spectrum' (Buzan, Wæver and de Wilde 1998, p. 24).

Despite being the subject of vibrant and extensive theoretical debate over the last decade (McDonald 2008; Stritzel 2011; Van Munster 2007), the majority of both empirical and theoretical works using the securitization model have been based on cases from within Western, and particularly European, contexts. With some notable exceptions (e.g. Wilkinson 2007; Coskun 2008; Vuori 2008, 2010), few studies have tried to utilize the securitization model to investigate non-Western security contexts, or to refine the model theoretically on the basis of such cases. In addition, most works have focused on examining the securitization of an issue, while some have sought to analyse an initial desecuritization of an issue. There are, however, not many studies that have sought to examine the full cycle of (de)securitization, tracing an issue from its initial securitization throught to its complete desecuritization. This study seeks to consider the full cycle of (de)securitization by investigating not only the precise moments of securitization or desecuritization, but also the constituted processes, discourse and practices in between them.

In this context, this study represents an attempt to comprehensively operationalize theories and models from Critical Security Studies to the study of a 'non-Western' power. It argues that when operationalizing theoretical models of security in non-Western contexts – and in order to garner a more comprehensive reading of how actors such as the Russian state conceptualize their security policy – it is important to take into account not only the local contexts in which they operate, but also these actors' readings of statehood and security and the way in which their security principles and priorities evolve across time. In so doing, this book seeks to re-engage Critical Security Studies with the changing landscape of the IR discipline.

Methods, sources and data analysis

In view of its post-positivist theoretical perspective, an inductive and qualitative analytical approach was adopted here. As noted by Checkel, post-positivists 'are committed to a deeply inductive research strategy that targets the reconstruction of state/agent identity' (Checkel 2004, p. 231). In other words, post-positivist research methodologies seek to faithfully reconstruct discourse within the context in which it was articulated. According to Bevir and Rhodes, researchers 'should treat data as evidence of the meanings or beliefs embedded in actions. They should not try to bypass meanings or beliefs by reducing them to given principles of rationality, fixed norms or social categories' (Bevir and Rhodes 2004, p. 203). Hence, only by reproducing the contextual normative significance of an actor's discourse, including its ideas and beliefs is it possible to fully comprehend their actions. Following this particular methodological assumption, discourse analysis should not only seek to 'recover agents' understandings in order to obtain an insider perspective on social life', but also 'put meanings into their intersubjective context' (Pouliot 2007, p. 365). Taking this into account, the aim of this book is to reproduce Russian official discourse by 'thickly inductive and empirical' discourse analysis (Hopf 2002, p. 3), so as to analyse this discourse according to the context in which it was articulated and from which it gains its meaning.

To illustrate the relationship between wider state and security agendas and individual security policies, the single 'case plus study' method (Hansen 2006) is adopted, by examining the evolution of a single case, in this case Chechnya, across an extensive period of time. In contrast to a neo-positivist use of case studies to test ideas or theoretical models deductively and provide verifiability of this study by replication in multiple cases or by a defined objective criteria (George and Bennett 2004, pp. 7–9), a single case study is here used in order to examine a particular subject in great detail. As argued by Hansen,

> One might ask why one large case study rather than a series of smaller ones was chosen, and the answer is that while ... discourse analysis can be

applied to a wide variety of topics, it is a form of analysis which requires extensive knowledge of the case in question and which therefore can only be undertaken in a small number of cases.

(Hansen 2006, p. 11)

Studies using the 'case plus study' method are not concerned with establishing causal relationships within and between case studies. Instead, the aim is to investigate the specifics of a particular issue in more depth, and to do so by analysing it in its own right. As outlined by Dessler and Owen (2005, p. 599) 'constructivists tend to develop and support their general claims about particular cases by working "upwards" from the details of these cases to theoretically informed claims that capture relevant patterns and relationships within them'. The evolution of Russia's discourse on Chechnya is, thus, used as a 'case plus study' for exploring both the evolution of Russia's state identity and security priorities under Putin and Medvedev, and the symbolic relationship between a single security issue and the wider national and security discourse within this context.

In this respect, a key element of the post-positivist research agenda is accounting for the 'historicization of meanings' of a discourse (Pouliot 2007). Or in other words, analysing how a discourse relates to the context – other contingent discourses at that moment in time – within which it was originally articulated. To this end, this study sets out to contextualize and trace the significance of Russian discourse on state identity, security agendas and its policy towards Chechnya across a period spanning the first two terms of the Putin Presidency, the Medvedev Presidency, and the first two years of Putin's third term as president. However, a certain degree of flexibility was introduced with regard to the temporal boundaries outlined above, in order to best capture and analytically conceptualize the contextual dynamics shaping this extensive period. Therefore, sources from autumn 1999, prior to Vladimir Putin becoming acting Russian President in January 2000, were included. These four months represented a critical juncture in Russo-Chechen relations (Souleimanov 2007), marking the restart of large scale military operations. Crucially, even during his Premiership, Vladimir Putin was viewed as the leading figure of the restart of the Second Chechen campaign. Not only was he heavily involved with the launch of military operations in Chechnya in 1999, his handling of this issue was seen by many commentators, at the time, as highly significant for his early popularity as President (Sakwa 2008).

According to Hansen, in analysing official discourse on foreign policy or, in this case, security policy, the discourse of 'the heads of states, governments, senior civil servants, high ranked military, heads of international institutions, official statements by international institutions' should be examined (Hansen 2006, p. 64). This seems appropriate in the case of Putin's Russia, which as many analysts have highlighted, has seen the Presidential office maintain a strong grip on Russian official discourse (Koltsova 2006). In turn, Ortmann suggests that by analysing state elites' official discourse in the public domain, 'the scripts and narratives producing the identity of the new Russian state can be traced' (Ortmann 2008, p. 366). Taking this into account, the source material for analysis was drawn from official Russian public sources. This included the key Russian ministries responsible for security issues and Chechnya, as well as key actors, such as Putin, Medvedev, the Kremlin, the Ministry for Foreign Affairs and the Ministry of the Interior, who articulated wider state identity and security discourse.

In selecting texts from these sources, this book followed what Hansen (2006) outlines are the two primary considerations for discourse analysis. First, that a text should come from the period under investigation; and second, that 'the body of texts should include key texts that are frequently quoted and function as nodes within the intertextual web of debate, as well as a larger body of general material' (Hansen 2006, p. 82). To this end, this study's analysis focuses primarily on policy documents, statements, speeches, articles and interviews, by the actors outlined previously, that had a strong resonance within the official discourse, which were identified as such by an ongoing review of both primary sources and the secondary literature.

In addition to documentary analysis of primary sources, analysis of secondary sources and fieldwork interviews were used to create methodological 'triangulation'. Triangulation, as defined by Bryman (2001, p. 274) is a process that 'entails using more than one method or source of data in the study of social phenomena' to widen and deepen the analyst's understanding of the context under study. As outlined, understanding the context within which discourses are articulated is central to this study's methodological approach.

This innovative step seeks to address the current shortcoming of some discourse analytical methodologies, which despite 'talking' about the importance of context in discourse analysis (Bevir and Rhodes 2004, p. 203), say little about how this knowledge of the context should be acquired (see Wodak 2001; Neumann 2002). To the end of understanding the context under study, the conduct and analysis of fieldwork is an important methodological step, as it enables the researcher to better 'read' and 'perspectivize' discourses/texts according to the context in which they have significance, rather than imposing their own a priori assumptions and biases onto the discourse. Taking this into account, as well as undertaking a thorough review of the secondary literature on Russia's state-building project and security agenda, 25 fieldwork interviews were conducted in Russia between April–May 2007 and April–June 2008, with practitioners from and experts on the foreign policy making bodies outlined above, analysts from leading think tanks, scholars from academic institutions and practitioners from NGOs.

These interviews were conducted using a flexible form of semi-structured interview technique (Bryman 2001, p. 314). This was the most appropriate approach since the aim was not to compare the answers of different respondents, but to collect as much contextual information about the topic as possible, which was then utilized to refine the researcher's analytical perspective on the corpus of official discourse, rather than being used as primary sources themselves. These interviews, in combination with the secondary literature review, were invaluable in elucidating the Russian context, in which the concept of 'security' itself has a different contextualized significance compared with its use in the IR literature. Hence, whilst the focus of this study is primarily on official discourse, these interviews provided important background knowledge from which the contextual significance embedded within these discourses could be reassembled.

In line with its inductive discourse analytical approach, rather than formulating a fixed hypothesis at the outset, this study placed emphasis on letting the discourse speak for itself. As Hopf (2002, p. 25) argues, in analysing discourse 'it is absolutely imperative that meanings remain what they mean and do not become what the researcher needs to test a hypothesis'. In other words, the hypothesis should emerge from the data rather than vice versa. In taking an inductive and interpretivist perspective on discourse analysis, the researcher should follow a series of analytical steps, to avoid the pitfalls of imposing a priori hypotheses and assumptions onto the corpus under investigation. First, the researcher should immerse themselves in the data, before proceeding to formulate an initial assessment of the key themes and trends within the discourse, in order to 'recover the subjective meanings', and establish some broad categorizations for analysing the discourse (Pouliot 2007, p. 369). The researcher should then repeatedly revisit and consider this initial reading and categorization, going backwards and forwards between the data collected and their analysis, until a clear sense of the context emerges. This process of analysis and reworking of key themes, categories and concepts continues until saturation point, when it is felt that the data has been analysed in full, and this process has been exhausted (Bryman 2001, p. 394).

Whilst in practice, documents are analysed, and often coded, individually, it is also critical to relate the discourse and its meanings from individual documents to the wider context in which they are embedded. In other words, texts and their meanings can only be made sense of in relation to other texts (Hansen 2006). Therefore, a process of intertextuality is vital, whereby the researcher relates their analytical understanding of different texts and discourses to one another, in order to recapture the wider context in which each text is situated and to provide a more nuanced and detailed reading and understanding of the discourse under study. As a researcher, it is therefore important to move not only between the data and their, constantly refined, analytical categories and concepts, but also between the different data being analysed throughout the research process, in order to build up an understanding of the interrelated contexts of different discourses (Bryman 2001, p. 381).

As inductive discourse analysis is not driven by aims of replicability and generalizability, instead of testing its authenticity in terms of reliability, a more appropriate test is one of 'confirmability' (Lewis and Ritchie 2003 p. 270). For discourse analysis, confirmability is seen in terms of whether another researcher looking at the same material would come to roughly the same conclusions. In light of this, inductive qualitative research must be very open and clear about the way in which a research project has been constructed and undertaken, to provide this confirmability. Taking this into account, a detailed list of sources analysed is provided at the end of the book.

To better account for the evolution of Russian official discourses over such a long period (2000–2014), the empirical analysis has been divided into four shorter time periods, in order to both enhance the clarity of the book and as an analytical aid for explaining the evolution of Russian state and security discourses coherently (Hopf 2002). These periods were identified by a preliminary analysis of the discourse and supported by a survey of the existent literature. These sub-periods are: Russia in crisis (1999/2000–2001); the rebuilding of Russia (2001–2004); Russia as a strong state and a great power? (2004–2008); and the modernization and resecuritization of Russia (2008–2014).

To illustrate the way in which Russia's overall security agenda impacted on the conceptualization of the Chechen issue, each of these temporal analytical categories are analysed in two chapters: the first, examining Russia's macro-state and security agendas; and, the second, investigating the way in which these changing agendas impacted on the specific policy towards Chechnya and the North Caucasus region more broadly.

Outline of the book

As outlined, the empirical analysis of Russia's state identity and security discourses, the interrelationship between these, and how this impacted on, and was impacted by, the approach to Chechnya under Putin and Medvedev is divided into four consecutive time periods, each comprising two chapters. However, before the empirical tracing of these discourses begins in Chapter 3, the next chapter sets out the book's conceptual framework.

Chapter 2, thus, details the main premises and assumptions of this study's post-positivist approach in greater detail, setting out the framework and concepts that will guide the analysis of the evolution of Russian security policy since 2000. This analytical framework takes into account the role of state identities, local contexts, the importance of policy clusters in the study of individual security policies, and the role of key turning points in the evolution of state security policies. Second, it demonstrates the way in which this approach can be operationalized in relation to three concepts, considered key for this study: weak/strong states, internal/external security, securitization/desecuritization. It is argued that rather than taking these binary conceptual divisions as objective principles for characterizing the strength of a state actor's statehood and the nature of its security context, they can be considered as discourses that are subjectively constructed by actors, which provide not only their analytical assessment of a given context, but can have real impacts on the shaping of their security policies.

The first empirical part of the book covers the 1999–2000 period, which saw Putin come to power and the initial programmes for Putin's Russia announced. Chapter 3 argues that in the early Putin years, Russian state identity centred on a construction of itself as a weak state that was threatened by a series of existential threats, in both its internal and external spheres. Chapter 4 illustrates the way in which this discourse served to structure the construction of Chechnya as one such existential threat, in which both Russia and specific context of Chechnya were depicted as failing and weak entities, experiencing fundamental security threats. It demonstrates how Chechnya was positioned at the heart of Russian state identity discourse and as a key security concern in both its domestic and foreign policy during the early 2000s. In other words, it outlines how the securitization of Chechnya between 1999 and 2001 came to symbolize Russia's overall weaknesses as a state.

Part II addresses the period from 2000–2004, in which the Putin regime sought to move beyond its initial prognosis for arresting Russia's decline into weakness, and elaborate their own vision for Russia's future. Chapter 5 suggests that having identified the key causes for Russia's weakness, the Putin regime then sought to systematically combat these problems in order to rebuild Russia both domestically, but also internationally. In Chapter 6, it is argued that this shift in the official discourse from portraying Russia as a weak state, towards it being a state in the process of 'rebuilding' itself, dramatically altered the earlier securitization of the Chechen issue. The Russian authorities increasingly argued that Chechnya, like Russia as a whole, was in the process of being rebuilt, through a series of desecuritization processes. At the same time, a parallel ongoing securitization of certain groups remained, in line with Russia's wider national and security priorities. In the wider context of Russian official discourse, Chechnya lost some of its salience as an issue, as other problems, notably tensions with the West and growing concerns with the security situation in the wider North Caucasus, came to dominate the central tenets of Russia's identity and security discourses.

The third empirical part covers the period from 2004–2008. Chapter 7 examines how official discourse now began to construct Russia as a 'strong' state, whereby ongoing security threats became articulated within, rather than in opposition to, Russia's image of itself as a 'strong' state. At the same time, there was a widening of the regime's image of its enemies to include any groups, actors or movements that appeared to challenge this hegemonic construction of Russia's identity. And, thus, the security of the regime became tightly interlinked with national security. Chapter 8 highlights the ways in which the official discourse on Russia as a 'strong' state directly impacted on the image of Chechnya, which was now constructed as a desecuritized republic. However, this desecuritization was closely intertwined and interconnected with the development of a 'strong' local regime, resulting in an increasing localization of power in Chechnya under President Ramzan Kadyrov. The desecuritization of Chechnya also marked a re-emergence of Chechnya in the federal discourse, with the image of a desecuritized Chechnya increasingly utilized, both internally and externally, to further Russia's image of itself as a 'strong' state.

The fourth empirical section covers both the Medvedev (2008–2012), and the first two years of the third Putin (2012–204), presidency. Chapter 9 outlines how the Medvedev presidency sought to address the consequences of the global financial crisis by placing a modernization drive at the centre of official discourse, but with little success and his term ending with large-scale protests erupting around the 2011 Duma and 2012 Presidential elections. In this context, the third Putin term as president has seen a reorientation of the regime's national programme towards the promotion and protection of 'traditional' Russian values, alongside the flaring up of anti-Western sentiments in the country. This has involved a wide-scale securitization of actors both within and beyond Russia (as seen during Russia's annexation of Crimea in March 2014 or the clampdown on independent media and internet in early 2014). These are said to be seeking to destabilize Russia, increasingly understood as the survival of the regime. Chapter 10 examines how in spite of a return to recognizing the ongoing violence and insecurity and a number of large-scale terrorist attacks across Russia, the instability in North Caucasus has been increasingly normalized within official discourse, and even detached and separated from state identity discourse for the rest of the country in light of the narrower 'nationalist' ideology promoted by the regime. Thus, in spite of it operating largely beyond federal control in many respects, Chechnya and the North Caucasus has come to play a low priority in comparison with popular protests within the rest of Russia, and developments in the wider post-Soviet region, notably in Ukraine.

The final chapter of the book outlines the conclusions reached from the tracing of Russian state identity, security and Chechnya policy discourse across the period from 1999 to 2014. First, it outlines the main changes and turning points within the Putin regime's construction of Russian state identity since 2000, detailing the key security priorities and considerations that have driven Russia's security agenda during this period, and highlighting how the two have been constructed in relation to another. This interrelationship is then considered in relation to the regime's specific policy discourse and practices towards Chechnya and the North Caucasus, assessing both how the relationship between state identity discourse and security policy played out in this issue area, and how the discourse and practices on Chechnya and the North Caucasus were not only shaped by, but also shaped, the nexus of these wider state identity and security agenda discourses. Second, its consider what implications can be drawn from this multifaceted and longitudinal approach to analysing Russian security policy, which treats domestic and foreign security policy as inherently interconnected and traces the evolution and changes within security discourse over time respectively, for understanding Russia as a security actor. Third, it examines the theoretical insights that can be taken from this study. It is suggested that a more interpretivist, post-positivist and longitudinal perspective is needed both to provide a more nuanced reading of the notions of 'weak' and 'strong' states within the existing IR literature, and in the application of the Copenhagen School's (de)securitization model to the study of security in non-Western contexts.

2 Analysing security in a non-Western context

In the last 30 years, the predominance of neo-realist and neo-liberal approaches within security studies has been increasingly challenged by post-positivist ontological approaches (Dannreuther 2007, pp. 39–42). Whilst there are differences between them, the neo-neo paradigm can be characterized as primarily focused on systemic developments at an international level. With the collapse of the Soviet Union, the neatly defined definition of a bipolar international system, which served as the background to the development of the paradigm, was lost. At the same time, more diffuse, less geographically-centred and more localized security threats were seen as having become more prominent. In response, many scholars have argued that the traditional rationalist conceptualization of security is too narrow[1] and problematic in today's security environment. Proponents of this view pointed to the difficulties that the traditional paradigm has in explaining the proliferation of civil and ethnic intra-state conflicts since the end of Cold War, and the rise in prominence of international terrorism (Smith in Booth 2005, p. 32). As a result, the discipline of security studies has sought to re-examine its previous assumptions about the nature of security (Krahmann 2003), and security has become an 'issue of reflection rather than a given', as it is in explicitly 'rationalist' approaches (Van Munster 2007, p. 235).

Post-positivist approaches to security thus rose to prominence by taking into account a wider range of security dynamics than military conflict, acknowledging that security referents function in more contexts than the systemic level between states, and considering internal security as a highly salient factor in a state's overall conception of security. In other words, such constructivist frameworks place the investigation of what an actor understands as 'security' at the heart of the analysis, because they take 'nothing for granted: the relevant actors, their interests and their understandings of the rules are all open to interpretation' (Martin and Simmons 2002, p. 198).

As will be argued below, a post-positivist approach is a highly relevant one for the study of non-Western regions and actors, for whom local contexts, frames of reference, worldviews and understandings of security are often markedly different from those commonly found in the Western literature. Hence, rather than making a priori assumptions about how security works in these alternative environments or applying theoretical models primarily designed and tested in the

Western contexts, a post-positivist approach allows us to recapture the way in which these particular actors have come to understand questions of security (Wilkinson 2007).

Identities and security

The post-positivist constructivist framework of analysis suggests that an actor's behaviour and hence security policy are not driven by objective interests and circumstances, but derive from an actor's reading of itself and its Others. In this way, constructivists suggest that identities, discourses and practices are cultural and social constructs that are established within an intersocial sphere (Finnemore and Sikkink 2001, p. 394). As a result, state interests, policies and priorities are drawn from a particular construction of a state's identity (Hopf 2005, p. 226).

An actor's security agenda and policies therefore derive from its reading of itself, other actors, and its place in relation to others and the world. To put it simply, identity enables an actor to make sense of the world, by telling it who it is, what sort of world it lives in (Frederking 2003), who the others in this world are (Honneland 1998, p. 281), as well as who it wants to be, who it is against (Rumelili 2004, p. 29; Greenhill 2008, pp. 344–345), and where it is going (Ringmar 1996, p. 76). As Hopf argues, 'in telling you who you are, identities strongly imply a particular set of interests or preferences with respect to choices of action in particular domains, and with respect to particular actors' (Hopf 1998, p. 175). Therefore, an identity positions an actor in the world both in terms of itself and in relation to others, providing the conceptual prisms through which it understands the world.

According to a constructivist perspective, this expression of a mutually-constituted identity can be located through an actor's discourse (Kassianova 2001).[2] However, the articulation of an actor's identity in discourse may be evident in more than a single discourse on a single subject (Hopf 2002). In other words, it is interrelationship between the various facets of an actor's discourse that form the generalized sense of its identity. Given the central importance of security to a state actor's sense of identity, there is often a strong inter-linkage between its security policy discourse and that of state-building or nation-building projects, with this playing a central role in an actor's conceptions of state identity by presenting visions for the future development of the state (Ringmar 2008). As noted by Katzenstein, a security identity evokes not only notions of security but is 'also a shorthand label for varying constructions of nation and statehood' (Katzenstein 1996, p. 6).

In investigating the interrelationship between Russia's official state identity, security agenda and position towards particular security policies such as Chechnya, this book's focus is primarily on the official security discourses and practices. As noted by Buzan, Wæver and de Wilde (1998) political elites are usually the main securitizing agents for state and national security, because they are the only agents that are widely perceived as legitimate in 'speaking security'. They are able to 'speak' security because state elites play the role of spokespeople of the state (Jepperson, Wendt and Katzenstein 1996, p. 59). Yerkel elaborates on this point further by stating that:

> State action is performed through the individuals that hold the position in the decision-making process. When referring to state identity, we actually imply the identity that is held by the individual or group acting on behalf of the state.
>
> (Yerkel 2010)

The state, however, is not an moderator of competing national discourses or an actor '"captured" by a particular identity narrative', but is 'the producer rather than the mediator or arbiter of the identity discourse' (Kassianova 2001, p. 825). In the Russian context, as noted by Ortmann, 'state elites' are 'a group of people who identify closely with the state and claim the legitimate power to speak in the name of the state. Furthermore, the 'state elite' in this sense refers to occupants of official positions within the Russian state, as well as a network of informal advisors and opinion-makers (Ortmann 2008, p. 366). While this discourse does not represent a national perspective, it does reflect what is considered the official discourse of the state, and thus acts as the official articulation of state identity, perceptions of the world and positions on individual issues.

Consequently, the discourses of these officials help shape perceptions of state identity in the eyes of its own citizens and beyond. In this way, although all possessing individual identities and perceptions, the officials composing a state leadership can be seen as acting as a loosely united single actor with a collective identity, projecting a common discourse on all manner of issues and hence a common articulation of state identity. Therefore, it is possible to

> assume the existence of state identity, not as a property of a state, but in the form of a concept perceived by individuals involved in foreign policymaking; that is a concept of what their country is and what it represents. The basis for this assumption is that such a state identity concept in the mind of policymakers operates on a state's action (undertaken by those policymakers) in the same manner that an identity of a person operates on that person's action.
>
> (Ashizawa 2008, p. 576)

In other words, it is possible to treat state identity analytically as a single collective identity. State identity, like individual identity, therefore, is not just a descriptive character of a state, but it is also a social and relational conception referring to the state in a way to reflect the existence, or identity, of Others (most likely other states) (Ashizawa 2008, p. 575). Hence, in the same way that identities shape an individual actor's interests and relationship with the outside world, 'a concept of state identity perceived by policymakers provides a specific value ... which in turn determines a policymakers' preference for a particular foreign policy' (Ashizawa

2008, p. 573). Therefore, in accepting that a state can be seen as a discrete actor with a discrete identity, a state's identity can then be analysed to see how this identity in turn determines its choice of policy. This choice will reflect a state's perception of its own identity, position in the world, and the way in which it develops a propensity towards viewing certain types of actions as 'appropriate'.

Context and the non-Western experience

A key feature of post-positivist approaches to security is the recognition that actors' identities and policies are shaped not by objective circumstances, but derive from within their local context. Rather than assigning an identity to a particular actor,[3] identities and interests emerge not only through interactions with external actors and developments (Wendt 2003), but are also heavily dependent on how an actor constructs its domestic context. In this respect,

> social experiences and interactions with Others are essential factors for shaping (and reshaping) identity, while environmental elements, such as cultures and institutional settings, within which such experiences and interactions take place, are also likely to be at work in constructing identities.
> (Ashizawa 2008, p. 575)

According to Hopf, analysing a state's understanding of its domestic context provides 'an account of how a state's own domestic identities constitutes a social cognitive structure that makes threats and opportunities, enemies and allies, intelligible, thinkable, and possible' (Hopf 2002, p. 6). By establishing the 'social cognitive structure that comprises the identities and discourse' of a particular context (which impacts on every member of the state, including policymakers), it is possible to infer a state's 'understandings of other states', which 'must necessarily involve the interaction between this complicated social Self and those external Others' (Hopf 2002, p. 20). Taking this into account, in order to understand an actor's identity and consequent behaviour, it is necessary to investigate the specific and different discourses and practices associated with the formation of an actor's identity and interpretation of a specific issue.

However, despite this long-standing recognition of the importance of the context in post-positivist approaches to security, until recently the study of the non-Western experience and security contexts tended to be relegated to post-colonial studies (Seth 2011; Jones 2006; Agathangelou and Ling 2009). However, there is now an ever-greater recognition that many of the concepts and models currently used in IR and security studies largely derive from the Western context and do not adequately take into account discourses and practices operating outside of this narrow geographical context (Bilgin 2008; Sabaratnam 2011; Hobson 2012; Hobson 2007; Barkawi and Laffey 2006). As a result, there have been calls to make greater efforts to take more into account the way in which international relations and security is viewed and practiced outside of the West (Acharya and Buzan 2007; Tickner and Wæver 2009; Shilliam 2010; Shani 2008).

18 *Analysing security*

This shift towards a greater inclusion and recognition of the non-Western experience in security studies has, to some extent, been bolstered by the contemporary debate about changing global order and the proclaimed rise of a number of non-Western states to become 'great' or 'global' powers, in the international system, most notably China, India and to some extent also Russia (see Zakaria 2011, Kupchan 2012; Zurn 2010; Murray and Brown 2012). With these non-Western powers set to play a greater role in the global security agenda, it has been seen as more important to gain a greater understanding of their security discourses and practices by taking into account their domestic context.

Drawing on the above, this book proceeds from the assumption that rather than seeing security discourses and practices in universal and objective terms, it is important to examine the way in which specific security concepts and practices come to be operationalized within their particular contexts and with what effect. In other words, it is necessary to place discourses and practices within the contexts from which they originate, as ideas and practices may have alternative meanings within this context than they do in the Western context, from which most of our conceptual and theoretical models are derived. Local readings of security and national identity must be taken into account when examining security discourses and practices of non-Western powers.

A comprehensive and multifaceted analysis of security policy

Methodologically, this book aims to provide a comprehensive and multifaceted analysis of individual security policies set within their political and security contexts. At present, there remains a tendency in the literature to examine individual security issues largely in isolation from wider security and national policy discourses and contexts. Similarly, the emphasis is often on the way in which a particular security policy is framed at a particular moment in time. This does not, however, provide a sufficiently nuanced reading of the incremental changes that security policies undergo, nor does it provide a comprehensive view on the wider ramifications and spill-over effects produced by individual policy decisions and choices. Thus, as well as analysing how individual security issues are framed, scholars should also consider three other aspects that are intrinsic to what constitutes a state policy, namely the role that individual security policy plays in wider state policy (Lupovici 2009, p. 213); the wider policy clusters within which individual security issues operate; and the evolution of a particular security policy across time. As noted by Bevir and Rhodes, a post-positivist interpretivist analysis must adopt a holistic approach that considers the wider web of beliefs and meanings of the context in which a discourse is articulated, and argues for 'the contingency of political life': the contingency of any given set of beliefs and meanings and their continual evolution and change across contexts and time (Bevir and Rhodes 2004, pp. 2–4).

As will be demonstrated in the case of Russia's policy on Chechnya, it is impossible to fully comprehend the nature and impact of a particular security policy, without also considering its wider place within wider national and security agendas. For example, a key feature of the Chechen issue was the way in which it became a symbol of Russia's failure and weakness in the late 1990s. Similarly, the subsequent desecuritization of Chechnya also went hand-in-hand with the Putin regime's changing position towards the Russian domestic space, and attempts to rebuild and stabilize the country. In other words, individual security policies and decisions are not made in isolation from their political and security contexts. Indeed, they are often interlinked and play a major role in other policy clusters and decisions, which must all be taken into account, in order to provide a more comprehensive security policy analysis.

In conjunction with this, in order to deliver a more comprehensive security policy analysis it is also important to examine the way in which particular security issues evolve across time. Drawing on the post-positivist assumptions that emphasize 'the fluidity and contextual nature of identities' (Abdelal et al. 2006, p. 697), security policies and practices can be seen as neither static nor permanent (Kratochvíl 2004, p. 4). Thus, in this book, rather than seeking to establish a 'positivist' causal relationship between state identity and its security interests, or 'objective' identifiable reasons for change, which as noted by Fierke are notions that are 'ultimately slippery' (Fierke 2007, p. 68), security agendas are considered as flexible constructions liable to change across time, contexts and social interactions. In turn, 'one way to establish covariance in a constructivist study is by executing a longitudinal survey' (Lupovici 2009, p. 209). Significant changes and tuning points in security discourses and practices can be ascertained through a process of discourse analysis and carefully executed process tracing (Bevir and Rhodes 2004, p. 9). As demonstrated in the subsequent chapters, external events and actors can and do have impact on a state actor's perception of itself, its security priorities and context, but often not in the way it was intended. For example, in the context of Putin's Russia, Western criticism of developments within the Russian domestic space did not result in a positive change from a Western perspective, namely more democracy and regime accountability, but, instead, led to a change of policy in a more restrictive and repressive direction, highlighted by the securitization of the West due to its perceived interfering and negative role in the post-Soviet space.

Hence, the exact impact of different modes of behaviours and developments is unpredictable and cannot be assumed a priori. A new event or issue may come onto the agenda and drastically alter an actor's understanding of its security agenda and context, and hence discursive constructions of other issues (Howarth 2000, p. 13). Conversely, a new event or issue may have a negligible effect on an actor's reading of its security agendas and priorities, if they are articulated in a way consistent with the prevailing discursive construction (Ezzy 1998). Events may also lead to an issue losing its salience or earlier role through a process of 'discursive disappearance' (Hansen 2006, pp. 44–45) in one area, whilst retaining it in another. Against this background, it is the analyst's job to identify which events have had an impact on a particular national and security agenda, and with what effect.

In summary, in order to ascertain how non-Western actors, such as Russia, view and articulate their security priorities, one must examine the way in which an actor constantly form and reinterpret its sense of self, its security interests and its position towards the context in which it operates. From this perspective, there emerges a set of guiding assumptions about what constitutes a security threat and what is not, which in turn conditions the debate on security within a particular context. Taking this into account, security policies and practices are not fixed, but can evolve in line with changes across the wider political and security agendas, both domestically and internationally. The role that particular security issues play within these wider agendas is also extremely fluid and liable to change across time. All of these elements and dimensions must be taken into account in the study of security policies in order to give a comprehensive and multifaceted security policy analysis.

Key concepts and analytical tools

In analysing the evolution of Russia's security policy, this book will draw on several concepts and theories from the existent IR literature, namely, constructions of weak/strong states, the nexus of internal/external security, and the theory of securitization and desecuritization from the Copenhagen School of Security (CS). However, these concepts and theories will not be adopted unquestioningly, but will be reinterpreted in light of the ontological and theoretical assumptions outlined above. Therefore, rather than viewing them as objectively derived concepts or theories, or as a set of fixed and ontologically separate binaries, they are rearticulated as discursive subjects in the manner of the post-positivist assumptions as described above. By reconceptualizing these concepts as without any inherent and essentialist meaning, it becomes possible to examine the ways in which these different models came to be operationalized and utilized across different contexts and time periods. Hence, the aim is to make sense of the way in which it was operationalized within the Russian security context, rather than imposing objectivist models of a context and assessing the degree of fit between the model and context. In so doing, this study demonstrates the limits of our current reading of securitization/desecuritization, weak/strong states and the internal/external security nexus.

'Strong' and 'weak' states

A key strand of the security studies' literature centres on characterizing the nature and behaviour of different states according to their regime structures and security priorities. In this vein, some scholars have advocated focusing on domestic security as a way of accounting for the context of countries beyond the 'West'. This agenda has been developed primarily by scholars of the 'third world' or 'weak' states (Ayoob 1995). These scholars argue that the concepts and ideas developed within system-wide theories do not fit with the reality of states beyond the Western liberal-democratic context, and thus do not aid analysis of such an environment.

As a result, these scholars have sought to develop alternative concepts and frameworks of the analysis for 'new' and 'weak' states. A prominent scholar of security in the less developed world, Mohammed Ayoob, has sought to distinguish between states on this basis. Although recognizing that all states differ, Ayoob has characterized less developed states as those that are 'weak' (lack of internal cohesion and legitimacy), vulnerable (marginalized and easily permeated by external actors) and insecure (susceptible to internal and interstate conflict) (Ayoob 1995, pp. 15–16). Indeed, this theme has been taken up by other scholars, including Desch who argues that 'strong' states are highly cohesive and tend to be maximal states; 'weak' states are divided and tend to be minimal states (Desch 1996, p. 241). Similarly, Rotberg argues that '*strong* states unquestionably control their territories and deliver a full range and a high quality of political goods to their citizens' (Rotberg 2003, p. 4). While,

> *weak* states include a broad continuum of states that are: inherently weak because of geographical, physical, or fundamental economic constraints; basically 'strong', but temporarily or situationally 'weak' because of internal antagonisms, management flaws, greed, despotism, or external attacks; and a mixture of the two (Rotberg 2003, p. 4).

Buzan and Wæver have also used a spectrum to classify states from 'strong' to 'weak' in terms of their 'degree of socio-political cohesion between civil society and the institutions of government' (Buzan and Wæver 2003, p. 22). Such scholars have thus sought to explain the difference in security perceptions between 'weak' and 'established' or 'strong' states on the basis that they are at different stages of development as nation-states (Ayoob 1995, pp. 27–28). From this literature, a criterion has emerged to distinguish 'strong' and 'weak' states according to the extent of internal challenges to the basic tenets of a state, national sovereignty and territorial integrity.

On the basis of this literature, the use of the terminology of 'strong' and 'weak' states, or equivalent terms, has become commonplace both in academic and international political communities. As highlighted by Atkinson and Coleman, the 'theoretical development and empirical research in comparative political economy over the past decade have been greatly influenced and stimulated by debates surrounding the theme of "strong" and "weak" states' (Atkinson and Coleman 1989, p. 47). Given the widespread acceptance of the conceptual difference between a 'strong' and a 'weak' state, discourses about 'strong' and 'weak' states have come to influence the development of state identities. Indeed, as evidenced by the Russian case study in this book, discursive constructions of the nature of a 'strong' and a 'weak' state can be very influential in state discourses.

While acknowledging both the need to contextualize theory and the commonplace usage of some conceptual terminology in the everyday practice of international and domestic politics, as an analyst it is nonetheless important not to superimpose fixed categorization by type, and one's reading of them, onto the actors under study, such as defining states as inherently and categorically either 'strong' or 'weak'. As such, this book rejects the notion that objective and fixed criteria for assessing a state as either 'weak' or 'strong' exist. Instead, it proceeds from the assumption that states come to perceive themselves and others as 'weak' or 'strong', on the basis of their reading and understanding of their own position, security interests and context. Hence, an actor forms its own specific sense of what a 'strong' and 'weak' strong might mean and consist of within a particular time and space.

Taking this into account, and contrary to the rationalist literature on 'weak' and 'strong' states that defines 'weak' states by internal vulnerabilities, an actor can still present itself as a 'strong' state while, at the same time, facing numerous internal security challenges. Indeed, this can be seen by countries such as the US and UK, in which internal terrorist threats are openly acknowledged, but which does not alter their self-perception as 'strong' states. Following this logic, an arbitrary classification of Russia as 'strong' or 'weak' does not aid our understanding of Russia's national or security priorities. However, Russia's understanding of the nature of 'weak' and 'strong' states in relation to itself and others is insightful for interpreting how security is framed within the Russian context.

As discussed above, an important component of identity is an understanding of where an actor considers it is going in the future. This aspirational element of state identity is at the heart of many state-building projects and national security agendas. The discourse of a state as either a 'weak' or 'strong' state plays an important role in shaping this, as it affects an actor's vision of the future. This is because 'if a state identifies itself as a great power, it will act to reproduce that identity in terms of prevailing norms regarding great power behaviour' (Lomagin in Kanet 2007, pp. 32–33).

In summary, this book utilizes the concepts of 'strong' and 'weak' states as discursive constructions, emerging out of the discourses of state actors as part of their nation and state building projects. These in turn structure their security agendas. The aim in this study is thus to examine the way in which these particular labels were appropriated and articulated by the Russian authorities in the construction of Russia's state priorities, and with what effect in relation to its security agenda and position towards particular security policies such as Chechnya.

Internal-external security nexus

Traditionally, security studies has focused on studying the external realm of state policy – foreign security policy. Indeed, for many years the mainstream perspectives of International Relations and Security Studies scholarship have treated foreign policy as distinct from the rest of state affairs. However, the emergence of social constructivism, with its emphasis on context and identity, challenged this idea.[4] From a constructivist perspective, the internal and external security spheres are interconnected, because they both derive from a state actor's reading of itself, its own context, interests and relationship with others. Therefore, developments in both the internal and external security contexts directly impact on states' reading of their national and security priorities. As Desch argues 'the correlation between very dramatic international changes on the one hand and very significant domestic developments on the other provides very compelling reason for exploring cross-level linkages in the realm of security affairs' (Desch 1996, pp. 237–238). Many scholars now acknowledge the need to analyse external and internal security as interrelated phenomena (Campbell 1998), whereby 'internal and external dimensions of security are inseparable' (Mishra 2007, p. 234).

In addition, empirical developments since the end of the Cold War have further propelled this change to recognizing the importance of the links between internal and external security. The rise in global non-traditional security threats, such as international terrorism, climate change, health pandemics, energy or cyber security, has challenged the assumption that security is essentially a static phenomenon, which only concerns inter-state relations in the international arena (Buzan and Hansen, 2009). In particular, the phenomenon of international terrorism and the development of the global 'war on terror' demonstrated that threats can operate simultaneously and in an interconnected fashion in the spheres of internal and external security. In turn, the measures adopted to deal with such threats have also had to be to be implemented not only at a national, but also a regional and international, levels. Indeed, 'as threats to the internal security of the EU were seen increasingly to arise from outside the Union, internal security concerns were turned into questions of external security' (Lavenex 2005, p. 128). As a result, there is now an ever greater recognition of the 'internal–external security nexus', whereby global security threats have a domestic impact and vice versa (Eriksson and Rhinard 2009).

However, as noted in the previous chapter, most of the current research on Russia's security policy tends to focus primarily on its external security agenda. And yet, in light of the greater recognition of the internal-external security nexus in security studies theory, it is critical to analyse developments in both the internal and external spheres in order to gain a more comprehensive reading of Russia's security priorities. In practice, many of Russia's security threats and problems are domestic, including domestic terrorism, a fear of extremism, concerns over internal cohesion, regime security and the survival of the current status quo. Indeed, the importance of internal security concerns was strongly recognized in the Russian National Security Agendas in 2000 and 2009.

Moreover, following the logic of the internal-external security nexus, developments and changes in both domestic and external circumstances have directly impacted on Russia's wider security agenda. For example, increasing frictions between Russia and the West in the mid-2000s led to a growing securitization of domestic Russian groups and NGOs that had direct links to the West. Similarly, Russia's involvement in the global war on terror was in part motivated by its domestic concerns with insecurity and the threat from Chechnya. It is therefore very difficult to practically and analytically separate domestic developments from external events in analysing Russia as a security actor. In light of this, this book sets out to investigate both the internal and external security spheres, and the interconnections between the two, in order to provide a nuanced and comprehensive analysis of Russia's changing security agenda.

Security in a non-Western context: discourses and practices of (de)securitization

To ascertain what constitutes security within Russia's contemporary context, this book draws on the Copenhagen School of Security's model of (de)securitization. In their now seminal work *Security: a new framework for analysis* (1998) Buzan, Wæver and de Wilde sought to reconceptualize our understanding of what is understood by security through the development of their concept of securitization (Buzan 1991; Buzan, Wæver and de Wilde 1998; Buzan and Wæver 2003; Wæver 1995, 1999, 2011). The securitization model challenges the assumption that security has an objective characteristic related to fixed number of issue areas, for example military is also security and security always involve military. Instead of an objective quality, securitization suggests that an issue becomes security when it is 'named' an existential threat by an actor.

Buzan *et al.* thus argue that to shift an issue from the realm of politics into that of security requires an actor to name that issue as a security threat to a particular referent object i.e. produce a 'speech act', and for this 'securitizing move' to be accepted by the relevant audience for this referent object. The movement of an issue from the status of 'securitized' to 'normal' politics represents a desecuritization, and follows the same process of a 'securitization' of an issue from 'normal' to 'securitized' but in reverse. It is therefore 'a process in which a political community downgrades or ceases to treat something as an existential threat to a valued referent object, and reduces or stops calling for exceptional measures to deal with the threat' (Buzan and Wæver, cited in Coskun 2008, p. 405). Within the CS framework, 'normal' politics and security are conceptualized as discretely distinct from one another 'by suggesting that while the former permits debate, the latter means the end of contestation and debate' (Acharya 2006 p. 250).

The implication of this model of security is that rather than taking for granted that certain issues or relationships are intrinsically and universally a security issue, the question of what a security issue becomes the subject of investigation (Buzan, Wæver and de Wilde 1998, p. 5). Thus, the key aim of (de)securitization theory is to identify what, when, where and how an issue is converted from the normal environment of politics to become a threat to security – and the other way around.

Despite its almost instant popularity, the CS securitization model has in recent years undergone a series of critiques and modifications, which have stemmed from both its staunch supporters, as well as its critics. As noted by Cuita, critique of securitization centres on three main strands: conceptual (structural issues particularly related to speech act theory and other necessary components of the model); epistemological (how securitization views contexts); and normative (related to the shift from securitization speech acts to practices of the political and the liberal) (Cuita 2009, p. 302). Alongside this animated, and at times heated, theoretical debate, the securitization model has also been applied to the empirical study of diverse security issues, ranging from the war on terror (Buzan 2006), immigration, trafficking and minority rights (Huysmans 1998, 2000; Aradau 2004; Sasse 2005; Jutila 2006); societal insecurity, human rights (Morozov 2002), environmental politics, HIV/AIDS (Elbe 2006) and EU security (Huysmans 2000; Balzacq 2008; Neal 2009).

Whilst most of the initial discussion surrounding the CS securitization model centred on establishing, negotiating and fixing the exact characteristics and principles of securitization, and its relationship with political and security contexts, desecuritization has not received as much attention in the literature (Coskun 2008, p. 393), at least not until recently. In the second half of the 2000s, however, scholars begun to delve more deeply into what it means to 'desecuritize' an issue and what a desecuritized issue would look like (see Åtland 2008; Aradau 2004; Aras and Polat 2008; Behnke 2006; Cui and Li 2011; Hansen 2012; Roe 2004; Wæver 1995; Oelsner 2005; Coskun 2008, Salter 2008). In this respect, a series of different theoretical conversations emerged, including whether or not the securitization model has an ontological preference for desecuritization over securitization politics (Wæver 1995; Roe 2004; Huysmans 1998; Aradau 2004; Floyd 2007; Abrahamsen 2005); whether or not 'desecuritization is desirable' (Roe 2004, p. 284); the wider normative biases of the (de)securitization model (McDonald 2008); or whether is is possible to ever truly achieve desecuritization in politics (Behnke 2006).

Besides these divergent critiques, Coskun also rightly points out that a major problem with the current desecuritization model, as set out in the original formulation of Buzan and Wæver, is that 'as far as the analysis of the desecuritization process is concerned, since the Copenhagen School does not suggest an explicit framework for its analysis as it has done for securitization, different scholars have interpreted and implied desecuritization differently' (Coskun 2008, p. 395). Much of the initial discussion regarding the nature of desecuritization, remained highly theoretical, often touching on the philosophical, aiming to conceptualize what constitutes the nature of politics and security within the (de)securitization model (Hansen 2012, p. 527).

Coming to this discussion from a more empirical perspective, an alternative set of studies chose instead to focus on the nature of (de)securitization processes in practice. In surveying the current literature, Hansen outlines four main readings of what constitutes a desecuritization from an empirical standpoint (Hansen 2012): first, those scholars that see desecuritization as primarily a form of 'détente' whereby it 'implies a rather slow move out of an explicit security discourse, which in turn facilitates a less militaristic, less violent and hence more genuinely political form of engagement' (see Wæver 2000); second, desecuritization as a 'replacement', whereby 'the combination of one issue moving out of security while another is simultaneously securitized' (see Bilgin 2007; Roe 2004; Aras and Polat 2008); third, desecuritization as a 'rearticulation' 'refer[ing] to desecuritization that remove and issue from the securitized by actively offering a political solution to the threats, dangers, and grievances in question' (Atland 2008); and finally, desecuritization as a process of silencing 'that is when an issue disappears or fails to register in security discourse' (MacKenzie

2009). Indeed, these divergent accounts of what constitutes a process of desecuritization would seem to support Coskun's claim that about the divergence of approaches currently at play and the conclusions reached in differing empirical analyses of desecuritization.

However, despite these divergent approaches, the question of what happens once the initial securitization (including the use of extraordinary measures) has been achieved has yet to be sufficiently investigated; how actors seek to manage these issues thereafter and how certain issues move from the realm of securitization politics back into desecuritization politics. In other words, an examination of the full process and cycle from the moment of initial 'securitization' towards the final 'desecuritization' of a particular security threat. Positioning itself as part of the more empirically-focused set of studies on (de)securitization, this book focuses on exactly this, examining the way in which the Chechen issue went from being securitized at the start of President Putin's period power to increasingly being desecuritized throughout 2001–2014. The Chechen issue is a particularly insightful case for investigating the relationship between securitization and desecuritization, as both processes of securitization and desecuritization were central to Russia's wider attempts to normalize the issue of Chechnya during this period and central to its attempts to remake itself from a 'weak' to a 'strong' state.

Alongside investigating the full cycle of the (de)securitization processes, another question that has yet to be resolved with regard to desecuritization theory is what it means to desecuritize a particular security issue/threat within an already 'securitized' domestic context. A major feature of politics in many non-Western contexts is that it is not centred on an open and deliberative democratic political process, but rather on the rule of a single political regime. From the perspective of the CS model, 'normal' politics itself has therefore already been distorted by the governing regimes, resembling a more closed and authoritarian model of governance than is assumed in the original securitization literature. As a result 'normal' politics and 'security' politics are much more intertwined that in the democratic Western context. Indeed, many scholars of securitization have warned of the power of securitizations to distort the functioning of 'normal' open and democratic processes even in the West. This problem is even greater in less democratic contexts, in which security politics often becomes the political 'norm', making it difficult to ascertain what it means to return an issue back from 'securitized' to 'normal' politics. Such a blurring of 'normal' and 'security' politics has been a particular feature of Russian politics during the last decade. Not only did the Putin regime seek to rebuild Russia from within, it also moved the Russian political landscape towards an increasingly authoritarian model of governance. In turn, the domestic sphere was securitized as a potential source of threat to the regime's survival. The 'securitization' and then 'desecuritzation' of Chechnya is therefore an illustrative and interesting case study in understanding how 'desecuritized' issues function within such generalized securitized political contexts.

In light of the assumptions about securitization theory outlined above, this book adopts the position that in order to fully comprehend and account for the nature of (de)securitization processes, it is necessary to analyse these processes in relation to the contextual reading by the (de)securitizing actors of both the relationship between these processes and wider security priorities, and the generalized nature of the divide between 'normal' and 'security' politics. To this end, it draws on what Stritzel (2011, p. 2492) has characterized as the 'second generation ... contextual securitization scholars' that place less emphasis on the formal aspects of the securitization model, but instead focus on drawing out and examining the interrelationship between security politics and its context. The aim being to 'construct a more comprehensive understanding of underlying processes' by focusing on the 'socio-linguistic and/or socio-political microdynamics of generating threats' (Stritzel 2011, p. 2492). Following this 'second generation' perspective, this book considers not just the interrelationship between the securitization and desecuritization processes of Chechnya within Russian official discourse, but also the way in which these processes were linked up with, and connected to, the wider political and security contexts within Russia from which they emerged. In other words, this study subscribes to the school of thought within securitization theory that assert the importance of situating investigation of (de)securitizations within the local meanings and understandings of what constitutes the security/politics divide of a particular context (for example of these types of studies see Balzacq 2005, 2011; Guzzini 2011; Salter 2008; Stritzel 2007, 2011; McDonald 2008). As outlined by Lupovici, this is necessary

> in order to acknowledge context in research we need to reveal the process in which it was constituted – how agents, ideational structures as well as social practices, influenced its creations – and to further establish that it is not an inevitable outcome
>
> (Lupovici 2009, p. 213)

Drawing on this inductive and empirically driven approach to (de)securitization theory, the aim of this study is to empirically reproduce and analyse the interrelationship between the wider contextual discourse of Russian security and state-building projects and the particular (de)securitizations policy towards Chechnya. Hence, rather than imposing objectivist models of what constitutes a particular form or concept of security/securitization and normal politics/desecuritization, this book aims to empirically investigate the way in which the Russian authorities sought to manage the Chechen issue across the 2000s, and how the processes of 'securitization' and 'desecuritization' that were pursued in this period – and their relationship to 'normal' and 'security' politics – came to be understood and practiced within this evolving context.

Notes

1 It is widely accepted that the research agenda has been broadened beyond the study of military threats and inter-state military conflicts, to incorporate factors such as economic and environmental issues, transnational crime, and the role played by ideas and identities. This has led to a splintering of sub-schools with divergent agendas within

28 Analysing security

the study of security seeking to account for these expanded agenda Buzan, Wæver and de Wilde (1998, p. 2).

2 Although, the expression of identity may take on forms of articulation other than spoken and written forms, for example visual, e.g. Putin's macho image, it is a methodological decision to focus on documented written and spoken discourse as representing the articulation of an actor's perception of identity, and that is the approach taken in this study.

3 Conventional constructivism assigns a fixed identity to a state actor, in order to make causal claims on the basis of this identity's reaction to the reality of the international system.

4 Social constructivism starts from the actor and not the systemic level, which enables the importance of the internal context that structures an actor's perceptions of security priorities and identities to be captured and investigated.

Part I
1999–2000

3 Russia in crisis 1999/2000

Immediately upon coming to power – first as Prime Minister in August 1999, then as acting President following the resignation of President Yeltsin on New Year's Eve 1999 and finally as an elected President, inaugurated on 7 May 2000 – Vladimir Putin set out to put his stamp on Russia's political landscape. Central to his political project was the realization that, at the turn of the millennium, Russia found itself a much weakened power than a decade previously. This was seen to be the result of major internal and external crises in the late 1990s. Putin suggested in his Millennium Manifesto in late 1999 that 'for the first time in the past 200–300 years, it [Russia] is facing the real threat of slipping down to the second and possibly even third rank of world states' (Putin 1999a). To deal with these major crises and weaknesses, he asserted that it was necessary to rebuild Russia from within, as only in this way could Russia become a major power once more.

Therefore, in many respects, Russia was presented by its political leadership as a conventional weak state, whose main security challenges came from internal, rather than external threats and dangers. The main thrust of Russia's insecurity was said to be its faltering economy, its dysfunctional and weak state apparatus, societal disillusionment and potential territorial disintegration in its southern regions. At the same time, Russia's international standing was also proclaimed to have been severely diminished by the late 1990s, whereby it was increasingly being sidelined in international affairs. The Putin regime continued to hold the ambition of Russia rejoining the ranks of other great powers on the international stage, but argued this could only occur once it had dealt with its internal problems.

Whereas conventional 'weak' states, as depicted in the literature, require external assistance in order to rebuild or secure themselves, the Putin regime argued that this was not the case with Russia. In its official discourse, Russia was portrayed more like a fallen great power than a weak state that needs external support in order to manage its own problems. Patriotism and a sense of pride in Russian cultural and historical heritage and belief in Russia's own strength and capacity to overcome its problems by itself were central to Putin's vision of Russia. Above all, in civilizational terms Russia was still very much presented as, if not a part of, then at least, on a par with the West.

The sense of disintegration and collapse conveyed by the Putin had direct ramifications on Russia's security agenda. The apocalyptic language of existential threats, and a fear that unless the authorities act now then Russia would disintegrate further, was at the heart of official security discourse. Russia's failures and fears were said to be so profound that the security agenda was expanded to include almost every aspect of policy, ranging from international terrorism and weapons of mass destruction to the demographic and economic crises. Dangers were said to be coming at Russia from all directions.

This chapter lays out the context of the first years of Putin's Russia, and how this directly impacted on the regime's readings of its immediate security threats and concerns, in both its internal and external spheres. It investigates the nature of Putin's political project and his particular reading of Russia as a 'weak' power in 2000, and outlines how this wider perspective was central to the way in which the Russian authorities chose to deal with individual security concerns, such as Chechnya. The securitization of Chechnya was therefore firmly embedded within the context of the time and followed many of the same logics and principles that the Putin regime had identified for Russia in general.

The crisis in the late 1990s and the rise of Putin

The emergence of Vladimir Putin, a relatively 'new political actor' (Dyson 2001, p. 330) about whom little was known, was greeted with both interest and trepidation by Russian and Western analysts alike. There were few clues about the future form, direction and ideology of this new regime. Indeed, Putin cut a contrasting figure to his ailing predecessor. By the end of his final term in power, President Yeltsin had become more associated with health and drink problems, long absences from the political stage, and political infighting, than with his previous role as Russia's energetic nationalistic leader, who had steered the country through the dissolution of the USSR and the tumultuous period of the early 1990s. So much so, that in most people's eyes, the hopes of the early 1990s that a prosperous and democratic Russia would emerge had long been left behind, replaced with concerns about the rise in lawlessness, oligarchs, the war in Chechnya, increased corruption and rampant criminality that had come to dominate Russia by the mid-1990s.

A relative unknown, Putin had come through the ranks: initially as an officer in the KGB posted to East Germany during the Cold War; as an advisor to the liberal mayor of St Petersburg in 1990; then moving through the administrative ranks in the federal administration in Moscow, becoming the head of the Federal Security Services in 1998 and prime minister in 1999. He was thus not seen as an obvious successor to Yeltsin. In fact, this was arguably precisely the reason for his appointment, whereby the ruling elites or the so-called Yeltsinites considered that they could manipulate Putin and thus retain their hold on power and influence (Sakwa 2008, pp. 70–73).

At the time, numerous attempts were made within the Western academic community to understand, characterize and conceptualize this change in Russian politics. Indeed many commentators tried to discern the direction in which he would take Russia from his past career choices (Herspring 2003, pp. 3–5; Pringle 2001, p. 545; Charap 2004; Hahn 2001). Some noted his pragmatism in international affairs, 'reflecting a cool, unsentimental appraisal of international realities, and his commitment to an alignment with the West' (Berryman in Kanet 2005, p. 31). Others characterized his presidency as a 'regime of consolidation', in sharp contrast to Yeltsin's 'regime of transition', noting that Putin had 'moved away from systemic transformation towards system management' (Sakwa in Ross 2004, p. 17). Putin's leading role, as prime minister, in the relaunch of the second Chechen campaign in September 1999, similarly brutal and devastating as the first Chechen conflict (1994–1996), can be seen as a forewarning of the direction and future development of his regime. At the time, however, Putin came across as a much younger, more energetic, pragmatic and realistic new leader, who would steer Russia into the new millennium.

Irrespective of their particular reading of this new Russian leader, most commentators agreed that during the late 1990s Russia had undergone a great crisis, in both its internal and external contexts, losing its sense of direction and purpose. As noted by Hill, by the end of the Yeltsin's era, 'morale was exceptionally low. The state was fundamentally weak. The mood was one of humiliation' (Hill 2008, p. 475).

In the internal sphere, Russia was suffering from a mass political, economic and societal dislocation (Treisman 2002, p.58–59). Russia's economic trajectory during the 1990s was marred with setbacks and failures, often stemming from the after-effects of the 'shock therapy' approach adopted years by the Yeltsin regime in the years immediately following the collapse of USSR, in order to shift Russia's macro-economic structures from a communist to a capitalist model. This resulted in the creation and rise of the so-called oligarchs, a powerful group of businessmen that had profited from the cheap sale of Russia's industries during the privatization programme in the early and mid-1990s. It also led to hyperinflation, wage freezes and a rise in poverty and unemployment for the average Russian. By the mid-1990s Russia's economic situation appeared to have begun to stabilize itself, but the global financial crash in August 1998 triggered a major economic meltdown. Russia defaulted on its IMF loans, and suffered massive inflation, currency devaluation, and the re-emergence of wage arrears on a scale not seen since the early 1990s, leading to the non-payment of taxes by both ordinary people and large enterprises, as well as whole regions of Russia (Sakwa 2008, pp. 241–243). Economically, by the late-1990s, Russia was thus on the brink of, if not already within, a major disaster.

Politically, the ailing health and diminishing standing and reputation of President Yeltsin, the growing power of the oligarchs, the increasing boisterousness of the regional governors (following the 1998 economic collapse), the weakness of political parties and the threat of a return of the Communist Party to power, further destabilized the nascent democratic spirit in post-Soviet Russia (Herspring 2003, pp. 6–7). As suggested by Shlapentokh, 'together, the governors and oligarchs created a climate of total disorder in the country and strengthened the ties between criminals and bureaucrats', which served to further criminalize the political and economic climate in the country (2001, p. 375). Socially, the high level of unemployment, declining life expectancy, poor health care system, unequal wealth distribution, corruption, and poor rule of law led to an increase in social discontent among the population at large and distrust of the political classes.

Externally, Russia's international standing was also being tarnished, with its foreign policy functioning on an ad hoc basis and increasingly in 'disarray' (Stent 2008, p. 1090). If, in the early 1990s, it had been suggested by the Kremlin that Russia could successfully join the international community as an equal and integrate itself into existing Western institutions and structures, by the late 1990s, this initial enthusiasm for the West and achieving this aim had dissipated. In part this was as a result of Russia's ongoing economic problems, which were largely blamed on the economic decisions made in the early 1990s by pro-Western political and economic reformers, such as Chubais and Gaidar, with the support of Western and global institutions, such as the World Bank and the IMF. At the same time, tensions between Russia and the West over key strategic and international questions increased through the decade, thereby decreasing the prospects for Russia's inclusion within the Western camp and international community more generally. The most problematic issues included the potential NATO eastern expansion to include Eastern European countries – which had not just been part of the Warsaw Pact, but, in the case of the Baltic state, also USSR, disagreement with the West's policy towards the wars in the former Yugoslavia, and in particular with regards to Kosovo (Dobriansky 2000, p. 135), the renegotiation of arms treaties and limitation on nuclear proliferation (Selezneva 2002, pp. 15–16), and tensions over Russia's policy towards Chechnya. However, an attempt to develop a more far-reaching and independent foreign policy trajectory centred on the principle of 'multipolarity', spearhead by Yevgeny Primakov in 1996, did little to improve Russia's international status. Hence, by the end of the 1990s, Russia's international standing was well short of its aspirations of becoming a great power on the par with the West.

In its relations with the former Soviet republics, Russia's policy also veered between ambivalence and attempts to exert its influence. For example, despite the establishment of the Commonwealth of Independent States (CIS) in 1991, Russia was frustrated in its attempts to develop this framework into a functioning and effective mechanism for regional integration in the post-Soviet space. Although most of the former Soviet republics choose to participate, many remained deeply distrustful about Russia's intentions towards it and them. Several CIS member states sought to stall any moves towards greater regional integration, at times even resorting to creating alternative regional integration groupings, such as GUAM (an initiative launched by Georgia, Ukraine, Azerbaijan and Moldova), to counteract the ongoing fear of Russia's power and influence in the region.

Russia's bilateral relations with its individual neighbours were also frequently difficult and problematic. Whilst it was successful in establishing cordial relations with some of its neighbours, notably Belarus, Armenia, Kazakhstan or

Tajikistan, tensions developed with others, including Georgia and Uzbekistan. Russia even had a complex relationship with seemingly its closest neighbour, Ukraine. The tendency of some of the former Soviet republics to develop relationships with European states and the US, and as such decrease the relative influence of Russia over their affairs, was exacerbated by the 1998 financial crisis. It encouraged these states to further diversify their trade and economic relations away from an economically faltering Russia towards other import markets, in particular the European Union (Kobrinskaya, in Smith 2005, p. 78).

The Putin project

Upon coming to power, Putin's regime, rather than shying away from these different crises, seemed ready and willing to face up to them. Indeed, when considered from a historical perspective, as suggested by Shlapentokh, the Putin regime followed in the footsteps of a number of Russian leaders (including Nicolas I, Alexander III, Brezhnev and Andropov) that advocated change, because they 'believed that the state was being jeopardized by plotters and revolutionaries' (2001, p. 374). The goal the new regime thus set itself was to remedy the situation inside Russia. In his approach, Putin came across as a 'disciplinarian reformer capable of combining a free market economy with rule exercised with a strong hand' (Rywkin 2003, p. 9). Critically, as suggested by White and McAllister, Putin was also a 'people's choice'. Not only did his support come from a cross-section of Russian society, including groups in rural and urban centres, but his regime was also representative of a cross-section of citizen's values and attitudes in this period (White and McAllister 2003, p. 384).

The Putin regime immediately set out to crystallize and articulate the sense of general societal dislocation of the late 1990s period within his new 'programme' for Russia. The president suggested that Russia faced a stark choice – to remain weak and feeble, or to rebuild itself from within and subsequently regain its position as a strong state and a great power.

In his 'Millennium Manifesto', a document published on the eve of Yeltsin's resignation in December 1999, Putin set out his vision for Russia. He outlined that the post-Soviet legacy and shifting international realities were to blame for Russia's current crisis. This had caused Russia to become domestically weak and internationally isolated, leaving it to face a series of key existential issues and questions. These had to be resolved before the country could begin to rebuild its strength, and were:

> How can we overcome the still deep ideological and political divisions within society? What strategic goals can consolidate Russian society? What place can Russia occupy in the international community in the twenty first century? What economic, social and cultural frontiers do we want to attain in 10–15 years? What are our strong and weak points? And what material and spiritual resources do we have now?
>
> (Putin 1999a)

In order to resolve these problems, he outlined, Russia first had to reconcile itself with its historical legacy and current circumstances (Sakwa in Ross 2004, p. 21), in three ways. First, in spite of the achievements of the Soviet Union, this episode in Russian history had pushed it 'away from the mainstream of civilisation'. Second, that 'Russia has reached its limit for political and economic upheavals, cataclysms and radical reform ... Responsible socio-political forces should offer the country a strategy for Russia's revival and prosperity ... implemented only by evolutionary, gradual and prudent methods'. Third, that 'mechanical copying of other nations' experience will not guarantee success either', as demonstrated by the damage done by Yeltin's adoption of the privatization programme of the early 1990s. As Lynch notes, 'a central theme running through Putin's policy' was 'recognizing Russia's weakness and diminishing its impact on domestic and foreign policy' (Lynch 2005, p. 143).

Although presenting Russia as a weak state, it was not suggested that it was part of the developing world, or that it sought any external assistance in order to rebuild itself. As noted in Chapter 2, the label of 'weak' states is often applied to states that are perceived to be part of the developing world, and are generally accepted as weak by themselves and others. These states are often also presented as significantly weaker than the West in global power terms. This was not the case with regards to Russia, at least in Putin's eyes.

Debates over Russia's civilizational identity – particularly with regard to its geopolitical orientation – re-emerged in this period. Indeed, discussions over whether Russia is a European, Asian or a Eurasian power have long featured within Russian intellectual thought, going back to the nineteenth century debates between the Westernizers and the Slavophiles (Neumann 1996[1]). As noted previously, by the time of Putin's ascent to president was complete, the initial hopes among many Russian politicians that they could join the post-Second World War Western camp and structure on an equal basis following the end of the Cold-War had been dashed, and a new ambivalence had set in concerning the geopolitical/civilizational direction that Russia should take.

As Smith writes 'great power mentality is at the core of Russian national identity',[2] and in this period Russia was depicted as a fallen 'Great Power', but a 'Great Power' nonetheless. Despite acknowledging that it had slipped down the hierarchy of global powers, Russia was still presented in its national discourse as a major world power 'with a centuries-old history and rich cultural traditions'.[3] According to Putin, Russia had to rebuild its strength, 'find its own path of renewal' and become an active participant in the international society of the future (Putin 1999a). As the National Security Concept argued:

> Despite the complicated international situation and difficulties of a domestic nature, Russia objectively continues to play an important role in global processes by virtue of its great economic, science-technological and military potential and its unique strategic location on the Eurasian continent.[4]

The Russian leadership thus drew a distinction between itself and what mainstream academic and policy analysis considers as a traditional 'weak' state,[5] and at times even sought to portray Russia as 'a metaphorical bridge between the G8 and the global South' for example in its relations with Africa (Jordan 2010, p. 83).

At the same time as detailing its perspective on current circumstances, the regime also put forward its expectations for Russia in the years ahead. This represented the aspirational aspect of the 'rebuilding' project, which while outlining past and present weaknesses, also presented a grand vision of Russia's future, whereby by overcoming its domestic problems it could re-emerge as a 'strong and self-confident' sovereign state in the future (Putin 2000a). The aspiration of becoming a strong state was therefore symbiotically welded with the image of Russia as a weakened and crisis-ridden state of the present. As noted in the National Security Concept 2000:

> Russia's national interests in the domestic political sphere lie in stability of the constitutional system and the institutions of state authority; in ensuring civil peace and national harmony, territorial integrity, the unity of the legal space, and law and order; in completing the formation of a democratic society; and in neutralizing the causes and conducive conditions for political and religious extremism and ethno-separatism, along with their consequences – social, interethnic and religious conflicts, and terrorism.[6]

The key challenges for Russia were how to deal with these different threats to its stability, in order to become a 'strong' state in the future.

Russia's security agenda

Within Putin's assessment of Russia as a 'weak' state, the question of 'security' played a pivotal role. As noted by Galeotti, 'it is not so much that security moved back into the heart of Russian politics – it was always there – as that the Kremlin adopted a far more comprehensive and consistent approach to building policy around its needs' (Galeotti 2010, p. 2).

Whilst Russia is conventionally presented as an actor that views security through rather traditional lenses, this is not an accurate reading of the nature of its security policy. In practice, the central focus of Russia's security agenda was on countering any issue or actor responsible for, or trying to exploit, Russia's current weaknesses, either domestically or externally. With dangers said to be looming from all directions, the Russian leadership adopted a very broad conception of security. As noted by Herd,

> this period reflects a gradual inclusion of non-traditional classical realist threats and state-centric responses to a wider appreciation that 'new' transnational threats can be non-military in nature and may require non-military and international rather than state-led responses.
>
> (Herd 2010, p. 11).

Consequently, the Putin regime's security agenda was defined by a hotchpotch of different concerns, some relating to external threats, others more to Russia's internal and domestic fears and insecurities. Russia, it was suggested, faced both traditional security threats, such as nuclear or military threats from other state actors, and a wide range of non-traditional security concerns, including an economic crisis, population migration and national depopulation, corruption and even the possibility of internal and regional conflict within Russia itself.[7] The inclusion of 'dangers' from the socio-economic and political sectors reinforced the wider Putin notion that the biggest threat was the current state of Russia itself. The domestic sphere was thus critical to Russia's security priorities in the early 2000s.

It did, however, retain a rather state-centric view of the management of security threats, remaining rather suspicious of any suggestions of pooling together of sovereignty or the notion that the human security agenda, an increasingly prominent topic on the global security agenda in this period, should trump or undercut state-security. As outlined below its participation in and promotion of multilateral organizations was limited to those forums that recognized the primacy of state sovereignty in global and regional affairs such as the UN, the OSCE or the Commonwealth of Independent States.

In 2000, the Russian authorities published concepts of National Security, Defence and Foreign Policy, in which the need for immediate action was spelled. At the same time, all three also accepted that Russia's security and foreign policies could only be developed in line with the current domestic circumstances.

Domestic security concerns

Within Russia's security agenda, internal insecurities and the domestic aftermath of the economic crisis of the late 1990s were prioritized over external security considerations. The mass economic collapse, societal and political turmoil and the lack of effective state governance, combined with the threat of international terrorism, were all said to be causing Russia's weakness. Rather than a source of stability and strength, the domestic context was re-articulated as a space fraught with difficulties and danger, and posing an existential threat to Russia. The 2000 National Security Concept suggested that the main security threats facing Russia were:

> The state of the economy, an imperfect system of government and civil society, the social and political polarization of Russian society and the criminalization of social relations, the growth of organized crime and increase in the scale of terrorism, the exacerbation of interethnic relations.[8]

Within this hierarchy of priorities, international terrorism and particularly events in Chechnya, were placed at heart of Russia's security priorities, as it was seen as a transnational phenomenon that transcended a simple division between the external and internal sphere. It was a danger that posed an existential threat to

Russia's sovereignty and domestic political, military, societal and economic sectors.[9] As noted by Putin: 'it is time to recognize that the plague of international terrorism has become a national problem for Russia' (Ustyuzhanin 1999).[10] In line with Buzan and Wæver's notion of securitization, these dangers were presented using the language of 'existential' threats, whereby these challenges were said to signal a potential disintegration of Russia unless remedial and immediate action was taken.

Instead of seeking external assistance to address these challenges, the Putin regime argued that the only way to overcome internal insecurities was by drawing on Russia's own resources and strengths. As outlined in the Millennium Manifesto, the solutions proposed to deal with these diverse threats centred on three basic principles. First, that the development of the country had to be centred on Russian ideas, which included patriotism and the concept of *derzhavnost* (the greatness of Russia). Second, that the rebuilding of Russia should be based on the principles of statism and social solidarity, whereby a 'strong' state was said to be 'the key to Russia's recovery and growth'. Third, that an efficient economy was necessary in order to alleviate the poor living standards and encourage dynamic growth, combat the shadow economy, and 'integrate the Russian economy into world economic structures consistently' (Putin 1999a). As concluded in the Millennium Manifesto the rebuilding of a 'strong' Russia would not come from outside, because 'nobody will do it for us. Everything depends on us, and us alone, on our ability to recognise the scale of the threat, to unite and apply ourselves to lengthy and hard work' (Putin 1999a). In this respect, Putin did not follow the classical model of a 'weak' state, as despite prioritizing its internal insecurities over external developments, he did not expect external assistance. To the contrary, the principles of self-reliance continued to dominate the official discourse on state-building and security.

As the principles outlined above suggest, the internal sphere was constructed as a fluid and tense space. On the one hand, it was a source of instability, insecurity and the root-cause of Russia's weakness. On the other, Russia was presented as a resilient actor that could use its own resources and strengths in order to rebuild itself from within. And although Russia was said to be a 'weak' state in the present, it was claimed that in the near future it could become strong again. In other words, both temporally and spatially the domestic sphere not only came to represent Russia's weakness, but was also articulated as a potential source of Russia's power and future strength.

External security concerns

Alongside this securitization of the internal sphere, Putin's regime also had concerns about threats to Russia's external security. These centred on three main factors: first, Russia's current weakened position in the international system; second, the threat posed by global dangers, such as traditional and non-traditional threats that were operating in the international sphere and impacting on both Russia's external security, but also its domestic stability; and third, tectonic shifts within the international system, which threatened to either further isolate Russia or prevent it from playing its role as a strong sovereign 'great power' in the international arena in the future. Hence, Russia's view of the international system and global security was intrinsically linked with its position and role as a 'Great Power'.

Aside from the domestic problems it has created, the crisis of the late 1990s was said to have left Russia isolated and grappling with its reduced status in a changing global system. Of particular concern was the changing nature of the international system and Russia's role within it (Legvold 2001). As noted in the Russian Foreign Policy Concept 2000, the aim of Russian foreign policy should be:

> To ensure reliable security of the country, to preserve and strengthen its sovereignty and territorial integrity, to achieve firm and prestigious positions in the world community, most fully consistent with the interests of the Russian Federation as a Great Power...[11]

Indeed, within this fractured and increasingly insecure international space, Russia's foreign security policy continued to emphasize the need to rebuild Russia's international status as a 'Great Power'. This was said to be important not only to ensure a more active international role for Russia, but also in order to rebuild its economic and domestic strength (Nicholson 2001, p. 871).

As in the 1990s, the role of the UN, and especially the UN Security Council, remained central to Russia's view of international system and global governance, which were presented as the lynchpin of international society.[12] Thus, 'the strengthening of the United States' position in the world as the main and only centre of power was named directly as a threat to Russian security' (Fedorov in Smith 2005, p. 16), as it was precipitating

> a growing trend towards the establishment of a unipolar structure of the world with the economic and power domination of the United States. In solving principal questions of international security, the stakes are being placed on western institutions and forums of limited composition, and on weakening the role of the U.N. Security Council.[13]

Indeed, the Putin regime remained suspicious of what it saw as the unipolar model championed by the US, and opposed any models of European security centred on the principles of 'NATO-centrism'.[14]

Aside from such traditional security concerns, it was also suggested that the global system was experiencing a rise in new security threats, such as organized crime, alcohol problems, and increased cruelty and violence. The issue of international terrorism, especially in relation to Russia's southern rim, was repeatedly talked about as a major security concern that had arisen due to the changes in the post-Cold War international environment and the growing power of globalization and insecurity across the world (Karev 2000).

Interestingly, and in sharp contrast to the previous and subsequent developments in Russia's foreign security policy, Russia's rise as a 'strong' state and 'Great Power' was presented as a process that could be achieved in harmony, rather than in disunity, with other Great Powers and the international community in general (Putin 2000a). Increased cooperation between Russia and the outside world was claimed not only to be possible, but also mutually beneficial. As noted by the Russian Foreign Minister Igor Ivanov during his speech to the French Senate on 27 October 1999, 'we are proposing building a world where there would be no wars or conflicts' (Ivanov 1999).

In this respect, the Putin regime reversed the trend within the previous administration's elite of widespread suspicion and hostility towards the international community, and in particular the West. If during the early Putin years Russia's failures were primarily blamed on its faltering domestic situation, prior to that most of the responsibility for the failure to reach Russia's great power ambitions was 'explained not as due to the ruler's own errors, but to the hostile intrigues of the West' (Fedorov in Smith 2005, p. 11). In this way, Putin's pro-Western stance was 'more radical than the overall mood in the country' (Baranovsky 2000, p. 457, also see Pravda 2003). As noted by Rywkin, 'given the current Russian financial situation, he saw no benefit in fighting Western economic penetration for purely ideological reasons … To him, it seemed more profitable to associate with the West wherever mutual advantage could be gained' (2003, p. 10).

Initially, it seemed that Putin would prioritize rebuilding relations with Europe (Stent and Shevtsova 2002–2003, p. 127, also see Lo 2003), but, following the events of 9/11, he emphasized Russia's relationship with the US. Whilst relations between Russia and the US under President Bush were initially cordial, if at times frosty, this changed rapidly following the events of 9/11. Following terrorist attacks on New York on 11 September 2001, Putin immediately moved to offer his sympathies to the American people and offered assistance to the US administration in tackling the perpetrators of the attacks. Putin's decision to align Russia with the US resulted in a reset in Russian-American relations. Not only were relations between the two sides more cordial, Russia even offered extensive practical assistance to the US-led campaign in Afghanistan in 2001, particularly in relation to the US military deployment in Central Asia. Putin also backed the US-led war on terror in other areas, such as in intelligence sharing, the opening up of Russian airspace and cooperation in search and rescue operations in Afghanistan, as well as participation in international antiterrorist initiatives. As such, Russia's counterterrorism policy in the external sphere was closely related to its stated aim of re-establishing frameworks of cooperation and coordination with the international community, in which Russia could play an active, rather than passive, role. To the end, the Russian government made regular statements suggesting that the global community should make a more concerted effort to develop a common approach to counterterrorism (Ishchenko 2001).

In addition, Russia was in favour of a greater engagement with the US on the issue of nuclear deterrence and arms control. As Mathers suggests, whilst Russia continued to utilize its 'nuclear power' to boost its international standing, this was also the start of a period of cooperation and engagement for Russia (2012, p. 497). With the likelihood of a future nuclear conflict deemed to be small, both the National Security Concept and Putin official speeches in 2000 supported the principle of a minimum nuclear deterrence and US and Russian joint reduction in their nuclear arsenals. Indeed, Putin personally came out in support of the ratification of the START II treaty with the US, as he also continued to express Russia's opposition to the US plans for a missile defence system, which it was said was not needed to make the US more secure (Mathers 2012, p. 502). Whilst sorely tested, Russia's willingness to cooperate and build good relations with the US was made clear by Putin's mild response to the US decision to unilaterally withdraw from the Anti-Ballistic Missile Treaty in 2001.

Together with moving Russia closer to the West, Russia's foreign policy also continued to champion the principle of multipolarity, from a perspective akin to that articulated by the then-Foreign Minister Yevgeny Primakov in the 1990s (Sakwa 2008). The Putin regime favoured efforts to continue diversifying Russia's foreign relations to include, and improve existing ties with, other international actors and regions of the world. In this vein, Russia took steps to strengthen its relations with China, which culminated in the signing of the Russian-Chinese Strategic Partnership agreement in 2001, and the creation of the Shanghai Cooperation Organization between Russia, China and four of the Central Asian states, namely Kazakhstan, Kyrgyzstan, Russia, Tajikistan and Uzbekistan.

With regard to the post-Soviet space, rather than adopting a 'neo-imperial and neo-colonial' (Dunlop 2000, p. 46) model, it was suggested that Russia should follow the path of any 'normal Great Power', with its own interests and areas of influence. On coming to power, Putin therefore sought to reinvigorate and reassert Russia's relationship with, and position in, the post-Soviet space. However, as noted by Sakwa, 'although Putin may have had a sentimental regard for the recreation of some sort of post-Soviet integrated space, his approach in practice was ruthlessly new realist' (2008, p. 294). Regional policy was to be aligned with national interests, and was no longer to be conducted without regard of the costs. In other words, Russia was no longer prepared to simply subsidize local regimes without a good return on its investments, as demonstrated in relation to Belarus and Ukraine. From this perspective, despite seeking to regain its strength and international standing, Russia's foreign security policy was mindful of its reduced status and position following the end of the Soviet Union (Lynch 2001, pp. 8–9).

Whilst acknowledging this reduced role, and the outlining of concerns by some within Russia that other countries may not automatically welcome back a 'strong' Russia, and that some foreign governments had a vested interest in keeping Russia down, in these initial years of the Putin presidency, official discourse expressed optimism about Russia's potential to once again become a 'Great Power' (Putin 2000a). Once Russia had rebuilt itself, it would become an accepted part of the international (read Western) society.

Conclusion

The depiction of the late 1990s as a crisis period played a pivotal role in the Putin regime's reading of Russia's immediate circumstances and priorities for the future. According to this logic, the first decade of the post-Soviet era had left Russia domestically weak and rife with internal insecurities and instabilities. Upon coming to power, Putin, a relative unknown political figure at the time, thus set out to not only make sense of this mass social, political and economic collapse, but also to put his stamp on Russia's future development. His political vision for Russia centred primarily on the principles of state and national rebuilding on the domestic front, coupled with regaining Russia's status as a 'great power' internationally, via more active engagement with the West.

With his emphasis on the importance of a strong state and a more pro-Western international stance, Putin portrayed himself as eager to reverse a number of long-terms trends that had developed over the course of the mid to late 1990s. He also made clear that despite categorizing early-2000s Russia as a weak state, his regime was determined to ensure that Russia would regain its power in the near future. This patriotism, central to his vision for Russia, also seemed to demonstrate that Putin continued to believe in Russia's national and historical power and strength, and thus under his Presidency, Russia would rebuild itself from within, without any help or support from the outside. And in this way, Russia would be able to rejoin the ranks of the other great powers on the international stage as an equal.

The primary threat to Russia's security and survival was therefore Russia itself. In this regard it was qualitatively different from what it perceived other great powers (read Western powers) to be i.e. strong internally and externally. Whilst, conventionally, Russia's security policy is read through its external security agenda, however, in this period, it was domestic security concerns that largely informed, shaped and drove its security agenda. Indeed, Russia was identified as a victim both of globalization and 'new' and emerging security threats in international security affairs such as international terrorism but also of its own domestic circumstances. Within this internal-external security nexus neither one of these two spheres could therefore be understood without reference to the other.

Despite acknowledging the shifting global security environment, the rise in non-traditional global insecurities and the need for greater multilateral mechanisms for combating these threats, at the turn of the millennium, Russia remained a 'modern' actor grappling with an increasingly post-modern world. It retained a rather traditional state-centric view of the management of security threats, particularly in its domestic sphere. Whilst this was not completely at odds in comparison with the majority of other actors across the international system, such as for example China, it did clash with the global perspective being promoted by the West.

However, even in this much weakened state, Russia did not allow for scrutiny or intervention into its sovereign domestic space – an issue that subsequently became an ever more prominent source of tension in its relations with the West. Since the principle ambitions for the regime was to regain sovereign control over its domestic sphere – the delegation or cessation of its sovereign rights was never on the agenda. At least in principle, Putin's ambitions for Russia followed the conventional model of a strong state – one that was strong internally and externally.

The next chapter examines the impact and effects that the official discourse on the crisis in the late 1990s and Putin's political programme had on the way in which the Russian authorities understood and dealt with particular security concerns of the time. It focuses on the central security concern of the early Putin years, which was said to be intrinsically intertwined with many of the wider trends the regime outlined on coming to power: Chechnya. The securitization of Chechnya in this period is an insightful case for gauging how Putin's new policy for Russia would play out in practice.

Notes

1. For more on this discussion on the role of Eurasianism in contemporary Russian nationalism see: Marlène Laruelle, pages 115–136 'The two faces of contemporary Eurasianism: an imperial version of Russian nationalism', *Nationalities Papers: The Journal of Nationalism and Ethnicity*, Volume 32, Issue 1, 2004, for a discussion about the impact this debate had on Russia's foreign policy see: 'Finding a Civilisational Idea: "West," Eurasia," and "Euro-East" in Russia's Foreign Policy', Andrei P. Tsygankov, *Geopolitics*, Volume 12, Issue 3, 2007 pages 375–399. On Putin's position towards Eurasianism see: Natalia Morozova, pages 667–686 'Geopolitics, Eurasianism and Russian Foreign Policy Under Putin', *Geopolitics*, Volume 14, Issue 4, 2009.
2. Hannah Smith, 'Domestic influences on Russian foreign policy: status, influence and ressentiment', in *Russia and its Near Neighbours*, Maria Raquel Freire and Roger E. Kanet, Palgrave Macmillan, p. 39. Also see *The social construction of Russia's resurgence: aspirations, identity, and security interests*, Anne L. Clunan, Baltimore: Johns Hopkins University Press, 2009.
3. 'Kontseptsiya natsional'noi bezopasnosti Rossiiskoi Federatsii', *Diplomaticheskii vestnik*, 2000, 2.
4. Ibid.
5. Russia saw traditional weak states as belonging to the regions of the 'South'. Russia also presented itself an active rather than passive international actor, and therefore offered its assistance to other weak states around the globe. This demonstrated that even within Russia's discourse there was a ranking of different weak state, which meant that Russia was presented as different from other weak states.
6. 'Kontseptsiya natsional'noi bezopasnosti Rossiiskoi Federatsii', *Diplomaticheskii vestnik*, 2000, 2.
7. 'Obsuzhdaem proekt voennoi doktriny. S uchetom vozmozhnostei strany', *Krasnaya zvezda*, 19 October 1999.
8. 'Kontseptsiya natsional'noi bezopasnosti Rossiiskoi Federatsii', *Diplomaticheskii vestnik*, 2000, 2.
9. These issues are discussed in more detail in Chapter 4 on the securitization of Chechnya.
10. This issue is discussed in more detail in Chapter 4 on the articulation of the Chechen problem.
11. 'Kontseptsiya vneshnei politiki Rossiiskoi Federatsii', *Diplomaticheskii vestnik*, 2000, 8.

12 Vladimir Sredina, Deputy Foreign Minister's statement 'Osnovnye napravleniya vneshnei politiki Rossii na sovremennom etape', *Diplomaticheskii vestnik*, 1999, 10.
13 'Kontseptsiya vneshnei politiki Rossiiskoi Federatsii', *Diplomaticheskii vestnik*, 2000, 8.
14 Vladimir Sredina, Deputy Foreign Minister's statement 'Osnovnye napravleniya vneshnei politiki Rossii na sovremennom etape', *Diplomaticheskii vestnik*, 1999, 10.

4 Russia's number one threat
The securitization of Chechnya

The Chechen issue, and the second Russian military and counterterrorist campaign in Chechnya that began in the late 1999, became one of the key issues of Putin's rise to power and his early years as president. It became both a symbol of Russia's failure, national tragedy and existential threats, and a source of hope that once it was resolved, Russia would be on its way towards rebuilding itself and returning to its previous position as a strong state domestically and a great power internationally. As Baev noted 'counterterrorism provides for a sufficient mobilization of the dysfunctional society around the regime and secures a better place in the U.S.-led effort at establishing a semblance of order in the unruly world' (Baev 2004, p. 348).

Dealing with the separatist and terrorist groups in Chechnya was thus one of the central issues in Russia's security priorities during the early Putin period. However contrary to other accounts, this chapter argues that the securitization of the Chechen issue in official Russian discourse did not simply emerge out of contemporary events in Chechnya and Russia, nor did it merely develop due to historical animosity between Russia and Chechnya. Neither was it simply a politically-orchestrated military campaign to gain more popularity for the Putin candidacy prior to the presidential election of May 2000 (McFaul 2000, pp. 19–21). Rather, it was structured by the Putin regime's reading of Russia's context, insecurities and immediate priorities at the time. This perspective also impacted on the 'solutions' and measures put forward for dealing with Chechnya.

The chapter begins by examining the way in which the Chechen issue was initially securitized by the Putin regime upon coming to power. It details that the main thrust of the official securitization discourse was premised on the notion of 'weakness' and 'existential threats' that stemmed directly from the Putin regime's characterization of Russia as a 'weak' state. The danger and insecurity said to be emanating from Chechnya were therefore proclaimed to be the result of it – much like Russia – becoming a failing and 'weak' entity during the late-1990s. In the case of Chechnya, this entailed succumbing to the forces of domestic and foreign terrorist groups. As a result of this, Chechnya was said to pose an existential threat not only to Russia, but also to itself. Despite this discourse of insecurity, Chechnya continued to be presented as an integral part of

Russia, both as a constituent part of the federation, but also in historic and cultural terms. The goals of the securitization, and the resulting security operations were said to be an attempt to localize and eliminate this existential terrorist threat and to re-establish Russian control over the territory. The resumption of Russian military operations in Chechnya, (following the ceasefire in 1996 of the first conflict in Chechnya and the subsequent signing of the Khasavyurt Accords in 1997) was hailed as a 'police counter-terrorist operation' to restore stability and order in Chechnya and Russia.[1]

In spite of the limited scope implied by the term 'police counter-terrorist operation', the securitization of Chechnya also played a much wider and crucial role in Russia's domestic and external security agendas. As noted in Chapter 2, securitization processes play an important role not only in the way in which particular discourses and security practices are articulated, but also in how they shape wider (re)structuring and symbolic power in terms of state-building and governance discourses, and the internal/external security policies of the securitizing actor. As well as symbolizing the sense of Russia as a 'weak' state articulated by the Putin regime, the securitization of Chechnya also functioned to create symbolic 'red lines', which could not be crossed or challenged by other actors – such as a continued rejection of any external interference from the West into Russian domestic policy towards Chechnya.

In addition, the particular form that the securitization of Chechnya took also suggests that securitization processes rarely function exclusively in either the internal or the external security spheres. Instead, as outlined in the remainder of this chapter, this securitization within Russia's internal sphere directly impacted on its behaviour in its external sphere. This highlights that it is important when analysing non-Western powers, such as Russia, as security actors, to take into account internal security concerns as part of, and together with, the external security dimension of these actors' security policies.

The securitization of Chechnya

A weak Chechnya in a weak Russia

A key aspect of the securitization of Chechnya was that rather than presenting it as a problem of a small secessionist republic seeking to gain independence from Russia,[2] the official discourse instead characterized it as a failed region, a 'quasi-state entity' (Putin 2001d). The notion that insecurity emerges as a result of lawlessness and weak statehood, which was already in evidence on the national level, thus served to structure the particular securitization of Chechnya, and the explanations given by Russian authorities for the increased insecurity and danger emanating from the republic. It was suggested that during the inter-war period (1997–1999), Chechnya had become seeped in lawlessness, instability and banditry and that by the late 1990s it had turned into a hotbed for terrorism, threatening the stability of the rest of the region and the entire Russian Federation. The interconnectedness of these different strands of discourses was aptly highlighted by Sergei Yastrzhembskii, a presidential aide, in an article investigating Chechnya's 10 years since 'independence', in which he stated that:

> For me the decade of independence of Chechnya symbolises first of all the destruction of one of the richest regions of the North Caucasus, the return of traditions from the middle ages, the loss of many innocent lives, the development of a terrorist enclave that had actually threatened the territorial integrity of Russia and the lives and safety of its citizens.
>
> (Yastrzhembskii 2001)

Indeed, the Russian authorities rejected alternative interpretations that highlighted the similarities between the First and Second Chechen campaigns (Golovin 1999; Golts 1999), questioned the legality of this campaign,[3] or viewed it as a cynical ploy by the Russian leadership to improve their chances in the parliamentary or presidential elections of 1999 and 2000. Thus, in response to the suggestion that the FSB was somehow involved in the Moscow apartment bombings in autumn 1999, which were officially attributed to Chechen separatists, the director of the FSB, Nikolai Patrushev, flatly rejected this claim, instead pointing to the context and nature of the terrorist threat in Russia. He argued that '[I]ts [the Moscow apartment bombings] organisers are not some mythical conspirators in the Kremlin, but are completely specific international terrorists who have embedded themselves in Chechnya under the benevolence of the Grozny authorities' (1999). In this respect, the Russian authorities drew a line between the two Chechen campaigns by suggesting that the current context was fundamentally different from the early 1990s.

Whilst the initial discourses about the unstable internal situation in Chechnya and the increasing Islamization of the republic were already present in the interwar period, this strand of discourse was galvanized to an even greater extent in 1999/2000–2001.[4] As noted by Bacon and Renz, the official discourse placed a lot of emphasis on the argument that the current lawlessness and economic deprivation in Chechnya, and that the growth of terrorism posed a great threat to the Chechen population, all of which had resulted in Chechnya becoming weak (Bacon and Renz 2006, p. 52).

The blame for the increasingly insecure situation within Chechnya was put on three key sets of actors: the Ichkerian administration of President Maskhadov, for failing to establish a viable state within Ichkeria between 1996–1999 (Soldatenko 1999b); international terrorists for taking advantage of the Chechen weakness; and the Russian state abandoning the Chechen republic without fully resolving this issue in 1996 and for not intervening sooner (Kozyreva 1999). The deterioration of the local security situation in the mid-late 1990s was alluded to by President Putin in September 2001:

> We had such a negative experience when Russia totally withdrew from Chechnya in 1996, it pulled out all its troops, all its armed units, its entire police; it dismantled everything. The result was a vacuum and an enclave

where bandits held sway. In fact we left the Chechen people at the mercy of the militants and allowed them to be humiliated by them. The vacuum was promptly filled by organisations preaching fundamentalist ideology and fundamentalists from various armed groups in the Middle East and other countries. Eventually it created the grave situation we have been trying to bring under control in Chechnya for a year and a half now.

(Putin 2001b)

President Putin also acknowledged Russia's earlier failures in providing an adequate response to the Chechen issue, stating that:

Since Russia has survived the unpleasant effects after the events of 1996, it did not respond to any of these crimes. All this, of course, only served to widen and radicalise the ambitions of those who were heading this territory and it led in the summer of 1999 to the large-scale attack on the neighbouring republic of Dagestan.

(Putin 2001a)

Furthermore, in addition to blaming the internal context and local actors, this securitizing discourse increasingly emphasized the growing influence of international Islamic terrorists operating from within Chechnya. For example, the official Russian media suggested that two-thirds of Chechen fighters were mercenaries from abroad with direct links to Bin Laden (Garin 1999). These discourses blurred the internal and external spheres, also present in Russia's wider security discourses, as the Russian authorities suggested that the same international terrorist Islamic organizations and Al Qaeda groups that operated in other areas and regions of instability, such as Afghanistan, were also active in Chechnya. For example in the article 'Fighters are helped from abroad', published in *Rossiiskaya gazeta* on 7 September 1999, Vladimir Lapskii suggested that Chechnya was too poor and too weak to be able to militarize itself from within and that instead 'Bin Laden sends weapons and technology to Basayev and Khattab through Afghani Taliban' (Lapskii 1999).

Spatially and normatively, these foreign fighters inside Chechnya were, in turn, presented as carriers of foreign norms and cultural traditions that were threatening not only security, but also both Russian and Chechen cultural and societal norms. Foreign forms of Islam, brought in by 'wahhabists' from Saudi Arabia, were presented as a dangerous and destructive influence threatening the Chechen way of life, by imposing their own norms on the local Chechen population. Indeed, foreign terrorist groupings were also often accused of not being real Muslims, and of using Islam as a cover for criminal interests and actions. As suggested by the Minister for Federal Affairs and Nationalities, Vyacheslav Mikhailov, 'the intentions of the fighters became clear, to create a number of zones of influence, under the cover of Islamic ideas' (Soldatenko 1999b). Within this discourse, the image of the threat centred on that of international terrorism as a threatening and hostile foreign influence, which was endangering both Russia and Chechnya.

In line with their ambition to reassemble and create a united 'strong' Russia, with a sense of pride in Russian history and heritage, the Putin regime's discourse on both wider state identity and the specific securitization of Chechnya constituted Chechnya, not as an entity separate from Russia, but as an integral part of it. Publically, the Putin regime always maintained that this 'counter-terrorist police operation' was not directed against Chechnya or Islam per se, but only certain elements of these groups (Putin 2000), even if in the long run the conflict severely damaged Russian-Muslim relations (Yemelianova 2002; Trenin 2002). Zelkina suggests that the conceptual divisions between official and unofficial Islam utilized by the Russian authorities, has a long tradition within Tsarist Russia and the Soviet Union, adopted as a mechanism of control of Islamic practices and Muslim groups by the Russian state (Zelkina 2007).

In societal and ethnic terms, a similar development occurred. A double identity for the Chechen people emerged with Russian official discourse, split between those deemed to be 'good' Chechens, who were prepared to collaborate with Russia and coexist peacefully within the Russian Federation, and 'bad' Chechens that had been influenced by external terrorists, and were fighting against the interests of the federal centre and the 'good' Chechens (Ivanov 1999).[5] Chechnya was, therefore, presented as a part of the 'Self' (i.e. the Russian Federation) in cultural, social, economic and political terms; whereas the security threat emanating from Chechnya was presented as a deviant form of the core identity of Chechens and articulated as the 'Other' in the official discourse.

In this way, the securitization of Chechnya evolved to play a role beyond that assumed by the Copenhagen School's model, whereby securitizations are only mechanisms of characterizing an issue as a security threat. It became a symbolic representation of Russia's failure as a sovereign state and a 'weak' state within wider Russian discourse on its state identity. These sentiments were clearly articulated by President Putin in his television interview with ORT in January 2000 when he stated that:

> I would not start changing anything, because I am absolutely convinced that we will not resolve any problems: not economic, social ones in a situation when the state is falling apart. Therefore, I think that there is nothing unusual that today we are devoting so much focus and attention to the problem of terrorism.
>
> (Putin 2000d)

Within the securitization discourse on Chechnya, the image of Russia as a 'weak' state and construction of internal and external insecurities was vital to the construction of the Chechen problem, the representation of its root causes and the articulation of the extent, and the main protagonists, of the threat to Russia stemming from it.

Proposed measures to deal with the existential threat of Chechnya

During the course of the second half of 1999, the threat from instability within, and terrorism originating from, Chechnya, was elevated to the status of an 'existential' threat to the Russian Federation in official discourse. This was precipitated, and reinforced, by a number of events. Between 2–7 August 1999, around 1,500 armed Chechen, Arab and Dagestani, mainly Salafi, fighters, invaded Dagestan, announcing the creation of an 'independent Islamic State of Dagestan'.[6] This was followed by the Moscow apartment bombings during September 1999. The invasion of Dagestan was constructed not only as a direct assault on Dagestan, and further proof of the destabilization and insecurity in Chechnya, but also an immediate security challenge to Russia's sovereign control over both republics, especially Chechnya, and an existential threat to Russia's national security and existence on a nationwide scale. These incidents in August and September of 1999 were not treated in isolation – but as part of a single existential threat posed to both Russia and Chechnya (Soldatenko 1999a). For example, in an interview with Mukhu Aliev, chair of the National Assembly of Dagestan, in *Rossiiskaya gazeta* on 11 September 1999:

> The aggression against Dagestan – is not simply an aggression against one of the republics of the Russian Federation. We consider it as aggression against Russia. Particularly using a moment when Russia is weakened and when many mistakes are made, also in regards to Chechnya.
> (Vorob'ev 1999)

Consistent with the presentation of the external influence of Islamic terrorism on Chechnya, the proponents of these acts were said to be an alliance of Islamic terrorists and former Chechen separatists set on attacking Russia and the rest of the civilized world (Snetkov 2007, pp. 1352–1355).

Inaction or non-response to the attack on Dagestan and the Moscow apartment bombings was presented as impossible, as they amounted to the main security 'hot spot' in Russia, as Putin characterized Chechnya in his speech at the Extended Session of the Ministry of Interior in January 2000 (Putin 2000b).

However, in spite of this portrayal of the threat from Chechnya as existential, the measures proposed to address it cannot be characterized as the 'extraordinary', as the Copenhagen School's model of securitization suggests will follow a successful securitization of an existential threat.[7] In practice, processes of securitizations often take different forms and necessitate different measures depending on the local contexts. In this case, the Russian authorities did not designate the threat from Chechnya as an 'emergency situation', which would have necessitated a vote in the Duma, choosing instead to use existing antiterrorist legislation that allowed the use of special terrorist operations and emergency measures to be implemented within a localized area for a finite amount of time.[8] According to the Presidential decree of 23 September 1999, this legal framework was sufficient to deal with the situation in, and threat from, Chechnya.[9]

In-line with the state-centric view of security evident in Russia's wider security policy, the securitization discourse on Chechnya suggested that the main measures to counteract the threat should be directed from the federal centre. Regional authorities and local Chechen groups were given a subsidiary role on the ground. In developing its plan of action in autumn 1999 to spring 2000, the Russian leadership drew parallels with NATO's experience in Kosovo and its use of force regardless of human suffering and loss. The leading Russian military scholar, Arbatov notes that Kosovo had taught Russia that 'ends justify the means' (Arbatov 2000, p. 32). Indeed, the actions of the West internationally were often alluded to in Russia's official justification of its use of particular military measures during the initial stages of its action in Chechnya, highlighting the inter-linkage between internal and external security spheres in the construction of Russia's official security discourse on Russia and Chechnya.

The military operations

The focus of the initial military operations in September 1999 was on pushing back the Chechen threat from Dagestan, through a mixture of Russian troops and local Dagestani militia. The attack against Chechnya itself began on 18 September 1999 and sought to initially create a 'cordon sanitaire', security zone around Chechnya (Maksakov 1999). In mid-September 1999, the Prime Minister argued for the launch of the security zone in Chechnya, stating that a 'quarantine around the whole perimeter of Chechnya is necessary' (Ustyuzhanin 1999).

Operations moved further into the Chechen territory during the second phase of the conflict, from mid-October to the end of November 1999. The Russian army sought to blockade Grozny and take control of this territory (Babaki 1999). As noted in a statement from the Russian government, the goals of this operation were 'to achieve the full restoration of the legality and rule of law on the whole territory of the Chechen republic, the liberation of Chechnya from terrorist and other bandit groups.'[10]

Large-scale military operations continued in December 1999 and January 2000, and centred on taking control of the capital Grozny via major bombings of the city. The end goal of the operation was to regain control of this territory. By spring 2000, the large-scale operations were over and Grozny was in some respects under the control of the federal authorities. At least in the immediate term, the Russian leadership proclaimed a victory in pushing back the terrorists, both in the republic and the country as a whole.

In turn, as noted by Pain (2005, p. 73), the early military victories in the Second Chechen campaign galvanized the Russian populace into believing that the failures of the 1990s could indeed be resolved by the Putin regime's administrative reforms and the creation of a strong centre, as outlined in official discourse. According to Pain,

> raids into Dagestan by Basayev's bands, the apartment bombings in Russian cities and the misunderstood 'Kosovo lesson' have released the pent-up

feelings of national humiliation and outrage: 'Nobody takes us seriously—not the Chechens, not the West'; 'nobody is protecting us'; 'the government and the military are good for nothing.' As the poet said, 'we long retreated in silence'.

(Pain 2000)

Addressing the challenge of Chechnya was presented as the first sign of Russia fighting back from its decline into weakness. In this way, the Chechen issue (alongside other issues) had become a vote winner, rather than a vote loser for the Russian leadership on the domestic front. Victory in Chechnya was presented as a key stepping stone towards Russia asserting its sovereign rights over its territory, and regaining its status as a confident and 'strong' domestic and international actor.

Non-military measures

After the initial phases of the conflict and large-scale military operations, the Russian leadership turned towards considering non-military measures to alleviate the security situation in Chechnya. In this respect, the Russian authorities linked the need to alleviate insecurity in Chechnya with their stated intention to rebuild Russia from within – not only in terms of security, but also economically and wider state-building. This was in line with the projects envisaged for the rest of the country, a trend which will be examined in more detail in the next chapter.

In a document published by the Russian government on the measures for alleviating the situation on the ground in Chechnya in October 1999, the Russian authorities laid out a set of 'solutions' for rebuilding Chechnya in the near future. It advocated the restoration of the Russian constitution within Chechnya, and the return of a peaceful and calm life to the Chechen population.[11] It also argued that military measures alone were insufficient to achieve these goals, and that negotiations and dialogue with the 'positive' elements within the Chechnya – groups that 'had actively condemned terrorism against the population of the Chechen republic, their neighbours in the North Caucasus region, and the whole population of the Russian Federation'[12] – was necessary.

A tense debate ensued within the Russian establishment regarding how best to rebuild Chechnya and what political system should be installed following the end of the large-scale military action.[13] As envisaged by the Copenhagen model of securitization, during the stage of the 'extraordinary measures' of the securitization, normal political structures and institutions in Chechnya were suspended. Instead Akhmat Kadyrov, a Chechen Muslim cleric and fighter, was appointed to head a provisional Chechen administration until such time that normal republican state structures, as per the Russian constitution, could be returned to Chechnya. In this respect, the Ichkerian administration under the leadership of President Maskhadov, elected by popular mandate in 1997, was sidelined.[14] Hence, the Putin regime's minimal dialogue with local groups betrayed Russia's ongoing paternalistic and federally-centred approach towards Chechnya. The appointment of Akhmat Kadyrov as the head of the provisional Chechen administration in 2000 was also a demonstration of the Russian regime's notion of 'good' and 'bad' Chechens. Despite participating on the side of the rebels during the first Chechen conflict, Akmat Kadyrov, as an opponent of 'Wahhabism' and the Salafi form of Islam, had refused to back the Wahhabist led invasion of Dagestan in 1999, switching his allegiances to support Russian federal policy from autumn 1999 onwards.[15] This illustrates that the definition of a 'good' Chechen in Russian official discourse is someone that, at this particular time, supports the federal authorities, even if previously they have opposed it, and rejects the influence of so-called 'foreign' forms of Islam, which do not have a long history of practice within the North Caucasus. Thus, Chechnya and its people were divided into those that were 'good' and those that were 'bad' (Boikov 2001) splintering the country into different camps, and it was the Russian authorities that were bestowed with the power to formulate these boundaries and decide who was accepted or kept out of the proposed state-rebuilding process in Chechnya.

Viewed with the Russian context of the time, the securitization of Chechnya followed the same logic as wider state-building and security discourses on the national level, which centred on the fear of a 'weak' state and internal instability and insecurity. The large-scale military operations and the establishment of the provisional Chechen administration under Akhmat Kadyrov were geared towards alleviating the danger emanating from Chechnya in the internal sphere, in same way that various other measure taken by the Putin regime in other areas were aimed towards restoring a strong central state and alleviating the instability that was said to permeate the late 1990s.

External sphere: the securitization of Chechnya as a global threat

Aside from being securitized in the domestic sphere, the issue of Chechnya also came to be presented as a major existential threat in Russia's external sphere by virtue of its association with international terrorism and the post-9/11 'global war on terror'. In this respect, the securitization of Chechnya played two key roles in Russia's wider external security policy. On the one hand, it fed into Russia's wider vision of what constituted the main security threats in the international system at the turn of the twenty-first century. On the other, it became a mechanism for alliance building. The Russian authorities sought to use the said connection between international terrorism and Chechnya in their attempts to re-engage with the West and to regain Russia's position as a major power within the international community, following its isolation in the late-1990s. Therefore, the securitization of Chechnya served not only to identify what constituted Russia's external security priorities, it also played a role in its wider foreign policy ambitions.

Chechnya and international terrorism: global threats

In the Russian context, the theme of external enemies seeking to infiltrate the Russian sovereign space pre-dated Putin's tenure as president. Even in the mid-late 1990s, the Russian leadership was already concerned about the threat of international terrorists operating both locally and internationally. They also feared the growing foreign influence inside Chechnya, such as the rising numbers of external fighters operating in the republic, but also the increasing Islamization of the republic via foreign clerics, and the growing impact of events and developments in the regions to the south of Russia, such as in Afghanistan (interview with Oleg Kusov, 20 May 2008, Moscow).

By placing such emphasis on the involvement of international terrorist groups on the territory of Chechnya, the Russian authorities seemed to be determined to demonstrate that this danger was not simply a discrete domestic problem of Russian-making, but was in fact a feature of the international system and the globalization of international threats. The Chechen issue therefore became a major external, as well as internal, security concern for Russia. It transcended the simple division of what constituted the external and internal security realms by posing a threat to both spheres at once and functioning within and across them simultaneously. As noted by President Putin, international terrorists operated in Chechnya

> under the slogan and for the purpose of getting additional territory from Russia and to establish a Muslim caliphate from the Black to the Caspian Sea – a United States of Islam.
>
> (Putin 2001a)

Within this nexus of global-local security threats, Russia's reading and understanding of what constituted the threat of international terrorism globally was, in turn, articulated through its domestic experience of terrorism in Chechnya (Polikovsky 2001). This interrelationship was alluded to, for example, in President Putin's response to the 9/11 attacks in the US. He noted that international terrorism 'is the plague of the 21st century. Russia directly knows what terrorism is and for that reason we understand the feelings of the American people' (Mereu 2001).

The dangers stemming from the global terrorist threat was not simply due to these actors' abilities to travel and attack targets in different geographical locations, but also from the growing links between local separatist movements and global and regional terrorist networks. For the Russian authorities, Chechnya came to represent one of the world hot-spots, in which such networks of separatists and terrorist grouping coalesced. Concerns over these links were explicitly made in a statement by Russia's Foreign Minister Ivanov in his speech to the French Senate in November 1999:

> As shown in practice, contemporary separatism directly connects with terrorism. Moreover, the tightest links are being laid down between different terrorist and separatist centres. The emergence of an open coordination of actions, the interflow of fighters and arms between the Balkans, Caucasus and Central Asia.
>
> (Ivanov 1999)

The securitization of Chechnya, hence, played a key role in Russia's understanding and position towards the problem of international terrorism in a global context. In this respect, the construction of its external sphere emerged directly out of its internal context and domestic security concerns.

Creating a common front between Russia and the West

Within Russia's discursive-construction of itself as a civilized and developed country with aspirations to become a great power, which is either part of, or at least on a par with, the West, the securitization of Chechnya served to strengthen the vision of Russia as a power on the frontiers of the fight between the civilized world and the world envisioned by 'wahhabist' terrorists (O'Loughlin et al. 2004, p. 4). The ongoing fight against terrorism inside Russia was therefore said to be carried out not only for the survival of Russia and Chechnya, but also for the survival of the prevailing international society. As noted, by the Head of General Staff of the Armed Forces, Valerii Manilov in September 2000, 'those guys, killed in Chechnya, are defending the whole of Europe from terrorism' (Kozyreva 2000). The Russian leadership justified its actions in Chechnya on the premise that it contributed to the wider security of the civilized world, and highlighted once more its wider foreign policy ambitions to re-engage with the West.

The Russian authorities sought to alert the international community to the danger of international terrorism in the late-1990s. For example, Russia initiated a series of UN resolutions aimed at security threats emanating from Al Qaeda terrorist cells in Afghanistan. In October 1999, Russia also sponsored UN Security Council (UNSC) Resolution 1267, which threatened to impose sanctions on the Taliban, unless it surrendered Bin Laden. UNSC resolution 1333 reiterated these demands in December 2000.[16] This discourse thus predated the launch of a similar rhetoric by US-led war-on-terror after 9/11. For Russia, international terrorism came to represent a security threat operating in multiple parts of the world, and it fell to the international community to establish a united front to counteract this global danger (Karev 2000).

At the same time, prior to the events of 9/11, the securitization of Chechnya played a negative, rather than a positive, role in Russia's relations with the West (Williams 2004, p. 198). The EU and the US refused to accept Russia's conflation of international terrorism with Chechnya, continuing to characterize it as a secessionist issue, whilst condemning the large-scale and destructive military operations in the republic. For example, the then republican Presidential candidate, George W. Bush famously suggested, in February 2000, that the IMF and Export-Import Bank should cut its loans to Russia if it continued its military campaign in Chechnya (Williams 2004, p. 198). In Europe, similar levels of criticism came both from various governments and various regional organizations, such as the EU, Organization for Security and Cooperation in Europe (OSCE) and the Council of Europe. For example, the EU threatened to review its assistance programmes to Russia. The EU External Relations Commissioner, Chris Patten, in December 1999, noted that 'we do want the best possible relationship with Russia. But the disproportionate use of force in Chechnya does not make it easier for us to have that sort of relationship' (Moore 2003).[17] Russia also failed to persuade the West that Islamic terrorism, particularly that developing around its Southern borders, should become a top priority for international security.

After 9/11, a shift in outlook was noticeable within the West. In response to the altered international environment, Putin galvanized this previously unsuccessful strategy of calling for the creation of a stronger international framework to deal with counterterrorism, and reiterated the link between Russia's experience in Chechnya and those of the US in relation to 9/11. Putin noted in one statement in September 2001 that,

> Following the barbaric terrorist acts in New York and Washington on September 11 this year, the world is still living under the impression of this tragedy...
> We also believe that what is happening in Chechnya cannot be viewed out of the context of the fight against international terrorism.
>
> (Putin 2001e)

Russia's attempts to participate in the US-led 'war on terror' coalition, however, drew mixed responses from analysts and academics in West. Some argued that the link between Russia's problems in Chechnya and the US 'war on terror' was an opportunistic move (Cornell 2003, pp. 167–168), a way to legitimize its campaign in Chechnya, (Kennedy-Pipe and Welch 2005), or purely a mechanism for restoring Russia's links with the West (Bosworth 2002), following the breakdown of relations in the late 1990s.

Nonetheless, on a bilateral level, at least in the initial stages, Russia did seem to gain wider international recognition of its problems in Chechnya, and was accepted as an important international actor in the 'war on terror' by the US. As noted by Lieven (2002, p. 249), Russia shared America's vision for the war on terror, as 'an alliance between states for the protection of states'. There was a marked decrease in US condemnation of Russia's actions in Chechnya, and in the US the issue of Chechnya became closely linked with what Williams calls the 'Chechen – Afghan – Al Qaeda' myths, especially in the American press in 2001 and 2002, which he notes became 'a veritable industry' during the Afghanistan campaign in the winter of 2001–2002 (Williams 2004, p. 204).

At a multilateral level, Russia sought to establish a degree of rapport with NATO around the issue of global terrorism, especially following the establishment of the NATO – Russia Council in 2002. Russia also became an active participant in the UN Security Council Counter Terrorism Committee (Lynch 2005, p. 150). The threat of international terrorism also became a mechanism for cooperation in non-Western multilateral organizations, such as the Collective Security Treaty Organization (CSTO) and the Shanghai Cooperation Organization (SCO) (Aris 2009, 2011).

However, despite attempts to create and/or participate in an international coalition against global terrorism, Russia remained very sensitive to any external assistance, interference, or overt criticism of its securitization of Chechnya and its policy in the republic.[18] External interference into its domestic space was seen as a further loss of control over territory, and as signalling a failure to function as the 'strong' sovereign state that it aspired to be.

This was particularly the case in Russia's relations with Europe. The European institutions and governments did not recognize Russia's discursive construction of Chechnya to the same extent as the US. Despite a muting of criticism by European countries immediately after 9/11, such discourses re-emerged rather swiftly at the Russia-EU summits in 2002. Europe continued to draw a distinction between Chechen rebels and Al Qaeda, insisting that Russia should negotiate with Chechen representatives, as outlined at the Russia-EU Brussels Summit of November 2002 (Herd 2002, p. 118).

Whilst its European partners attempted to put pressure on it regarding events in Chechnya, and to hold it to account on humanitarian issues, such as human rights, the level of abuse at the hands of the Russian army, and the plight of Chechen refugees in neighbouring republics (OSCE memo 2000), Russia flatly refused to be told what to do in Chechnya. This refusal was aptly demonstrated by its response to the attempts to exclude it from the Council of Europe in April 2000 due to its actions in Chechnya. Rather than conceding to international pressure, Russia instead blamed its European partners for undermining the dialogue between the two sides, and vowed to carry on with its policy towards Chechnya regardless.[19] From the Russian perspective, its aspirations of becoming a strong state meant that external interference into its internal space would not be tolerated for fear of a loss of power and sovereignty rights over its territory.

The securitization of Chechnya thus played multiple roles in Russia's external security policy. On the one hand, the fusion of Chechnya and international terrorism enabled Russia, in some respects, to initiate a re-engagement with the international community and the West in particular. While on the other hand, the West's frequent criticism of Russia's securitization practices in Chechnya led to growing tensions between Russia and the West. Despite achieving some of its initial aims, in the form of an alliance with the US-led 'war on terror', the securitization of Chechnya remained a source of friction between Russia and the West.

Conclusion

During the initial securitization of Chechnya, this issue became the lynchpin of Putin's wider national agenda of presenting Russia as a 'weak state' rife with insecurities and instability in its domestic and external spheres. The sense of societal, political and economic collapse and insecurities were writ large in Chechnya. The work of rebuilding Russia had to start in Chechnya and the mass security operations launched against the republic in late 1999 were meant to achieve that goal. However, in many ways the regime also betrayed its sense of conservatism. This was not only because it sought to preserve Russia's unity and control over the republic, but because much of this securitization discourse was also couched in the language of patriotism and pride in its national and historical traditions, with Chechnya said to form a historical link with Russia. In practice, however, the precariousness of the conceptual separation between the good and the bad Chechens was often 'lost in translation', and did not abate either the rising ultra-nationalism or the anti-Caucasian feeling in the country. Nonetheless, as discussed in a later chapter, it was precisely this separation that structured Russia's subsequent attempts to co-opt certain Chechen groups into its 'normalization' project, highlighting once more the incremental and piecemeal nature of securitization and desecuritization processes. Rather, than a deviant case, the securitization of Chechnya was therefore emblematic of wider processes in Russia at the time.

More broadly, the war in Chechnya and Russia's fight against international terrorism formed part of Russia's wider debate regarding the shifting nature of the global security agenda, the nature of globalization and Russia's role and position towards this. In particular, the regime was adamant that the second Chechen campaign was not a 'local' secessionist conflict lingering on from the previous era, but formed part of a much wider changing global security context in which non-traditional threats such as global terrorism operate without fixed borders or addresses and could strike anyone at anytime. In this regard, Russia was very much painted as a victim both due to its post-Soviet legacy and from the forces of globalization i.e. global terrorism. However, particularly following the events of 9/11 and the launch of the global war on terror, the regime also saw this as an opportunity to boost its position internationally, to rejoin the international community and in particular to rebuild its relations with the West, after the wilderness years in the late 1990s.

From Russia's point of view, its participation in this broader multilateral coalition to combat global terrorism did not, however, equate to a loss or weakening of its sovereignty rights. If Russia's sovereignty had already been undermined by its domestic collapse and forces of global terrorism it was not prepared to erode them further. The Chechen issue sorely tested these assumptions, nonetheless, at this stage, Russia remained optimistic about its capacity and ability to re-engage with the international community but on its own terms.

The next chapter sets out the way in which Putin's project moved to the next rebuilding stage, resulting not only in a growing sense of power and strength intertwined with growing disillusionment and defensiveness against the West, but also a growing focus on the preservation of regime security in both its domestic and foreign security agendas.

Notes

1 The focus of this book is on the official version of events in relation to the Chechen incursion into Dagestan in August 1999 and the apartment bombings in September 1999. These two events have raised a great deal of controversy and debate both in Russia and in the West in relation of what 'actually' took place on the ground, especially in relation to the role that Putin and the FSB may or may not have played. However, due to the lack of space the focus of this piece is exclusively on the official

discourse rather than these alternative interpretations. For alternative versions of events see Felshtinsky and Litvinenko (2007); Bennett (2007); Criticism of such conspiracy theories was put forward by other scholars such as Sakwa (2008). For a discussion of the different version of events see Hale (2004).
2 This was the image of Chechnya in the First Chechen conflict, for more information see Gall and de Waal (1998).
3 'Memorial and Demos (2006) ' "Counterterrorism Operation" by the Russian Federation in the North Caucasus throughout 1999–2006', *Memorial*, January, available at: www.memo.ru/hr/hotpoints/N-Caucas/dkeng.htm, accessed 14 April 2007.
4 Prior to Vladimir Putin's ascension to power, there was a proliferation of official discourse about the growing insecurity in Chechnya, and the use of public executions, the adoption of Islamic tradition, and the general Islamization of Chechnya under Maskhadov's regime, (interview with Panfilov, May 2008, Moscow).
5 These two discursive constructions of traditional 'indigenous' versus foreign and new forms of Islam, and 'good' versus 'bad' Chechens, were often operationalized together in the official securitization discourse, particularly when officials sought to highlight the differences between 'our Chechens' versus the threatening foreign Islamic influence. For example in 2000, in his interview with the German journal 'Focus', Putin merged these two discourses together when stating that more should be done to protect this 'indigenous' form of Islam. He noted 'I feel great failure that we cannot more effectively protect the peaceful population and representatives of traditional Islam from terrorist acts on the part of fundamentalists' (Putin 2001b).
6 For more details on this initial period of the Second Chechen campaign see Souleimanov (2007, pp. 147–171).
7 In the Copenhagen School of Security's approach to securitization, a successful securitization should be followed by the removal of an issue out of the realm of normal politics, into the realm of security where extraordinary measures are applied, see Buzan, Wæver and de Wilde (1998).
8 Interview with Cherkassov, Moscow, April 2007.
9 Presidential Decree of the Russian Federation N1255c on 23 September 1999, 'On measures for increasing the effectiveness of the counter-terrorist operation on the territory of the North Caucasus region of the Russian Federation'.
10 Russian Government, 'Zayavlenie Pravitel'stva Rossiiskoi Federatsii o situatsii v Chechenskoi Respublike i merakh po ee uregulirovaniyu', *Rossiiskaia gazeta*, 23 October 1999.
11 Russian Government, 'Zayavlenie Pravitel'stva Rossiiskoi Federatsii o situatsii v Chechenskoi Respublike i merakh po ee uregulirovaniyu', *Rossiiskaia gazeta*, 23 October 1999.
12 Russian Government, 'Zayavlenie Pravitel'stva Rossiiskoi Federatsii o situatsii v Chechenskoi Respublike i merakh po uregulirovaniyu', *Rossiiskaia gazeta*, 23 October 1999.
13 Other suggestions, which were not adopted, were made about the future of Chechnya, favoured by key influential persons in the Russian elite and presidential apparatus such as the Plenipotentiary Envoy of the President of the Russian Federation to the Southern Federal District, key figures in the FSB and Nikolai Koshman, the government envoy of the Russian Federation in Chechnya. This plan involved the establishment of a Russian General Governor in Chechnya, which would install a direct vertical of power from the centre to the republic, and ensure direct control, as well as implementation of political, economic and social reforms. For a longer discussion about the different political options put forward for dealing with Chechnya in this period see Souleimanov 2007, p. 189.
14 Some officials and ministers, such as the Minister for Nationalities Affairs emphasized the urgent need for a meeting between Putin and Maskhadov, because Maskhadov 'must be helped' because he was unable to control the situation in the

republic, see ('Ministr po delam natsional'nostei schitaet neobkhodimoi skoreishuyu vstrechu Putina i Maskhadova', *Polit.ru*, 18 September 1999, available at: www.polit.ru/news/1999/09/18/536951.html, accessed 18 February 2008); others, such as the *siloviki*, held Maskhadov responsible for the current security situation in Chechnya, and were reluctant to negotiate with the Ichkerian government or the halting of military operations in favour of political settlements (Korotchenko 1999). In the end, despite the development of different negotiation plans, which proposed a more active engagement between the leaders of Ichkeria and Russia, this idea did not come to fruition.

15 For a longer discussion regarding the reasons for Ahmat Kadyrov switching sides in 1999 from supporting the rebels to backing the Russian federal policy in Chechnya see Souleimanov, 2007, pp. 191–194.
16 The text of the UN Security Council Resolution 1333 available at: www.un.org/News/Press/docs/2000/20001219.sc6979.doc.html, accessed 20 November 2008.
17 Russia's voting rights in the Council of Europe were removed for the period 2000–2001.
18 Interfax 'Poseesh veter – pozhnesh' buryu' *Rossiiskaya gazeta*, 18 November 1999.
19 Statement from the Ministry of Foreign Affairs', 7 April 2000, *Diplomaticheskii Vestnik*, May 2000, available at: www.ln.mid.ru/dip_vest.nsf/99b2ddc4f717c733c325 67370042ee43/e9c96e639cff38b1c32568ef0027c966?OpenDocument, accessed 5 January 2009.

Part II
2000–2004

5 The rebuilding of Russia

At the heart of Putin's ambitions in 2000 was to transform Russia into a secure, strong and confident power both domestically and internationally. By the time that most of the initial 'ambitions' and goals of this rebuilding programme across the four pillars of reconstruction, identified in 1999/2000: economic growth, state making, nation building and regaining Russia's position and standing internationally (Sakwa 2007) had been put in place at the end of 2004, Russia, at least in the official discourse of the regime, had indeed become a more confident, and to some extent a stronger but still rather insecure power. Despite managing to deal with and alleviate the major existential crisis of the late 1990s, the process of implementing this rebuilding programme, the growing authoritarianism of the Putin's system and the increasingly difficult relationship with the West, together with the fallout from the 'colour revolutions' in Georgia (2003) and Ukraine (2004) meant that the search for greater 'security' remained a rather illusive and constantly moving target for Russia. Furthermore, this process of 'rebuilding' did not result in the creation of a more open and democratic Russia, as had been hoped for in the West, but the emergence of a much more authoritarian and overbearing system, with the Putin regime at the heart of it.

The focus of this chapter is therefore not on the whether or not the Putin regime had succeeded in rebuilding Russia as a strong state by 2004. Rather it traces the way in which the regime's perception of strength versus weaknesses, security versus insecurity evolved and with what effect, as the country was being rebuilt both domestically and internationally. In this regard, Putin's rebuilding project for Russia produced a much more complex picture of Russia, one in which its growing sense of confidence and strength in some areas, particularly in economics remained tightly intermixed with its ongoing sense of insecurity, such as regarding 'internal' enemies or in its relations with the West.

Indeed whilst the regime appeared to be 'proud' of its successes in bringing the country back from the brink of a general collapse in the late 1990s, it remained very fearful that its project for Russia, an issue closely interconnected with its own ambitions of gaining and retaining control and power in the country, could be derailed or swept aside. The more that the Putin regime sought to gain greater control over the domestic sphere and to boost its position internationally the more it came to see any deviation or alternative positions to its vision for

Russia as a direct threat. It was this sense of duality that was translated into the regime's representation of Russia as simultaneously a much stronger and confident and yet still insecure actor.

In this respect, as argued below, the interrelationship between Russia's internal and external spheres remained very strong, as developments in one area such as for example the worsening relationship with the West or the colour revolutions in the post-Soviet space (in Ukraine in particular) directly impacted on events and perceptions in the other. The exact evolution of Putin's programme for Russia did not, however, follow a tight blueprint but developed in conjunction with and in response to events and changing circumstances domestically and internationally.

This chapter now turns to examine the key tenets of Putin's rebuilding programme for Russia, it then considers Russia's changing foreign relations, particularly its growing disillusionment with the West, the effect of the colour revolutions and the impact this had on its perceptions of the domestic sphere. It then moves on to examine Russia's changing security agenda and the way in which despite Russia's rebuilding efforts insecurities domestically and internationally remained a key feature of its domestic and foreign politics. It argues that not only did the West now carry a much more negative image for Russia by the end of this period, but also that domestically, as the regime sought to accrue greater control over the system it remained fearful that its efforts would be derailed either domestically and internationally, and a much wider set of threats and insecurities emerged under the umbrella notion of the image of *obraz vraga*.

From a weak state to a power rebuilding itself

Rather than a halfway house between pinpointing Russia's problems or publicizing its strengths, the rebuilding project rolled out during 2000–2004 was a political agenda in its own right, centred on a series of macro-structural changes, particularly in the economic, political and social sectors. In turn, as the pace of change quickened, supported by Russia's growing economic stability, more emphasis was placed on highlighting the successes of the 'rebuilding' efforts. By the end of 2004, the main goals of this rebuilding programme had been achieved, the main pillars and structure of the Putin system had been put in place and Russia was ready to enter the next stage of its development.

On the economic front, despite structural weaknesses and institutional problems (Hansen 2003, p. 380), the reform proposals of Economics Minister, German Gref led to a restructuring of the Russian economic space. These changes included tax reform, deregulation, land and judicial reform (Åslund 2004, p. 398), devaluation of the rouble and prudent monetary and fiscal policy (Hansen 2003, p. 380). These reforms coincided with wider global shifts, such as the increase in energy prices, which led to an annual growth rate of 6.5 per cent. According to Rich, Russia emerged as an energy superpower, rather than its traditional role as a military superpower (Rich 2009, p. 294). As a result, Russia's economic and social indicators witnessed substantial improvements in standard of living, decreased national debt and a stronger internal and external economic position.[1] Economic successes became central to Russia's overall construction of itself, as a state successfully 'rebuilding' itself and were frequently noted in public discourse.[2] An example of this was President Putin's praise of recent economic successes, at the Meeting with the Cabinet Members, the Heads of the Federal Assembly, and State Council Members, on 5 September 2005, in which he stated 'let me remind you that over the past five years, Russia's economy has grown by almost 40 per cent. This rate provided macroeconomic stability.' (Putin 2005b).

Alongside economic growth, the Putin regime moved towards strengthening Russia's internal space, through the principle of state building, dramatically altering the Russian political landscape (Lavrov 2005a). As noted by Okara, this new political idea focused primarily on Russia's internal problems in an attempt to legitimize, 'the young political regime and fixed the power-wielding camp's exclusive status regarding the heritage of Yeltsin's era marked by a collapse of the state, the rule of oligarchs, chaos and total de-modernization' (Okara 2007, p. 14).

Taylor suggests that Russia's state building centred on three key principles: state integrity (Chechnya), state capacity (federal reforms) and state autonomy (attacks on oligarchs) (Taylor 2003, p. 1) to be underpinned by a 'dictatorship of the rule of law' (Sharlet 2001). All of these sought to deal with the state failures inherited from Yeltsin's administration that were blamed for Russia's weaknesses in 2000. The Putin regime therefore continued to define itself against the Yeltsin regime, especially in relation to federal control, by suggesting that the previous regime had little control over the country. Whilst, Taylor is critical of the successes of this state-building programme suggesting that the end result did not produce the 'democratic, law-based, capable, federal state' but left 'serious deficiencies … in both the capacity and especially the quality of the state' (Taylor 2011, p. 3), the goal of state rebuilding was nonetheless a central trope in the official discourse of the regime. As discussed in a later section, it also had a very real impact on its wider set of relationships, particularly with Chechnya and the West.

In the first wave of federal reforms, the creation of seven federal districts (and the presidential representatives, *polpredy*, for each district), the harmonization of the legal space between the centre and the periphery,[3] and the strengthening of the executive vertical, the non-renegotiation of the bilateral federal-republican treaties was established. In September 2004, following events in Beslan, the ending of elections for regional governors was announced marking a second wave of reforms to strengthen federal control over the regions. All of these different reforms aimed at repositioning the federal centre and state authority at the heart of the Russian federal system (Hahn 2003, pp. 114–117).

Simultaneously, the Putin regime thus sought to acquire a greater control over the political arena, increasingly centred on the principle of 'managed democracy', or what Balzer has characterized as the emerging new system of 'managed pluralism' (Balzer 2003). Electoral and party reforms since 2001 such as the party law in 2001 (amended in 2004) and electoral law in 2005 (unveiled in 2004 following events in Beslan) ushered in a series of changes to the electoral rules. Most notably they signalled the end of regional parties or blocs of parties being able to compete in federal elections, the end of the system of 'first past the post' and the raising of the threshold for parties to be elected to the Duma form 5 to 7 per cent. This period also witnessed the growing influence of the party of power: United Russia, as exemplified by its dominant performance at the December 2003 parliamentary elections, in which it gained 37.57 per cent of the popular vote and 223 out of 450 seats in the State Duma. By contrast, liberal parties such as Yabloko and Union of Right Forces, and even the more left-wing Communist Party fared a lot less well at the polls.[4] Finally, Putin's re-election on 14 March 2004 for a second presidential term with 71 per cent of the vote and without much opposition demonstrated yet again the emerging power of the regime in the Russian political. As noted by Sakwa, during the 2003–2004 electoral cycle 'the authorities fought to ensure not only the survival of the particular individual at the head of the system but also to preserve the incumbency of the regime as a whole' (Sakwa 2005).

The Putin regime was also increasingly set on gaining control over alternative and independent groups and centres of power in the system. The crackdown on the oligarchs and independent media (particularly independent television stations), as exemplified by the attacks against business and media tycoons such as Vladimir Gusinsky, the founder of the Media Most and owner of the independent television channel NTV, and Boris Berezovky in 2000, and the Yukos affair (Russia's biggest oil company at the time) and the arrest and subsequent sentencing to jail of its CEO Mikhail Khodorkovsky in 2003 on corruption and embezzlement charges.[5] Alternative voices and spheres of influence were therefore not welcomed within this restructuring and rebuilding project.[6]

Many analysts were now characterizing the emerging system, in which democratic political processes, institutional and business relations became fused with regime politics, as increasingly authoritarian and an antithesis of the regime's initial goals for the rebuilding programme.[7] Others suggested that Russia was undergoing a civilizational shift, which they characterized as a negative, stemming from the increasingly authoritarian and dangerous nature of the Putin regime (Whitefield 2005, p. 155) that was to the detriment of the country and its people.[8]

By contrast, the official discourse coming out of the regime displayed a growing sense of accomplishment over the course of this period. For example, the Russian Foreign Minister Sergei Lavrov characterized the achievements over the course of this period as,

> today, we are striving to create a normal modern State. It's only a question of time. The most important thing is that we are headed in the right direction, which is widely acknowledged … Such consensus has been achieved in Russia today, and the consistently high rating of President Vladimir Putin testifies to that.
>
> (Lavrov 2005a)

This was also very noticeable in the changing themes within Putin's Annual Addresses to the Federal Assembly. For example in his 2002 Federal Address, President Putin stated that: 'people look to the future with more confidence' (Putin 2002a). This optimistic tone contrasted sharply with the more sombre and negative assessments of Russia's position in his Annual Address in 2000 and the Millennium Manifesto of 1999.

Indeed, by the end of 2004 the Putin regime argued that the bulk of the rebuilding programme in the domestic space had been achieved with success. Remaining domestic problems, – amongst others, issues of social welfare, poor living standards, high crime, poor housing, tax collection, poor infrastructure, high mortality rate and poor health provisions and slow modernization of the Russian army – were constructed as part of, rather than an existential challenge to, the overall direction of this 'rebuilding' project, in sharp contrast to the previous period. At the same time, it was suggested that no dramatic changes were needed to address these issues, because the regime had already chosen the right path for the country to follow. This was the message in President Putin's Annual Address to the Federal Assembly in 2004 when he noted that alongside the progress made in 'rebuilding' Russia, more effort should be made to deal with the remaining problems and weaknesses (Putin 2004a). This theme was also present in his end of year review and press conference in December 2004, when Putin explained:

> Administrative reform is not a rapid process, but we are moving in the right direction, I think. Of course, the government has not done enough yet, but it has begun moving in the right direction.
>
> (Putin 2004c)

Despite continuing to experience significant problems in its domestic sphere, belief in Russia's own abilities to rebuild itself without recourse to external assistance persisted. This blurred the boundaries between what is considered by positivist models to be a 'weak' or a 'strong' state.

Foreign policy, relations wih the West and the impact on the domestic sphere

Alongside the 'rebuilding agenda' in the internal sphere, this project was also carried out in Russia's external relations. As argued earlier, Russia's three key foreign policy goals for rebuilding itself were economic modernization, global competitiveness and regaining its status as a Great Power (Trenin 2004). Within this framework, debates emerged as to where Russia's strength and greatness should come from, either from its energy and economic power, a greater engagement with the post-Soviet space, through a more active role on the international stage or from its historical heritage, national norms and identity (Trenin 2004, p. 63). In its foreign affairs, the Putin regime adopted a flexible, multifaceted and pragmatic policy (Lavrov 2005b). As argued by Lo, Russia operationalized different identities towards different external spaces and actors, whereby Russia: 'is European in Europe, transcontinental "strategic partner" when dealing with the United States, Asian and Eurasian in Asia, and cautiously integrationist in the CIS', (Lo cited in Duncan 2005, p. 293). In part this developed from the regime's ongoing affirmation of the multifaceted civilizational position of Russia as a great power. Sergei Karaganov, Foreign Policy Advisor to the Deputy Head of the Presidential Administration, for example argued in 2003 that Russia,

> exists in a different geopolitical reality, as it finds itself lodged simultaneously, as it were, on the cusp of two socio-political fractures. On the one hand, it is positioned somewhere between the rich and the poor nations of the world. On the other hand, it is caught between an Islam that is currently losing a cultural-historical battle, and Western society, which appears to be winning so far. This gives Russia the advantage of being in a better position than most other nations to recognize new challenges, and more importantly, the imperative to cope with them in a decisive manner.
>
> (Karaganov 2003)

In line with its desire to re-establish its external role, and promote its interest abroad, Russia sought to re-engage with the West, both institutionally through the creation of the Russia-NATO Council, membership of G8 or on a more bilateral basis. A sense of achievement in rebuilding Russia's international standing was noted by the First Deputy Foreign Minister of Russia Vyacheslav Trubnikov, in 2003, when he suggested that,

> Russia has strengthened its positions in the international arena, consolidated its reputation as a responsible, constructive and predictable member of the world community. This has strengthened our security, created favorable external conditions for tackling the social and economic development tasks in Russia, for implementing the necessary reforms and improving the well-being of the citizens.[9]

Despite proclaiming its successes in domestically rebuilding itself, Russia continued to seek recognition of this successful rebuilding project from what it saw as the key referent actor in the international system, namely the West. Indeed, as noted previously, it was assumed that this recognition would naturally be given once Russia had begun to rebuild itself. However, this recognition was not forthcoming, which in turn led to increasing tensions and disillusionment about its relationship with the West from the Russian side, particularly in the latter half of this period.

On the one hand, this lack of recognition was attributed to the West's refusal to acknowledge Russia's successes in 'rebuilding' itself. The West's ongoing criticism of Russia's internal policy and increasing authoritarianism (Trenin 2004), including the anti-oligarch campaign, state rebuilding practices, election campaigns, and Chechnya were singled out in this regard. On the other hand, the rising friction between the two sides was also blamed on Western actions in the external sphere. These were said to be challenging Russia's vision of the international system and its own role within it. Notably, the decision of a US-led coalition to invade Iraq in 2003, without a UN Security Council resolution, was presented as setting a dangerous precedent that 'poses a real threat of the break-up of the established architecture of the existing world orders, one that is based on compromise and has far from outlived its usefulness' and potentially weakened the rule of international law (Bessmertnykh 2003, pp. 28–29). Continued disagreements over NATO expansion, energy wars, nuclear disarmament, Russia's entry into the World Trade Organization (WTO), stationing of US troops in the post-Soviet space, and the events surrounding the 'colour revolutions' in Georgia, Ukraine and later in Kyrgyzstan all compounded these tensions.

In response to such external developments, in particular the 'colour revolutions', the need to protect Russia's sovereignty emerged as an even stronger central strand in Russia's official discourse. These developments resulted in what Lukyanov calls 'passions over sovereignty' and a period in which Russia began to question whether its values were compatible with those of the West (Lukyanov 2005). This shift in Russian foreign policy perceptions was aptly summed up by the Russian Foreign Minister, Sergei Lavrov, when he accused some powers of using the 'banner of democracy' to promote their own national interests, abandoning the principles of multilateral cooperation to create a monopoly of norms. He went on to argue that these same powers were responsible for restarting the competition of the Cold War era and engaging in active interference in the internal affairs of sovereign states (Lavrov 2005b). Thus, over this period, less and less value was placed on integration with the West, and more on the promotion of international norms in line with, rather than against, Russian perceived national interests.

The West, 'colour revolutions' and Russia's domestic space

In relation to the above, and owing to a perception of the ongoing interconnectedness of the internal and external spheres, concerns over potential external interference in actors' internal space, questions of sovereignty and fear of domestic non-state actors allying themselves with external forces became a prominent feature of Russia's domestic policies. In particular, events, such as the 'colour revolutions', were constructed as 'key' developments for Russia and the regime now placed more emphasis on creating a common front between the regime and the nation. As noted by Igor Ivanov, the secretary of the Russian Security Council, on 1 December 2005:

> Government, recognising its high responsibility for the fate of the country, is prepared to collaborate with civic society, active and all-embracing support for setting up and strengthening its institutions. Exactly this position creates the necessary conditions for the affirmation of the new model of partnership between the state and civic society.[10]

This was said to be necessary both in order to prevent the emergence of independent groups from within civil society that were hostile to the Putin regime and to rebuild the weak relationship between the regime and society. As noted by Evans, this gradual development merged together Russian traditional values and universal values, resulting in a vision 'of a pseudo-civil society in which social organizations are subordinated to the authority of the state and express demands that are consistent with the programme of the regime itself' (Evans 2005, pp. 108–109). This notion of civil society was, however, at odds with the Western model, under which civil society should be an independent and dynamic force, holding the state to account, rather than aimed at directing society's concerns through official and controlled channels (Evans 2005, p. 111).

Overall, during the early-2000s, a series of new themes and issues were added to the Putin regime's project for 'rebuilding' Russia. In practice many of the themes that became central to the official discourse by the mid-2000s were not even in view in the early stages of this period, such as sovereignty projection, growing concerns over regime security and increasing tensions with the West. Hence, rather than developing along a teleological path, from a 'weak' to a 'strong' state, this political project developed along its own trajectory and in response to shifting domestic and external circumstances.

Russia changing security agenda

The development and trajectory of the Putin regime's 'rebuilding' project for Russia also led to the repositioning of security perceptions and articulation of threats on the official level. Whereas, in 1999/2000, security threats centred on weakness with Russia presented as an existential threat to itself, by 2001–2004 this construction had altered. Security threats were now presented either as the remnants of those threats from the previous period, as actors or issues seeking to undermine or derail Russia's rebuilding project or those actors (particularly in the external sphere) that failed to recognize Russia's changing domestic circumstances and stronger international position.

Within this altered construction, an ever-expanding range of security threats were now occupying Russia's security agenda. Externally, Russia became increasingly concerned with the behaviour of the West, whilst domestically a growing number of non-state actors were seen to pose an actual or potential security threat. The position, and the salience of the role, that security threats occupied within wider Russian state discourse also changed. First, as Russia was no longer identified as an existential threat to itself, security ceased to be the main gathering mechanism of Russia's self-identification (Ivanov 2002). Second, in view of its growing strength, security threats were now increasingly presented as dangers that could be dealt with, rather than existential challenges to Russia's very existence. Even in the case of terrorism, despite suggestions that this danger was growing across both the internal and external spheres, Russian authorities now presented this danger as one that Russia could work to overcome (Ivanov 2005). At the same time, a focus on the internal-external security nexus persisted

The rebuilding of Russia 73

as events and developments in both of these spheres drove the evolution of Russia's security agenda.

Domestic security concerns

A key shift in Russia's security discourse, as noted earlier, was that Russia was no longer presented as an existential security threat to itself.[11] As suggested by the Duma Banking and Finance Committee Chairman, Valerii Zubov, on 3 January 2005: 'The country is not in crisis, neither in politics, nor in a crisis of federal relations, nor in economic crisis, there is not a single crisis'.[12]

Despite such achievements, it was acknowledged that internal security threats, such as international terrorism, crime or corruption, persisted. However, as in the case of the other remaining weaknesses and ongoing problems, these dangers were now articulated through the prism of Russia 'rebuilding' itself, as actors or issues seeking to derail Russia's 'rebuilding' efforts. For example, following the terrorist actions in Nazran in June 2004, Putin characterized these attacks as undertaken by 'the bandits [who] do not like the fact that the leadership of the Republic of Ingushetia has spent the last year and a half working to create normal conditions there.' (Putin 2004b). Ongoing problems such as in the North Caucasus were now couched in and read through the prism of Russia's wider rebuilding efforts, almost regardless of actual developments on the ground.

There was, however, a major change in the types of threats about which the regime was most concerned. In the previous period, most of the threats and dangers were perceived to be emanating from or as a result of the large structural weaknesses inside Russia, such as state collapse or economic failure. In this period, with the regime arguing that most of the large structural problems in Russia were beginning to be dealt with, the image of the threat also changed. Whilst to some extent concerns with long-standing problems, such as corruption or terrorism, remained, there was much more emphasis on 'dangerous' groups or individuals than previously. The danger was thus increasingly said to be stemming not from the way in which Russia's domestic space was evolving and rebuilding itself, but rather from isolated groups within it, which had to be curtailed.

The apparent successes in Russia's rebuilding efforts together with external events, most notably the colour revolutions, brought about greater anxiety with the possibility of non-state actors, in conjunction with external actors (i.e. the West), bringing about a change of regime.[13] The Putin regime became increasingly alarmed about links between state and non-state actors, such as civil society actors that could potentially result in the overthrow of ruling regimes (Lukyanov 2005a). Acknowledging that certain groups may be interested in replicating a colour revolution in Russia, the leadership became adamant that this would not be allowed to take place. Vladislav Surkov, deputy head of the presidential administration and a chief ideologue of the Putin regime argued on 20 June 2005, that:

> These were not revolutions. In these countries ... There will be no uprisings here. Of course we are aware that these events have had a big impact on

many of the local politicians. And we also see many foreign NGOs, who would not be against repeating this scenario in Russia ... Coup attempts will happen without a doubt. But they will not succeed.

(Mauer and Kussmann 2005)

A wider discursive umbrella of '*obraz vraga*'[14] emerged to include any group that actively rejected or were assumed to reject the Putin regime's project for Russia. Groups such as the oligarchs, independent media, liberal political parties and NGOs working on sensitive issues were increasingly added to Russia's security agenda. This also resulted in the selective application of certain legislation, and security efforts targeting those groups deemed to be a potential threat to the regime, whilst others remained untouched (Sakwa 2008). Similarly in relation to the media, growing state control and official criticism of independent reporting was also evident.[15]

As a result of the interconnectedness between the internal and external security spheres, Russia's worsening relations with the West also directly impacted on the shifting notion of internal security. The growing prominence of the image of the West as an actor potentially challenging Russia's 'rebuilding' efforts was evident in internal affairs, as well as the external context. Vladislav Surkov, raised this issue on 28 September 2004, when he noted that:

In fact in the surrounded country there developed a fifth column of left and right wing radicals. The fake liberals and real nationalists have more and more in common. Joint sponsors from abroad. Joint hatred. Towards Putin's Russia as they say. But in reality towards Russia as it happens.

(Kaftan 2004)

Russia's domestic security agenda thus underwent substantial changes over the course of this period, with security issues from the previous period downgraded, whilst a wider set of new issues said to be challenging Russia's 'rebuilding' process were now included. External threats continued to play an intrinsic role in shaping the internal security agenda, although it became less clear whether the prime external threat to Russia domestically was international terrorism or the West.

External security concerns

At same time as new groups and priorities were appearing on the internal security agenda, a similar shift was also taking place in Russia's external security conceptions. On the one hand, the Putin regime increasingly presented Russia as a growing and progressively stronger actor in international affairs as a result of its 'rebuilding' efforts. It was suggested that Russia, as a result of its increasing internal solidity, should be able to alleviate its insecurities on an international level from the first period, simply through the promotion of its national interests. On the other hand, events and the shifting context of the external sphere, as seen by the Russian leadership, led to it remaining an uncomfortable space for Russia despite the proclaimed success in its efforts to rebuild itself.

At the start of this period, Russia's external security concerns were very similar to those found in the previous period and stemmed from apprehensions about being left out of the group of Great Powers, the changing nature of the international system and from the proliferation of non-traditional security threats, such as international terrorism. However, as Russia's sense of its own improved position and domestic circumstances developed, so too did its perspective towards its external sphere and security concerns. As noted earlier, the West was increasingly presented as a security 'Other', alongside previously identified global threats such as international terrorism.

The Iraq crisis not only altered Russia's foreign policy, but also its security perceptions. In the eyes of the Russian authorities, it signalled the West's readiness to use unilateral force bypassing international law and disregarding the principle of sovereignty and multilateral global governance, as well as the apparent hollowness of the principles and norms espoused by the West.[16] As a result, the West was increasingly characterized as trampling over the principles and notions of current international order, resulting in a more insecure world.

The 'colour revolutions', particularly in Ukraine, increased Russia's concerns about its external space and the post-Soviet space in particular, as well as the role the West played in these events and within Russia's perceived 'zone of privileged interests'. Not only did 'the colour revolutions' demonstrate that no political regime was immune, they also emphasized the West's perceived negative, but nonetheless real influence in relation to Russia's interests and power in the post-Soviet space (Lavrov 2005b).

Hence, Russia's external security agenda evolved not only in relation to the Putin regime's aspirations for Russia, but also in response to developing circumstances, in this case the West's apparent failure, in Russia's eyes, to fully recognize and appreciate its national interests. Thus, it was the West that was said to be losing Russia, and perhaps the rest of the global community, rather than the other way around. As Trenin suggests 'Iraq and Chechnya, YUKOS and Ukraine have brought the [Russia-West] relationship to even lower depths at the close of 2004 than Kosovo five years earlier' (Trenin 2005). This change of emphasis, and perception that the international context had altered, was evident in a statement by the Secretary of the Russian Security Council Igor Ivanov in October 2004, when he outlined that the Security Council is 'developing a new national security concept ... not because the old one is bad, but because the security situation has changed' (Felgenhauer 2004). As will be discussed in a subsequent chapter, what came next was a much more belligerent and anti-Western Russian foreign security agenda than has been seen under Putin up till this point.

Conclusion

Reversing the failures and weaknesses of the previous period were the central focus of the Putin regime in the early–mid 2000s. While Putin was a relatively unknown political figure at the start of his period, by the end, he had clearly begun to succeed in imposing his own vision onto the country. Alongside a boom in the economy, in large part helped by soaring global energy prices, and the restructuring of the state, an increasingly undemocratic political regime was emerging in Russia, centred on the figure of Putin and focused on increasing its control over all aspects of Russian politics, economics and society. Nonetheless, by the end of 2004 the main goals of this rebuilding programme were said to have been achieved and a new system was now in place. This 'new' political project was less interested in developing a Western-style democracy, and more in constructing the regime's control over the country. At the same time Russia became a much richer and more confident and self-assured actor.

In the course of this evolution, two key developments took place in Russia's security agenda. On the domestic front, amidst the increasing sense of confidence and triumphalism about the way in which Russia was rebuilding itself, the beginnings of a wider securitization of the domestic space began to emerge. As the regime sought to accrue an ever-greater control over the domestic space, alternative voices and centres of power were increasingly squeezed out of the public sphere. Despite its earlier hopes and aspirations, the rebuilding project did not in effect eliminate the regime's concerns with domestic security, but accelerated them. If Putin began by focusing on Russia's domestic difficulties and the domestic causes for these, by the end of 2004 the regime was beginning to revise its approach by increasingly blaming external actors for seeking to criticize and put pressure on Russia from within. Internationally, there was a growth in Russia's sense of pride in itself, at the same time as its relationship with its key partners, namely the West, began to falter. It was suggested that the international community, and the West in particular, did not want to see a rebuilt and powerful Russia but would rather it had stayed weak and insecure. Developments taking place in its vicinity were now also increasingly a source of concern, such as the after-effects from the colour revolutions, particularly in Ukraine.

However at this stage, the regime still remained hopeful that once the rebuilding programme was complete that domestic insecurities would disappear and that Russia could still become the 'strong' state it aspired to be in 2000, i.e. internally and externally secure. Insecurities were still presented as temporary failures that had to be dealt with in order to achieve a more stable future. Nonetheless, they had to be eliminated in order to ensure the implementation and sustainability of Russia's rebuilding efforts.

In the next chapter, the impact that these changes in Russia's national and security priorities had on the securitization discourses and practices vis-à-vis Chechnya is examined, and the question of whether or not this issue retained the same role and symbolic salience in this 'new' 'rebuilding' Russia as it had in the previous period is considered.

Notes

1 As noted by Trenin 'From 2002, doubling the GDP within eight to ten years has become almost an obsession with Putin. Foreign policy's principal task was officially set as helping provide outside resources for Russia's supreme national task of modernization' (2005).
2 'Kudrin has no doubts that Russia will restore its competitive power', News Section, *RIA Novosti*, available at: http://en.rian.ru/onlinenews/20040512/39915991.html, accessed 20 September 2010.
3 For more information on the impact of these federal reforms on Russia's centre-periphery relations see: ed. by Reddaway and Orttung 2005; for their impact on presidential power in Russia see: Hyde, 2001.
4 For more information on the changing political regime in Russia see: Robinson 2012.
5 For more information on the anti-oligarch campaign and its impact on security affairs see: Shlykov 2004; for a detailed discussion of the impact of the Yukos affair on Russian economic, political and institutional relations see: Sakwa 2009; Tompson 2005; Fortescue 2006.
6 For the impact on these developments on freedoms and civil rights in Russia see: Mendelson 2000.
7 For example Hashim notes that the 'concentration of state power in the absence of horizontal accountability and an effective state bureaucracy will only consolidate a non-democratic regime incapable of implementing its proclaimed public policy goals', Hashim 2005, see Shevtsova 2004, Hale 2006, Mendras 2012.
8 It was also argued that the norms and practices developed by this regime now made Russia qualitatively and perhaps civilizationally different from the West to the detriment of the country and its people (Duncan 2005, p. 294).
9 'Interview with First Deputy Foreign Minister of Russia Vyacheslav Trubnikov to ITAR-TASS News Agency', Ministry of Foreign Affairs, 15 Janury 2003, available at: www.ln.mid.ru/Brp_4.nsf/arh/8498405114D9D09C43256CB0002E6BA8?OpenDocument, accessed 20 September 2010.
10 'Statement from the Secretary of the Security Council at the All-Russian Conference 'Problems of strengthening national and societal security. The role of civil society actors', *Security Council*, 1 December 2005, available at: www.scrf.gov.ru/news/63.html, accessed 19 September 2010.
11 As was the case in the period 1999–2001 – as argued in Chapter 3.
12 'Interview with First Deputy Secretary of the Duma Committee on banks, financial and credit markets, conducted by Valerii Zubov', Litsom k Litsu, *Radio Svoboda*, 3 January 2005, available at: http://archive.svoboda.org/programs/ftf/2005/ftf.010305.asp, accessed 18 September 2010.
13 'Interview with the deputy Foreign Minister Aleksander Safonov on the issue of the fight against international terrorism, bulletin of the Russian Ministry of Foreign Affairs', Ministry of Foreign Affairs, 21 January 2004, available at: www.mid.ru/ns-rkonfl.nsf/ac72b85191b0db0643256adc002905c1/30e74d191e2478f9c3256e7600478 1a7?OpenDocument, accessed 26 January 2008.
14 Russian term for the image of the threat that was often used in the wider national discourse in this period.
15 The desire to increase official control over the media was noted by the Russian Foreign Minister, Sergei Lavrov at one of his speeches in the US, in which he noted that,

> as for the mass media, our experience of the 90's has demonstrated that they can easily become an instrument of private or group interests to the detriment of the public interests and the democratic process itself. An objective and unbiased analysis of Russian electronic and print media shows that the authorities face much harsher criticism in Russia, than in many Western countries.

Sergei Lavrov, 'Main points of the Address by the Foreign Minister of the Russian Federation at Stanford University, San Francisco', Ministry of Foreign Affairs, 20 September 2005, available at: www.mid.ru/Brp_4.nsf/arh/8CD3437CC7575184C325 7086002DB677?OpenDocument, accessed 20 September 2010.

16 'Transcript of Russian Minister of Foreign Affairs Igor Ivanov Interview with TVTs Television Company, Moscow', Ministry of Foreign Affairs, 25 January 2003, available at:www.ln.mid.ru/Brp_4.nsf/arh/1D1C016B1F8D675943256CBC0053750A?OpenDocument, accessed 10 September 2010.

6 The 'normalization' of Chechnya

Having set Russia on a new course, the Putin regime moved towards formulating a new 'normalization' programme for Chechnya. The nature, source and level of the threat emanating from Chechnya were all reinterpreted in line with Russia's shifting national and security priorities. Indeed, the processes advocated in Chechnya mirrored those on the federal level. The 'rebuilding' programme replaced the earlier securitization strategy as the main conceptual prism for understanding the situation inside Chechnya. Within this process, dual policies of desecuritization and ongoing securitization were deployed parallel to each other in a two-pronged approach of normalizing of Chechnya. Both were said to be necessary in order to stabilize the situation in the republic.

A major part of the initial securitization of Chechnya was the central symbolic role it played in representing Russia's weakness and vulnerability to existential threats in internal and external spheres. However, as argued in Part II, in the internal sphere, the process of Russia 'rebuilding' itself resulted in perceived previous weaknesses, such as Chechnya, being increasingly downgraded and losing their earlier salience and symbolic role. The Chechen issue was also increasingly removed from the political agenda as the major source and reason for the ongoing occurrence of terrorist acts on Russian territory that was increasingly blamed on the worsening situation across the North Caucasus region.

At the same time, however, the Chechen issue retained some form of its earlier role in Russia's foreign security priorities due to Russia's ongoing concerns with international terrorism. In spite of lull in tensions with the West over Chechnya, as part of the joint Russia-Western alliance in the global war on terror in 2001, the issue of Chechnya re-emerged as a point of contention between Russia and the West. Nonetheless, within Russia's wider security discourse there was a shift towards emphasizing its problems with the West, whereby the Chechen issue was beginning to lose its salience as both the Russian and Western focus shifted elsewhere.

In tracing the evolution of the securitization discourse on Chechnya against wider Russian state discourse, this chapter also addresses two relevant interrelated issues for the theory of securitization: what impact do changes in national and security agenda have on the reading and management of individual security concerns, and what happens after governments manage to successfully securitize an issue and have implemented extraordinary measures for dealing with it.

The rebuilding of Chechnya: policies of desecuritization

In the early-, and especially the mid-2000s, the Putin regime sought to move away from the initial securitization discourse and process towards Chechnya, which had deployed between 1999/2000. Indeed, a key feature of Russia's official policy on the normalization of Chechnya became a dual approach of desecuritization alongside an ongoing securitization. Despite representing seemingly contradictory aims and forms, the duality of these discourses were advanced as a necessary part of a comprehensive strategy to rebuild and stabilize Chechnya. Putin himself, for example, pointed to this duality when he defined the situation in Chechnya in February 2002 as 'seriously stabilizing' and noted that 'large-scale acts by fighters are almost excluded now' (Putin 2002). In this way, these desecuritization and securitization policies played a different role than would be assumed by conventional securitization theory. In the Russian context these two sets of discourses and practices were not mutually exclusive, as desecuritization and securitization are often assumed to be in the Copenhagen theory, as well as in some of the literature on Chechnya (for example see Bacon and Renz 2006, pp. 58–68). Instead they served as twin and interrelated policies, drawn from Russia's wider national discourse of Russia 'rebuilding' itself (Snetkov 2011). In fact the Russian authorities were adamant that only by deploying this twofold approach would the normalization of Chechnya be achieved (Putin 2004a).

In practice, the Putin regime's desecuritization strategy functioned as a multi-faceted set of discourses, interlinked with Russia's varied ambitions for Chechnya. These were not only connected with removing Chechnya from the realm of security, but also with 'rebuilding' the situation on the ground. The federal authorities now suggested that following the end of the large-scale military operations on the ground, Chechnya was becoming increasingly normalized (Lukov 2005). For example, the Russian Minister of Defence, Sergei Ivanov described the changes in Chechnya, in February 2003 as:

> Now, things start looking up in Chechnya, with the economy being regenerated, the educational institutions rebuilt, health care revamped, preparations for a referendum on the Constitution of the Chechen Republic, previewed on March 23, 2003, well underway, and local elections to be held.[1]

Russia's normalization strategy centred on 'the stabilization of the situation in the republic, reconstruction of its economy, return of refugees and the holding of a referendum on adoption of the republic's Constitution [in 2003]'.[2] The restoration of the 'normal' political space in Chechnya also became an important pivot within this policy. The holding of parliamentary and presidential elections in 2003 and 2004 were hailed as significant steps towards the re-establishment of a normal situation in Chechnya (Putin 2003 cited in Bacon and Renz 2006, p. 61).

Within this process of political normalization, the process of a 'Chechenization' of the local political space, or the return of local political controls to the Chechens was considered an integral part of this restructuring process. Galvanized by its earlier discursive constructions of 'good' and 'bad' Chechens and traditional and non-traditional Islam, the Russian authorities now argued that some Chechens should be included into the 'normalization' process. The need to get the sympathetic local Chechen population directly involved in this 'rebuilding' project was noted by President Putin in 2002, when he stated that:

> It is crucial to restore normal life to the Chechen republic not only through the federal authorities ... [but also] local authorities and the system of republican organs of power, even the law enforcement ones.
> (Putin 2002b)

The significance of this approach became more pronounced with the nomination of Akhmat Kadyrov as the temporary head of Chechnya in 2000, and as President in 2003, and again with the nomination of Alu Alkhanov in 2004 following the assassination of President Kadyrov in May 2004. As it subsequently became apparent, with the emergence of the Ramzan Kadyrov as President in the mid-2000s, Russia's choices in siding with a particular group in Chechnya was not a neutral decision. Instead it had the potential to give a significant amount of power to one particular group in Chechnya at the expense of others. The process of desecuritization, therefore, not only served to 'normalize' Chechnya within Russia's political space, but also had the effect of restructuring the social basis for power inside the republic.[3]

Similarly to the 'rebuilding' project on the federal level, economic development and the rebuilding of infrastructure also formed part of federal authorities attempts to 'normalize' the situation in Chechnya. This ordering of priorities stemmed from the principle that poverty breeds weakness and insecurity, which was also apparent in the rebuilding project for the rest of Russia (Putin 2002d). In this context, economic rebuilding was presented both as a central component of the wider process of desecuritization/normalization and as a mechanism to alleviate security threats said to be fuelled by lingering poverty in the republic. According to Borisov,

> if Chechens feel that they are really returning to rebuild houses, that conditions are being created for peaceful work, then the stream of those who want to go to the mountains [i.e. join the terrorists] will dry out.
> (Borisov 2002)

A vital part to this development-security nexus approach was the large subsidies allocated to Chechnya, which constituted the majority of its local economy and revenues. For example in 2004 over 90 per cent of total revenues in Chechnya came from federal subsidies. Other rebuilding projects, such as restoration of housing and other public services in Grozny, the rebuilding of banking services in Grozny, payment of compensation to 39,000 citizens in Chechnya due to loss of housing and possessions, were also undertaken (Vendina *et al.* 2007, p. 179).

The second pillar of Putin's 'normalization approach' was the persistent, prolonged and deadly counterterrorist securitization strategies that continued to be carried out by Russian security forces, and increasingly also by the local Chechen authorities. Despite this remaining insecurity in Chechnya, it was suggested that the situation was not on the same scale as in the years prior and that by 2002 Chechnya was progressively moving towards stabilizing itself.[4]

Unlike in the past, even the targeting of terrorist groups was said to be no longer simply about identifying certain groups as threats, but was presented as another mechanism for 'rebuilding' and normalizing Chechnya (Pilipchuk 2003). In line with changes in wider national security constructions, security tensions were no longer exclusively blamed on Chechnya's weaknesses. Instead these were reconceptualized as groups acting against Russia's 'rebuilding' efforts and trying to derail progress made in normalizing the situation. This link was highlighted by the Minister for Chechen Affairs, Stanislav Ilyasov, in Paris in May 2003 who noted, 'the situation in Chechnya is changing for the better that is why the terrorists are trying to implant nervousness and panic amidst the population' (Nizamutdinov 2003).

Critically, insurgency groups and members of Maskhadov's former administration continued to be conflated with Russia's wider security concerns regarding international terrorism and the 'war on terror'. For example in September 2004, *Rossiiskaya gazeta* suggested that terrorism in Russia 'is linked with the worldwide terrorist Islamic movement ... and Chechen separatists are nothing more than errand boys for them' (Zakatnova 2004). Conflating international terrorism with the previous Ichkerian administration also sought to remove the latter's connection to, and legitimacy within, the Chechen domestic sphere. According to Putin, 'they [separatists and the previous Chechen administration] don't have anything in common with the interests of Chechen people' (Putin 2002b).

Despite some discussions about, and even partial, if botched, attempts at, establishing talks between the two sides, the Russian authorities largely refused to negotiate with the Maskhadov administration. Ongoing terrorist attacks inside Chechnya and large-scale attacks within the wider Russian space, such as the high profile terrorist acts of the Dubrovka Theatre siege in 2002 and the Beslan hostage taking in 2004, were therefore attributed to and blamed on the Ichkerian administration of President Maskhadov, which had to be stopped. For example, in November 2002, Putin argued that 'specifically he [Maskhadov] brought Russia and Chechnya to war'. Maskhadov was therefore personally linked and blamed for the events of the Moscow Theatre tragedy in October 2002 (Wilhelmsen 2005, p. 51).

In turn the Russian military continued to carry out its counterterrorist special operations in Chechnya.[5] It was suggested that the only solution for dealing with those fighters refusing to put down their arms, was their elimination. As noted by the Russian Defence Minister, Sergei Ivanov, during a meeting in July 2003 'at the present time, on the territory of Chechnya there are around 1200–1300 active fighters, irreconcilable bandits, with whom the only form of conversation is their elimination'.[6] The Russian military also strengthened the border between North Caucasus and Georgia, through operations such as 'Echelon-2003', to prevent the movement of fighters and supplies in and out of Chechnya.[7]

At the same time as this dual approach was being deployed on the ground in Chechnya, the Russian authorities came under severe and repeated criticism from a wide spectrum of opinions and groups in Russia. These groups rejected the official suggestion that the situation in Chechnya was normalizing and that the republic was gradually being rebuilt. Such voices ranged from the liberal groups and human rights NGOs, such as Memorial, the Helsinki Group and Committee of Soldiers Mothers of Russia,[8] to diverse groups across the political spectrum such as the liberal, nationalist, but also communist groupings. In their 2007 analysis of the Liberal, Communist and Nationalist press, Kolossov and Toal found that all these groups questioned the extent to which the Chechen conflict was actually being resolved (Kolossov and Toal 2007, p. 217).

Most of these critical voices pointed to the gap between the official line and the situation in Chechnya. Latynina had characterized this gap as the story of two Chechnyas, one seen on television and the other, 'the concentration camp in Khankala and the bomb attack near Avtozavodskaya metro station. For the Kremlin, this Chechnya does not exist' (Latynina 2003). Furthermore, analysts and human rights groups at the time challenged the extent to which any actual reconstruction took place on the ground. In this light, Vendina *et al.* called Chechnya 'an economic unknown', because of the sparse information about its economy and finances (Vendina *et al.* 2007, p. 179).

Despite these criticisms, the Russian authorities refused to alter their discourse on and policies towards Chechnya, even at times of major *terakty*.[9] Instead, as noted in the next section, opposition and independent groups, such as the media and NGOs, that were involved with and continued to work on the issue of Chechnya were increasingly securitized themselves as part of Russia's widening security agenda in its domestic sphere.

In the case of events such as large-scale *terakty*, the Russian authorities were forced to publically articulate their position towards the Chechen problem (Snetkov 2007). However, whilst such *terakty* often resulted in the Russian authorities placing key strategic assets, and especially large cities, such as Moscow and St Petersburg on high security alert,[10] they did not signal a change in the content of the official discourse on Chechnya or a greater prioritization of this issue on the political agenda. Some of the most well-known incidents were the Dubrovka Theatre siege in October 2002, the July 2003 bomb at a rock festival outside Moscow, which killed 15 people, the train crash in December 2003 killing another 40 people in southern Russia, the February 2004 explosion on the Moscow metro killing 40 people, the killing of the Chechen president Akhmat Kadyrov during Victory day celebrations in Grozny in May 2004, and the August 2004 explosion outside a Moscow metro station. In spite of the high-profile media coverage, these events did not act as key turning points in the official construction of Chechnya. Instead, a determination among the regime to continue along the same path prevailed.

In fact the Russian authorities suggested that any deviation from the chosen course would severely undermine the normalization project in Chechnya. Illustrating Russia's 'zero-sum-game' approach to terrorism, the Russian authorities suggested that any change in their approach would signify that the terrorists had won. This was an outcome to be avoided at all cost. Particularly during times of *terakty*, the Russian authorities were eager to demonstrate their resolve and strength in the face of this danger. For example, the refusal to concede to terrorist demands during Dubrovka *terakt* 23–26 October 2002,[11] unlike during the 1995 and 1996 terrorist acts,[12] was presented as a major victory for the Russian government. According to Kichin, the Dubrovka Theatre crisis was meant to become Russia's 'new' Stalingrad (Kichin cited in Vorob'ev 2002). Even the assassination of the pro-Russian Chechen president, Akhmat Kadyrov, on 9 May 2004 was not enough to shake the Russian authorities' determination to continue with their stance towards Chechnya. Instead, the regime refused to call for a state of emergency, seeking to downplay the magnitude of this event, and turned instead to publicizing the achievements of his Presidency, vowing to continue the course of normalization.[13]

The functionality of both the desecuritization and securitization strategies were thus much broader than simply identifying whether an issue was an 'existential security' threat or a 'normal' political issue. Both sets of policies became part of a wider state-led attempt to deal with insecurities on the ground in order to 'normalize' the Chechen republic. Critically, the Russian authorities refused to accept any criticism of their normalization policy in Chechnya, or acknowledge that developments on the ground did not correspond to the official version of events.

Chechnya's changing role in Russia's domestic agenda

Alongside the multifaceted normalization process that was being rolled out, the role of Chechnya in Russia's wider domestic agenda was also changing. As would be expected by securitization theory, a move towards, if only a partial, desecuritization resulted in the Chechen issue losing its salience and symbolic power in Russia's domestic context. And yet an implicit, if not explicit, role remained, albeit in different a form. The discourses and practices of (de)securitization began to function differently depending on which sector and political level is examined. In this respect, Chechnya' role in Russian domestic political and security agendas underwent three major transformations. First, Chechnya was increasingly sidelined as a policy issue on the official level; second, the Russian authorities attempted to increasingly and actively silence this issue in the Russian public space; and third the Chechen issue continued to impact and play a role within Russia's widened domestic security agenda, albeit in a more implicit rather than explicit form, particularly around the issue of the North Caucasus. This emphasizes that securitization and desecuritization discourses and practices are diverse processes, which cannot be examined in isolation from wider political and security developments taking place in domestic and international contexts.

As part of the wider change in the Putin regime's construction of Russian national identity from a 'weak' state to one that was 'rebuilding' (Snetkov, 2012), Chechnya lost some of its 'exceptional' (read: symbolic power) status of the previous period, and was increasingly pushed out of the Russian political agenda. Instead other policies and national priorities, such as the economic rebuilding of the country and political developments in Russia increasingly took its place.[14] And the rebuilding processes in Chechnya now followed, rather than structured Russia's domestic political sphere.[15] The shift towards some form of desecuritization discourse did not result in Chechnya as an issue returning to the realm of normal politics, as would be expected by the classic model of securitization. It did, however, lead to it being increasingly sidelined across Russia's political sphere.

Second, this process of disarticulation was taken a stage further by the Russian authorities', as part of their attempts to silence all discussions regarding Chechnya not only in terms of political debate, but also on the public stage at large, including in the media. An important arena of this new securitization of Chechnya became what Mendelson has called the 'creeping securitisation of information' (Mendelson 2002, p. 64). This development had already begun towards the end of previous period, but was accelerated and became more pronounced now.[16] Putin continued to link security and the conduct of the media, as demonstrated during his speech at the World Congress of News Agencies, in 2004 stating that:

> the mass media cannot simply stand on the sidelines ... the information community can and should design such a model of work that would make the media an effective tool in the struggle with terrorism.
>
> (Putin 2004d)

In practice, this resulted in those media dealing with, or reporting on, the Chechen issue needing to acquire special accreditation from the Ministry of Interior, in order travel to the region and report on developments there. During such trips, journalists had to stay in special accommodation and were accompanied by security personnel at all times, whilst the foreign media were increasingly cut off from reporting from the region or communicating with separatist groups (Koltsova 2006, p. 7). The media was also reprimanded over their reporting of major *terakty*. For example, the editor of the newspaper *Izvestia* was sacked following the paper's coverage of the Beslan siege in 2004 (Dejevsky 2004).

The Russian authorities continued to link information dissemination with the promotion of terrorism. In particular, websites and internet portals published by pro-separatist, terrorist groups, such as Kavkaz Center, were targeted.[17] As a result of these measures, the extent of coverage of Chechnya in Russian media was greatly reduced, as only a small number of journalists working for alternative newspapers, such as *Novaya Gazeta* and *Nezavisimaya Gazeta* continued to report on this issue. From the point of view of the official media discourse, Chechnya as a security issue was more or less successfully silenced over the course of this period.

It was only at times of large-scale terrorist actions, such as the theatre siege of Dubrovka in 2002 and the school siege in Beslan in 2004 that the issue of Chechnya returned to the front pages and remerged in the Russia's official state discourse. However, as noted earlier, rather than turning points, these events became opportunities for the regime to reiterate once more that the normalization strategy in Chechnya was the correct policy both for the republic and the country at large (Snetkov 2007). Furthermore, the Chechen issue quickly disappeared from the front pages back into obscurity.

Third, despite these developments on the national level, the process of normalization of Chechnya remained tightly interlinked with other securitization discourses and processes developing across Russia's ever-widening domestic security agenda. This was particularly the case on the regional level, whereby by 2004 a creeping securitization of the wider North Caucasus emerged alongside the discourse of desecuritization/securitization of Chechnya.[18] Indeed, the North Caucasus region saw an increased level of terrorist activity during these years, particularly in Dagestan, Ingushetia and Kabardino-Balkaria. This included events such as the Nalchik siege in August 2004 and the Beslan school siege in September 2004.

A critical juncture point for this change of discourse became a series of events in the North Caucasus in the summer of 2004, and especially the events surrounding the Beslan school hostage crisis in September 2004. This was the first time that such a major *terakt*, with widespread national and international resonances, was constructed as emanating from instability in the North Caucasus, rather than Chechnya specifically. In fact, the Russian Foreign Minister, Sergei Lavrov acknowledged this change in an interview with foreign journalists after the Beslan siege, noting that: 'as to the criminals, neither the President Vladimir Putin, nor other officials, said it was an attack by Chechens' (Lavrov 2004b). The North Caucasus came to play the role, initially occupied by Chechnya, of the epicentre of terrorist activity in Russia, leading to security forces conducting counterterrorist activities carried out across the whole region (Lynch 2005, pp. 141–142).

Despite the shift of the geographical loci of this terrorist threat and processes of desecuritization, Chechnya continued to play a negative security role in Russia's security construction, especially in creating an escalation in insecurity in the rest of the North Caucasus region, albeit in more subtle ways. First, the desecuritization of Chechnya and the securitization of North Caucasus were said to be intertwined processes. This spatial shift was said to be taking place because terrorist and insurgency groupings were being squeezed out of Chechnya due to the successful Russian 'rebuilding' project underway there, and were relocating to other part of the North Caucasus (Putin 2005d).

Second, many of the key discursive constructions and policies initially linked with Chechnya were now superimposed onto the increasingly insecure situation in the rest of the North Caucasus.[19] As before, these groups continued to be painted as an alliance between foreign fighters and carriers of non-traditional, foreign forms of Islam[20] and deviant local groups jointly engaged in acts of global terrorism.[21] The 'local' context and indigenous factors particular to each of these different republics, Dagestan, Ingushetia or Kabardino-Balkaria in which these insurgency groups developed and operated (O'Loughlin *et al.* 2011) were also largely absent from the official representation of the widening insurgent threat. Instead the use of the same securitization lexicon enabled the Russian authorities to present the spreading insurgency threat as originating firmly from Chechnya (and abroad) rather than having roots within the North Caucasus itself.

Thus, despite the diminishing role of Chechnya in Russia's wider security discourses and state policies, this issue continued to have a latent impact on the securitization of the North Caucasus region.

In turn, the increased securitization of the North Caucasus led to a reconfiguration of Russia's security policy in the region.[22] Calls for an integrated security system to combat terrorism across the whole of the North Caucasus, and the appointment of Dmitry Kozak as the new plenipotentiary envoy to the Southern Federal District to deal with this region as a whole (Lynch 2005, pp. 141–142), all signalled a shift in the focus of the Russian authorities.

Thus, despite being the subject of a policy of normalization, Chechnya continued to play a negative, if at times more latent, security role in the region. Therefore, contrary to the expectations of securitization theory, the desecuritization of Chechnya did not end its security or discursive role in Russia's security agenda, especially in relation to its regional policy towards the North Caucasus. In fact, Chechnya was instrumental to the securitization of the North Caucasus.

Away from the North Caucasus, on a national level, the widening securitization of the internal space, as discussed in the previous chapter, also touched other actors associated to Chechnya, such as NGOs working on human rights issues in Chechnya. The Russian authorities often publicly criticized reports coming out of different NGOs about the situation in Chechnya, arguing that rather than supporting they were undermining Russia's efforts in the republic. As noted by Mendelson, this was not a new policy for Putin, who even as head of the FSB, in an interview in July 1999, argued that most environmental NGOs in Russia were linked with foreign intelligence agencies (Mendelson 2002, p. 62).

The Chechen issue, together with the associated images of the terrorist threat, and that of the increasingly the unstable and insecure North Caucasus region, also continued to play a role in the discursive construction justifying the growing centralization, political authoritarianism and strengthening of the Putin regime across the domestic political space. Whilst Chechnya had lost much of its political salience, major events surrounding it, and particularly *terakty* such as Beslan (2004) were nonetheless often utilized in order to promote the regime's political power in the country. As noted by Vladimir Putin at the Enlarged Government meeting with the Government and Heads of Regions, 'the war on terrorism is a national task. It is a task that requires the mobilization of all resources. And it is clear that a unity of actions of the entire executive power vertical must be ensured here unconditionally' (Putin 2004f). The abolishment of direct elections of governors, the change of electoral rules towards complete proportional representation in the Duma, the creation of a Public Chamber, were said to be measures necessary in order to deal with the terrorist threat and to further strengthen the state.

In this way, shifts in Russia's national and security priorities and the normalization process inside the republic led to a change in role for Chechnya within the Russian domestic agenda. On the one hand, this issue was increasingly sidelined and silenced on a national level, at the same times as it was said to be continuing to play a negative regional role. Chechnya therefore retained some of its salience of the previous period, albeit as a less significant focal point than before.

Chechnya – a difficult international issue

As outlined in Chapter 4, the issue of Chechnya played a dual, and at times conflicting, role in Russia's external security agenda when President Putin first came to power. On the one hand, it was securitized not only as a domestic, but also a global security threat. Whilst, on the other, the Russian authorities tried to use it as a way of re-engaging with the international community around the global war on terror. In this period, the shift in Russia's domestic policy towards Chechnya and its wider foreign security policy perceptions and priorities again impacted on the role of Chechnya in the Russian external security agenda. Despite, Russia's ongoing attempts to build a common front around the global war on terrorism, Chechnya came to play a major part in Russia's growing disillusionment with the West.

One of Russia's key stated foreign security policy priorities in 2000 was to re-engage with the international community, and particularly the West, following a period of isolation. The issue of international terrorism became central to its ambitions to build an in-group dynamic between itself and the rest of the developed world around the communality of threats from international terrorism. During the early-2000s, terrorism (both domestic and international) continued to be presented as a global and transnational phenomenon, or as Yuri Tchaika, the Russian Justice Minister, characterized it an 'invisible threat without borders' (Yamshanov 2004). In turn, domestic terrorist attacks were used as moments of opportunity to create a conceptual link between events within Russia's domestic context and developments around the world, most notably the West's experiences and policies in the 'war on terror'. For example, following the events of Beslan in 2004 the Foreign Minister, Sergei Lavrov noted that 'the terrorist acts that have been continuing in Russia, Israel, Spain and elsewhere require of us all an intensification of efforts' (Lavrov 2004b).

The Chechen issue also continued to feature in Russia's attempts to rebuild its position internationally and to shape (direct) the future of the international system. Particularly, in the early–mid 2000s,[23] this issue remained closely related to Russia's attempts to create a multilateral coalition around this issue. Russia sought to build a degree of rapport with NATO around the issue of terrorism, particularly within the framework of the NATO-Russia Council (NRC), established in May 2002. At the first NRC meetings in Moscow in 2003 and in December 2004, the comprehensive NRC Action plan on terrorism was approved, which 'aimed at improving overall coordination and strategic direction of NRC cooperation in this area'.[24] Joint exercises, nuclear-weapon-accident-response field exercises were hosted in Russia in 2004, followed by counter-narcotics training, missile defence, the Cooperative Airspace Initiative, military to military cooperation, submarine-crew search and rescue amongst others.[25] Russia also joined the US-led Proliferation Security Initiative established in May 2003, which focused on preventing the global proliferation of weapons of mass destruction (WMD).

On the multilateral level, Russia continued to argue that the UN should be at the heart of any future counterterrorist cooperation in line with its wider desire to retain the UN as the main instrument of international affairs. Russia became an active participant in the UN Security Council Counter Terrorism Committee (Lynch 2005, p. 150). The need to ensure that the global 'war on terror' continued to be based on 'firm foundations of international law', re-emphasizing the vital role of the UN in international affairs, was frequently noted by Russia's top leadership.[26] Russia also made recourse to the UN at times of domestic *terakty*, in order to bolster legitimacy for both its internal and external policies. For example, following the events in Beslan in September 2004, Russia drafted a Security Council Resolution, within the UN, to facilitate the handover of individuals with a refugee status who supported terrorism, alluding to the ongoing friction over Russia's attempts to get Akhmat Zakayev extradited from the UK.

The ongoing securitization discourse about Chechnya also formed part of Russia's attempts to diversify its foreign policy by building greater rapport with other regions in the world. For example, concerns over international terrorism and developments in Chechnya formed part of its attempts to re-engage with the post-Soviet space. These issues became a mechanism for cooperation in regional organizations, such as the Collective Security Treaty Organization (CSTO) and the Shanghai Cooperation Organization (SCO).[27] Within these institutions the Chechen issue, especially in the early part of this period, remained at the heart of Russia's agenda and seemed to be a driving factor behind their efforts to position counterterrorism as a critical issue within these organizations (Aris 2009). Russia thus continued to link its internal security problems with its wider external ambitions.

Dannreuther outlines that following the US invasion of Iraq (2003), the Chechen issue also formed part of Russia's attempts to rebuild its relations with the Middle East, as actors such as Turkey and Saudi Arabia had become increasingly disillusioned with the position and actions of the West (2010, pp. 119–120). In the past, this issue had been a major irritant in Russian-Saudi Arabian relations, with Russia accusing the Saudi Kingdom of sponsoring Chechen rebels, particularly in the late 1990s and early 2000s. However, as noted by Katz, following the Iraq crisis, the Saudis moved towards greater acceptance of

Moscow's policy in Chechnya. The Saudi regime even went as far as to condemn the Beslan terrorist hostage action as an act of terrorism and backed Russia to become an observer member at the Organization of the Islamic Conference (Katz 2008). The culmination of this policy to rebuild its relations with the Middle East was seen when Russia was accepted as an observer member of the Organization of the Islamic Conference (OIC). The OIC had previously objected to Russia's actions and policy in Chechnya (Levesque 2008).

Nonetheless, after the post-9/11 lull, the issue of Chechnya re-emerged as a source of tension with the West. This source of tension was threefold – first over the nature and direction of the 'war on terror'; developments on the ground in Chechnya; and the question of external assistance/interference into Russia's domestic space.

As noted in the previous chapter, a key feature of Russia's wider foreign policy context was the growing tensions with the West due to divergent visions for the 'war on terror', the international system, laws and the role of unilateralism for dealing with global security problems. In particular, the Russian authorities complained that the West was not taking seriously enough Russia's position that insecurity in Chechnya was directly linked with the 'global war on terror'. For example, the Russian authorities criticized the West for repeatedly failing to give them sufficient support for combating pro-Chechen groups operating in the West. One such issue was Russia's failed attempts to extradite key Chechen figures back from the West. This lack of results was said to be as a result of the West using one set of rules for themselves and another set for Russia. Indeed the Russian First Deputy Foreign Minister, Trubnikov complained about the double standards applied to the Chechen issue in the West, he noted:

> Even now we are confronted with manifestations of political shortsightedness and lack of statesmanship or appeasement of terrorists and double standards. There is no other explanation of the fact that terrorist Zakayev moves unhindered from Denmark to Great Britain.... Herein lies an answer to the question of whether everyone realised, then as now, the seriousness of the threat of international terrorism.
>
> (Trubnikov 2003, p. 39)

Repeated complaints were also made that the Western media continued to show certain Chechen independence groups in a positive light.[28] The Russian authorities were also left disappointed at Western governments' failure to close down the internet sites of the Ichkerian administration and other groups, such as the Kavkaz Center, in their domestic spaces (Kamynin 2005). The Russian authorities also criticized their European partners over the hosting of the World Chechen Congress in Denmark in October 2002, at the time of the Dubrovka siege. This led to the Council of Europe summit in November 2002 having to be moved from Copenhagen to Brussels following protests from the Russian Ministry of Foreign Affairs (Volkhonsky 2002).

Indeed, the Russian leadership now argued that the 'war on terror' was not a global effort, but a Western-led project run according to its own interests and norms. Russia accused the West of betraying the initial principles and purpose upon which this alliance was created.[29]

Similarly, Russia's domestic policy in Chechnya became a source of tension. The main point of contention was the West's ongoing refusal to accept the Russian authorities' description of, and approach toward, Chechnya. The lull in Western criticism of Russia's policy in Chechnya immediately after 9/11 was therefore short-lived. Despite conceding that this was largely a domestic issue,[30] Russia's Western partners became vocal in their disapproval of Russia's policy of normalization in Chechnya. In particular they criticized the gap between Russia's official rhetoric regarding the rebuilding of Chechnya and the reality on the ground, its use of force and military tactics in its counterterrorist operations and frequent disregard for human rights and media freedoms, all of which came under heavy criticism from its Western partners. For example the representative of the US State Department, Richard Boucher, in January 2002 criticized Russia's operations in Chechnya for their 'excessive use of force' against civilians and human rights violations.[31] This scepticism about Russia's official discourse was also demonstrated by the EU's launching of a motion to the UN in May 2004 to condemn Russia's human rights violations in Chechnya, to which Russia retaliated by imposing a ban on EU meat exports in June 2004; or the OSCE refusal to observe the Chechen elections in 2003 and 2004 (Timmins 2004, p. 368).

Disputes regarding Chechnya and the North Caucasus, in turn, clouded Russia's view of European institutions, even those of which it was a member. Despite its initial enthusiasm for the Organization for Security and Co-operation in Europe, the Russian view of the organization soured as it made repeated attempts to both monitor and question developments inside Russia vis-à-vis Chechnya. In Russia's eyes, the OSCE was now a politicized organization having cast aside its founding principles of non-interference and state sovereignty towards an increasingly selective application of double-standards against some of its member-states regardless of the local context and norms, as highlighted by the statement from the Commonwealth of Independent States in July 2004 (CIS Member Countries 2004).

Tension over the best strategy for increasing security and stability in Chechnya was another bone of contention, particularly when it came to the issue of possible negotiations between the Russian and Chechen sides. In the West, the Chechen conflict continued to be seen as a secessionist problem, with the Ichkerian administration under Maskhadov largely presented as the other side in this dispute, and therefore representing an acceptable negotiating partner for Russia to deal with in order to restore peace in the republic. However, the Putin regime saw the Maskhadov regime very differently. In their view, Chechnya was just another link in the chain of global jihadism and the Maskhadov administration the equivalent of the Taliban in Afghanistan, which had to be eliminated rather than negotiated with. All suggestions that the Russian authorities should negotiate with such insurgency groups were interpreted as yet another example of the

West using double standards against Russia. As noted by Yuri Ushakov, the Russian Ambassador to the US following Beslan in September 2004 'child-killers come closer to Osama Bin Laden ... It is unimaginable that any US administration would ever negotiate with Al Qaeda' (Ushakov 2004). From the Russian side, as Morozov suggests, the

> message [from Russia] is quite straightforward: either you accept that Russia's conduct in Chechnya is right and refuse to deal with separatists, or you become one of them, end up on the other side of the boundary separating Good from Evil.
>
> (Morozov 2002, p. 424)

By 2004, as suggested by Kuchins, a sense of disillusionment had set in and 'to expect that the US-Russian relationship will grow in importance in each capital on an anti-terror basis does not appear very promising at present' (Kuchins 2004, p. 1).

Furthermore, the Russian authorities complained that the West was disregarding its position as a sovereign state by seeking to influence and interfere in its domestic policy in Chechnya. Frictions over Chechnya thus highlighted wider disagreements between Russia and the West over the rules of the game in the international system. Kalland characterized these as tensions between 'norms of interference ... against the norm of non-interference' (Kalland 2004, p. 2), stemming from their very different interpretations over what constitutes a 'strong' state. As Lynch notes Russia's policy towards the EU continued to rest on foreign rather than domestic policy, in other words Russia did not want the EU to play a role in its internal policy. This however was at odds with the EU model, developed on its experience with other East European states, which granted the EU the right to interfere and restructure domestic affairs, in order to ensure that these actors comply with the regulations and principles of the EU. This created a sharp division between the EU and Russia. As noted by Lynch, 'the EU has now become an obstacle to Russia's pursuit of a European system in which Moscow enjoys an equal and independent voice' (Lynch 2004, p. 105).

Within this mounting catalogue of tensions, the salience of the single issue of Chechnya became increasingly diluted. This was compounded further, by the West's growing concerns regarding political developments inside Russia and what it saw as a growing drift towards authoritarianism. Chechnya was now just one of many issues seen as illustrating that the Putin regime was heading in this direction, alongside others such as the Yukos affair, the lack of independent media in Russia, the conduct of parliamentary and presidential elections in Russia, all of which became 'cause[s] for concern'. In fact, the West increasingly argued that it was the Putin regime that was posing the biggest threat to Russia, both in its domestic and foreign affairs. As argued by Vershbow 'the [American] perception of Russia is changing, the reliability of Russian partners is being questioned' (Torbakov 2005).

In Russia, the West was also increasingly presented as a source of insecurity and threat. The lines began to be blurred between whether it was international terrorism or the West that posed the biggest security concern for Russia. This blurring was particularly prominent at times of internal terrorist crises in Russia, such as Beslan in 2004. At this time, the Russian authorities even went as far as to argue that the West's response to the 'war on terror' and Chechnya was part of a conscious effort by the West to weaken Russia. This line of argument was evident in President Putin's post-Beslan speech, in which he described this blurring of threats as:

> Some would like to tear from us a "juicy piece of pie". Others help them. They help, reasoning that Russia still remains one of the world's major nuclear powers, and as such still represents a threat to them. And so they reason that this threat should be removed.
> (Putin 2004a)

By the end of this period, both Russia and the West were questioning their earlier attempts at a rapprochement, casting doubts on whether their cooperation could ever be based on firm foundations or mutual understanding. As noted by former US Ambassador to Russia, Aleksandr Vershbow in January 2004, 'we expect our relations to be based not only on the commonality of interests but also on the commonality of values' (Torbakov 2005) – this however was not forthcoming. Problems with the West were thus increasingly presented alongside international terrorism as the main security threat to Russian aspirations to rebuild itself. Within this macro-discourse, tensions over Chechnya contributed to the overall disillusionment with one another on both sides.

Conclusion

During the mid-2000s, Chechnya became a much less important or significant issue within both official state and security discourse. Indeed, whereas discourse on Chechnya had played a strong shaping role within wider official discourse in the early Putin years, during this period its role was much less as a shaper and rather followed the wider security agenda. In this respect, in spite of a number of high-profile terrorist acts, continued violence and ongoing insecurities within the republic, the Putin regime's discourse on and policies in Chechnya mirrored the overall trajectory that it was putting forward the federal level. Within this context, Chechnya was perhaps a very 'extreme', but not a deviant, case for contemporary Russian politics and security.

Following the wider 'rebuilding' discourse, in which Russia was presented as well on the way to becoming 'strong' again, the regime's policy towards Chechnya was dominated by its 'normalization' programme. Reflecting the federal rebuilding discourse, this concentrated on emphasizing the return of 'normal political processes and institutions', or at least what became 'normal' politics under the Putin regime, economic development to address security concerns and identifying those Chechens that sided with the regime as the true representatives of the republic, and, hence, marking a break with the previous 'deviant' regimes and actors within Chechnya. At the same time, this did not mean that the Chechen issue was fully desecuritized. Extensive and large-scale military and security operations continued alongside the discourse about 'normalization'. Hence, the extent to which Chechnya could be said to have been desecuritized was dependent on whether the focus was on Chechnya as an existential threat to Russia's security, or a more localized security threat. It was also dependent on whether or not the discussion of Chechnya was taking place on a domestic or international level.

Indeed, in line with the regime's domestic security agenda, which increasingly identified and securitized a wider range of actors and spaces as concerns for the regime and their model for a rebuilding, those voices inside Russia that sought to highlight that in spite of the 'normalization' discourses, military operations and a state of insecurity were ongoing within Chechnya were themselves securitized, with the regime seeking to limit the access of journalists and human rights activists to Chechnya. This was part of a wider silencing of the Chechen issue within federal discourse, which was only broken at times of high-profile *terakty*, and even then this did not lead to a change in the 'normalization' discourse. There was, however, a relocation of many aspects of the lingering securitization discourse from Chechnya to the wider North Caucasus, with the terrorist threat now said to be originating from across this wider region.

In addition, following the 9/11 terrorist attacks in the US, the Chechen/North Caucasus threat was also claimed to be part of a transnational phenomenon of international terrorism, with radicals from abroad inciting, organizing and carrying out operations in the North Caucasus and attacks within the rest of Russia. This coincided with the beginnings of an official discourse on security that identified Russia as suffering from the actions of foreign actors interfering in and destabilizing the Russian domestic space. This paved the way for efforts from the regime to paint the security issues in Chechnya and the North Caucasus as part of a wider international problem, one which should serve as the basis for cooperation with both the West, who was seen as facing similar problems, and for the development of regional mechanisms to tackle terrorism with other post-Soviet states. However, rather than laying the ground for cooperation and recognition from the West, Russian policies in Chechnya, by the mid-2000s, became a renewed source of contention, with Western criticism of Russian actions on the ground in Chechnya, the refusal by several European states to extradite Chechen leaders in exile, and the bringing of criminal cases against the Russian government by Chechens in European courts. Yet, in spite of this role in generating tension between Russia and the West, the issue of Chechnya became a lot less important within their relationship over the course of this period.

Interestingly, from a comparative perspective, Russia's dual approach of overlapping securitization and desecuritization discourses and practices towards Chechnya seemed to mirror a number of global trends in relation to how best to deal with difficult spaces and problematic regions. For example, the two-pronged approach that combined both security measures and development/state-building strategies has also been practiced in other cases, such as China's attempts to deal with instability and frontier security in its Western region provinces (Cui and Li 2011). It also resembled the counterinsurgency strategies deployed by the Western-led coalitions in Afghanistan and Iraq (see Betz and Cormack 2009; Dixon 2009; Lopez 2007; Metz 2003). Others have also noted a growing emphasis on such inter-linkages between security policies and development programmes, particularly in the case of international humanitarian assistance in relation to new wars in Africa, the Balkans, Central Asia (Duffield 2001, cited in MacKenzie 2009: 243). Whilst in each of these cases success as measured in restoring normal life on the ground to these difficult contexts is debatable (Slim 2004), such an approach nonetheless represents a larger trend in the 'doing' of security/peace-building/development in the 2000s. Thus, perhaps surprisingly, it would seem Russia's approach towards 'normalizing' Chechnya was not the exception, but the norm in global security terms.

Notes

1 'Concerning the Holding of a Republican Referendum in Chechnya', Ministry of Foreign Affairs, available at: www.mid.ru/Brp_4.nsf/arh/116684CEB052E226C3256 EC9001CD30D?OpenDocument, accessed 10 June 2010.
2 Concerning the Holding of a Republican Referendum in Chechnya. Ministry of Foreign Affairs, available at www.mid.ru/Brp_4.nsf/arh/116684CEB052E226C3256E C9001CD30D?OpenDocument (accessed 10 June 2010).
3 An issue addressed in the next chapter.
4 Interview with Russian Minister of Defence, Sergei Ivanov, 'Na territorii Chechni deistvuit okolo 1300 aktivnyikh boevikov' *Newsru.com*, 16 July 2003, available at: www.newsru.com/russia/16jul2003/boeviki_print.html, accessed 23 August 2010.
5 Interviyu I. O. Ministra vnutrennikh del Chechenskoi Respubliki Ruslana Shakhaevicha Alkhanova po itogam operativno-sluzhebnoi deyatel'nosti v 2004 godu. Ministry of Interior, 28 July 2004; available at www.mvd.ru/press/interview/2825/, accessed 2 August 2010.
6 'Na territorii Chechni deistvuet okolo 1300 aktivnikh boevikov', *NEWSru.com*, 16 July 2003, available at: www.newsru.com/russia/16jul2003/boeviki_print.html, accessed 13 June 2010.
7 'Rossiiskie pogranichniki provodyat na granitse Gruzii i Chechni operatsiyu "Eshelon-2003"', *NEWSru.com*, available at: www.newsru.com/russia/15jun2003/esh_ print.html, accessed 20 August 2010.
8 These groups suggested that large scale hostilities continued on the ground, repeatedly criticized the policy of *zachistki* and the ongoing problems with human security. They also questioned Russia's state rebuilding efforts, the slow tempo of the reconstruction programmes, the loss of funds and the lack of openness and transparency of events in Chechnya. As noted by the Representative of the Committee for the Human Rights, Lyudmila Alekseeva on 13 January 2003, the ongoing hostilities meant that 'neither referendum, nor elections can give real results'. NEWSru.com, available at: www.newsru.com/russia/11jan2003/ref_pr_print.html; also see 'Human Rights Watch (2002) Russia, Chechnya, Swept Under: Torture, Forced Disappearances, and Extra Judicial Killings during Sweep Operations in Chechnya', *Human Rights Watch* 14:2.
9 *Terakt* became a Russian term for terrorist actions, coined by putting these two English words together, used to describe the Chechen terrorist actions in this period.
10 'V svyazi s teraktom v Groznom militsiya v Moskve i oblasti perevedena na usilennyi rezhim sluzhby', NEWSru.com, 27 December 2002, available at:www.newsru.com/ russia/27dec2002/force_print.htmlNEWSru.com, accessed 10 September 2010.

11 For more information on the events surrounding the Dubrovka Theatre siege in October 2002 see Dolnik and Pilch (2003).
12 In June 1995 Chechen insurgents took hundreds of hostages in a small town of Budennovsk in southern Russia. Over 100 people died during the rescue operation. A similar incident took place six months later in Dagestani city of Kizlyar in January 1996. This time, Chechen rebels under the command of Salman Raduyev took 3,000 people hostage in a local hospital.
13 'Duma pledges to step up anti-terrorist fight', *RIA Novosti*, 12 May 2004, available at: http://en.rian.ru/onlinenews/20040512/39916031.html, accessed 20 September 2010; Filippov, Yu. 'Kadyrov's legacy put to the test', *RIANovosti*, 12 May 2004, available at: http://en.rian.ru/onlinenews/20040512/39915969.html, accessed 20 September 2010.
14 Interv'yu Sekretarya Soveta Bezopasnosti Rossiiskoi Federatsii I.S Ivanova zhurnalu 'Strategiya Rossii'. News and Information, Russian Security Council. 4 May 2005; available at www.scrf.gov.ru/news/98.html, accessed 10 September 2010.
15 'Interv'yu Zamestitelya Sekretarya Soveta Bezopasnosti Rossiiskoi Federatsii N Spasskogo "Rossiiskoi gazete" "Mi zalozhniki svoego proshlogo"', News and Information, Russian Security Council, 5 October 2005, available at: www.scrf.gov.ru/news/70.html, accessed 13 September 2010.
16 For more information on the framing of the terrorist issue in the official Russian media see Simons 2010; for a discussion about the way in which the terrorist issue was reported and framed during the 2003–2004 electoral cycle see Oates, Lee Kaid and Berry (2009).
17 'Russian Foreign Ministry Spokesman Mikhail Kamynin's Interview with Interfax News Agency on Various Aspects of Cooperation of Russia with Foreign Countries and International Organisations in Struggle Against Terrorism', 12 September 2005, available at: www.ln.mid.ru/Brp_4.nsf/arh/C4F8E3C6B8D77BFFC325707B002550A7?OpenDocument, accessed 13 July 2010.
18 'Interv'yu zamestitelya Ministra vnutrennikh del Rossii general-polkovnika militsii Arkadiya Edeleva gazete "Shchit i Mech"', Press Service, 6 October 2005, available at: www.mvd.ru/press/interview/3708/, accessed 2 September 2010.
19 'Interv'yu zamestitelya Ministra vnutrennikh del Rossii general-polkovnika militsii Arkadiya Edeleva gazete', *Shchit i Mech*, 6 October 2005; available at www.mvd.ru/press/interview/3708/, accessed 2 September 2010.
20 According to Walker, following the attacks in Nazran and Beslan 'the Putin administration has apparently ordered a crackdown not only on Islamist groups but all forms of unofficial Islam in the North Caucasus as well', Walker (2005, p. 268).
21 'Interv'yu zamestitelya Ministra vnutrennikh del Rossii general-polkovnika militsii Arkadiya Edeleva gazete "Shchit i Mech"', Press Service, 6 October 2005, available at: www.mvd.ru/press/interview/3708/, accessed 2 September 2010.
22 Crucially, the opposition discourse did not witness the same shift, and generally continued to identify Chechnya as the source, and not just the location, of instability. For example, writing in *Vremya Novostei*, Novoprudsky (2004) discussed the roots of the 'Chechen', not 'North Caucasian', conflict. Some opposition media in 2004 actually blamed President Putin for failing to fulfil his promise to keep Russia safe and resolve the Chechen issue. Ryzhkov, a liberal member of the *Duma*, was quoted in *Nezavisimaya gazeta* as arguing that 'the president was given a contract to keep order in the country and to safeguard people's security. Now we see that this contract has been violated' (Ryzhkov 2004). Ryzhkov also rejected the discourse on international terrorism suggesting that 'this is an utterly lame excuse and cannot be taken seriously' and questioned whether the president would fundamentally alter his policy on Chechnya. Thus Chechnya continued to play a key political role in the discourse of the independent media in 2004. However, this was not reflected in the official Russian discourse.

23 By mid-2000s the image of North Caucasus took over from that of Chechnya as the epicentre of terrorist activity inside Russia.
24 NATO's relations with Russia', North Atlantic Treaty Organization, available at: www.nato.int/issues/nato-russia/topic.html, accessed 12 October 2009.
25 'NATO's relations with Russia', North Atlantic Treaty Organization, available at: www.nato.int/issues/nato-russia/topic.html, accessed 12 October 2009.
26 Keynote Speech by Sergey Ivanov, Minister of Defense of the Russian Federation, at the 39th Munich Conference on Security Policy, press service, Russian Ministry of Foreign Affairs, 8 February 2003, available at: www.mid.ru/Brp_4.nsf/arh/C361362C B0E593A0C3256EC9001D196C?OpenDocument, accessed 1 September 2010.
27 Keynote speech by Sergey Ivanov, Minister of Defense of the Russian Federation, at the 39th Munich Conference on Security Policy, press service, Russian Ministry of Foreign Affairs, 8 February 2003, available at: www.mid.ru/Brp_4.nsf/arh/C361362C B0E593A0C3256EC9001D196C?OpenDocument, accessed 1 September 2010.
28 'Regarding the Showing on Czech Public TV Channels of a Film in Support of Chechen Terrorists', Press Release, Russian Ministry of Foreign Affairs, available at: www.mid.ru/brp_4.nsf/e78a48070f128a7b43256999005bcbb3/b2417df92e6e2c43432 56c6a0028e072?OpenDocument, accessed 12 June 2010.
29 Igor Ivanov interview in *Times* 28 November 2003, cited in Statements and Commentaries, Memorial, available at: www.memo.ru/hr/hotpoints/caucas1/rubr/3/l200312. htm, accessed 10 June 2010.
30 The West's acceptance of this narrative was demonstrated by the US President George Bush, following the Dubrovka siege in November 2002. He argued '*In relation to Chechnya we continue to hope that a solution will be found in peaceful way. This is an internal Russian problem.*' Bush: problema Chechni – vnutrenee delo Rossii, NEWSru.com, 21 November 2002, available at: www.newsru.com/world/21nov2002/ bush_print.html, accessed 3 May 2010.
31 'Vpervie posle teraktov 11 sentyabrya SSHA kritikuyut deistviya Rossii v Chechne', NEWSru.com, 11 January 2002, available at: www.newsru.com/world/11jan2002/ usa_chech_print.html, accessed 2 May 2010.

Part III
2004–2008

7 Russia as a strong state and a great power?

By the mid-2000s, the Putin regime's political project was entering its 'third phase', in which Russia was presented as a 'strong' state and a great power. This was a period of both domestic economic growth and increasing prosperity, growing concerns about dislocation between the regime and the general populations, and rising tensions and frictions between Russia and the West. With regard to the latter, many commentators, particularly in the West, began to talk of a 'new' Cold War developing between Russia and its Western counterparts by the end of 2006. By the mid-2000s, Russia's official agenda was, on the one hand, dominated by a strong sense of triumphalism and renewed power, while, on the other hand, concerns about internal tensions, fear of a lack of cohesion between the regime and society and ongoing frictions with the West rose to the surface.

As a result, an ever 'widening' of the *obraz vraga* (image of the threat) emerged, with more and more actors represented as potential security threats to Russia. However, whereas in 2000 such security threats were said to be the major causes of Russia's weakness, they were now accepted as part of the new image of Russia as a 'strong' state. Within this framework, the internal and external security agendas continued to be tightly interconnected, with the fear of hostile and often invisible enemies in both spheres seen as threatening Russia's position as a 'strong' state. This resulted in the development of a complex, multifaceted and, perhaps more, problematic image of a 'strong' Russia.

The reality of what constituted a 'strong' Russia in the mid-2000s was therefore very different from the expectations of internal harmony and international recognition set out by the Putin regime upon its coming to power. Instead, this 'new' identity of a Russia as a 'strong' state presented by the Putin regime was developed in conjunction with the key principles as set out in the early 2000s, but adapted in response to events and changing circumstances within both Russia's internal and external agendas. This reaffirms the assertion of this book that one cannot adequately make sense of the evolution of Putin's project for Russia by referring to a fixed objectivist models of what constitutes a 'strong' and a 'weak' state.

This chapter examines these issues in more detail, by first outlining the key principles and parameters of this new state identity, and, second, the way in which it impacted upon Russia's security agenda and priorities.

Russia as a strong state

By the mid-2000s, all talk of Russia as a 'weak' state, rife with internal and external security threats, had disappeared from public discourse. In its place, a new image of Russia as a 'strong' state emerged, underpinned and supported by the notion that Russia had successfully rebuilt itself from the difficulties of the late-1990s. The overall message from the Russian authorities was one of self-confidence. Russia was presented as an energy power, satisfied with its economic progress (Putin 2006e) making it 'one of the world's ten-biggest economies' (Putin 2007a), with a strong state and a united country and people. In turn, following an initial emphasis on restructuring and the resultant successes in socio-economic and political spheres, the focus of Russia's governing elites increasingly turned to future and longer term developments, as the problems of the early 2000s were considered as having been overcome. In September 2005, a number of long-term national social programmes were launched in four key areas: health care, education, housing and agriculture (Putin 2005b), whilst in September 2007, the Russian authorities launched the 'Concept of Long-term Socio-economic Development of the Russian Federation to 2020'.[1]

At the same time, weaknesses and problems (particularly those identified in the first years of Putin's administration) were increasingly confined to the past. This process of historicization meant that all of Russia's previous ills and weaknesses were relegated to the era of President Yeltsin and the general societal collapse of the 1990s (Sakwa 2008). As Petersson notes:

> with regard to order, the vitality and dynamics of the Russian great-power myth has to be seen in conjunction and contrast with another potent political myth: the myth of the cyclically recurring "times of troubles" (sing. smuta) that inhibit Russia's aspirations to realize its rightful great-power potential and in domestic and international recognition
>
> (Petersson 2014, p. 33).

Drawing on these fears, the Russian authorities suggested that any deviation from the course set by the Putin regime would result in a return to the 'bad old 1990s', and the general instability endured at that time. In remembering the Yeltsin period, Putin, in May 2007, drew a sharp contrast between that period and the current political and social situation inside Russia, noting:

> Our country at that time was deeply divided by complex social conflicts, confrontation between parties and ideologies ... We have worked together for many years to overcome the serious consequences of the transition period, to overcome the negative effects of far-reaching but not always straightforward transformation. In untangling the complex knots of social, economic and political problems, we have at the same time built a new life. As a result, the situation in the country is gradually, slowly, step by step, changing for the better.
>
> (Putin 2007a)

Despite constructing a discourse about the dangers of a return to the difficult years of the Yeltsin period, the Putin regime also remained very anxious about maintaining the momentum within its project for Russia. Concerns were increasingly raised about the 'ideological emptiness' (Popescu 2006, p. 1), or void between general society and the political sphere. This played into the regime's fears about the potential for a 'colour revolutions', similar to those that had swept across the post-Soviet space in 2003–2005, in Russia during the electoral 2007/2008 cycle. In this context, some people raised questions about whether the political elites possessed the legitimacy necessary to sustain them in power.

In response to such concerns, the Putin regime made a conscious and public political shift from promoting a discourse of 'managed democracy'[2] towards one of 'sovereign democracy', as the conceptual centre-point of Russia's political order and aspirations. As publicized by Vladislav Surkov – a key ideologist of the Putin regime, the concept of 'sovereign democracy'[3] harked back to Russian historical traditions (Krastev 2006; Averre 2007). In particular, it rested 'upon the notion that for a state to have political sovereignty, it must have economic independence, national political and economic elites and military might, the ultimate guarantor of sovereignty and territorial integrity' (Herd in Galeotti 2010, p. 9) Furthermore, Okara suggests that this notion was drawn mainly from conservative/revolutionary political philosophy (Okara 2007). In keeping with the emphasis on the interconnectedness of internal and external security evident in Putin's Russia, 'sovereign democracy' 'highlighted international problems in the first place' and fused together two ideas: that,

> we [the existing regime] are a party wielding state power and a sovereign elite, and the sources of our legitimacy are found in Russia, not in the West ... being a power-wielding force we are the guarantors of Russia's sovereignty and survival in the context of globalization and other external superthreats.
> (Okara 2007, p. 14)

Thus, in Putin's Russia, the discourse of a 'strong' state was increasingly linked with other discourses on greater state control over society, and the closing down of spaces for open public debate. The newly proclaimed status of a 'strong' state did not involve a greater openness or more emphasis on liberal and democratic principles, as is sometimes assumed in objectivist conceptual models for measuring a 'strong' state. Indeed, the principle of 'sovereign democracy' seemed to further elaborate the notion of a social contract between the Russian government and people, whereby a loss of political freedom was exchanged for growing economic prosperity (McFaul and Stoner-Weiss 2008). Or what Petrov *et al.* have termed an 'overmanaged democracy', which

> combines a high degree of state centralization with the gutting of democratic institutions, and their systematic replacement with substitutions that are

intended to serve some of their positive functions without challenging the incumbent leaders' hold on power.

(Petrov *et al.* 2010).

A shift towards greater control of Russia's political system by the regime has already been present in the early-2000s. Now these trends were accelerated further. New initiatives to disseminate the regime's key ideological principles were implemented, such as the creation of youth movements, primarily *Nashi* in 2005, and the promotion of political technologists, such as Pavlovskii or Kolerov, who from March 2005 headed a department to promote Russia's influence in the former Soviet Space (Krastev 2005, p. 3). In April 2005, the Public Chamber was created,[4] whilst in June 2005 a programme entitled '[t]he patriotic education of citizens of the Russian Federation for 2006–2010' was launched to encourage 'an expansion of patriotic subject matter in television programming, the publications of the patriotic press and in works of literature and art'. This programme was allocated R497.8m over the course of this period, highlighting the state's growing interest in building and fostering a greater sense of patriotism within Russia.[5]

Domestic circumstances continued to play a major role in defining official Russian state perceptions of itself as an international actor, in turn, Russia's newly-found domestic strength signalled a Russia 'on the upgrade' internationally (Lavrov 2007a). As suggested by the Russian foreign minister, Sergei Lavrov in 2006, 'the most important thing that we ourselves sensed is that the role of the Russian factor in international affairs has considerably grown' (Lavrov 2006a). Within official discourse, Russia was therefore increasingly presented as a 'great power' in the international system, capable of defending its position and interests, and which was no longer prepared to be sidelined in major international events. As part of this self-defined rehabilitated international status, the Putin regime criticized the West for continuing to operate according to an old-style Cold War mentality in relation to Russia, outlining that this was an outdated view of twenty-first century Russia and calling instead for a new relationship of equals.[6]

There was a reinterpretation of constituted symbols of a 'strong' international status. In view of the worsening of relations with the West, the importance of gaining acceptance or recognition from the West for Russia's status as a great power was now downgraded. In its place, the furthering of Russia's foreign policy interests according to its own national traditions and culture was prioritized (Aksenyonok 2008), and said to illustrate a strong international presence. Focus also shifted towards 'the forming of a new Russian national ideology, the new emphasis of Russian global foreign policy and the radical shift of the Russian-CIS policy' (Poti 2008, p. 39). Alongside the efforts to establish a seat at the top table of the international system, ensuring that Russia's national interests were placed at the heart of international affairs,[7] and in relation to other international actors, such as the UN,[8] NATO[9] or the OSCE[10] took centre-stage.

Russia's new assertive position in its foreign policy sent shockwaves through political, policy and academic circles in the West. Debates and discussions followed as to the primary drivers of this new discourse of a 'strong' Russia, and about the nature of its key security interests and worldview. A variety of positions were put forward to account for this new tone in foreign policy, some arguing that Russia was driven by realist and isolationist principles, with others suggesting that Moscow sought to play a more active role in the existing international system. The central questions asked were whether this new Russia was a revisionist power or a follower; was it a great power or a failing power (Sakwa 2008, p. 244)? Perhaps, the most persuasive explanation for this new foreign policy stance was simply that the Putin regime was no longer looking to Washington or other Western capitals for their acknowledgement and approval. As noted by Trenin, the central notion driving Russia's foreign and security policy became that

> Russians no longer recognize U.S. or European moral authority. Moscow is prepared to deal with its Western partners on the basis of its interests or agree to disagree and compete where necessary.
> (Trenin 2007, p. 95)

In this way, a much more antagonistic view of Self-Other relationship between Russia and the West was evident in the eyes of Russian elites during Putin's second term. On this basis, some commentators suggested a return to the 'Cold War' or a 'new' Cold War (Sakwa 2008). Morozov highlights the primary issues of tension between Russia and the West, outlining that

> sovereignty and democracy stand out as the two most prominent keywords in this controversy, with both sides insisting on their understanding of these notions as being self-evident and universal, and dismissing the other's vision as ideological and distorted
> (Morozov 2008, pp. 152–153)

In this context, Russia's relations with the West reached their lowest-point since the end of the Cold War during the mid-2000s, with both sides seeing few avenues for an improvement in the relationship.

Russia's security agenda

The Putin regime's new political discourse of strength, stability and achievements also became the dominant themes in security discourse. The overall message was that Russia could deal, or at least could continue to manage, with threats to its security, in both the internal and external security realms.[11] Two key themes emerged, first, a greater acceptance that security risks would remain ongoing, but would not hinder or dramatically undermine Russia's view of itself as a 'strong' state; second, that the location and nature of these threats now centred more on ongoing insecurity in the North Caucasus and the threat from external forces (i.e. the West) in undermining Russia from within.

In 2000, a key message and argument put forward by the Putin regime was that once Russia is 'strong', it will no longer face security threats. By the mid-2000s, this assumption of a stark contrast between 'security' and 'insecurity' had disappeared. While the security agenda evolved during the period, it also became increasingly apparent that security threats and insecurity could not be eliminated outright. At the same time, a reorientation in the discursive imaginary outlining a 'strong' Russia, enabled the ongoing prevalence of such threats to be incorporated within this discourse.[12]

Alongside this general acceptance that low-level insecurity will remain even within a 'strong' Russia, changes in the official discourse on national identity impacted on which security concerns were now prioritized. In addition to a continued highlighting of external security threats, such as the proliferation of nuclear, chemical and biological weapons, local conflicts, traditional state-to-state confrontation, international terrorism amongst others,[13] new threats and actors were attributed significant emphasis within the Russian security agenda, because they were said to be trying to derail and undermine Russia's new found strength and prosperity. These actors included those that the regime expected to, but had not, recognized Russia's position as a 'strong' state. As noted by President Putin in April 2007:

> Some, making skilful use of pseudo-democratic rhetoric, would like to return us to the recent past, some in order to once again plunder the nation's resources with impunity and rob the people and the state, and others in order to deprive our country of its economic and political independence.
>
> (Putin 2007a)

As outlined in the previous chapters, Russia's growing concerns about the West's role in international affairs and the 'colour revolutions' in the post-Soviet space resulted in a sense of fear within official discourse about the possibility of similar events happening inside Russia. In response, the regime widened its *obraz vraga* to include any actor or group – domestic or foreign – that questioned the course and direction chosen for Russia by the Putin regime. The president of the Academy of Military Sciences Army General, Makhmut Gareyev, characterized the main threats to Russia's security and the world as

> [t]o begin with, if we were to generalize about the numerous and versatile threats we face today, the list would include above all the efforts of certain international forces and leading countries to encroach on Russia's sovereignty and prejudice its economic and other interests; different forms of political and informational pressure and subversion, as was the case in Ukraine, Georgia, and Kyrgyzstan; and territorial claims along the entire length of our borders.
>
> (Litovkin 2007)

Within this vaguely defined *obraz vraga* to challenge the regime's security became synonymous with challenging Russia itself.

Domestic security concerns

The official position on Russia's internal security threats radically altered in the mid-2000s. Despite a partial desecuritization of the internal space and a move away from presenting internal insecurities as immediate major and existential threats, certain elements of internal space and activity remained securitized. Indeed, an ever wider and less specific list of internal security threats were named, gathered around the notion of the 'enemies' that threatened to assail Russia's strength and stability. Whereas in previous periods the debate on internal security was structured in terms of Russia's own weaknesses or the threat from international terrorism, the authorities now suggested that any group that challenged the Putin regime's direction of development was an enemy of the country. Thus, in the internal sphere, the notions of Self and Other were redefined to represent those with and those against the Putin regime, rather than centring on those defending and challenging the territorial or national integrity of Russia, as in the early 2000s.

The notion of the *vrag* [enemy] became increasingly diverse, malleable and highly ad hoc in nature, often reflecting developments not only in the internal, but also the external sphere. Russia's experience and developments in the external sphere continued to structure the regime's reading of internal insecurity. In addition, many of these security threats were externalized along normative, geographical and increasingly temporal axis. As noted by Vladimir Putin during his annual Address to the Federal Assembly in April 2007 that:

> There has been an increasing influx of money from abroad being used to intervene directly in our internal affairs...
>
> Some are not above using the dirtiest techniques, attempting to ignite inter-ethnic and inter-religious hatred in our multi-ethnic and democratic country. In this respect, I ask you to speed up the adoption of amendments to the law introducing stricter liability for extremist actions
>
> (Putin 2007a)

The Russian leadership increasingly rejected what it saw as the imposition of Western 'values', and challenged the notion of Western-inspired universal norms, whilst emphasizing the importance of Russia's own national values, culture and interests (Lipman 2006a). By extension, any groups that positioned themselves, potentially or actually, against the Putin regime, supported Western criticism of Russia or were independent from the regime were presented as actors seeking to undermine and crush Russia's new found stability and prosperity. The nature of such threats was predominantly constructed around a fear of extremism, rather than terrorism, as in the previous periods. Putin suggested at his meeting with students from Moscow State University on 25 January 2005 that '[t]he state and society must jointly fight any type of extremism and radicalism.'[14] Similarly, as suggested by the Secretary of Russia's Security Council Igor Ivanov in March 2007:

> In place of traditional threats, developed out of the bipolar confrontation, there emerged a new generation of threats: the rise in political extremism under the cover of religious and ethnonational principles.
>
> (Ivanov 2007)

Geographically, security threats were decreasingly linked with the threat of international terrorism and increasingly associated with symbolic and direct Western influence on Russian domestic affairs (Putin 2007a). Whereas in the past, it was the image of international terrorism that was used as a scapegoat for Russia's ills, this role was now filled by the image of the threatening West.

As a result, the regime portrayed domestic liberal opposition movements and non-governmental organizations associated to the West as threats to Russian internal stability, and subsequently targeted them. Protests and meetings of groups, such as 'The Other Russia' before the G8 summit in July 2006, were quashed by the authorities with passports confiscated and foreign officials and representatives warned that their attendance would be deemed as 'an unfriendly gesture' (Lipman 2006b). Pressure was also applied to nationalist groups not supportive to the Putin regime's programme through the use of anti-extremism legislation, and in 2007–2008 at least six trials ended with convictions for xenophobic activities (Kozhevnikova 2008).

Temporally, a process was undertaken to historicize internal security threats to fit within the image of the chaos of the 1990s, and thus the Russian leadership reacted strongly to any suggestion that the situation might revert to the instability and uncertainty of that period (Putin 2007a). Frequently, actors that questioned the political and ideological course chosen by the Putin regime were labelled as enemies that wanted to see Russia return to the problematic period of the 1990s.

The shifts in threat construction also resulted in a change in the security practices advocated and implemented. The trend, noted in the previous period, of using administrative and legislative mechanisms, rather than advocating extraordinary measures for dealing with international terrorism was accelerated. A series of new administrative measures and counterterrorism laws were enacted, such as the 2006 Counter Terrorism Law and the creation of the National Anti-terrorist Committee with local branches throughout the Russian Federation. These new security measures sought not only to counteract existing security threats, but also prevent these threats from arising in the first place. As such, increasing emphasis was placed on preventing actors from operating independently within Russia, as exemplified by the 2006 law on NGOs, under which the Russian state sought to reinstate its control over all non-state activity.

The overarching effect of this reconceptualization of security threats was a new discourse, which conflated domestic insecurities with independent activity and influences from the West. This was highlighted by Aleksandr Torshin, deputy chairman of the Federation Council and a member of the National Anti-terrorist Committee (NAC), when he stated that 'foreign NGOs often turn into platforms for recruiting terrorists and extremists. What is particularly alarming is that in most cases they recruit young people'.[15] He also suggested that foreign, especially European governments not only did not clamp down on such activity in their countries, but also operationalized the information disseminated by such NGOs for their own propaganda purposes.[16]

This change in approach was a reflection of the change in the regime's grand-identity discourse from that of a 'weak' state threatened by internal instability and thus requiring extraordinary measures, to a 'strong' state that can cope with some elements of internal instability through its normal structures and practices. In this way, within the Putin regime's representation of Russia as a 'strong' state, the widening of administrative systems to prevent the emergence of enemies to the interconnected image of the regime and state became the central focus of Russia's internal security agenda.

External security concerns

From the leadership's perspective, Russia had now regained the status of a 'strong' state by virtue of the relative success of their internal rebuilding project. Indeed, an analysis of the 2008 Foreign Policy Concept suggests that Russia's position on strengthening international security centred primarily on the assertion of Russian national interests within international affairs and matters of governance in the international system, rather than the direct defence of the Russian state from external challenges. In this regard, and as part of its interest in international economic and resource cooperation, the regime sought to emphasize Russia's importance as an energy and resources provider, and suggested that due to this there was a need for Russia's greater integration into world economy, whilst, at the same time, 'taking into account the need to ensure economic, energy and food security of the country'.[17]

Consequently, Russia expected its status as an important international actor to be recognized externally, particularly by its Western partners. However, as noted previously, this acknowledgement was not forthcoming. In turn, the Putin regime became increasingly vocal about how the return of a 'strong' Russia to the international system was 'not to everyone's taste'.[18] This also led to a reconfiguration of the key actors threatening to Russia, with the image of global terrorism losing much of its salience and the construction of an increasingly threatening West coming to the fore in Russian official discourse (Trenin 2006).

Frictions between Russia and the West – already present – were aggravated further by a plethora of new tensions, including energy geopolitics, oil and gas disputes with Ukraine, Belarus, Georgia, Moldova between 2006–2008; the potential expansion of NATO to include Georgia and Ukraine; the positioning of US Missile Defence in Poland and Czech Republic; bilateral friction between Russia and US/EU together with the friction over the CIS space.

From the Russian perspective, perceived Western unilateralism was now seen as destabilizing the international system more immediately than international terrorism (although this security concern continued to be constructed as a significant threat internationally). This point was exemplified by Putin in 2007, 'today we are witnessing an almost uncontained hyper use of force – military force – in international relations, force that is plunging the world into an abyss of permanent conflicts',[19] and by its suspension of its involvement in the Treaty on Conventional Armed Forces in Europe in July 2007.

At the same time, the Russian leadership became increasingly disillusioned with the West's lack of acknowledgement that their actions violated key Russian national interests. This was evident in the frequent references to what Russia proclaimed as Western 'double standards', between the West's own behaviour and the expectations the West placed on how Russia should behave (Aksenyonok 2008). The Russian official position betrayed disappointment and, to some extent, resignation with regards to the West. This was the sense conveyed by Lavrov's article in the April–June 2007 issue of the journal *Global Affairs*, in which the West appeared to have been securitized by Russia:

> The novelty of the situation is that the West is losing its monopoly on the globalization process. This explains, perhaps, attempts to present the current developments as a threat to the West, its values, and very way of life … Russia is against attempts to divide the world into the so-called 'civilized mankind,' and all the others. This is a way to global catastrophe.
>
> (Lavrov 2007c)

As Sakwa notes, as well as being based on political, strategic and security issues, these tensions with the West were also underpinned by the promotion of alternative 'intellectual' and 'cultural' principles about how both individual nation-states and the international system should be organized (Sakwa 2008b, p. 264). By the end of this period, Russian-Western relations had degraded into a deeply negative spiral of mutual suspicion, which in turn gave way to threats and counter threats. Russia's domestic struggles were projected onto interstate rivalries. Indeed, the scholar Dmitry Furman argued that '"there is only one opposition to Putin at present – other countries"' (Sakwa 2008b, p. 253). As in the internal sphere, there was a hardening of the distinction between the Self (Putin's Russia) and the Other (opponents to this particular vision of Russia).

In the context of this tense relationship, the regime began to be concerned that the West may attempt to directly interfere in Russian politics, via financial, social, political and moral support of certain candidates in the 2008 Presidential elections,[20] as they believe the West to have done at the end of regime change during the 'colour revolutions'. Thus, as in previous periods, events in the external sphere were said by the regime to have a direct and profound effect on Russia's domestic space. Also, in spite of its proclamations to the contrary, at the start of the 2000s, the change in state identity discourse from depicting Russia as 'weak' to a 'strong' state, resulted in external security threats coming to be seen as more of a priority than internal security threats.

Conclusion

By 2008 many of the initial assumptions that were made when Putin initially came to power within Russia's political and security agendas had been reversed. The vision that a 'strong' Russia would be a Russia that had managed to deal with all of its insecurities disappeared, and a new discourse articulated that a 'strong' Russia was one that would have to cope with certain ongoing security risks and threats. In this way, Russia became a strange hybrid of a 'strong' and 'weak' state: on the one hand, a much more assertive and confident actor, but, on the other, a more fearful and insecure one. The official state identity and security discourse at the end of Putin's second term conveyed an almost paranoid image of a 'strong' Russia, surrounded by enemies, from within and beyond.

During this period, buoyed by economic growth driven by oil and gas exports, Russia's sense of patriotism and pride reached a new height, as it was suggested that, for the first time in the post-Soviet period, Russia had found its own path to success. Whilst this sense of optimism proved to be rather short-lived, it nonetheless represented a key moment in post-Soviet development. At the same time, and in spite of high levels of economic growth, strong popular approval rating, and a newly found gravitas and confidence on the international stage, the after-effect of the 'colour revolutions' caused the Putin regime to become ever more concerned that a similar development could also take place in Russia. Thus, in domestic politics, while Putin remained popular with the electorate, regime security and a preoccupation with clamping down on any non-state activity that could be deemed as a potential threat to the preservation of the regime came to play an increasingly central role in Russia's domestic security agenda. This was connected with activities of an increasingly threatening West interfering in Russia's internal matters. Thus, a renewed sense of power and strength sat side-by-side an increased sense of paranoia on the part of the regime about challenges to their legitimacy.

In international affairs, Russia's disillusionment with the West and its role in the international system – a process that had already began in the previous period – was accelerating by the mid-2000s. Disagreements over the rules of the game, the West's continued refusal to take Russia seriously as a great power, and – according to the Russian elites – the West's disregard for global norms resulted in relations between Russia and the West evolving within a downward spiral. Whilst the West remained a key referent Other for Russia, and whose recognition it continued to seek, it rejected what it saw as its claims about the universalism of its norms and values.

By the end of Putin's second term, the regime had achieved most of the aims it had set itself on coming to power at the turn of the millennium, most notably taking the official construction of Russia's state identity from that of a 'weak' to a 'strong' state. However, in the process of realizing these aims, the regime had made Russia into a much more isolated and insecure actor. Yet, so long as wealth and economic successes continued to improve, this system based on a social contract of more state political control for generalized economic gain continued to function. However, as will be discussed in the final section of this book, the dual impact of the presidential change-over from Putin to Medvedev and back again four years later, together with the global recession of 2008–2009, placed this system under severe stress, and the regime sought to find new tools to manage Russia in these changed circumstances.

Notes

1 For more details on this new initiative see: 'Putin utverdil Kontseptsiyu sotsial'no-ekonomicheskogo razvitiya Rossii do 2020 goda', NewsRu.com, 25 November 2008, available at: http://txt.newsru.com/finance/25nov2008/conception.html, accessed 16 April 2009. Whilst the effect of the recent global economic crisis has forced the Russian government to somewhat re-examine the feasibility of such socio-economic as well as military programmes in the immediate future, these have been renegotiated, put back by a few years, but as yet not suspended outright, see: 'Pravitel'stvo RF rassmotrit kontseptsiyu razvitiya strany do 2020', *RIA Novosti*, available: www.rian.ru/economy/20081001/151746239.html, accessed 16 May 2009.
2 Petrov and McFaul have argued that managed democracy under Putin was primarily about the state (and the Putin regime) adopting a top-down approach to controlling the state and the country, in the form of controlling: a strong presidency and weak institutions; state control of the media; control over elections allows elites to legitimize their decisions. Petrov and McFaul (2005).
3 Surkov, Rossiya i demokratiya', *Ekspert*, 3 July 2006, available at: www.expert.ru/printissues/expert/2006/25/news_surkov_rossiya_i_demokratiya/, accessed 20 August 2014; Gromov (2006).
4 For more information see, 'Obshchestvennaya palata' available at: www.oprf.ru/rus/about, accessed 6 June 2010.
5 Russia moves to inculcate greater patriotism', Interfax, Johnson's Russia List, #16 – JRL 9204, available at: www.cdi.org/russia/Johnson/9204-16.cfm, accessed 19 September 2010.
6 Russian Foreign Minister Sergey Lavrov's Interview with the Newspaper Vremya Novostei, Published on 26 December 2007, Press Service, Russian Ministry of Foreign Affairs, available at: www.mid.ru/brp_4.nsf/e78a48070f128a7b43256999005bcbb3/dc07853785fc201ec32573bd005e7190?OpenDocument, accessed 3 June 2010.
7 Article of Russian Minister of Foreign Affairs Sergey Lavrov, 'The Foreign Policy of Russia: A New Phase', Published in the journal *Ekspert* on 17 December 2007, Press Service, Russian Ministry of Foreign Affairs, available at: www.mid.ru/brp_4.nsf/e78a48070f128a7b43256999005bcbb3/969279ee85a9b046c32573b60048c175?OpenDocument, accessed 20 December 2009.
8 'Russia's Activities at the UN: Results of 2006', Russian Ministry of Foreign Affairs, available at www.mid.ru/brp_4.nsf/e78a48070f128a7b43256999005bcbb3/281ee0e34a13b1a8c325726f0047c561?OpenDocument, accessed 4 June 2010.
9 'Russian MFA Spokesman Mikhail Kamynin Interview with RIA Novosti on the Upcoming Russia-NATO Council Meeting', Russian Ministry of Foreign Affairs, 6 December 2007, available at: www.mid.ru/brp_4.nsf/e78a48070f128a7b43256999005bcbb3/d8913d1dfe5358e7c32573aa00235f77?OpenDocument, accessed 5 June 2010.

10 'Russian MFA Spokesman Mikhail Kamynin Interview with RIA Novosti on the Upcoming OSCE Ministerial Council Meeting in Madrid', 27 November 2007, Russian Ministry of Foreign Affairs, available at: www.mid.ru/brp_4.nsf/e78a48070f128a7b43256999005bcbb3/abea360a8970ac2fc32573a300219f37?OpenDocument, accessed 10 June 2010.
11 Vladimir Putin, 'Speech at a Meeting of the Board of the Federal Security Service (FSB)', 7 February 2006, available at: http://archive.kremlin.ru/eng/speeches/2006/02/07/1946_type82912type82913_101157.shtml, accessed 20 June 2010.
12 Vladimir Putin, Annual Address to the Federal Assembly, 10 May 2006, available at: http://archive.kremlin.ru/eng/speeches/2006/05/10/1823_type70029type82912_105566.shtml, accessed 10 June 2010.
13 Vladimir Putin, Annual Address to the Federal Assembly, 10 May 2006, available at: http://archive.kremlin.ru/eng/speeches/2006/05/10/1823_type-70029type82912_105566.shtml, accessed 10 June 2010.
14 'Putin calls for more resolute struggle with manifestations of extremism among young people', RIA Novosti, 25 January 2005, cited by Johnson's Russia List, #20 – JRL 9033, available at: www.cdi.org/russia/Johnson/9033–20.cfm, accessed 4 June 2010.
15 Aleksandr Torshin, Deputy Chairman of the Federation Council, quoted in RIA Novosti, 8 April 2008, cited in 'Foreign NGOs support terrorism in Russia – senior senator' in Johnson's Russia List, #24 – JRL 2008–72, available at: www.cdi.org/russia/johnson/2008–72–24.cfm, accessed 1 May 2009.
16 Aleksandr Torshin, Deputy Chairman of the Federation Council, quoted in RIA Novosti, 08 April 2008, cited in 'Foreign NGOs support terrorism in Russia – senior senator' in Johnson's Russia List, #24 – JRL 2008–72, available at: www.cdi.org/russia/johnson/2008–72–24.cfm, accessed 1 May 2009.
17 Russian Foreign Policy Concept, Russian Ministry of Foreign Affairs, 12 July 2008, available at: www.mid.ru/ns-osndoc.nsf/1e5f0de28fe77fdcc32575d900298676/869c9d2b87ad8014c32575d9002b1c38?OpenDocument, accessed 4 June 2010.
18 Vladimir Putin, Annual Address to the Federal Assembly, 26 April 2007, available at: www.kremlin.ru/eng/speeches/2007/04/26/1209_type70029type82912_125670.shtml, accessed 16 February 2009.
19 Vladimir Putin, 'Speech and the Following Discussion at the Munich Conference on Security Policy', 10 February 2007, available at: http://archive.kremlin.ru/eng/speeches/2007/02/10/0138_type82912type82914type82917type84779_118123.shtml, accessed 3 June 2010.
20 Personal communication with Dr Peter Duncan, 3 March 2009.

ated Chechnya as a symbol of its successful programme of rebuilding Russia

8 A 'rebuilt' Chechnya in a securitized North Caucasus?

Alongside the rebranding of Russia as a 'strong' state, in which the fundamental structural domestic weaknesses identified in 2000 were said to have been resolved, from 2004/2005 official discourse began to suggest that the authorities' primary goals for their normalization of Chechnya project had been achieved. Having taken the initial steps between 2001 and 2004, Russian officials, by and large, argued that the macro-processes of normalization and counterterrorism had significantly reduced the threat posed by Chechnya to Russia. The image of Chechnya, therefore, began to be reconstructed from that of a failing entity to a rehabilitated republic. This representation of Chechnya as no longer a significant threat saw them remerge in official federal discourse, after a period of silencing. Indeed, in a full circle transformation, the regime began to talk of the rehabilitated Chechnya as a symbol of its successful programme of rebuilding Russia from weakness to strength.

However, at the same time, this representation did not convey the full complexity of the ongoing process of desecuritization of Chechnya. The emergence of the increasingly authoritarian Kadyrov regime in Chechnya certainly did not mirror the Copenhagen School's ideal type of desecuritization, in which a security issue is moved back into democratic-pluralistic 'normal' politics. Furthermore, in contrast to the early 2000s, in which the independent-minded Chechnya was considered a fundamental threat to Russia, the transfer of authority and control over security functions to the seemingly independent Kadyrov regime was depicted in official discourse as a sign of the 'normalization' and rehabilitation of the republics into a strong Russia.

To examine the complexity and specificity of the desecuritization process, this chapter begins by investigating Russia's policy towards Chechnya on the local level. In parts two and three, Chechnya's role across Russia's wider domestic and foreign political and security agendas is examined.

Desecuritization of Chechnya on the ground

Across Putin's second term, his regime increasingly asserted that the political foundations for Chechnya to function as a normal republic within the Russian Federation had been successfully laid down. The bulk of security threats on the ground were said to have been dealt with and Chechnya proclaimed to have made strides in its economic and social development. This 'new' stage in Chechnya's development was noted by Vladimir Patrin, from the United Press Centre of the Operative Headquarters in the Chechen republic in March 2008,

> in the last few years the Chechen republic has achieved great successes. The process of rebuilding the economy destroyed by the war is smoothly transitioning into a new phase: of economic and resource development and growth. It appears that soon Chechnya will take its deserved place amidst other prosperous regions of the Southern Federal region and the rest of Russia.[1]

As a consequence, the focus of official policy turned towards capitalizing on these gains and developing them further, as seen in the official bulletins on Chechnya, produced by the Ministry of Interior. In 2008, one read,

> Provision has been made for the rebuilding, reconstruction and restoration of all sectors of economic and social sphere in the Chechen republic.[2]

This change of image was not simply cosmetic, but informed the focus of the large-scale state programmes for Chechnya. One such programme entitled the 'Socio-economic development of the Chechen Republic 2008–2011', was allocated a budget of 120.6 billion roubles, and identified the key priorities for Chechnya's development: an increase in employment and economic growth, development of production and service sectors, restoration of large-scale infrastructure and communication and transport networks as well as the provision of new housing in the republic.[3]

Whilst the socio-economic situation in Chechnya remained rather precarious in places, for example, unemployment remained at 70–80 per cent and the republic's health service in dire straits (Lunze 2009), major redevelopments were now taking place. Most notably, the rebuilding of Grozny, which was named the best CIS city of the year in April 2008, due to the success if its restoration.[4] Similarly, both officials and independent analysts returning from Chechnya during this period noted the major significant improvement in infrastructure and security in Grozny.

On the political front, the desecuritization of Chechnya continued to mirror trends at the federal level. The same logics and norms of defining what constitutes 'normal' politics in Russia under President Putin, were also evident in the structuring of political developments in Chechnya. The tightly interlinked notions of a 'strong' state and 'normal' politics were primarily defined by the existence and operation of formal state institutions, the reintegration of former fighters and the re-emergence of a 'strong' local leader based on the Putin model for wider Russia. This heavy emphasis on formal political institutions, rather than the practice of politics was evident in Putin's speech in 2006, at a press conference for the Russian and foreign media, in which he argued that:

With the election of parliament this process has been brought to a close and the Chechen Republic has fully returned within the constitutional sphere of the Russian Federation. Of course, many economic and social tasks remain and tasks concerning creating local authorities. But the problem of forming state authorities has been resolved.[5]

Hence, following the re-establishment of formal institutions in Chechnya, Russian official discourse no longer featured the 'extraordinary' nature of the Chechen political regime, but rather the 'ordinariness' and 'normalness' of the day-to-day workings of the Chechen political system.[6]

This desecuritized Chechnya was, in other words, in the process of re-entering the 'normal' politics of contemporary Russia, which, in contrast to the assumptions of traditional securitization theory, was not an open liberal democratic polity. Within Chechen politics, authoritarian trends, such as the barring of opposition candidates at elections and the appointment without election of Ramzan Kadyrov as the Chechen President in spring 2007, were not discussed either in Russian or Chechen official discourse and associated media outlets. Nor was there any political or wider societal discussion about what 'normal' politics in Chechnya should involve. The return of 'normal' politics was thus centred primarily on the formal trapping of democratic-politics, and not, as will be discussed further on, the 'normal' workings of politics as it commonly understood within the Western-centric theories of (de)securitization.

Security risks

As was the case in terms of the political realm, official discourse on security in Chechnya mirrored that of the wider federal discourse, which meant a change in the language and practices of 'existential threats' had been replaced with that of 'security risks'.

The deaths of the central figures of the Ichkerian resistance movement, namely Maskhadov in March 2005 and Shamil Basayev in July 2006, were portrayed in the official discourse as marking an end of an era and final page in the history of the second Chechen conflict.[7] Whilst in the first half of the 2000s, the Ichkerian administration of Maskhadov continued to be presented as a major existential threat, by 2006, with most of the key figures of this movement had either eliminated (Maskhadov and Basayev), in exile abroad (such as Zakayev) or incorporated into the pro-Russian Chechen administration (Kadyrov), they were no longer considered a threat of 'existential' significance.

Indeed, to some extent, the Ichkerian movement had been replaced. The creation of the Caucasus Front in May 2005, headed by Shaykh Abdul Khalim Sadulaev, previously the so-called leader of the Ichkerian resistance, re-orientated the focal-point of terrorist activity away from Chechnya towards the other North Caucasus republics. The Front comprised a much wider group of North Caucasus republics, namely Adygea, Dagestan, Ingushetia, Kakabardino-Balkaria, Karachevo-Cherkessia, Krasnodar, North Ossetia and Stavropol. Upon his death in 2006, Sadulaev was replaced by Doku Umarov as the head of the Caucasus Front.

The remaining insecurity in Chechnya was presented as 'banal' with little wider significance. Instead of presenting Chechnya as posing a credible and coherent threat, as in first half of the decade, outbreaks of violence and terrorist actions were explained as small-scale actions by the remnants of the previous resistance groups, splintered and unspecified bandit groups,[8] or as a result of the wider regional dislocation affecting the whole of North Caucasus. In other words, the joint policies of normalization and the ongoing counterterrorist operations were said to have successfully reduced the level of instability and insecurity.[9]

On an operational level, the discourse altered from favouring large-scale military operations to the maintenance of vigilance to ensure that the situation did not flare up again. Although disagreements between different official bodies as to the precise number of remaining fighters continued, most agreed that security in Chechnya had greatly improved and that it was now under greater control than before (Panchenkov 2008). Ignoring the remaining concerns of some official voices, particularly on the part of the power ministries, Chechnya was now discussed as enjoying a new level of stability and was thus 'desecuritized', opening up the possibility for a partial withdrawal of federal troops and a substantial shift of command from the federal forces to local Chechen controls.[10]

From 2006–2008, significant numbers of the federally controlled forces were pulled out of Chechnya. As noted in the August 2006 decree, together with 3,000 border guards, only a brigade of 7,000 interior troops and a 15,000-strong brigade of the Defence Ministry remained, thus halving the number of soldiers operating in Chechnya (Muradov 2008). Furthermore, many of the remaining troops rarely left their barracks. Nonetheless, heightened vigilance was, for example, deemed necessary during sensitive events, such as the parliamentary elections in 2007, when the federal authorities increased their security presence.[11]

Despite suggestions that Chechnya's legal system was now fully operational, the federal Duma rejected proposals for the reintroduction of trial by jury in November 2006, choosing to postpone this issue for three years by suggesting that the situation inside the republic remained unstable, creating the potential for the prejudicing of trials.[12] Access to Chechnya remained difficult for certain groups, such as foreign journalists, which was explained in the official discourse as due to the danger from the ongoing security risks on the ground.[13] Concerns were also raised regarding the possibility of future instability re-emerging, particularly in the event of these terrorist groups obtaining more substantial funding from abroad or benefiting from increased recruitment locally.[14]

Decentralization of Chechnya and the emergence of a federal-local alliance

Alongside political normalization and the downgrading from existential threat to risk, a third element in the official Russian desecuritization of Chechnya was decentralization. A process that had begun with the policy of 'Chechenization' in the early 2000s, with the support of the local Chechen regime of Akhmat Kadyrov, reached its peak in 2007 with the instalment of Ramzan Kadyrov's as President. The importance attributed to the establishment or a 'strong' Chechen leader loyal to Russia was evident in Vladislav Surkov's statement that:

> Stability in the Caucasus today rests on the shoulders of people like Ramzan Kadyrov...
> As long as people like Kadyrov are around, we can rest assured that constitutional order in the republic will prevail and every possible effort will be made to ensure peace, stability and prosperity in Chechnya.[15]

As the Russian regime stepped back from direct micro-management of Chechnya, the local Chechen regime became the main securitizing and desecuritizing actor in the republic. This included the ceding of significant autonomy to the local regime. For example, Kadyrov successfully lobbied to replace the head of the Federal Operational-Investigative Bureau (OSB), which was subordinated to the MVD's directorate in the Southern Federal *Okrug*. Kadyrov was also able to replace the republic's Chief Prosecutor, Valerii Kuznetsov, with a local civil servant more compliant with his regime (Slider 2008, p. 191). Furthermore, the dismantling of the *Vostok* and *Zapad* battalions of the Russian Defence Ministry's 42nd Motorized Division in November 2008 removed the last bastion of federal Ministry of Defence control over Chechen security agencies.

However, in contrast to the predictions of many analysts, a 'strong' local Chechen regime was not interpreted as a threat by the Russian authorities. Indeed, rather than ignoring this development, the Russian officials both acknowledged and endorsed the emergence of the 'strong' nature of the Kadyrov regime. The president of the Russian military commanders' club, General of the Army Anatoly Kulikov, acknowledged the federal-Chechen tandem relationship and security arrangement, when he stated in February 2008 that, 'the presidents of Russia and Chechnya have taken a firm and consistent position, and that largely helped turn the situation for the better.'[16] Even the Russian Interior Minister, Rashid Nurgaliyev noted that:

> Today, the Chechen interior ministry is probably one of the most effective fighting units of the Russian police, and the testimony to this may be seen in the results in the prevention of terrorist threats and in strikes against the members of illegal armed formations.
>
> (Are 2008)

Federal Russian authorities thus largely accepted this decentralization process and the growing role of the local authorities in combating insecurity and terrorism within Chechnya.[17] In fact, the local republican forces were even described as more suited to the job of guaranteeing security in Chechnya than federal forces, due to their local and cultural awareness and knowledge.[18]

This new-found centre-periphery pattern of relations also showed a degree of resilience, in the face of clashes and tensions between the Kadyrov regime and the representatives of the federal power ministries, such as between Kadyrov and the Yamadayev groupings in April 2008. Events which in the past may have resulted in the resecuritization of Chechnya or relaunch the discourse of Chechnya becoming too independent or too powerful went largely unnoticed or at least passed with minimum fuss. Neither the discussion over Chechen prisoners in Russian prisons,[19] nor accusations of the Kadyrov regime's use of its military power to eliminate its political and even more importantly economic opponents, such as Baysarov and the Yamadayevs outside the Chechen borders,[20] set off alarm bells in the official federal construction of developments in Chechnya.

This led some commentators to suggest that Chechnya under Kadyrov amassed more autonomy than it had even under Maskhadov during the period of independence (1996–1999) (Zakayev 2008). This perspective was reinforced by the fact that this form of localization of power was not confined to issues of security, but was also evident in other areas, such as social services, education, health and other local affairs.[21] In practice, the rule of the regime of Ramzan Kadyrov was akin to a personal fiefdom, with many characterizing this period as the 'Ramzanification' of Chechnya.[22] The Kadyrov regime also attempted to exert a greater influence over reconstruction and economic policies, such as over the issue of revenues from the Chechen oil,[23] and to regain control over the Chechen agricultural land and civilian facilities used by the Russian federal forces.[24] As argued by Malashenko the local regime's power in Chechnya was 'centred on three closely interwoven cables: a regime of personal power, a clan-based structure and loyalty to Moscow' (Malashenko 2007, p. 2). Slider characterized this new form of desecuritization/decentralization as '"illiberal federalism"—decentralization to the benefit of a regional leader who, in effect, was a warlord with unlimited powers' (Slider 2008, p. 190). Therefore the 'return' of Chechnya to the 'normal' politics of the Russian Federation was firmly embedded within the structured and restructured milieu created by the Putin regime: an authoritarian local regime, founded on the fusion of regime security[25] and the provision of socio-economic benefits in return for declining personal liberties became the perfect conduit for desecuritization.

However, whereas the independent Maskhadov regime 1996–1999 was perceived as a threat to Russia's security, leading to the securitization of Chechnya, the growing independence of the Kadyrov regime was not presented as a threat to Russia, in 2006–2008. Owing to the way in which the Russian authorities constructed the Kadyrov regime and its own state identity, the Kadyrov regime was presented as enhancing federal control over Chechnya, despite its growing local control and power over the local population.[26] The coexistence and growing use of Kadyrov's regime and their discourses to alter the image of Chechnya demonstrated the full extent of the changing discourse on Chechnya. What emerged was an image of a 'strong' Chechnya with a strong Chechen local leadership, which was no longer mutually exclusive to the discourse of a 'strong' Russia, but could in fact be complementary and coexist. Therefore, a 'strong'

Chechnya within a 'strong' Russia now rested not only on desecuritization, but also the localization, of Chechnya in the hands of the powerful local regime of Ramzan Kadyrov, which operationalized Russia's policy and discourses on the ground.

Chechnya's role in the domestic political and security agenda

The generalized rehabilitation, 'normalization', desecuritization and localization of the Chechen issue within Russia's wider national and security agenda led it to play an increasingly positive role in the Putin regime's wider discourse about the domestic security situation in Russia. Although never regaining the pre-eminent role it held within state discourse during the early Putin period, the regime no longer insisted on silencing discussion of Chechnya, as it had done in the middle years of Putin's first two terms in office. This suggests that it is not only instances of securitization that can have symbolical political significance, but desecuritizations may also have a role in wider political agendas (Balzacq 2008).

As outlined by Moore and Wills, during the mid-2000s the image of Chechnya underwent a period of rebranding by both federal and republican elites (Moore and Wills 2008, p. 260), or what this book characterizes as a process of rehabilitation. Not only was Chechnya no longer considered a 'forbidden' or 'unspoken' issue, but it was now presented as a rehabilitated part of the Russian Federation that had successfully shed its previously negative image. Improvements on the ground were frequently noted in official meetings between Russian officials and Chechen groups. A growing number of reports and eye-witness accounts highlighting the increasing pace of reconstruction and the return to normal life in the republic also began to appear in official sources and media.[27]

Critically, there was also a change in the official spokespeople for Chechnya within the national-level discourse, as the Kadyrov regime established itself as the accepted voice for Chechnya.[28] For most of his first two terms in office, Putin, the presidential administration and select federal bodies, such as the Power Ministries, had played this role. The growing power of the Kadyrov regime and its authority within the official federal discourse was not, however, presented as a threatening or dangerous development,[29] but as a natural component of the new 'strong' Russia. Indeed, the Kadyrov regime regularly outlined its support for Putin staying on for a third presidential term.[30]

As part of the wider process of historicization of Russia's past weakness, and in conjunction with the rehabilitation of Chechnya, the image of Chechnya as an existential threat to Russia and the region was now relegated to the past. For example, during Putin's Annual Address to the Federal Assembly in 2005, he dismissed talk of the threat from international terrorism and from Chechnya as only relevant to 'Russia's most recent history'. As a result of this process of historicization, Russian officials began to refer to two distinct periods in recent Russo-Chechen relations. The first marked the initial securitization of Chechnya, the second the process of normalization. This periodization of two periods, one of securitization and the other of desecuritization, was evident in Putin's statement that,

We couldn't repeat the mistakes of the past; we couldn't begin reconstruction before the main questions of security had been resolved.[31]

Within this re-periodization of the Chechen conflict, the time of instability and insecurity was now presented as taking place almost exclusively in the 1990s, with little reference made to the large-scale military operations that continued to be carried out throughout Putin's first term in office.[32] This was in line with the wider discourse in Russian politics – noted in the previous chapter – whereby Russia's weaknesses and failures were now firmly relocated to the 1990s under President Yeltsin.

Hence, as in the case of the political system put in place in Chechnya, there was no attempt to initiate a wider discussion in society about the impact of the second Chechen conflict. Nor was there any re-examination or real discussion of Russia's policy and actions in Chechnya, either in the early 2000s or during the 1990s. For example, Deputy Minister of the MVD Arkady Edelev, suggested that 'the blood was split on Chechen soil not in vain ... and there should not be any enclaves, set up on religious intolerance and religious confrontation'.[33] By the end of Putin's second term, Chechnya had been reinterpreted as a more positive element in Russia's wider identity discourses, while the second Chechen conflict had been confined to the pages of Russia's recent history.

As well as its rather complex role within Russia's national political agenda, Chechnya also retained a significant position within Russia's domestic security agenda, particularly in relation to North Caucasus. Within the 'performative geopolitical script' of internal security agenda,[34] Chechnya continued to be constructed as part of the unstable region of North Caucasus that was associated with the potential risk of terrorism and security tensions (Medvedev 2008). This discourse informed regional policy in the North Caucasus and was related to its ongoing concerns about continued terrorist activity across Russia, especially in its southern region.

In the period 2004–2005, Chechnya was still said to have a negative influence on the rest of the region, as the federal rebuilding efforts in Chechnya caused those intent on creating insecurity to relocate to the other republics of the North Caucasus. Following the raid on Nalchik, the capital of Kabardino-Balkaria by the insurgent groups on 13 October that resulted in 142 deaths, Putin highlighted the shifting location of terrorist activity as:

> As you can see, the terrorists have ever less opportunity to act effectively in Chechnya itself and so they are trying to expand their activities into other regions of the Caucasus, but they will not succeed in this objective for we will not let them.
>
> (Putin 2005d)

On this basis, Chechnya continued to be included within Russia's wider counter-terrorist and security operations in the region. One such example were the command and staff exercises during 31 July–9 August 2007, which included

Chechnya among exercises in North Ossetia, Ingushetia, Dagestan and Chechnya and the Stavropol Krai.

Other republics in the North Caucasus, namely Dagestan, Ingushetia, Kabardino-Balkaria and increasingly also Karachevo-Cherkessia, were now becoming the focal points for the counterinsurgency strategy. Sticking to the securitization script first deployed in relation to Chechnya, the official position continued to largely exclude the complex interconnection between local, regional, national and even global factors driving the insurgency in the region. Most of the emphasis, both on the official and insurgency side was now placed on the figure of Doku Umarov, who in 2007 announced the establishment of the Caucasus Emirate to replace the Caucasus Front.[35] This development marked the end of the 'Ichkerian idea' (Markedonov 2008), with many of the previous leaders of the Ichekerian administration, such as Zakayev, distancing themselves from this new project (Shlapentokh 2008, 2010). In turn, as Sukhov notes, the insurgency changed from being a single conflict between rebels and federal forces to becoming a 'series of separate attacks by small armed groups, usually aimed at corrupt local officials and police and inspired by the general idea of an Islamic jihad' (2007). This new challenge was, however, constructed by the Russian state as a less coherent and more fluid movement, akin to a patchwork of insecurities and risks, rather than an existential danger (Pchelov 2008).

Conceptually, within the official discourse, the focus remained primarily on terrorism and radical Islam as the key driving factors behind the ongoing insecurity.[36] Some recognition was given to socio-economic problems such as corruption, clan politics, societal problems for fuelling the discontent and resulting insurgency in the region.[37] However, the Russian authorities were less ready to discuss the impact that the violent tactics used by the law enforcement operatives had on the ongoing insurgency in the North Caucasus, or whether the overall strategy in the North Caucasus was itself fuelling the insurgency rather than solving it (Sagromoso 2007).[38]

In turn, the Russian authorities used the same types of strategies put forward in Chechnya in the early 2000s in order to eradicate the insurgency in the North Caucasus, namely counterinsurgency operations, the promotion of official Islam and local cultural traditions and attempts at socio-economic development.

The Russian authorities moved to carry out extensive counterinsurgency operations across the region throughout this period.[39] Furthermore, in July 2005 Putin announced the deployment of mountain brigades to the North Caucasus, as well as plans to secure the Russian southern border, although the implementation of these proposals ran into problems and was repeatedly postponed (Blandy 2007, p. 3). Special operations targeting both the leaders of the insurgency but also the rank-and-file supporters were also regularly carried out across the region.[40] In 2006 a series of new counterterrorist legislation was launched such as the creation of the new National Anti-Terror Committee to coordinate the work of the different agencies involved in counterterrorist activities, together with a new Counterterrorism Law. By 2007 the authorities lauded their successes by announcing that 192 militants and insurgents had been killed that year with 700 people arrested in antiterrorist operations.[41] Despite such announcements, insurgent violence continued to flare up in the region with persistent regularity.

Alongside such counterinsurgency measures, the Russian authorities conceded that the dire economic situation was a contributing factor for the instability in the region.[42] As in the case of the normalization strategy in Chechnya, economic development was presented as the other side of the coin to the counterinsurgency operations, at least in word if not in practice. Unusually, in a leaked report in June 2005, Dmitry Kozak, the presidential envoy to the Southern Federal district, made a candid acknowledgement of the dire economic, political, security and social situation in Federal district, and particularly in the North Caucasus.[43] Indeed, as demonstrated by Gerber and Mendelson, in their 2006 survey of young males in the North Caucasus 'economic conditions and poor governance' rather than 'radical Islam or ethnic animosity', continued to be the main concerns for the local population (Gerber and Mendelson 2009). In practice, in the period 2000–2010, the Russian authorities allocated $30 billion to the region to lift it out of its poverty (Alexseev 2011), although Chechnya continued to be the largest recipient of aid in this period, followed by Ingushetia (Kuchins *et al.* 2011). However, it is debatable how effective this strategy proved to be, as the region continued to suffer from high incidents of unemployment, poverty and socio-economic problems together with the ongoing violence.[44]

In order to alleviate some of the political problems on the gorund, the federal authorities also moved towards political reschuffles in this period, replacing the heads of North Ossetia, Kabardino-Balkaria and Dagestan. In Kozak's proposed plan for the stabilization of the North Caucasus in 2005 importance was attributed to the need 'to break the regional power of the clans and strengthen federal control'.[45] However, as noted by Stanovaya this was an 'almost impossible task of solving the systemic crisis in a stepwise fashion without disrupting the current fragile balances, thereby preventing the escalation of conflict in the region.'[46] Political reshuffles did not, however, end the problems of corruption, poor governance or inefficient political institutions, nor did they succeed in preventing the ongoing insurgent violence in the region.

Finally, in order to tackle the spread of radical Islam across the region, the Russian authorities moved towards the promotion of the official forms of Islam.[47] Using the conceptual frames initially constructed to explain the phenomenon of radical Islam in Chechnya, it was argued that 'good' traditional Islam should be encourage whilst 'bad' 'new' and foreign forms of Islam, said to be promoted by the radical Islamists should be eradicated. Unfortunately, as argued by Yarlikapov the mosaic of forms of 'traditional Islam' in the region made it difficult for the authorities to designate which particular groups or practices should be encouraged and which banned. Nonetheless, the federal authorities sought to promote Islamic education in the region, such as through the establishment of Islamic higher institutions of education and universities, whilst attempting to clamp down on unofficial forms of Islamic worship and scholarship.[48] Overall, the arbitrariness and confusion within this official policy that often targeted non-radical forms of worship alongside the more radical forms of Islam did nor abate but instead fuelled the ongoing violence in the North Caucasus.

By the end of this period, however, a dramatic shift took place in Chechnya's image and role as a regional player. Instead it changed from being presented as a regional threat to a potential model for regional stability. As the normalization and desecuritization process inside the republic gathered pace, and particularly with the coming to power of Ramzan Kadyrov, Chechnya was no longer considered as the epicentre of regional instability. Sukhov suggested that 'paradoxically, Chechnya now serves as a model of centre-region relations' (Sukhov 2008). The Deputy Interior Minister of the Russian Federation, Arkady Edelev, also alluded to this development in February 2007,

> Today, almost everyone recognises that key positive developments have taken and are taking place in the Chechen Republic ... And now Chechnya is no longer, so to speak, a leader in instability across North Caucasus ... Ingushetia, Dagestan and Kabardino-Balkaria are [leaders]. In Kabardino-Balkaria there are two well trained and very hidden terrorist groups. These are the groups of Astimirov and Mukozhev and that of Solpagarov.[49]

In this respect, the Chechen leadership themselves sought to position Chechnya as the leader of counterterrorism in North Caucasus, by offering to give direct assistance to the other North Caucasus republics. Talking in relation to Ingushetia, Ramzan Kadyrov outined that, 'if we are given the order, we will impose order as surely as two times two makes four. It is only a small republic' (Leahy 2009). In spite of the tension this caused in Chechnya's relationships with the other North Caucasus republics, this served to alter Chechnya's image within the federal discourse. Ironically, Chechnya thus regained some remnants of its prior symbolic role in domestic security discourse, but this time as model of resolving a security challenge, rather than as a security threat.

Chechnya's role in the external security agenda

On the foreign policy stage, Russia took an increasingly self-assured approach during Putin's second term. The interaction between this more assertive foreign policy direction and the desecuritization of Chechnya on the ground impacted on Chechnya's role within the Russian national discourse. As in the internal sphere, Chechnya was rehabilitated as a more positive tool in Russia's external foreign and security policy.

As is expected within the classical model of securitization, a key part of the desecuritization process of Chechnya was its disassociation with other security concerns on Russia's foreign security agenda. This was partly due to internal developments within Chechnya itself, but also reflected wider changes in Russia's external security agenda, and an increasing focus on the West rather than international terrorism as Russia's major security 'Other'.

With Chechnya no longer presented as the epicentre of international terrorism in Russia, its role in Russia's foreign policy declined significantly. Indeed, the Russian leadership seemed actively pleased that Chechnya was now being downgraded from its foreign policy agenda, as shown during a meeting between the Italian Prime Minister, Silvio Berlusconi, and Putin in April 2008. Putin noted the lack of journalists questions on Chechnya, and remarked 'thank God, no one is asking questions about Chechnya anymore'.[50]

At the same time, the generalized downgrading across Russia's policy agenda did not mean that Chechnya lost all of its symbolic power in foreign affairs. It now became an image of Russian policy success that the Putin regime wished to project. Russian officials ran organized trips for foreign journalists to visit Chechnya, in order to document the changes taking place.[51] Similarly, it was included in the Russian-Chinese Business Communities' Economic Forum in March 2006, as one of the Russian regions developing ties with Chinese businesses.[52]

The Russian state also sought to project Chechnya as a positive influence in its developing and more proactive Middle Eastern policy (Malashenko 2007).[53] Russia's links with the Organization of the Islamic Conference continued to grow, with this organization increasingly giving positive assessments of developments in Chechnya and of Russia's normalization policy (Putin 2006c). Russian officials used the Chechen issue to promote positive external relations with Lebanon, by, for example, sending a Chechen battalion to Lebanon to help with rebuilding infrastructure. In an interview with the Arab Satellite TV Channel Al Jazeera in February 2007 President Putin justified this decision as,

> we decided that since our servicemen would be working mostly in the Muslim areas of Lebanon, it would be good if the unit providing the security for our engineers was made up of Russian citizens from Chechnya, which, as is well known, has a primarily Muslim population ... Moreover, this decision also illustrated that great changes are taking place in Chechnya itself. We have complete confidence in those who are carrying arms to defend the interests of their people in Chechnya.
>
> (Putin 2007b)

Therefore, unlike in the past, the Chechen issue was utilized as part of Russia's representation of its strength, rather than weakness.

Nonetheless, Russia's attempts to promote the successes of its desecuritization strategy in Chechnya internationally were not without tensions, particularly in its relations with the West. Familiar themes such as the inappropriateness of Russia's policy towards Chechnya, the plight of human rights workers and organizations in the region (Penketh 2007) and the information blockade on reporting in the region continued to be intermittently raised by Russia's Western partners (Havel *et al.* 2006). A wider culture of animosity between the two sides was also in evidence with regards to other high-profile cases relating to Chechnya. Issues, such as the movements and actions of Zakayev, continued to cause disagreement between Western and Russian officials[54] and the high profile assassinations of Anna Politkovskaya in Moscow and Aleksandr Litvinenko, which the Russian officials related to the Chechen question,[55] also became focal points in the friction between Russia and the West.[56] In both cases, Russia disputed the West's interpretation of these events, refusing to concede to the West's demands.

New issues also emerged, notably the cases brought to the European Court of Human Rights by Chechen claiming the payment of compensation for suffering caused by the Russian counterterrorist operations. Despite the tacit acceptance of these judgements as a member of the Council of Europe, in practice Russia was reluctant, or at least very slow, to pay out to individual claimants and to implement the recommended changes to avoid further structural and systemic abuses ongoing in North Caucasus.[57] Indeed, Russian official discourse questioned the validity and authority of the court, and argued that it was unfairly singling out Russia as part of the growing 'new' Cold War atmosphere between Russia and the West. As argued by the Russia judge, Anatoly Kovler: 'We (the Russian Federation) appear in the role of a watchdog, and no one loves a watchdog'.[58]

The Putin regime thus explained Western criticism of its actions in Chechnya as symptomatic of the West's wider rejection of Russia's new found position as a 'strong' state, rather than something specifically linked with Chechnya itself. Tensions over Chechnya therefore fed into the larger image of the 'threatening' West in the Russian security agenda. Whilst Chechnya was no longer a major issue within Russia-West relations, it did serve as additional fuel to the fire of their already tense relationship.

Chechnya: a growing international player under President Kadyrov

The increasing localization and decentralization within Russia's domestic policy and discourse on Chechnya as a form of desecuritization, outlined previously, also had an external dimension. As it established itself as an increasingly autonomous actor, the Kadyrov regime began to develop its own independent voice in the external sphere, although remaining within the overall parameters of Russia's foreign security agenda. Elements of the local regime's position vis-à-vis the international sphere were pertinent to the nature of the desecuritization of Chechnya and its interconnection with Russia's national and security priorities.

In keeping with its strong support for Putin in domestic politics, the Kadyrov regime endorsed the official Russian portrayal of developments and policy regarding Chechnya vis-à-vis the West. For example, they adopted a similar position and rhetoric towards the Parliamentary Assembly of the Council of Europe (PACE), rejecting a new PACE investigation in Chechnya into investigate human rights abuses in March 2007.[59] In this way, a united front seemed to emerge both relationally and constitutively, between the Russian and Chechen leadership in the identification of common external enemies, in this case the West.

While remaining within the confines of the Russian foreign policy agenda, the local Chechen administration became increasingly instrumental in structuring the image of a desecuritized Chechnya abroad. The Kadyrov regime took a proactive approach to normalizing relations with the Chechen diaspora living outside Russia, and encouraging their return to the 'desecuritized' and 'normal' Chechnya (Fuller 2009).[60] The Chechen administration also took the lead in opening Chechnya up to the wider world as part of 'rebuilding' process.[61] This was seen in Chechnya's hosting of the 'International Peace-making Forum: Islam – religion of peace' in August 2007, bringing together representatives from Saudi Arabia, Iraq and Azerbaijan among others. This strand of policy was justified by Chechnya's Representative to the Russian President, Ziyad Sabsabi Moslem by arguing that, 'countries are willing to invest in the Chechen economy, and we are talking about the implementation of these projects. Our republic can set an example of expanding ties with these states and attracting investments in the economy'.[62]

Aside from some attempts on the federal level, it was largely the local regime that actively tried to showcase Chechnya's rehabilitation internationally by bringing in foreign visitors. Officially sponsored visits were organized for world famous figures, such as the boxer Mike Tyson in September 2005, who in turn made public declarations about how much the situation in Chechnya had changed in recent times.[63] During an interview, Kadyrov explained this strategy:

> Why do we bring them to Chechnya? They travel around the world and we want them to tell objective stories about Chechens, that they are not bad people, that they are not killers, that they like this world too, they love life, they want to live in peace.[64]

Conclusion

The Putin regime's normalization policy that was focused on Chechnya was further developed, and most significantly, expanded in scope during Putin's second term in office. The course of this expansion followed the trends in wider national and security discourses, which among other things saw an increasing focus on a discourse asserting Russia's successful progression from 'weak' to 'strong' states, controlling the domestic political space as a means of countering the risks threatening to undermining this newly established strength, and a shift towards seeing West rather than international terrorism as the primary external challenge to Russia. The desecuritization process on the ground centred on three interconnected, and wide-ranging dynamics that reflect the national discourse: desecuritization as a form of a return to normal politics within what was now a much more authoritarian and securitized political and social context in Russia; desecuritization as a reduction in threat perception, articulated through the language of security risks rather than existential threats; and desecuritization as a form of delegation of security controls and oversight from the federal to local authorities.

In this way, the desecuritization of Chechnya functioned as more than simply a way of presenting this issue as having returned to 'normal' politics, and a normal relationship between republic and federal centre, as is suggested in the classical securitization model. It also had resonance and significance for wider state discourse. Indeed, Chechnya began to reappear as a symbol within Putin's political project for wider Russia, although without ever regaining the same salience or symbolic power it had in early Putin period. In contrast to 1999–2001, it was now a symbol to illustrate a 'strong' Russia, rather than a 'weak' one as in the previous period. In both the domestic and foreign policy spaces, the Putin regime tried to utilize the Chechen issue to publicize its success in re-establishing Russia's power and strength. Critically, in relation to the rest of the North Caucasus – as the regional instability grew, by the mid/late 2000s, Chechnya was no longer presented as the epicentre of insecurity. Nonetheless, many of the tropes initially employed in the securitization of Chechnya continued to be utilized by the Russian authorities, in explaining the ongoing regional instability. Rather than articulating this phenomenon as specific to the particular context and circumstances of each of the different republics in the North Caucasus, the Russian authorities continued to present the violence there as part of the same phenomenon of radical Islamic insurgency and terrorism spreading from the republic. By the final stage of the desecuritization of Chechnya, thus, had several functions beyond that of presenting Chechnya as a 'normal' issue within the Russian Federation.

A key development, in this period, was the growing decentralization of Chechnya. In some respects, this approach would seem inherently contradictory and, therefore, perhaps unsustainable in the long run. At the same time as Putin was suggesting that Russia had succeeded in normalizing the situation in Chechnya and Chechnya's position within the wider Russian political and security space, his regime was also in the process of sanctioning a shift of power and control away from the federal centre to the increasingly autonomous-minded and repressive Kadyrov regime in Chechnya. During his second term in office, Putin's more authoritarian model of governance centred on regime security became all pervasive not only on the federal level, but also at all levels in Russia. Whereas in the past a republican regime like that of Kadyrov's, which was centred on a single authoritarian leader with almost unlimited powers, was seen as an aberration in Russia, this was now the norm. The close relationship between Putin and Kadyrov served as an indication of the degree to which politics in this period became highly personalized, driven more by the personalities of the leaders than the democratic process.

Notes

1 'Chechnya derzhit kurs na ekonomicheskogo razvitie', News, Russian Ministry of Interior, 25 March 2008, available at: www.mvd.ru/news/15015/, accessed 20 June 2010.
2 'Segodnya v zasedanii MVD po Chechenskoi Respublike sostoyalos' Koordinatsionnoe soveshchanie MVD Rossii po voprosu "Ob uchastii organov vnutrennikh del Chechenskoi Respubliki po obespechenii realizatsii prioretetnykh natsional'nykh proektov i federal'nykh tselevykh programm, rasrpredelenii kompensatsionniykh

vyplat za utrachennoe i razrushennoe zhil'e', News, Russian Ministry of Interior, 31 July 2008, available at:www.mvd.ru/news/18090/, accessed 3 June 2010.
3 Text of the Programme the 'Socio-economic development of the Chechen Republic 2008–2011', Russian Federal Agency for print and mass communication, available at: www.fapmc.ru/activities/chechenrepublic/, accessed 4 June 2010.
4 'Grozny wins best CIS city contest for successful city restoration', *ITAR-TASS Daily*, 7 April 2008, available at: http://dlib.eastview.com/browse/doc/13842980, accessed 10 July 2010.
5 'A major press conference given by President Vladimir Putin for the Russian and foreign media has taken place at the Kremlin, Moscow, January 31, 2006', Russian Ministry of Foreign Affairs, available at: www.mid.ru/Brp_4.nsf/arh/784A0038F85F DA38C325710A002B086F?OpenDocument, accessed 15 June 2010.
6 Vladimir Putin, 'The opening of the Meeting with the Leadership of the Republic of Chechnya', 21 December 2005, available at: http://archive.kremlin.ru/appears/2005/12/21/1949_type63374type63378type82634_99215.shtml, accessed 30 June 2010.
7 'Wrap: Russia's terrorist no. 1 Basayev killed in south Russia operation', RIA Novosti, 19 July 2006, available at: http://en.rian.ru/russia/20060710/51142822.html, accessed 10 June 2010.
8 Typical descriptions and reporting of events in Chechnya in the official media centred on unidentified groups operating in the republic. For examples of such reporting see, 'Serviceman and local resident killed in Chechnya', Itar-Tass Daily, 29 June 2008, available at: http://dlib.eastview.com.ezproxyd.bham.ac.uk/browse/doc/18545355, accessed 20 August 2010.
9 Also see 'Illegal armed groups still operating in Chechnya – commander'. Interfax, 20 May 2008, posted on Johnson's Russia List; available at: www.cdi.org/russia/johnson/2008-99-19.cfm, accessed 30 June 2010.
10 'Illegal armed groups still operating in Chechnya – commander'. Interfax, 20 May 2008, posted on Johnson's Russia List; available at www.cdi.org/russia/johnson/2008-99-19.cfm, accessed 30 June 2010; 'Vosem' let vremennoi operativnoi gruppirovke organov i podrazdelenii MVD Rossii', News, Russian Ministry of Interior, 22 April 2008, available at: www.mvd.ru/news/15621/, accessed 4 September 2010.
11 'Chechenskaya Respublika nakanune vyborov', News, Russian Ministry of Interior, 13 November 2007, available at: www.mvd.ru/news/13215/, accessed 3 September 2010.
12 'State Duma backs delay in introducing jury trials in Chechnya', RIA Novosti, 15 November 2006, available at: http://en.rian.ru/russia/20061115/55674530.html, accessed 5 September 2010.
13 'Lavrov says Chechnya still unsafe for foreign journalists', RIA Novosti, 23 January 2008, available at: http://en.rian.ru/world/20080123/97602605.html, accessed 6 September 2010.
14 'Interv'yu zamestitelya Ministra vnutrennikh del Rossiiskoi Federatsii general-polkovnika militsii Akradiya Edeleva "Rossiiskoi gazete"', News, Russian Ministry of Interior, 2 February 2007, available at:www.mvd.ru/news/10468/, accessed 7 June 2010.
15 President Kadyrov's official website, available at: www.ramzan-kadyrov.ru/position.php, accessed 15 June 2010.
16 'Terrorist activity in North Caucasus eases – General Kulikov', *ITAR-TASS Daily*, 20 February 2008, available: http://dlib.eastview.com/browse/doc/13462804, accessed 17 June 2010.
17 'Illegal armed groups still operating in Chechnya – commander', Interfax, 20 May 2008, posted on Johnson's Russia List, available at: www.cdi.org/russia/johnson/2008-99-19.cfm, accessed 30 June 2010.
18 A major press conference given by President Vladimir Putin for the Russian and

foreign media has taken place at the Kremlin, Moscow, 31 January 2006, Russian Ministry of Foreign Affairs, available at: www.mid.ru/Brp_4.nsf/arh/784A0038F85F DA38C325710A002B086F?OpenDocument, accessed 15 June 2010. For more information about the clash between the Kadyrov and Yamadayevs groups in April 2008 see Bigg (2008).
19 31 August–2 September 2006 following a brawl in a restaurant called Chaika between ethnic Russian and Chechen groups. Local Chechen families had to be evacuated, while local groups called for all Caucasian families to be removed. President Kadyrov suggested that such clashes would threaten the fabric of Russia, 'Zayavlenie Predsedatelya Pravitel'stva Chechenskoi Respubliki, sekretarya regional'nogo otdeleniya "Edinoi Rossii" Ramzana Kadyrova', 4 September 2006, available at: www.ramzan-kadyrov.ru/press.php?releases&press_id=391, accessed 5 June 2010; 'Ramzan Kadyrov: Kontakti Chechenskoi Respubliki cs drugimi rossiiskimi regionami razvivayutsya planomerno I prinosyat vzaimnuyu vigodu', *President Kadyrov website*, 22 September 2006, available at: www.ramzan-kadyrov.ru/smi.php?releases&smi_id=18, accessed 4 June 2010.
20 Interview with Friederike Behr, Moscow, 23 April 2007.
21 'Russian President's envoy tours Chechnya', Interfax, 29 May 2008, Johnson's Russia List, #21 – JRL 2008–106, available at: www.cdi.org/russia/johnson/2008–106–21.cfm, accessed 14 April 2010; This form of localization of powers in Chechnya was also seen in relation to health facilities in Chechnya, it was suggested that sufficient legislation has been passed on the federal level, and this issue should now be addressed in agreement with the Chechen administration. As noted by the Public Health and Social Development Minister Mikhail Zurabov in 2006, 'the situation with cancer treatment is quite complicated at the moment in Chechnya. This means that once the first part of the project is completed, the question will remain of building the second phase in order to make available the necessary equipment so that the full spectrum of cancer treatment services can be provided within Chechnya. We don't see any problems that need to be settled at presidential level. The government has already signed the relevant instruction. We held additional consultations with the Chechen leadership last week and they are happy with the solutions proposed for these issues', see, 'Transcript of Meeting with the Government Cabinet', 13 February 2006, available at: http://archive.kremlin.ru/appears/2006/02/13/1647_type63378type63381_101589.shtml, accessed 4 April 2010.
22 Large billboards with Ramzan Kadyrov's portrait were erected around the capital Grozny, a large fleet of cars, his friendship with the Moscow millionaire circle, the renaming of the Victory Prospekt to Kadyrov Prospekt after his late father, all seemed to elevate Kadyrov to the position of a national hero, in a society where egalitarianism was the norm and considered a virtue. Matveeva characterizes this rising cult of personality around Ramzan Kadyrov as Ramzan adopting 'the ways of a traditional Caucasian hero: merciless to his enemies, generous to his subordinates, respectful of tradition, but also enjoying a fast car and knowing how to have a good time' (Matveeva 2007, p. 7).
23 The Kadyrov regime sought to regain control over the revenues from Chechen oil, most of which was currently taken by the federal authorities. In an address in July 2007, President Kadyrov noted that:

> Today, 95 percent of the total volume of industrial production belongs to the oil-producing branch ... But this industry does not provide the return, which is so necessary for our economy. It is necessary for us to develop such a policy with the federal center so that the financial revenues from oil worked for the Chechen economy

from the 'Poslanie Prezidenta Chechenskoi Respubliki Ramzana Akhmatovicha Kadyrova narodu i Parlamentu Chechenskoi Respubliki', 9 July 2007, Ramzan

Kadyrov Presidential website, available at: www.ramzan-kadyrov.ru/press. php?releases&press_id=1032&month=07&year=2007, accessed 4 June 2010.
24 As noted by the Chechen Minister of Property Relations and Land Use Supyan Lechkhadzhiev, which he argued was because 'Every month, the republic incurs a loss of more than 15 million roubles, since most of the land is not used for its intended purpose' see 'Ramzan Kadyrov Frees Chechen Lands', 21 July 2008, *Kommersant*, available at: www.kommersant.com/p914433/r_527/Chechnya_Ramzan_Kadyrov/, accessed 5 July 2010.
25 In spite of improvement in economics and stability the situation, political freedom was people increasingly curtailed. In an interview with Friederike Behr from Amnesty on 23 April 2007 she mentioned that lawyers who travel to Strasbourg with Amnesty International note that they cannot say things today that they could a year ago for fear of persecutions (interview with Friederike Behr, Moscow, 23 April 2007).
26 President Kadyrov's official website, available at: www.ramzan-kadyrov.ru/position.php, accessed 15 June 2010.
27 For example, it was noted during a meeting between President Putin and the representative of various societies on 16 May 2007, that a trip by a group of doctors to Chechnya had illustrated its progress, stating that, 'We have come back, eight doctors from Chechnya, and you know Vladimir Vladimirovich, the impression is a very happy one, because the city of Grozny is transforming itself into a garden-city'. 'Stenograficheskii otchet o vstreche s chlenami Soveta Obshchestvennoi palaty Rossii', Russian President website, 16 May 2007, available at: http://archive.kremlin.ru/appears/2007/05/16/2214_type63376type63381_129310.shtml, accessed 10 July 2010.
28 In fact, the discourse and opinions of the Kadyrov regime was increasingly adopted by the official federal narrative to construct a narrative of Chechnya and its role in Russia. An example of this was a report on the number of militants killed in 2007 run by RIA Novosti, an official Russian news agency in January 2008, which read,

> Chechen President Ramzan Kadyrov assessed the work of the Interior Ministry in 2007 as positive. The Interior Ministry provided order during elections to the State Duma [Russian parliament's lower house] and public security during a number of important public and political events in the republic. They were all held without any violations ... In 2006 more than 600 militants in Chechnya and adjacent provinces reportedly surrendered their arms in response to a six-month amnesty declared by the Russian government on July 15 of that year for those not involved in any serious crimes.

'Law enforcers killed 72 militants in Chechnya in 2007', 16 January 2008, *RIA Novosti*, available at: http://en.rian.ru/russia/20080116/97117813.html, accessed 30 June 2010.
29 An example of the change was seen in Russian official media coverage prior to the 2007 federal parliamentary elections. As part of the campaign, the federal sources cited the Kadyrov regime rather than the federal authorities as the main actor in Chechnya, but also as the main actor supporting the party of power, United Russia, in Chechnya. As reported by RIA Novosti in December 2007:

> Russia held elections to the State Duma, Russia's lower house of parliament, on Sunday. According to preliminary national data, with 85% of the vote in, the United Russia party, whose candidate list was headed by President Putin, has received 63.3% of the vote nationwide. Chechen President Ramzan Kadyrov had previously told foreign journalists that he saw no need for any official opposition parties in the southern Russian republic. The Chechen leader had also urged Chechens to vote for United Russia at a rally in the republic on November 27. 'We have to prove on December 2 that we fully support Putin and his party by voting 100 percent for him,' he said. Turnout in Chechnya was the by far the highest in Russia, with 99.2% of registered voters participating in the election

see 'United Russia wins over 99% of vote in Chechnya – preliminary data', *RIA Novosti*, 3 December 2007, available at: http://en.rian.ru/russia/20071203/90609389.html, accessed 17 August 2010.
30 'Chechen president insists Putin should stay for third term', *RIA Novosti*, 12 July 2007, available at: www.cdi.org/russia/johnson/2007-153-10.cfm, accessed 4 July 2010.
31 'Stenograficheskii otchet o vstreche s chlenami Soveta Obshchestvennoi palaty Rossii', Russian President website, 16 May 2007, available at: http://archive.kremlin.ru/appears/2007/05/16/2214_type63376type63381_129310.shtml, accessed 10 July 2010.
32 'Segodnya v Chechenskoi Respublike otkryt memorial'nyi pamyatnik', News, Russian Ministry of Interior, 11 October 2007, available at: www.mvd.ru/news/12711, accessed 30 July 2010.
33 'Segodnya v Chechenskoi Respublike otkryt memorial'nyi pamyatnik', News, Russian Ministry of Interior, 11 October 2007, available at: www.mvd.ru/news/12711, accessed 30 July 2010.
34 A performative geopolitical script is what a foreign policy leader draws upon to articulate, explain and state foreign policy, see O'Loughlin *et al.* (2004, p. 6).
35 For more information on the structure and operations of the Caucasus Emirate see: http://csis.org/files/publication/110930_Hahn_GettingCaucasusEmirateRt_Web.pdf.
36 'International terrorists seeking to aid militants in N. Caucasus', *RIA Novosti*, 24 January 2007, available at: http://en.rian.ru/russia/20070124/59612643.html, accessed 10 April 2014.
37 'Russian Defence Minister Sergei Ivanov in an interview with Frankfurter Allgemeine Zeitung, Germany', *RIA Novosti*, 6 February 2006, available at: http://en.rian.ru/analysis/20060206/43377957.html, accessed 10 April 2014.
38 For an alternative view on the relationship between an indiscriminate use of violence and insurgent attacks see Lyall (2009).
39 'Interior Ministry focuses on anti-terror operations', *RIA Novosti*, 9 March 2005, available at: http://en.rian.ru/onlinenews/20050309/39699027.html, accessed 10 April 2014.
40 'Russian Interior Ministry on special operation results in North Caucasus in June–August', *RIA Novosti*, 11 August 2005, available at: http://en.rian.ru/russia/20050811/41137147.html, accessed 10 April 2014.
41 'Almost 200 militants killed in North Caucasus in 2007', *RIA Novosti*, 10 April 2008, available at: http://en.rian.ru/russia/20080410/104757694.html, accessed 10 April 2014.
42 'Situation in Dagestan tense – Russian senator', *RIA Novosti*, 12 July 2005, available at: http://en.rian.ru/russia/20050712/40896126.html, accessed 12 April 2014.
43 Aleksandr Khinstein, 'Prodaem kavkaz. Torg umesten' ['We are Selling the Caucasus: Bargaining is Appropriate'], mk.ru, 15 June 2005. Cited in Dunlop and Menon (2006); also see 'Kremlin studying Kozak's recommendations for changes in the North Caucasus', *RIA Novosti*, 21 June 2005, available at: http://en.rian.ru/analysis/20050621/40563954.html, accessed 12 April 2014.
44 For a more extensive discussion about the effect of subsidies on the region see Alexseev (2011).
45 For more information on the role of the clans in the North Caucasus see: 'Kremlin must do something in North Caucasus', *RIA Novosti*, 20 July 2005, available at: http://en.rian.ru/analysis/20050720/40938485.html, accessed 12 April 2014.
46 'The North Caucasus: a knotty problem', *RIA Novosti*, 1 July 2005, available at: http://en.rian.ru/analysis/20050701/40827421.html, accessed 12 April 2014.
47 For more information on the role of Islam in the insurgency see 'Terror in Dagestan has religious roots', *RIA Novosti*, 25 July 2005, available at: http://en.rian.ru/analysis/20050725/40969497.html, accessed 20 April 2014.

48 A. Yarlykapov, 'Separatism and Islamic Extremism in the Ethnic Republics of the North Caucasus', *Russian Analytical Digest*, No 22, available at: www.isn.ethz.ch/Digital-Library/Publications/Detail/?ots591=0c54e3b3-1e9c-be1e-2c24-a6a8c7060233&lng=en&id=31618, accessed 13 April 2014.
49 'Interv'yu zamestitelya Ministra vnutrennikh del Rossiiskoi Federatsii general-polkovnika militsii Akradiya Edeleva "Rossiiskoi gazete"', Ministry of Interior, 2 February 2007, available at:www.mvd.ru/news/10468/, accessed 7 June 2010.
50 'Talks between Vladimir Putin and Silvio Berlusconi continued after a working breakfast at Villa Certosa, Sardinia, April 18, 2008', Press Service, Ministry of Foreign Affairs, available at: www.mid.ru/Brp_4.nsf/arh/EA4328F5B48B03D0C32574320024A071?OpenDocument, accessed 1 July 2010.
51 'Foreign Journalists' Trip to the Chechen Republic', Press Release, Ministry of Foreign Affairs, 28 February 2006, available at: www.mid.ru/Brp_4.nsf/arh/841DDFECB4FB29D1C3257123005D14C0?OpenDocument, accessed 5 September 2010.
52 President Putin noted that

> More than 60 Russian regions are today involved in business ties with the People's Republic of China. Russia's central and southern regions have shown increasing activeness in developing ties with China of late and China's southern Guangdong Province has been seeking to expand its presence on the Russian market. It is important that more and more Russian regions become drawn into this process, including regions in the Caucasus. The first agreement on investment cooperation with the Republic of Chechnya was signed during this visit.

See Vladimir Putin, 'Vystuplenie na Rossiisko-Kitaiskom ekonomicheskom forume', Presidential website, 22 March 2006, available at: http://archive.kremlin.ru/appears/2006/03/22/1123_type63376type63377type82634_103471.shtml, accessed 5 July 2009.
53 In one official letter Vladimir Putin acknowledged this rapprochement between Russia and Saudi Arabia on the Chechen issue by writing:

> I have warm recollections of our meeting in Riyadh in February. The agreements we reached have made it possible to intensify the political dialogue between Russia and Saudi Arabia, begin taking practical steps towards comprehensively developing our trade and economic, military-technical, investment, and other forms of cooperation and consolidate our work together in combating international terrorism. Russia and Saudi Arabia are together in their support for work to improve the situation in the Middle East and are working actively to help settle crisis situations and strengthen security and stability in the region. The open and constructive discussions I had recently with Prince Bandar bin Sultan confirmed the closeness of our positions on the main international and regional issues. I would like to thank you for receiving President of the Republic of Chechnya R. A. Kadyrov as a guest of the Government of the Kingdom of Saudi Arabia. I see this as yet another confirmation of the friendly relations between our two countries.

See Vladimir Putin, 'Nachalo vstrechi s general'nom sekretarem Soveta natsional'noi bezopasnosti Saudovskoi Aravii printsem Bandarom ibn Sultanom', Presidential website, 2 August 2007, available at: http://archive.kremlin.ru/appears/2007/08/02/1541_type63377_139461.shtml, accessed 5 June 2010.
54 'Russia demands explanation over Zakayev's visit to Strasbourg', World, *RIA Novosti*, 29 June 2007, available at: http://en.rian.ru/world/20070629/68062369.html, accessed 6 July 2010.
55 'Russia says Litvinenko visited Chechnya to kill for Berezovsky-1', Russia, *RIA Novosti*, 1 June 2007, available at: http://en.rian.ru/russia/20070601/66514612.html, accessed 10 July 2010.
56 For example Russia was criticized over its official investigation of Anna Politkovskaya's murder by the West, such as for example the 34 parliamentarians of the

PACE, October 2007, 'PACE urges international probe into Politkovskaya murder', *RIA Novosti*, available at: http://en.rian.ru/society/20071005/82677496.html, accessed 14 July 2010.

57 'Russia: Prosecute Rights Violations in North Caucasus: European Court Has Issued 104 Rulings Against Moscow Over Killings, Other Attacks', *Memorial*, 4 June 2009, available at: www.memo.ru/2009/06/05/0506092.htm, accessed 5 July 2010; also see 'HRW Says Russia Ignoring Chechen Rights Rulings', Radio Free Europe, 28 September 2009, available at: www.rferl.org/content/HRW_Says_Russia_Ignoring_Chechen_Rights_Rulings/1838563.html, accessed 30 July 2010.

58 'Za neispolnenie reshenii Strasburgskogo suda Rossiyu mogut vremenno vygnat' iz Soveta Evropy', NEWSru.com, 2 March 2009, available at: http://txt.newsru.com/russia/02mar2009/eurosud_kovler.html, accessed 18 July 2010.

59 The coalescence between the official and Russian position was demonstrated for example by the statement from the Chechen parliamentary speaker, Dukuvakha Abdurakhmanov, in March 2007, in response to this announcement. He stated that,

> it is time for European politicians to close 'the Chechen issue', especially now tat the situation in our republic allows them to do so without any qualms ... We've had enough of PACE's commissions trying to find non-existent faults in Chechnya ... The Chechen people have taken the situation under control. They now have a leader who many people trust. Towns and villages are rapidly being restored, and law enforcement officers are working hard to provide security in the republic.

See 'Time for Europe to close "Chechen issue" – speaker', *RIA Novosti*, 30 March 2007, available at http://en.rian.ru/russia/20070330/62867861.html, accessed 17 June 2010.

60 President Kadyrov highlighted his desire to reassemble the Chechen people during his visit to Jordan in January 2008, reiterating his sense of communality with the diaspora and concerns over its welfare and desire for a more united Chechen people,

> When I was on a visit to Jordan the issue of a meeting with the diaspora was discussed. I said that all those who think badly of us should be invited. I brought everyone together who was unhappy about what is happening in the republic. There were people there whose children had fought with Khattab and Basayev and were killed. I told them that they can ask any questions. I am not a politician, I do what the people need, and I follow the direction which the people want.

See 'Interv'yu Prezidenta Chechenskoi Respubliki R.A. Kadyrov telekanaly "Russia Today"', President Kadyrov website, 28 January 2008, available at: www.ramzan-kadyrov.ru/smi.php?releases&smi_id=52&month=01&year=2008, accessed 19 June 2010.

61 An example of this was the signing of bilateral treaties with Middle East partners, such as the Jordanian-Chechen treaty on healthcare, education restoration in February 2008 see 'Jordanian – Chechen treaty on healthcare, education restoration to be fruitful', *ITAR-TASS Daily*, 29 February 2008, available at: http://dlib.eastview.com/browse/doc/13524359, accessed 5 June 2010.

62 'Chechnya seeks to attract more foreign investments in 2008', *ITAR-TASS Daily*, 4 February 2008, available at: http://dlib.eastview.com/browse/doc/13377341, accessed 5 July 2010.

63 'Boxer Tyson welcomed in Chechnya', BBCNews, 15 September 2005, available at: http://news.bbc.co.uk/2/hi/europe/4250126.stm, accessed 10 June 2010.

64 'Chechnya: "If You're A Leader, People Should Fear You"', Radio Free Europe, 27 February 2007, available at: www.rferl.org/content/article/1074952.html, accessed 10 June 2010.

Part IV
2008

9 Modernization, resecuritization and patriotic fervour

Medvedev and Putin

By the end of its consecutive terms during the 2000s, it appeared that the Putin presidency had succeeded in its macro-programmatic aim – at least in words, if not in deeds – of rebuilding Russia from its proclaimed weakened state during the late 1990s into a stronger and more powerful actor, both domestically and in terms of its international position. With this transformation established within the official discourse on state identity and security, the Medvedev presidency (2008–2012) followed and by the return to the presidency of Putin in 2012 had been marked by three major counterpoints to the mid-to-late 2000s: the modernization agenda pursued the Medvedev presidency; the impact of the global financial and economic crisis; and the mass protests around the 2011–2012 electoral cycle and return to the presidency of Putin, accompanied by an attempt to redefine Putin's Russia centred on a more aggressive patriotic platform.

Although this period cannot be said to be fully synonymous with that of the late 1990s that the Putin regime had characterized as a time of weakness, it was, nonetheless, marked by tension, with the Kremlin uneasy about the future and the survival of their regime. The 'new' political agenda advanced by both Presidents in response to this unease was made-up of an amalgamation, or perhaps more accurately a hotchpotch, of the different concerns identified and voiced over the course of 2000–2008. However, the rudderlessness following Putin's initial return to power in 2012 was swiftly replaced with a new focus on populist patriotism, which became the new central tenet for the regime, as demonstrated in Russia's aggressive position towards Ukraine in 2013–14. Under the banner of patriotic fervor, the Putin regime sought to plaster over many of the existing structural and systemic problems and weaknesses in Russia, whilst a wide-sweeping wave of resecuritization was launched both at home and abroad – as the regime attempted to retain its dominant position in Russia following the mass electoral protests in 2011–12.

The 2008 changeover: Putin to Medvedev

According to most political analysts, during its two-terms in office, the Putin-led regime had transformed the Russian state into something akin to a 'network state' (Kononenko and Moshes 2011) or 'dual state' (Sakwa 2011). In other words, a system based on both the formal constitutional state and an informal behind-the-scenes competition for influence within the regime with Putin as the central figure and arbiter. Hence, Putin's role within the Russian political system was considered to have far exceeded that of a constitutionally elected head-of-state. As Russian constitutional law prevents presidents from serving more than two consecutive terms in office – meaning that Putin could not stand for re-election in 2008, speculation mounted during the second-half of Putin's second term about the future of the regime, as it was seen as representing more than a simple change of elected head of the political system, but also as potentially leading to a radical alteration in the political order and system itself.

The speculation about Putin's successor was brought to end in December 2007, when Putin announced that he would step aside as president and that he was nominating Dmitry Medvedev, the then deputy prime minister, as his successor. Upon accepting Putin's nomination Medvedev, in turn, signalled both his allegiance to Putin and to the existing regime by stating that if elected, he would nominate Putin as his prime minister. Although Putin's support for Medvedev as president did not come as complete surprise, many saw Medvedev as too liberal and pro-Western to lead an increasingly authoritarian and anti-Western regime.

As with Putin in 2000, as the 'regime's nominee' Medvedev was duly elected on 2 March 2008 with 70.28 per cent of the vote, and as promised, Putin was given the post of Prime Minister. The Medvedev presidency was faced with two sets of immediate challenges: ensuring the coherence of the existing political order, and coping with the 2008 global financial crisis and recession.

The first set of challenges were thus political, and revolved around managing the transition in president and establishment of a new tandem arrangement with Medvedev as president and Putin as prime minister in terms of both the unity of the existing political regime, and its economic and social appeal and legitimacy amongst the wider populace. Indeed, commentators questioned both the nature and longevity of the tandem arrangement, with many suggesting that this system would be inherently unstable and thus unsustainable (Reddaway 2009).

In practice, although some commentators cast Medvedev as a lame-duck and Putin as wielding power on his own, the tandem arrangement proved to be not only durable, but provide the regime with certain advantages. As argued by Overland (2011, p. 3), the Putin-Medvedev tandem

> made it possible to appeal simultaneously to two different parts of Russian society: Prime Minister Putin appealed more to conservatives, patriots and people in rural areas; President Medvedev tended to be more popular among liberals, city-dwellers and people with higher education.

While Putin remained a pivotal figure in both the regime and national politics, the official image of the regime's political project was, to a certain extent, widened from primarily being centred on a single man in the figure of Putin, to becoming much more of a 'team' (Whitmore 2011). Indeed, as suggested by Monaghan, this tandem became a 'broadly stable ruling group or leadership team—one that draws together the state and big business and blends formal structures with informal networks—[and] is perhaps the most important development in Russian politics over the last few years' (Monaghan 2012, pp. 15–16).

While the new political tandem of Medvedev and Putin proved relatively stable and oversaw the successful management of the potential problems associated with the change of leadership envisioned within regime politics – although somewhat less successful in terms of the wider populace, the financial crisis of 2008–2009 provided a sterner economic 'stress-test' of the regime and the prevailing economic and social order (Belaeff 2009). Indeed, with the impact of the 2008–2009 global financial crisis, it could be said that the Russian economy had gone full circle from when Putin first came to power: from bust-to-boom-to-bust. Whilst, as outlined by Gaddy and Ickes, the 2008–2009 financial crisis was not as devastating for Russia as the 1998 economic crisis, it did have a similar effect of laying bare the major weakness and problems within Russia's economic system, and reinforced its dependency on energy exports (Gaddy and Ickes 2010).

Although the Russian economy was not as interconnected to the sub-prime mortgage schemes in the US that triggered the global crisis as in some other countries, the fluctuation in financial markets, drop in the price of oil, reduction in consumer demand in Europe and general global recession it caused had a significant impact on the Russian economy. The severity of this impact was slightly delayed with 2009 becoming the most arduous year, and unemployment rising to 10 per cent in March; the rouble devalued by 40 per cent, the value of the Russian stock market falling by almost 400 per cent and GDP shrinking by 8 per cent (Johnson 2012). In addition, inflation rose to 11.6 per cent in September 2009,[1] with industrial output dropping by 10.3 per cent in December 2009.[2] The 2009 crisis illustrated that the economic gains made in the 2000s could easily be swept away and that an upward economic trajectory could not be guaranteed in the future.

The combination of challenges from domestic politics and stresses from the global economy proved especially prescient in the post-2008 Russian security context. As already argued, the success and management of the Russian system under Putin rested upon the establishment of what some have termed a 'social contract' between the regime and society. According to the terms of this contract, in return for delivering the population with economic growth and prosperity, the Putin regime had been able to restructure domestic political-social and economic space, imposing substantial limits, or at least boundaries, on democratic freedoms in the process. With the economy faltering and future growth uncertain, the sustainability of this social contract and thus the legitimacy of the regime came into question. In this way, the end of Putin's second-term marked the beginning of a period of greater political and economic uncertainty, with Russia facing a new set of problems the like of which had not been witnessed since the late 1990s.

Medvedev – a modernizing Russia?

Whilst Putin's solution for the crises facing Russia in the late 1990s was a state 'rebuilding' project, the Medvedev administration adopted a 'modernization' programme. In both cases, the focus was on rebuilding Russia from within, whilst ensuring its foreign policy served to bolster these domestic efforts. Despite initially focused on absolving the regime from blame for the impacts of the global financial crisis asserting that the root causes came from the US's mismanagement of its domestic finances,[3] official discourse soon began to acknowledge the need, and the regime's responsibility, to take actions to manage and deal with the dire economic circumstances in which Russia found itself. The Medvedev administration quickly moved to set out its own agenda and programme for Russia's economic development. Despite its lack of success on the ground (outlined in the next section), this 'new' political project represented an attempt to address the domestic weaknesses and failures revealed by the 2009 economic crisis in Russia.

In a manner akin to Putin's Millennium Manifesto in 1999, Medvedev's interpretation of the problems faced by Russia and his vision and priorities for resolving them were set out in an article entitled 'Go Russia' in September 2009. He compared the need for modernization to what he characterized as the two other major instances of modernization in Russian history – Peter the Great in the seventeenth century and the Soviet period in the twentieth century, suggesting that

> an inefficient economy, semi-Soviet social sphere, fragile democracy, negative demographic trends, and unstable Caucasus represent very big problems, even for a country such as Russia.
>
> (Medvedev 2009)

This modernization project thus suggested that Russia suffered from having an economic base that was both out-of-date and over-dependent on energy exports. He also described the economy as held back by the high-levels of corruption, the ineffective execution of political orders and regulations and the lack of independent implementation of the rule-of-law by the judiciary.

To address these problems, Medvedev outlined a programme that centred on two main points: the need to combat economic backwardness, and the need for 'economic diversification away from a primitive resource-oriented economy' (Medvedev 2009). More emphasis was to be placed on securing and promoting new technologies, efficient energy use; nuclear technology; information technology; medical technology and pharmaceuticals; and space technology, and a move towards e-government and greater use of technology in schools.[4] In May 2009, a Commission for Modernization and Technological Development of Russia's Economy was set up, charged with developing venture capital and supporting the innovation of new technologies, by coordinating resources, linking up associated services, expertise and consultancies, developing local financial markets and creating favourable conditions for foreign investment and coordinating resources.[5] The regime also pushed for the establishment of free-economic-zones, in order to attract foreign investment and increase innovation. The push to develop innovation was showcased by the announcement of the *Skolkovo* project on 12 November 2009, which involved the creation of a specialized area for the development of innovative technology businesses and research in the outskirts of Moscow.

Alongside economic modernization, Medvedev's programme for the presidency focused on tackling the endemic corruption within Russia's politics, economy and society. In his inauguration address in May 2008, Medvedev announced that:

> We must fight for a true respect of the law and overcome legal nihilism, which seriously hampers modern development.[6]

A series of new bills were introduced, including the May 2008 decree on anti-corruption measures, the creation of the Anti-Corruption Council in July 2008, the Anti-Corruption plan, the Law On Corruption Counteraction on 25 December 2008, the April 2010 National Anti-Corruption Strategy and the Federal Law on Amendments to the Criminal Code and the Code of Administrative Offences of the Russian Federation to Improve State Anti-Corruption Management in May 2011.

The level of state involvement in private businesses and large enterprises was also highlighted, with the Medvedev regime laying out a five-year plan for greater privatization of actors within industries from energy to agriculture, and banking to transportation sectors.[7] Furthermore, in December 2010, Medvedev demanded that regional governors adopt privatization plans for 'non-core assets' in their regions.[8] As part of the anti-corruption drive, it was also suggested that government members should not sit on the boards of state-controlled companies.

With the regime, changes in personnel and key political figures around the Presidential apparatus – such as the replacement of the head of the Federal Security Service Nikolai Patrushev with Alexander Bortnikov, the Minister of Justice Vladimir Ustinov by Aleksandr Konovalov; the Minister of Energy Viktor Khristenko with Sergei Shmatko – seemed to indicate that the power of the *siloviki*, central to Putin's regime, had been weakened somewhat.

Empty promises of modernization

Official discourse, thus, presented Medvedev's modernization project as centred on restructuring Russia across a wide-variety of spheres of activity in both public and private life. However, beyond this discourse, the modernization drive remained superficially and ineffectively enacted in practice. While identifying weakness and the need to diversify Russia's economy, the project provided little detail about how the mechanisms through which the Russian state would in practice address these endemic problems. Furthermore, even the official discourse neglected the problems caused by creation of a network or dual state during the Putin presidency. Indeed, in spite of the Medvedev-Putin tandem holding numerous consultations, talks and working groups with experts to devise policies in order to modernize Russia during the course of 2008–2012, in practice the economic agenda they set out was, as noted by Delyagin, full of 'half measures' (Delyagin 2012). In October 2011, the Russian Audit Chamber criticized their modernization programme for being overly optimistic, and not taking into account the need for implementing real economic and social change.[9] While, the vagueness of the proclaimed 'modernization drive' was highlighted by the Deputy Director of the Higher School of Economics' Development Center, Valery Mironov, who noted that

> [t]hese points migrate from one speech to the next, but it remains unclear just how they'll be executed and how the nation's leadership see the structure of this process as a whole as well as the order in which the unveiled plans should be implemented.[10]

As well as scepticism about the overall programme, there has been criticism of specific reforms for failing to enact the fundamental changes required. For example, the reforms of the police were said to fall short of addressing key issues, such as the demilitarization into a more civilian organization, the disclosure of police structure and activities and the demarketization of police activities (Kosals 2010).

Furthermore, an admission of the failure of his modernization programme was evident in Medvedev's own speeches. In January 2011 during a meeting of the Anti-Corruption Council, he conceded in terms of tackling corruption 'that our successes in this sphere have been limited'.[11] Thus, by the end of Medvedev's period in power, the regime had failed to reach its proclaimed aim of structurally altering the social-political and economic context. Instead, Medvedev's Russia was one in which the political regime had remained, if not had become further, detached from the formal political system, the economy continued to be riddled with inefficiency and corruption with large state-controlled enterprises resisting modernizaiton, and endemic corruption continuing to pervade all levels of society. However, as will be discussed below, while Medevedev's modernization project did not bring tangible structural change, it did serve to generate a sense that it was imperative for Russia to modernize in order to for it move forward.

The protest movement and the 2011–2012 electoral cycle

The official discourse about modernization acted as a broad umbrella idea, under which a variety of societal groups who had previously been politically passive came together. These groups included the educated middle-classes that either did not have a stake in the Putin regime, whose conditions had deteriorated significantly following the 2009 economic crisis or who had simply outgrown the social contract of economic prosperity for political passivity. For these groups, the image of modernized Russia with an inclusive and pluralistic participatory system, held out by Medevedev's project, crystallized the need to change the Russian political, economic and societal agenda. This was transformed into action during with creation of a protest movement, and the mass demonstrations that took place during the electoral cycle of 2011–2012. These extensive public street protests from December 2011 till June 2012, and thereafter, demonstrated that a large section of Russian society had listened to and connected with the message of modernization that Medvedev had put forward, and were responding to it by expressing their displeasure with a return to the status quo system that Putin was seen as representing. In this way, the modernization campaign of Medvedev can be seen as playing a role in empowering certain groups in society to come out onto the streets and protest.

The fact that such widespread protests seem to make relatively little impression on the existing political order is an illustration less of the lack of support for the protest movement's aims, and more of the power of the prevailing regime, which continues to be centred around Putin. Indeed, the 2011–2012 electoral protests represented the first time in the 2000s that the idea that prevailing regime could be overturned by public protest was entertained. Under the slogan, 'For Fair Elections', the protest movement – made up of a mixture of groups with diverse political persuasions, encompassing liberals, nationalists and communists – called for a re-run of the parliamentary elections held on 4 December 2011, in which the regime's official party, United Russia, were awarded 49.32 per cent of the vote, and held 52.88 per cent of Duma seats. Protestors were mobilized through local groups, political parties and, for the first time the internet, via websites such as LiveJournal and Twitter. They came out onto the streets not only in Moscow, but in St Petersburg, Novosibirsk, Yekaterinburg and cities across Russia. Large-scale protests continued up to and including the Presidential elections on 4 March 2012. However, most commentators agreed that, in spite of their scale, the protests did not lead to the emergence of a clear alternative to the existing regime, nor any sense as to where change to the system would come from, nor the intended end point of such a structural change (Shevtsova 2012a; Evans 2012, p. 234). Indeed, ultimately, in spite of this show of collective support for change from certain sections of Russian society, Putin was re-elected as President with 63.60 per cent of the vote.

The regime's response to the protests

Following the Presidential elections, the protest movement sought to keep the pressure up on the Putin regime, with a new round of demonstrations, notably the 'March of the Million' that took place on 6 May in Bolotnaya Square, Moscow. The official response, as noted by Koesel and Bunce, centred on three main tactics: undermining the opposition, restoring the image of the regime and implementing democratizing reforms to stave off the thrust of the anger following the accusations of fraudulent elections (Koesel and Bunce 2012, pp. 415–416). Critically, however, the Medvedev and Putin camps within the regime appeared to be split as to the exact nature of the regime's response.

Medvedev appeared to be more forthcoming in negotiating with the protestors, going as far as to call for an investigation into the accusations of electoral fraud and asserting the need for greater transparency in the Russian political process and the introduction of reforms to democratize the Russian political system (Medvedev 2011). While still president, in December 2011, Medvedev introduced a number of reforms to the electoral system and practice, including reintroducing the direct elections of regional governors, changing the regulations governing the official registration of political parties to run in elections, and the creation of an independent television channel. All in all, Medvedev appeared to take a rather conciliatory tone with the opposition, whilst continuing to call for calm and restaraint, noting in December 2011 that 'Russia needs democracy, not chaos' (Medvedev 2011).

By contrast, whilst Putin recognized the right of people to express their opinion,[12] and disassociated himself from the now-discredited party of the regime 'United Russia', the thrust of his response was to prevent any change to the *modus apparatus* of the prevailing system. He quickly reverted to talking about familiar themes regarding the need for stability and the actions of foreign enemies seeking to stir up a 'colour revolution' in Russia.[13] Furthermore, as Shevtsova notes, Putin drew on the example of Viktor Yanukovych in Ukraine, by seeking to shore-up support for the regime in the provinces, even seeking to undermine the urban and middle-class protestors by supporting pro-Putin rallies in rural area (Shevtsova 2012b), in an attempt to create a sense of US-versus-THEM by characterizing the protest movement as anti-Russian (Koesel and Bunce 2012, pp. 415). As suggested by Makarkin, 'it was a conservative strategy under the banner of stability', which emphasized stability, traditional values and orthodoxy (Makarkin 2012). These values were then repositioned as the cornerstones of his third term in power.

Putin 3.0

The tumultuous and controversial manner in which Putin won re-election, opened up questions about the type of political agenda he would follow in his a third presidential term. Would Putin return to the discursive structure of a strong Russia with a strong state as seen in his first term, embrace the modernization agenda put forward by Medvedev, or pick up where he left off in 2007–2008 following an anti-Western agenda, focused on regime politics and an ever enlarging securitization of the Russian domestic sphere?

In practice, at least initially, the regime – for the first time since the late 1990s – appeared to lack a coherent ideological programme. There was a shift from an emphasis on modernization towards stability, and a retrun to 'aggressive nationalism and Anti-Americanism' (Felgenhauer 2013), but the overriding impression was that the regime's political project was incoherent, splintered and ad hoc. As outlined by Lukyanov, the difference between Putin's stability in 2000 and Putin's stability today. Stability in 2000, in fact, represented action. You might have different views on what he did, but he was undeniably active in establishing a new model for Russia, in repairing the state after the 1990s, in implementing governance mechanisms and so on. That was a stability that meant some activity, some doing. Today stability is self-preservation. Non-doing. A 'do not touch' mentality'.

(Lukyanov 2012a)

The regime's initial agenda became a fusion and hotchpotch of tried and tested ideas from earlier periods, incorporating such diverse notions and ideas as Russia as a weakened state in which 'domestic rather than external, factors constitute our main development risks' and that must be rebuild from within,[14] the need to modernize the economy through diversification and opening up to investors, rampant and rising anti-Westernism, and a growing emphasis on patriotism and assertions of Russia's civilizational identity.

As in the early Putin period, in the first few years upon Putin's return, the domestic space was prioritized over the international sphere. Despite increasingly anti-Western rhetoric, the focus of the regime was primarily on domestic developments, as it was suggested that Russia's foreign policy and global role must be developed in line with, and in order to benefit, Russia domestically. This was particularly evident in economic affairs. Whilst the term 'modernization' now fell into disuse, discussions continued over the need to restructure and diversify the economy, in particular to overcome dependence on commodities and energy exports, and attract greater foreign investments into Russia.[15] As under Medvedev, the regime acknowledged that the model of growth followed in the pre-financial crisis period was unsustainable in a changing global economy, which continued to witness a drop in Western consumer demand and energy prices and with the looming possibility of the shale-gas exploration dramatically changing the global energy market to the detriment of Russia's hydro-carbon based reserves.[16] The challenges to economic growth were outlined by Medvedev in January 2013 at the Expanded Government meeting:

I am talking about the predicted decrease in the economically active population, the low quality of public administration, the need to improve the investment climate, diminishing domestic consumption growth rates and the need for budget consolidation. Obviously, those factors which ensured our economic growth in the previous decade are no longer always adequate. The potential of development in line with the traditional export-oriented model has also been virtually exhausted.[17]

Other themes from the Medvedev's presidency were also retained, including the need to improve Russia's investment climate, increase its economic links with the EU and its regional partners, such as via the Customs Union between Russia, Belarus and Kazakhstan.[18] However, also like the experience of the Medvedev presidency, implementation did not match announcements, and was restricted by both the difficult economic climate and the whims of the Putin regime.

In social terms, the Putin regime continued to emphasize traditional Russian norms, whilst outlining concerns about the impact of Russia's negative demographic changes on the country's future projected economic growth. In October 2012, plans to create an agency to promote Russian patriotism, the Directorate for Social Projects, were announced.[19] The danger of the imposition of externally (read Western) models of society on Russia was expressed regularly within official discourse, with the regime maintaining that Russia's system of democracy must be developed in-line with its own historical traditions. Malinova argues that Putin began to rely on more references to Russia's national traditions in communicating this discourse, stating that '[t]he collective past is used in presidential addresses to both firmly establish the present political course in the national tradition and to justify it through a critical reassessment of previous experience' (Malinova 2012). Indeed, Putin noted in his address to the Federal Assembly on December 2012 that:

> In the 21st century amid a new balance of economic, civilisational and military forces Russia must be a sovereign and influential country. We should not just develop with confidence, but also preserve our national and spiritual identity, not lose our sense of national unity. We must be and remain Russia.
>
> (Putin 2012a)

As detailed, even before the 2012 Presidential elections, the regime had proposed a number of changes to the political system. These included returning a degree power to the regions from the federal centre by reinstalling the election of regional governors, and a draft bill proposing changes to the Duma electoral procedure to establishing a mixed Duma election system, and a lowering of the threshold for party to win seats in the Duma from 7 per cent down to 5 per cent of the popular vote.[20] However, many have noted that these changes were intended to give the impression of a move towards meeting the demands of the protestors, but in practice represent only minor revisions to politics in Russia. Hahn has characterized the reforms as a

> two-tier strategy of carrot and a stick in relation to the opposition. On the one hand there is the carrot: the electoral system is being opened up, and the possibility of real opposition forces taking a significant number of seats in the Duma exists. On the other hand there is the stick of continued harassment and the possibility of potential imprisonment of opposition leaders and activists.
>
> (Hahn 2013)

Aside from changes to the formal regulations governing electoral practice, a prime focus in 2012–2013 became whether the hybrid formal/informal system of

Modernization, resecuritization 147

governance put in place during the 2000s by the Putin regime was under threat. A greater number of public divisions within the regime's elite were commented upon analysts and opposition media alike. According to Sakwa, 'the division now is beginning to take on an overtly political form, with regime-sponsored ideational programs giving way to more openly ideological conflict over development strategies and modernization plans' (Sakwa 2012). This perspective was supported by the Minchenko Consulting group's report entitled the 'Big Government and the Politburo 2.0', which identified six different blocs at the centre of the Putin regime, namely the *siloviki*, business, political-bloc, systemic opposition, technical-bloc, leaders of administrative clans, such as Chechen President, Ramzan Kadyrov. The report argued that these blocs represent 'a conglomerate of clans and groups that compete with one another over resources' and the regime's policy agenda and its implementation, including the privatization programmes, the introduction of new controls on the fuel-energy sector, development of Siberia and Far East, regulations related to the management of Gazprom.

Analysts described the new sense of incoherence and instability within the regime in 2012–early 2013 in terms similar to the late-Yeltsin period, which the Putin regime had cast itself in contrast to during the 2000s, with the state-building programme initiated in 2000 framed as a response to rectify the situation created by the Yeltsin regime. Indeed, Hahn characterized 2012 as 'a year that began with democratic reforms and promises of progress towards a democratic regime transformation is ending in a cacophony of incompetent governance, pervasive and massive corruption scandals, petty infighting, and a petite repression' (Hahn 2012). In this way, and in contrast to the official discourse of the second Putin presidency that asserted Russia had found its path to returning of the pantheon of 'great powers', the prevalent public mood a few months into the third term of Putin presidency was that Russia was back 'at a crossroads, from where it could start to quickly climb upward or descend into stagnation'.[21]

However, by mid-2013 to early 2014, this initial uncertainty as to the direction of the third Putin presidency gave way to a growing consensus that the regime's new platform centred on a traditional notion of patriotism and, in so doing, was aimed at appealing to the 'ordinary' and largely 'unheard' Russians. This new version of Russian patriotism was based much more on chauvinism and traditionalism than discourse of patriotism previously espoused by the regime. In the 2000s, Putin's use of patriotism was connected to ideas such as modernization and progress, and thus sought to appeal to as wide a range of society as possible, including the educated urban middle classes in St Petersburg and Moscow. Whereas, in his third term as president, the discourse of patriotism were specifically geared towards defending so-called traditional Russian values. In spite of its overarching failure, the modernization project and discourse that took centre-stage during Medvedev's presidency had succeeded in creating a relative consensus, at least among the urban middle-classes, that Russia needed to concentrate on modernizing its economy, opening up to the global economy and addressing endemic corruption. The patriotism being espoused by Putin in mid

2010s outlined a political vision for Russia that stood in contrast to this modernization perspective, drawing on historical imagery of a Russia that was an independent and proud nation that functioned beyond global developments and that does not bow down to the West.

The Putin regime's adoption of a more patriotic and nationalist perspective can be seen as an attempt to win back support lost to nationalist opposition figures, such as Navalny, who had mobilized much of the protest and opposition movement during the electoral cycle in 2011–2012. With this move, the regime sought to set the nationalist agenda, rather than allowing the non-regime nationalists to do so. Yet, in the first year or so of his third term as president, Putin's patriotism differed somewhat to the version that had gained significant support for some nationalist opposition figures. It was not as chauvinistic and ethnic-Russian centred as the views of many right-wing nationalist groups, such as the Russian Public Movement, the Russian Civil Union, the Moscow Defence League and the Slavic Union. These groups were particularly critical of the cost of state programmes to stabilize and develop the North Caucasus, and perspective that was crystallized in Navalany's endorsement of the campaign 'stop feeding the Caucasus'.[22] In contrast, the regime's notion of patriotism sought to appeal more to a sense of state patriotism, which was not tied to a strictly ethnic-Russian centred standpoint, but based on a view of Russia as a multi-ethnic and multi-denominational state. However, as his third term as president evolved, Putin's regime increasingly moved towards an interpretation of patriotism that contained elements of the nationalism it had previously distanced itself from. This was most evident in the regime's discourse around the annexation of Crimea in March 2014, which is discussed below.

The regime's focus on patriotism and generating pride for Russia's strength was linked up with the Sochi Winter Olympics in February 2014. Indeed, from the very beginning, the Olympic mega-project was directly associated with and led by Putin (Müller 2011), who by taking direct control over the Olympics sought 'to communicate that he is still a vital and dynamic force' (Petersson 2014). In this way, the Sochi Olympics were intended to project both Russia's and Putin's sovereign strength and power, both domestically and internationally, and in particular to assert what Makarechev and Gronskaya (2014) have termed Russia's 'normalcy and security'. As set out by Deputy Prime Minister, Arkadii Dvorkovich, the 'hosting these international events gives us a chance to show as many people as possible that Russia is a normal country' (Gronskaya and Makarychev 2014, p. 47). And, hence, the successful hosting of the Sochi games, in spite of the concerns voiced by both domestic and foreign commentators regarding its cost, human rights issues and a lack of security in the region around Sochi, was heralded by the regime as evidence of both its effectiveness and competence and the pride that Russians should have in their country's capabilities and international standing.

However, the Ukraine crisis and Russia's annexation of Crimea in March 2014 quickly superseded the Sochi Olympic games, simultaneously serving to boost and crystallize the regime's new patriotic programme and undo much of

Modernization, resecuritization 149

good-will won among Russia's foreign partners during the Olympic Games. Although many of themes within Russia's official discourse on the Ukraine crisis were not new, these events served to position the focus on Russia's historical greatness, patriotism, and the need for Russia to protect itself from the malign intentions of the West, as the ideological centre points of both domestic and international policy. In this vein, Putin utilized many historical analogies in situating the crisis, such as depicting Russia as historically being a victim of the West, noting that 'we have every reason to assume that the infamous policy of containment, led in the 18th, 19th and 20th centuries, continues today'.[23] Alongside this, the regime put forward a version of a shared history between Russia and Crimea since Catherine the Great, at the same time as denouncing Khurschev's supposedly illegal decision to reallocate the territory of Crime to the Ukrainian Soviet republic in 1954. Drawing on these historical discourses to appeal to a sense of patriotism, Putin noted that 'everything in Crimea speaks of our shared history and pride'. And that

> in people's hearts and minds, Crimea has always been an inseparable part of Russia. This firm conviction is based on truth and justice and was passed from generation to generation, over time, under any circumstances, despite all the dramatic changes our country went through during the entire 20th century.[24]

As will be outlined in more detail in the section on Russia's foreign security agenda further on, while Putin's stance on Ukraine and the annexation of Crimea was met with great concern by the West, domestically it galvanized much of the population to support the regime's notions of patriotism, nationalism and sense of responsibility for Russian compatriots abroad. Notably Putin's approval ratings jumped to 80 per cent, levels that had not been seen since the mid-2000s. Simultaneously, these events and the sense of patriotic fervour that emerged around the regime, also saw other issues and priorities, such as Russia's economic problems and governance issues, slide down the agenda. Thus, at least temporarily, the Putin regime succeeded in mobilizing much of the support that it had seemed to have lost since 2008, and was once again in strong position domestically.

The security agenda under Medvedev (2008–2012) and Putin 3.0 (2012–2014)

Despite the controversy surrounding Russia's foreign security policy with regard to the 2008 Russia-Georgia war and the debate over international intervention in the Syrian civil was (2011–2013), the main focus of both the Medvedev and the Putin regimes' security policy, until the crisis with Ukraine, was on domestic issues. Indeed, in light of their growing concern about the popular legitimacy of the regime and the need to modernize the economy, the regime considered that the role of foreign policy was to contribute to domestic stability, rather than functioning as a standalone agenda on international issues. However, in practice, aspects of foreign security policy came to lead domestic policy.

Internal security concerns

Whilst the change in president from Putin to Medvedev in 2008 did little to structurally alter Russian political life, it had a significant impact on the overall tone of domestic security, away from a generalized securitization of external enemies. This was largely a consequence of the greater preoccupation with addressing macro-structural problems, via the modernization programme. This, in turn, led to a de-escalation in the extents of the perceived threat to regime and national security from both domestic and international actors. However, the return of Putin to the presidency, in conjunction with the after-effects of the 2011–2012 electoral protests, led to a sharp resecuritization of a wide-range of actors and issues across the full range of political, economic and social spectrums, with the regime seemingly having run out of ideas for preserving and advancing its state-building project. This also entailed a return to emphasizing that external actors were attempting to interfere in Russian domestic affairs. As noted by Lukyanov (2012b) in relation to Putin's address to the Federal Assembly in December 2012: 'the external and the internal were inseparably intertwined; one fed the other, creating a turbulent "swirl"'. As a result, mitigating external risks in order to ensure stability, development and prosperity domestically became once more critically important.

Medvedev: a less securitized domestic context?

The coming to power of Dmitry Medvedev led to a thaw in the regime's securitization discourse within the domestic sphere. Not only was Medvedev's regime more prepared to acknowledge the inherent structural weaknesses within Russia's contemporary governance system, economy and society in connection with his modernization project. It also made less use of discourse securitizing the domestic sphere, in order to bolster support for the regime and target potential opposition groups.

Despite softening the tone, Medvedev becoming president did not a signal a full desecuritization of the domestic political and social sphere. Indeed, most of the groups targeted under Putin during the mid-2000s continued to be put under pressure by the state. For example, in December 2008, the offices of the human rights NGO, Memorial, were raided by law enforcement agencies. Opposition rallies continued to be targeted and dispersed by OMON forces, a notable example being the May 2010 rally at Triumfalnaya Square in Moscow.[25] Several reports suggested that the Russian government continued to leverage extensive pressure on liberal-independent and pro-Western candidates during mayoral and local elections, including against the campaign of Boris Nemtsov to become mayor of Sochi in April 2009.[26] Despite highlighting deficiencies within the judicial system and problems with corruption amongst the police, the death of Sergei

Magnitsky in November 2009 – while in custody on what many commentators argued were fabricated charges – reinforced perceptions about informal collusion between elements of the regime and the state beyond the scope of the formal rule-of-law.

Terrorism remained a prime internal security threat. The Medvedev administration more openly and more publically acknowledged ongoing difficulties with terrorism. Indeed, Medvedev labelled terrorism and instability in the North Caucasus, as the 'single biggest internal threat to Russia'. Indeed, rather than being cast as 'extraordinary' threat to Russian society, by 2008–2012 domestic terrorist attacks had become to be seen as 'ordinary' (i.e. a fact of everyday life) by both the regime and the public.[27] Indeed, the reach of the terrorist threat beyond the North Caucasus became firmly established during the period of the Medvedev presidency. A number of high profile *terakts* targeting transport infrastructure in and around major cities occurred. These included the derailment of the high-speed train travelling between Moscow and St Petersburg on 27 November 2009; a suicide bombing on the Moscow metro on 29 March 2010, which killed 40 people and injured another 100; and the bomb detonated in the international arrivals' terminal of Russia's largest airport, Domodedovo, in Moscow, which killed 37 and injured dozens on 24 January 2011.

Unlike in the previous period, the Russian authorities did not seek to link this incident exclusively to the ongoing insurgencies and instability in the North Caucasus, instead focusing on the 'global' aspects of the terrorist threat. As such, the regime called for a greater determination across the world in the global fight against terrorism, and highlighted the need to focus on the ideological and economic basis of terrorism.[28] In line with his modernization ethos, Medvedev cited the obvious 'systemic failures in ensuring people's safety' in relation to the Domodedova attack.[29] To counteract the terrorist threat, the powers of the FSB were expanded in July 2010, as the regime expressed concerns about the failure of the power ministries to curtail domestic terrorism.[30]

Aside from terrorism, issues of economic and food security emerged as major issues on the internal security agenda. The economic slump coupled with rising food prices produced a fervent cocktail of anger with the regime among the general population.[31] Also, a number of environmental protests made headlines, such as the campaigns against the building of the Gasprom tower in St Petersburg in 2009–2010[32] and the proposed plan to build a motorway through Khimki Forest.[33] Protests about other issues, such as non-payment of wages, became regularly occurrences, and were symptomatic of the general dissatisfaction with the conduct of local authorities and business-owners in certain industries. Indeed, the regime viewed this societal frustration that occasionally spilled over into protect with such concern that Putin chose to personally intervene in some of these disputes, including in June 2009 when the employees of Oleg Deripaska's Basel Cement Company staged a dramatic strike over wage arrears and unpaid benefits.[34]

With the benefit of hindsight, these sporadic social protests can be seen as a precursor to mass demonstrations following the December 2011 Duma election.

In security terms, the protest movement that emerged around these issue-specific demonstrations were already being presented as a threat to Russia's stability and critically the regime. Indeed, even prior to the 2011 Duma elections, the regime was certainly concerned about a 'colour revolution' taking place in Russia, especially against the background of the 'Arab Springs' removing authoritarian regimes across the Middle East from the beginning of 2011.

Putin's return: a resecuritization of Russia's internal space?

Upon returning to the presidency Putin oversaw a sharp resecuritization of the domestic space. Seemingly picking up from where it had left off in early 2008, during 2012 the regime set about characterizing a new range of groups and sections of society as internal security risks to national and regime stability. The presumed aim was to curtail civil society groups, particularly those linked with protests in 2011–2012. Aside from a use of force by the police to disperse the 5 December 2011 protest against the conduct of the Duma elections, the regime had kept law enforcement agents in check during the regular protests held between the Duma elections of early December 2011 and the Presidential elections in early March 2012. However, this changed following the inauguration of Putin as president in May 2012. Almost immediately, the power ministries moved in to arrest protestors, most notably during the Bolotnaya protest on 6 May 2012 (see O'Flynn 2012). The clampdown on protestors was followed by the targeting of key figures in the opposition movement, such as Alexei Navalny, Sergei Udaltsov, Ilya Yashin and even Ksenia Sobchak. Indeed, the leaders of the opposition movement were arrested and detained repeatedly and their homes raided by law enforcement agencies (see Kelly and Gutterman 2012). Furthermore, a range of new legislation was passed that sought to curtail the activity of independent political voices, such as increasing the fine for, and limiting the right to, public assemblies and the recriminalization of libel in August 2012.[35]

In view of the increased prominence that use of the internet played in both disseminating information and uniting the opposition movement during protests, the Russian authorities also sought to tighten the regulation governing internet content through the creation of a single register of banned websites in June 2012. This was in theory a measure to prevent child pornography on the internet, but in practice also provided the possibility to increase pressure on certain opposition websites.[36] In addition, harassment of independent journalists and opposition groups continued throughout 2012, with the Press Freedom Index placing Russia a lowly 148 out of 179 states in its 2013 list.[37]

Much of this resecuritization of the domestic space was closely inter-linked with the rising anti-Westernist rhetoric of the Putin regime, which not only became a feature of foreign, but also domestic discourse. As Trenin outlined, '[w]hen Putin declared himself the winner of the presidential election at a public rally in the evening of 4 March 2012, his words sounded like a declaration of victory over a foreign enemy and its collaborators inside the country' (Trenin 2013). While the proclaimed role played by Western actors and their Russian proxies in destabilizing the Russian domestic political and security space had been a feature of discourse at various stages in the preceding decade, it now became a high priority and very visible theme. As such, the Putin regime sought to cut and discredit any influence wielded by Western governments or non-governmental organizations within Russia's political and social life. This notion of the regime standing up against foreign interference aimed at destabilizing Russia was a common theme in defending their policy of securitizing large sections of the domestic space. As suggested by Putin in his Federal Address in December 2012: 'Any direct or indirect foreign interference in our internal political processes is unacceptable.' While Putin's spokesperson Dmitri Peskov stated that,

> We have heard numerous times the word in Washington that Russia's domestic affairs are not satisfactory ... Unfortunately these voices cannot be taken into account here, and we cannot agree with them. We are a genuine democratic country, and we are taking care of ourselves.
> (Peskov cited in Herszenhorn and Kramer 2013)

Combining elements of the moves to reassert control over the domestic space and the discourse of anti-Westernism, the Foreign Agents NGO Law was introduced, which stipulated that all NGOs connected with political activity must declare themselves as foreign agents if they receive funding from abroad. While, in October 2012, the Russian authorities widened the definition of espionage and treason to sanction criminal action against any persons or group carrying out advocacy on international human rights issues. And, in April 2014, several laws were passed in the Duma applying restrictions on the internet information space in Russia. These laws required all social media websites to operate on servers located within Russian territory and all bloggers with more than 3,000 daily visitors to register with the state regulatory media agency, Roskomnadzor, and once registered these bloggers would be subject to the same legal constraints and responsibilities and mass media outlets.[38] In explaining these new restrictions and regulations on social media communication in Russia, connections were made to the use of such forums and technologies by the West to shape events inside Russia. At a media forum following the passing of this legislation, Putin highlighted that the 'the Internet first appeared, as a special CIA project. And this is the way it is developing'. And that as 'everything goes through servers located in the United States' with everything 'monitored there', it was has been agreed 'that servers need to be moved and information has to be closed'.[39] Hence, official discourse drew a direct relationship between the West and actors and media considered as undermining Russian stability and challenging the regime.

This use of 'anti-Western' discourse and generalized securitization of the domestic sphere had a negative impact on Russia's relationship with the West, particularly in relation to a number of clashes over the implementation of these securitizing measures inside Russia that Western observers and officials suggested were evidence of the increasingly authoritarian and repressive nature of the Putin regime. In turn, the regime responded aggressively by outlining that outside actors had no authority to comment on events inside Russia and that their motivation for doing so was to destabilize Russia in general or the regime in particular. Such tensions were notable around the sentencing of Pussy Riot,[40] with Putin reacting negatively[41] to the widespread criticism by the West of the lengthy verdict handed down to two members of the group;[42] the Magnitsy list, issued by the US, with the support of European states, banning the issuing of visas to, and freezing the assets of, any persons allegedly involved with the death of Magnitsy, and the subsequent expelling of USAID from Russia by the Putin regime. Furthermore, the targeting of certain social groups, such as the LGBT community, on the grounds of morality that provoked widespread criticism from the West, suggested that the Putin regime was not only moving in an anti-Western direction, but also increasingly adopting a populist patriotic and conservative agenda.

The dual effects of this extensive resecuritization of the domestic sphere and the promotion of a more patriotic, traditionalist and populist agenda for Russia became particularly evident around the fallout from Russia's role in the Ukraine crisis and the Russian annexation of Crimea in March 2014. Similarly to the regime's domestic response to the colour revolutions (the Rose revolution in Georgia (2003); Orange revolution in Ukraine (2004); Tulip revolution in Kyrgyzstan (2005)) between 2003 and 2005, this crisis also precipitated an increased securitization of the domestic sphere, an expression of concern about regime security and appeals to patriotic fervour. Whilst most of the media and analytical attention was devoted to Russia's external security policy in Ukraine and the Crimea, the regime undertook several steps to tighten its grip over domestic affairs, in particular over media and public discourse. Indeed, some critics of the official discourse on the annexation of the Crimea were sidelined, most notably in the case of the removal of Professor Andrei Zubov from his position at the Moscow State Institute of International Relations (see Kravtsova 2014), and the sacking of the editor of the Lenta.ru news website, Galina Timchenko, in March 2014. Other media and internet came under increased pressure not to challenge the official discourse.[43] These developments reflected an intensified version of an ongoing process to strengthen the regime's influence over Russia's information space. Indeed, this process was even outlined by RIA Novosti in relation to its own relaunching as Russia Today in December 2013, suggesting that this 'move is the latest in a series of shifts in Russia's news landscape, which appear to point toward a tightening of state control in the already heavily regulated media sector'.[44]

As well as seeking to increase its control over media, the regime also took steps to keep protest leaders in check around the Ukraine crisis. Alexey Navalny was placed under house arrest in February 2014 in relation to embezzlement charges, and banned from using the internet (Navalny 2014). In this way, the regime – as following the 2004 Orange revolution – seemed to equate developments in Ukraine with those in Russia, and considered it necessary to take steps to prevent the development of a common cause between the nationalist and liberal agenda, as in Ukraine. This concern about the emulation of the events in Kiev in Russia was, however, more acute than in 2004, because such a coming together of opposition movements had, to some extent, already been witnessed during the 2011–2012 election cycle protests, and during Navalny's Moscow mayoral campaign in 2013 (Frolov 2014).

However, it was not only the societal groupings and cleavages that had previously been considered as opposing the Putin regime and its programme – pro-Western groups, liberal media outlets and nationalist leaders – that came under increased pressure and scrutiny from the regime around the Ukraine crisis, and in relation to the wider move toward a new patriotic agenda. The regime's focus on patriotism also entailed a debate and reconsideration of what constitutes a Russian patriot, and which groups are for and which are against a patriotic vision for Russia. Within official discourse, a number of new groups and individuals came under suspicion of not being Russian patriots. Against the background of the greater emphasis on the West's role in undermining Russian domestic stability, official discourse suggested that element of the Russian elite were not patriots working for the Russian cause. Instead, due to their conducting of business abroad and their holding of Western bank accounts, properties and in some cases citizenship, that they had been co-opted by the West and were thus not working for Russia's best interests. In his December 2012 address to the Federal Assembly, Putin outlined that the notion of '*deoffshorizatsiya*' should be a priority for Russia's economic development, whereby Russian companies and businessmen should not be able to opaquely conduct and register their businesses and hold assets within foreign jurisdictions, which saw the capital generated and taxes owed leave Russia.[45] While in April 2013, state officials and employees were given three months to close any foreign bank accounts and sell foreign assets, after which time any official found to have such foreign holdings would be removed from their post (Clover 2013). This securitization of elites with ties to the West as potential Trojan horses for Western efforts to destabilize Russia was evident in the regime's response to the imposition of targeted sanctions on Russian elites by Western actors due to the annexation of Crimea, with the regime suggesting that the elite should not hold foreign assets in any case.

In addition, official newspapers and television suggested that the actions of some groups and actors within Russia in challenging the regime's policy in Crimea, were those of a fifth column acting according to their own or external interests, rather than those of the nation. In line with this notion of patriotism, a website called traitor was set up, on which anyone accused of criticizing Putin's policy in Crimea could be listed. In this way, much of the public debate became preoccupied with whether people were for or against the regime, and whether or not they were patriotic, with supporting the regime equated with patriotism and vice versa. In this context, in which an ever wider array of actors and spaces had become securitized, societal divisions appeared to widen between those in favour and those against the status quo of the Putin regime's increasingly patriotic and securitized agenda.

External security concerns

Medvedev: modernization of foreign policy?

Upon coming to power, Medvedev set out what he understood as Russia's key priorities in foreign security policy on 31 August 2008, namely ensuring the pre-eminence and importance of international law, the benefits of multipolarity, avoiding isolation, the belief in Russia's right to protect its citizens both at home and abroad, and retaining Russia's privileged interests within its own region. The modernization discourse that Medvedev developed with respect to domestic affairs also touched upon foreign policy and the external security agenda. Discourse about the importance of economic security and economic development rose up the agenda. Medvedev outlined at a Security Council meeting on Russia National Security Strategy in March 2009 that '[w]e understand security not only in light of our foreign policy environment and ensuring our defence, but also in terms of economic security. We believe that economic security is a component of the National Security Strategy'.[46]

Indeed, with Medvedev as president, a number of commentators outlined their hopes for a change in foreign security policy. Galeotti noted that

> the Medvedev presidency ... offer [ed] a genuine opportunity for Russia to articulate a new approach to security policy, one which steps away from the expectations and prejudices of its imperial and superpower past and sees security as something best attained through genuine collaboration, transparency and democratic accountability
>
> (Galeotti 2010, p. 2).

However, as outlined by Trenin, irrespective of who is president, Russia's foreign policy suffers from the duality of its interpretation of the contemporary world, whereby it is formulated as 'if they [Russia] exited the twentieth century through two doors at the same time: one leading to the globalized market of the twenty-first century and the other opening onto the Great Game of the nineteenth century' (Trenin 2009).

Russia–Georgia war August 2008

The Russia–Georgia conflict over South Ossetia in August 2008 cast a long shadow over Medvedev's presidency. Despite regular frictions between Russia and other former Soviet republics throughout the 2000s, these had not turned into conflict. In this respect, the Russia-Georgia conflict should be seen as the culmination of a various strands of tension between Russia and certain states within what the Russian foreign policy establishment considers as its 'region', with the West often seen by Moscow as playing the role of an agitator either overtly or in the background, during the two terms of the Putin presidency and even prior to this. Thus, whilst the conflict took place under Medvedev's watch, its genesis harked back to tensions and concerns built-up during the previous decade around sense that Russia was losing power and influence within its 'region of privileged interests'.

The relationship with Georgia had arguably been most tense and conflictual of any of Russia's relationship with post-Soviet states since the collapse of the Soviet Union, particularly after the 2003 Rose revolution brought the Saakashvili regime to power and adopted an increasingly Western orientation. Tensions between the Putin and Saakashvili regime were evident during the frictions over Russia's actions in South Ossetia in August 2004, a dispute of gas in 2006; Georgian rejection of Russian peacekeepers in Abkhazia and South Ossetia; Russia's import ban on Georgian wine; spying scandals; the deportation of Georgians from Russia; Georgia's appeal to the European Court of Human Rights in 2007; and Russia lifting of sanctions against Abkhazia. Georgia's offensive in South Ossetia during July and early August, led to Russian military response against Georgian forces in South Ossetia, and then deep into Georgian territory.[47]

While leading to strong international criticism of their actions, for the regime the Georgian episode came to be seen as evidentce of what a strong Russia was capable of, and, as subsequently suggested by Medvedev, served as warning to the West against the expansion of NATO to include states bordering Russia.[48]

The issue of recognition thus continued to play a central role for the political regime under Medvedev, with the need for stated Russian national interests to be taken into account both regionally and globally playing a pivatol role within its wider national project. In this respect, the legacy of the post-Soviet legacy of the concerns over Russian international position continued to permeate Russia's security agenda despite the change of leadership from Putin to Medvedev and the apparent shift from a more aggressive international stance to a more conciliatory modernizing agenda usually perceived to have been more pliant to the international context and the need to build bridges with Russia's international partners.

Foreign relations

In response to changing domestic and global realities, Medvedev advocated both a rebuilding of relations with the West, and a widening and deepening of relations with non-Western powers seen as 'rising powers' as part of the modernization discourse.[49] In his 'Go Russia' article, he noted that

> the issue of harmonising our relations with western democracies is not a question of taste, personal preferences or the prerogatives of given political groups. Our current domestic financial and technological capabilities are not sufficient for a qualitative improvement in the quality of life. We need money and technology from Europe, America and Asia. In turn, these countries need the opportunities Russia offers. We are very interested in the rapprochement and interpenetration of our cultures and economies.
> (Medvedev 2009)

Under Medvedev, attempts were made to repair relations with the EU and the US, which had seen rapid deterioration in the second half of Putin's second term.

With regard to the EU, Medvedev advocated an initiative to create a continent-wide security treaty between Russia and the EU as part of moves towards a EU-Russian 'Partnership for Modernization'.[50] However, this proposal was not met with any enthusiasm in Europe, as tensions over the EU's Eastern Partnership, visa-free travel negotiations, and the EU's concerns over the targeting of opposition and civil society activists inside Russia continued to dominate the relationship (Moshes 2012, pp. 17–19). Some progress was, however, made with regard to Russia's relations with the Council of Europe, with the regime ratifying the Protocol on the Convention for the Protection of Human Rights and Fundamental Freedoms in February 2010 (Kaczmarski 2010), whilst bilateral relations with some European partners also improved, notably with Denmark, Norway, the Baltic states and Poland, despite frictions regarding the 1940 Katyn massacre. While not amounting to the resolution of many of the key sources of tension in the EU-Russia relations, Medvedev's modernization policy at least reduced the tense atmosphere built up under Putin.

Efforts by both Russia and US to improve their relationship made a promising start, encapsulated by the US discourse of a 'reset' in the relationship with new presidents in both states. This saw an intensification in dialogue regarding missile defence and the START negotiations, but also the establishment of a US-Russia Bilateral Presidential Commission and negotiations over Jackson-Vanik Amendment. Yet, in spite of finding agreement on START in April 2010, with both sides committing to deploy no more than 1,550 strategic warheads on up to 800 strategic nuclear delivery vehicles, talks over missile defence in Eastern Europe stalled. In November 2008, the Russian authorities threatened to place the Iskander missile system and radar-jamming facilities in Kaliningrad in retaliation to the US plans to position missile defence in Eastern Europe, whilst in November 2011 Medvedev admitted that the 2008 war with Georgia was carried out in order to prevent NATO expansion into the region. As Legvold notes, against the background of the last half-a-century, Russia sees US actions as 'part of a conscious and coherent strategy to weaken Moscow' (Legvold 2009). Tensions soon proliferated from the nature of the US's role in the world, to the announcement of the ISAF-NATO withdrawal from Afghanistan by the end of 2014 (Karaganov and Bordachev 2009). Nonetheless, as in the case of the EU, Russia's relations with the US could be characterized as warmer under Medvedev than they had been in the last years of the second Putin term.

As part of its attempts to modernize Russia and its role position in the world, the Medvedev regime set out to strengthen its relations with the countries seen as 'rising powers', so that Russia could find itself in a position in which it is connected to both the West and the 'rising' East and thus can balance its economic risk against major financial or economic crisis in either. The need to diversify Russia's relations was articulated in relation to the principle of 'network diplomacy', whereby Russia sought to inscribe itself in a wider range of forums and international groupings. Economically, Russia began to play a more active role in major international forums, such as the G20 forum, and via the success in 2012 of its efforts to join the WTO over the last two decades. Geopolitically,

Russia had a lead role in the creation of the BRIC, now BRICS, forum, an initiative comprising the main so-called rising powers, namely Brazil, Russia, India, China and, since 2010, South Africa. Building on efforts during Putin's presidency, Russia continued to focus on developing its relations with other regions, most notably Asia and in particular with China. Indeed, the new Chinese president's first visit abroad was to Russia in March 2013. In addition, the SCO continued to be presented as a major foreign policy achievement for Russia. Furthermore, Russia has sought to develop its relations with Japan and South Korea in East Asia, as well as India in South Asia and Indonesia and Vietnam in South East Asia. In 2012, Russia hosted the APEC summit in Vladivostok (see Sumsky and Kanaev 2014; Richardson 2014; Kozyrev 2014).

The 2008 Russia–Georgia war was watched with some concern by other former Soviet republics, with fears that it marked the beginning of a more aggressive and militaristic Russian approach to its region of 'privileged' interests. However, it soon became clear that this scenario was not on the horizon, and the conflict with Georgia, at least until the events in Ukraine, was an exception rather than a new rule. Indeed, Russia's refusal to intervene in the Osh riots in Kyrgyzstan in June 2010, in spite of a request for such intervention by the interim president served to harden the view that Russia's policy towards its region continued to be governed by pragmatism, whereby if Moscow did not see strong political or economic benefit in it expending resources in the region then it was unlikely to do so. Russia's strategic approach to relations with its region remained based on a combination of promoting multilateral integration projects and bilateral realpolitik. From Moscow's perspective, an important component to its promotion of multilateral projects in the post-Soviet space was seeking international, and especially Western, recognition of these frameworks, and as such, in the eyes of the regime, of Russia's predominant role in region. Thus, Russia actively promoted CSTO cooperation with NATO, and cooperation between the Single Economic Space and the EU. However, the regime was disappointed by the lack of active recognition by both NATO and the EU, which was interpreted as another signal of the West's agenda in interfering in Russia's region.

The Arab Spring and the Libya crisis 2010–2012

The events of the 'Arab Spring' of 2011, and thereafter, in the MENA region had several effects on Russian domestic and foreign policy. It exacerbated the regime's already existing concerns, related to the 'colour revolutions', about the possibility of similar developments taking place in Russia. It also caused discomfort about a lessening of Russian influence in the MENA region and a spread of Islamic radicalism from this region to Russia and its immediate neighbours. Moscow had built rapport with several of the regimes that fell, and in some cases, replaced in part by Muslim groups that advocate the spread of an Islamic revolution to areas of the post-Soviet space. In addition, Russia looked on with concern at what it saw as the West's role in interfering in, and disregarding, the national sovereignty of several states, most notably the campaign to gain an UN sanction for a 'no-fly zone' in Libya, and subsequent military role aiding the opposition's advance to achieve regime change in 2011.

Putin's return 2012–2014

By the time of the changeover in president from Medvedev to Putin, many analysts had begun to highlight a generalized narrowing of opinions within Russia's foreign policy community. Kuchins and Zevelev suggest that although Medvedev was conventionally characterized as in the liberal camp, and Putin was normally associated with the more hard-line 'great power' faction, the differences between them in practice should not be overstated (Kuchins and Zevelev 2012, p. 158). Nonetheless, whereas under Medvedev Russia's foreign policy discourse became permeated with the language of modernization and the need for 'resets' in relationships, the return to power of Putin brought back a much harder tone. As in the domestic sphere, many of the discursive strands and constructs from the early Putin presidencies reappeared, in particular with regards to relations with the West.

In a series of articles published prior to his return to power, Putin set out his future priorities in foreign (Putin 2012b) and security affairs (Putin 2012c), which reiterated the focus during his second term on the centrality of power and strength to foreign policy by noting that: 'Russia is only respected and has its interests considered when the country is strong and stands firmly on its own feet'.

Upon his return to power, anti-Western rhetoric quickly re-emerged, identifying the US in particular as acting to prevent Russia's regaining 'great power' status on the international stage. Russia's Federal Security Service declared on 14 February 2013 that 'last year saw an escalation in geopolitical pressure on Russia on behalf of the United States and its allies, who still regard our state as a rival on the international arena'.[51] Many of the familiar discursive constructions present during Putin's second term were redeployed, with Putin labelling NATO as driven by 'bloc mentality', and characterizing its approach to international security as 'missile-and-bomb democracy' (Putin 2012b). This anti-Western discourse served as a frame for interpreting the continued tensions between Russia and the West over the international recognition of Kosovo, Iran's nuclear programme,[52] the Arab Spring, energy security,[53] Western criticism of the regime's governance of Russia's domestic space, disparity between 'Western' global norms and regional one in Russia and 'zone of privileged interests', and ongoing allegation by Moscow of what it considered to be the West's 'double standards' (Karaganov 2012).

Disagreement over the appropriate international response to the Syrian civil war brought to the fore the high level of distrust and gulf in assumptions about the norms governing international relations between Russia and the West. Russia resisted the efforts of the US, UK and France to international community, and crucially the UN Security Council, to support an intervention led by them to bring the conflict under control and to prevent the Assad-regime from using chemical weapons against the rebels (Putin 2012b). Furthermore, the Syrian issue came to be seen as a 'line in the sand' moment by Russia's foreign policy established, particularly, after Iraq and Libya, whereby they felt they needed to oppose a general trend of intervention in domestic conflict situations by the West, and in particular the US, since the end of the Cold War, which they saw as undermining the centrality of the principle of 'non-intervention in the domestic affairs of sovereign states'. Russian Foreign Minister, Sergei Lavrov, openly acknowledged that Russia saw the Syrian issue as having wider implications and that its approach to this particular issue was seen against the background of earlier precedents, when he stated that for Russia it was

> a fundamental issue of contemporary international politics, directly related to the issue of the future world order. I do not mean to say that Russia resists Western influence by force of habit or that it 'out of spite' throws sand in the wheels of projects initiated by the West. The point is that the policy of promoting democracy 'by blood and iron' simply does not work. We have seen this over the last year and a half and even over the last decade. We all know about persistent problems faced by Iraq. No one really knows what will happen in the Middle East.[54]

Whilst analysts have argued that Russia remains unable to articulate any other role for itself in the world than that of a superpower, which included viewing it relations to the West in zero-sum terms and mainly as a counterpoint (Kozlovsky and Lukin 2012; Spasskiy 2011), Lukyanov notes that Putin's anti-Western discourse of 2012 differed to that of 2007. He outlined that it was more defensive than offensive in nature, as 'Putin understands he cannot close down the country. He is trying to achieve equilibrium – to isolate politically, but to engage economically' (Lukyanov 2012a). Hence, despite the increasing animosity in its relations with the West and attempts to diversify its range of international partners away from the West, the West continues to be a top priority in Russia's security agenda, and an important part of the Putin's regime economic strategy.

However, the attempt to cordon off economics cooperation from the increasing intensity of the anti-Western discourse in both foreign and domestic security policy has led to an extremely incoherent policy, and has ultimately proven an unsuccessful approach. Whilst Putin continued Medvedev's efforts to attract more capital investment from the West into Russia, promote economic deals with the US and European states, the ongoing disagreements over the appropriate response to the Syria crisis, and animosity over other issues such as surrounding the Magnitsky Law,[55] have limited the scope for such economic coordination.

Alongside Putin's new fervour in resisting perceived Western interference in Russia's development, his prime focus in 2012–2013 had been on trying to reinvigorate multilateral integration with amenable states in the post-Soviet space. Ahead of the presidential election, in November 2011, Putin published an article that outlined the creation of a Eurasian Union by 2015, a primarily economic integration mechanism built in on the existing framework of the Russian-Belarusian-Kazakhstsani Customs Union, and which in the future sought to attract other major participants from the post-Soviet space, notably Ukraine.[56] Within official discourse, the Eurasian Union was compared to the European Union. Indeed, while initially seen by many commentators as a retrograde step to create a neo-USSR, the Eurasian Union is increasingly being seen as a manifestation of Russia's attempt to modernize its economy and develop itself into a modern regional, if not global, economic power.

In spite of the Putin regime's attempts to isolate its economic policy and foreign policy in relation to global security concerns from developments in domestic political affairs, most notably the mass protests around the electoral cycle December 2011 to March 2012, these three different policy agendas remained tightly interlocked in Russia's external policy. While the high-profile nature of the disputes with the West on issues of global governance and intervention, particularly over the Syria crisis, suggested a prioritization of global affairs, the primary focus of Russia's external policy and relations was on its perceived region of 'privileged interests'. Furthermore, even Putin's increasingly anti-Western and anti-US stance was connected more to developments in its domestic sphere than the West's actual or perceived role on international affairs. Nonetheless, the return of Putin and his anti-Western discourse resulted in a worsening in relations between Russia and the West.

Russia–Ukraine crisis 2013–2014

Whilst the regime seemed partially interested in continuing to balance these multiple agenda strands within foreign policy during the initial period following Putin's return to the presidency, this changed in early 2014, with its response to the crisis in Ukraine crisis, and in particular the decision to annex Crimea in March 2014.

The initial crisis in Ukraine developed as a result of President Yanukovich's decision to reject an EU Association agreement in favour joining the Eurasian Union. This led to large-scale popular protests against both this decision and the Yanukovich regime, under the banner 'Euromaidan', most significantly in Kiev and the Western cities of Ukraine. These protests continued until the ousting of Yanukovych, and the formation of an interim government in Kiev under the premiership of Arseniy Yatsenyuk in February 2014. Following these events, counter-protests against the 'Euromaidan' protests and the ousting of Yanukovych began to occur in the Crimean peninsula. This saw the storming of the government offices in Sevastopol in Crimea by pro-Russian, or anti-Euromaidan, groups in late February, and was followed by the massing of Russian forces on the borders of the peninsula. In this context, a referendum was held in Crimea on 16 March, which saw a majority vote for Crimea to secede from Ukraine and accede to the Russian Federation. Following the accession of Crimea into Russia, various groups opposed to new government in Kiev and with separatist ambitions in eastern Ukraine, seized control of governmental buildings and declared independent authority for their towns, cities and region. Russia continued to voice support for such groups and caution the new Ukrainian government against military suppression of these groups, outlining the consequences for doing so would be severe.

These events precipitated one of the most significant security crises in Europe in decades, as European states, the EU, the US, NATO and other Western actors strongly condemned Russia's role in supporting separatist groups in Crimea and anti-government groups in eastern Ukraine, and its choice to incorporate Crimea into the Russian Federation. If the Russia–Georgia war in 2008 cast a long shadow over the Medvedev presidency, then the Russian annexation of Crimea became the most pivotal event of Putin's third presidency in terms of external relations. Russia now found itself in a diplomatic impasse with the acting regime in Ukraine, and its relations with the West at a new low point, with the US and EU applying sanctions, in the form of asset freezes and visa bans, on Putin's inner circle in the wake of its annexation of Crimea in March 2014 (Mason and Kelly 2014).

The regime's response to these events, reflecting a gradual trend since 2013, saw the more bellicose and patriotic strands in foreign security discourse come to predominate over the more economically driven modernization agenda, developed under Medvedev, and which necessitated cordial relations with Western and regional foreign policy actors and investors.[57] This also represented a switch in emphasis in terms of the stated interconnections between Russia's internal and external security concerns. The traditionalist, patriotic and assertive discourse that had been evident within the domestic sphere for several years, was now operationalized in Russia's external relations. Several major pre-existing strands of discourse became intertwined and 'radicalized' to create a new form, particularly in relation to the justification of the annexation of Crimea.

Notions of legitimacy, legality and order – usually reserved for the domestic space and high-level international disputes, such as in the UNSC – were articulated as central to understanding the crisis in Ukraine. Indeed, not only were elements of discourse previously reserved for the domestic sphere supplanted onto foreign security policy, but also – as during the period of the Orange revolution in 2004 – the Russian leadership presented 'events in Ukraine through the prism of its own domestic politics and is anxious to prevent the type of democrats-and-nationalists alliance that brought down Yanukovych' (Goode and Laruelle 2014). Against the background of the general discrediting of independent voices and civil society actors within Russia itself over the course of the 2000s, the Putin regime argued that Yanukovych was the legitimate political leader of Ukraine, who had been overthrown by the illegal groups of Euromaidan, unleashing disorder within the Ukrainian domestic space. Hence, the regime challenged the Euromaidan and Western discourse that the protests that led to fall of Yanukovych were a legitimate expression of popular grievances by the Ukrainian people. In February 2014, Medvedev outlined that: 'Some of our foreign, Western partners think otherwise. This is some kind of aberration of perception when people call legitimate what is essentially the result of an armed mutiny.'[58]

Indeed, within Russian official discourse, the image of the protest movement in Ukraine was presented as sponsored by the West. The depiction of the protests as being driven by the extremists and orchestrated from abroad by the West, was presented as evidence of its illegitimacy, whereby the protestors could not be considered an authentic representation of the Ukrainian people, but rather as actors who had been bought-off by the US and EU.[59] In this way, it was suggested that the West was a revisionist and aggressive actor, eager to support an illegitimate and illegal armed mutiny, in order to undermine Russia's legitimate interests in Ukraine and within its wider region. This image of disorder in Ukraine, provoked from afar, was contrasted to the stability, and freedom from foreign agitation, within Russia. As Coalson outlines, official Russian state-television presented a picture whereby 'Russia is an oasis of calm good governance in a world of chaos. Fascism is on the march in the world and Russia must be vigilant. The motif of "Europe in flames"' (Coalson 2014).

Alongside painting the Euromaidan as illegitimate, official Russian discourse focused on the perils of disorder created by their illegitimate removal of the Yanukovych regime. This theme was strongly taken up in relation to the discourse about Russia's responsibility to protect and ensure the rights of Russian compatriots living in Ukraine. This was manifested in the support of activities of groups in Crimea and eastern Ukraine opposing the illegitimate change of regime in Kiev, and their attempts to assert their own local political rule in the face of repression and discrimination from the new regime. A Russian Foreign Ministry statement on 13 April outlined that:

> The self-proclaimed Kiev authorities, following a coup d'etat, took action to suppress popular protests and reacted by completely ignoring the legal interests of the population of South-Eastern regions by using direct threats and violence against those who do not agree with the dominance of the national radical, chauvinistic, Russo-phobic, Anti-Semitic actions of the coalition, operating in Kiev with direct support of the United States and the European Union.[60]

Furthermore, historical imagery and notions of fear that had become a familiar part of the Putin regime's official discourse in domestic politics and security were also drawn upon in the discourse that sought to question the 'legitimacy' of the new Ukrainian leadership and ratchet up the threat posed to Russian compatriots by the crisis in Ukraine. The Russian leadership utilized the familiar lexicon of fascism, based on the historical memory of Western Ukraine's collaboration with the Nazis in the Second World War, to paint the protest movement in Ukraine as a Russophobic and arrogant group of violent right-wing extremists threatening stability in Ukraine, including targeting minority groups, such as the Jews. Historical discourses were also drawn upon to elaborate a notion of nationalism more centred on ethnicity than previously, as the regime utilized the historical precedence of certain parts of Ukraine having been located within the Russian Empire. While the theme of Russia's responsibility for protecting

Russian-speaking communities abroad had been present within Russian foreign policy since the collapse of the USSR, its usage as justification for the annexation of Crimea and support for the separatist movements in eastern Ukraine represented a more traditional understanding of Russian nationalism and patriotism than before. This traditional and patriotic version of nationalism was in line with the regime's discourse in the domestic sphere since Putin's return to the presidency in 2012.

The crisis served as another flashpoint in Russia's relationship with the West, with the Russian authorities accusing its Western counterparts of orchestrating the crisis for their own interests, which were said to be pushing back against Russia. Thus, despite the success of the Sochi Olympics and the attempts to create some form of a bridge with the West over Syria, during the Ukraine crisis, the Russian leadership returned to its familiar discourse of an aggressive West seeking to undermine Russia's legitimate interests, whilst seeking to stir up trouble in its neighbourhood.[61] In addition, the West's decisions to impose sanctions on Russia, the suspension of all NATO cooperation with Russia,[62] the stripping of the rights of Russian representatives of the Council of Europe was met with even more virulent anti-Western discourse from the Putin regime. And Russia's veto of the UNSC resolution to condemn the annexation of Crimea,[63] alongside Russia's criticism of the EU and US diplomatic and financial support of the new Ukrainian government brought the relationship to a new low.

However, a novel element within official Russian discourse was the emphasis placed on the extent to which Russia and the West are co-dependent. The notion of co-dependency with the West has long been part of Russian politics and foreign policy, in particular in terms of the desire to gain the West's recognition of Russia's equal status and similarity to the West. However, in the context of the greater concentration on economics in the post-global 2008 financial crisis international landscape, the directionality of co-dependency came to be seen as more equally distributed, especially in terms of the EU and European states. In other words, that these actors were as reliant on Russia, as Russia was on them. Hence, alongside the discussion about whether Russia could absorb the sanctions imposed by the West, emphasis was also placed on whether European actors were really prepared to punish Russia economically for its actions vis-à-vis Ukraine, due to the reciprocal economic impact it would likely have on them. Indeed, it was suggested that following the Euro crisis that the European powers had realized that they themselves are greatly dependent on emerging markets, such as Russia, for rebuilding their own economic stability (Jordan 2014).[64]

In spite of the breakdown in relations with the new Ukrainian administration and the West, and the impact of the imposition of economic sanctions, in the domestic sphere, the Putin regime successfully created a hegemonic discourse in representing the crisis and justifying and legitimating their position towards it.[65] Whilst some pockets of the populace, primarily in Moscow and St Petersburg, publically spoke out against the regime's position, as noted already, domestic approval ratings of Putin as President increased significantly during the crisis. Indeed, despite the international fallout from the crisis, domestically Putin had managed to galvanize the public and unify them around the Crimea issue,[66] reversing the initial low popularity of his return to the presidency in 2012.

Conclusion

By 2013, official discourse presented an image of Russia with multiple personalities: a weak state, a strong state and a modernizing state. It thus seemed to combine all of elements of state identity advanced by the regime during the previous two terms of Putin presidency. This attempt at reconciling discourses about Russia as both a weak and a modernizing strong state, resulted in an official discourse that was composed of a colourful but incoherent kaleidoscope of ideas and agendas about the future direction of the regime and country.

Indeed, this contrasted sharply with the vision presented by the previous Medvedev administration's modernization project that despite remaining largely on paper provided a radically different popular vision for the future direction of Russia. Emerging out of the upheavals of the global financial crisis, its focus centred primarily on the modernization drive of Russia's domestic sphere and the need to revitalize Russia from within, particularly in economic terms with foreign policy becoming an added extra, in spite of high-profile disputes over international security issues. Indeed, as in the previous eras when Russia felt weakened, particularly in economic terms, in foreign affairs the Medvdev regime in fact appeared to be more conciliatory with its Western partners, as characterized by Medvedev's call for the creation of a new common European security architecture. In this respect, the Medvdev regime continued to follow the logics outlined elsewhere in the book that greater domestic insecurities appear to result in a more conciliatory Russian policy abroad. At home, the focus on modernization saw a softening in the tone of the securitizing discourse about domestic opponents, threats and enemies, and, indeed, an acknowledgement of some of the problems and shortcomings that these actors sought to advance against the regime. However, there was no end to expansion of actors and activity deemed as internal threats, which had been ongoing since the mid-2000s, nor a desecuritizaiton of the domestic space. Indeed, concerns about popular protests due to the downturn in the economy saw economic and food security came to the foreground of the domestic security agenda, alongside terrorism, which was increasingly said to be a global phenomenon, rather due to specific issues in the North Caucasus.

By contrast, while initially the returning Putin regime's put forward a project that appeared to lack a coherent and clear internal logic and sense of direction, it increasingly moved towards an ever-more aggressive and a rather confused discourse about 'patriotism'. This was manifested in the regime's revival and intensification of anti-Westernist discourse, an emphasis on the importance of the future being built on the basis of traditional Russian civilizational and cultural values, and a return to tried-and-test discourse form the early 2000s about the importance of Russia being rebuild from within. In this respect, the Putin regime seemed to be actively isolating Russia from the wider international community, as demonstrated by its actions towards Ukraine, which appeared to stand in contradiction with its stated goal of modernizing and diversifying the Russian economy.

Indeed, despite its increasing focus on patriotism and re-envigorated securitization of the domestic sphere, the Putin regime had retained some of the original concerns, vocalized during the Medvdev's presidency, over the Russian present and future economic prospects. As part of this rebuilding mantra, initial attempts have been made to open Russia up internationally by way of better and more varied relationships to other states and forums. Similarly to Medvedev's modernization, official discourse, particularly in the first couple of years after Putin's return in power, noted the need to bring investments in, develop new technologies, diversifying its foreign relations especially within the Asia-Pacific, at the same time as emphasizing a focus on the core of Russia's domestic weaknesses. In an attempt to somehow connect these two avenues, a renewed focus on multilateral integration within its main partners in the post-Soviet space become evident, in particular via the Eurasian Union and the CSTO.

However, there appeared to be a major tension between Russia's stated economic needs and interests and its apparent resecuritization discourses, both domestically and internationally, which serve to undermine and preclude the building of a positive investment climate inside Russia or good relations with key economic partners such as the EU. As highlighted by Medvedev – as part of his modernization discourse – aspects of Russia's economy and societal governance are antiquated, slow and corrupt, and the regime is aware that it can no longer count on the proceeds from exporting its energy resources to fulfill its part of the Putin social contract – economic growth for limited political participation – in light of the fall in energy prices associated to the global financial crisis, and with advancements in mining of shale gas threatening to transform the energy markets in a direction unfavorable to Russia. However, the regime's concern with their own survival and tendency, as part of the 'strong state' model advanced by Putin, to seek greater political control over all sectors of social life is contributing significantly to perceptions that Russia does not have a healthy climate in which to invest. The renewed securitization of the domestic space with the return of Putin in 2012 would not seem to signal any reversal in this trend.

A similar contradiction is evident on the international stage, as while Russia seeks to build strong economic relationships with a variety of actors, including the West, the conflictual nature of the relationship with the West on politico-security issues works to undermine this. Indeed, Putin's desire to re-establish Russia as a 'great power' appears rather one-dimensional in practice, because Russia lacks the power to back up such claims apart from the use of its permanent veto on the UN Security Council. In addition, foreign policy decisions, such as over Ukraine and Crimea served only to reinforce further the image of Russia as an aggressive, hostile and unpredictable international partner, particularly vis-à-vis the West. In this way, Russia can be characterized as different to other 'rising powers', whose emergence onto the world stage is built on economic capacity, not hard political power.

Notes

1 'Markets & Data', September 2009, *The Economist*.
2 'Industrial Output Falls By 10.3% in December', *Moscow Times*, 26 January 2009.
3 Medvedev outlined, in June 2008 at the St Petersburg Economic Forum, that:

> 'The failure to properly assess risk by the largest financial corporations, combined with the aggressive financial policies of the world's largest economy, have led not only to losses for those corporations ... but unfortunately have impoverished the majority of people on the planet', see 'Russia: Medvedev Blames U.S. For Economic Crisis, Offers Moscow's Help', Radio Free Europe Radio Liberty, 7 June 2008.

4 See Official Website of the Council for the economic modernization and innovative development of Russia under the President of the Russian Federation, available at www.i-russia.ru/.
5 See 'Opening remarks at meeting of Commission for Modernization and Technological Development of Russia's Economy', Official Website of the President of the Russian Federation, 27 July, available at: http://eng.kremlin.ru/transcripts/673, accessed 17 October 2011.
6 'Speech at Inauguration Ceremony as President of Russia'. Official Website of the President of the Russian Federation, 7 May, available at: http://archive.kremlin.ru/eng/speeches/2008/05/07/1521_type82912type127286_200295.shtml, accessed 16 March 2010.
7 'Russian government approves 5-year privatization plan', RIA Novosti, 21 October, available at: http://en.ria.ru/business/20101021/161034056.html, accessed 7 March 2011.
8 'Medvedev orders regions to adopt privatization plans by July', RIA Novosti, 7 December, available at: http://en.ria.ru/business/20101207/161670761.html, accessed 11 February 2011.
9 'Russia's 2020 economic strategy "too optimistic"', *Russia Today*, 4 October 2011, available at: http://rt.com/politics/putin-strategy-economic-development-005/, accessed 4 January 2012.
10 'Medvedev pitches Russian modernization to investors at Davos', *RIA Novosti*, 28 January, available at: http://en.ria.ru/analysis/20110128/162345571.html, accessed 17 March 2012.
11 'Opening remarks at meeting of the Council for Countering Corruption', Official Website of the President of the Russian Federation, 13 January, available at: http://eng.kremlin.ru/transcripts/1598, accessed 15 February 2012.
12 'Predsedatel' Pravitel'stva Rossiiskoi Federatsii V. V. Putin provel zasedanie Koordinatsionnogo soveta Obshcherossiiskogo narodnogo fronta', Official Archive of the Government of the Russian Federation, 8 December, available at: http://archive.today/3M4K#selection-161.0–161.131, accessed 14 February 2012.
13 'Putin makes first comments on weekend's poll' *RIA Novosti*, 15 December, available at: protests'http://en.ria.ru/russia/20111215/170267350.html, accessed 17 March.
14 'Expanded Government meeting', Official Archive of the Government of the Russian Federation, 31 January, available at: http://archive.government.ru/eng/docs/22596/, accessed 7 June 2013.
15 See 'Expanded Government meeting', Official Archive of the Government of the Russian Federation, 31 January, available at: http://archive.government.ru/eng/docs/22596/, accessed 7 June 2013.
16 'Expanded Government meeting', Official Archive of the Government of the Russian Federation, 31 January, available at: http://archive.government.ru/eng/docs/22596/, accessed 7 June 2013.
17 'Expanded Government meeting', Official Archive of the Government of the Russian

Federation, 31 January, available at: http://archive.government.ru/eng/docs/22596/, accessed 7 June 2013.
18 'Dmitry Medvedev attends the session "Russia in the Global Context" during the World Economic Forum meeting in Moscow', Official Archive of the Government of the Russian Federation, 14 October, available at: http://archive.government.ru/eng/docs/21136/, accessed 4 March 2013.
19 'Presidential Social Projects Directorate established', Official Website of the President of the Russian Federation, 20 October 2012.
20 In theory this would allow for more parties to participate in the political process. It was unclear, however, what these new reforms meant for the future of the political system or the relationship between the regime and the opposition.
21 Pavel Andreev cited in 'Russia is on the verge of change, say Valdai Club experts', *Valdai Discussion Club*, 18 November 2011, available at: http://valdaiclub.com/politics/49000.html, accessed 1 May 2013.
22 Nationalists demand Moscow 'stop feeding the Caucasus', *Russia Today*, 29 September 2011, available at: http://rt.com/politics/moscow-stop-feeding-caucasus-651, accessed 14 April 2014.
23 Address by President of the Russian Federation, 18 March 2014, available at: http://eng.kremlin.ru/news/6889, accessed 25 March 2014.
24 Address by President of the Russian Federation, 18 March 2014, available at: http://eng.kremlin.ru/news/6889, accessed 25 March 2014.
25 31 May 2010, *Gazeta.Ru*, available at: www.gazeta.ru.
26 For more information about the mayoral race in Sochi prior to the elections on 26 April 2009 see 'The Circus Comes To Sochi', Radio Free Europe/Radio Liberty, 16 March 2009, available at www.rferl.org/content/The_Circus_Comes_To_Sochi/1511167.html, accessed 16 April 2009.
27 In a Levada opinion poll in January 2011 around 48 per cent of respondents agreed that terrorist acts have become part of everyday life in Russia, and 34 per cent agreed that the frequency of terrorist acts in Russia will remain the same in the future.
28 'Dmitry Medvedev addressed the World Economic Forum in Davos', Official Website of the President of the Russian Federation, 26 January, available at: http://eng.kremlin.ru/news/1684, accessed 12 April 2012.
29 'Terrorism remains the main threat to Russia's security', Official Website of the President of the Russian Federation, 25 January, available at: http://eng.kremlin.ru/news/1675, accessed 8 April 2012.
30 FSB officers to give warnings to people on future crime and arrest for 15 days if they don't follow the orders. 'Federation Council approves bill broadening FSB powers', *Russia Today*, 19 July 2010, available at: http://rt.com/news/federation-council-fsb-bill/, accessed 19 April 2012.
31 The heatwave and wildfire in the Moscow region in the summer 2010 resulted in a spike in wheat and bread prices in the same year Russia had to stop exporting grain abroad, in order to ensure that domestic markets were satisfied. For more information on this see: Welton (2011) and Rozhnov (2010).
32 For more information on the Gazprom tower protests in St Petersburg see: Zakharov (2010).
33 For more information on the protests see: 'Clashes, Camp Attacks Occur As Battle Over Russia's Khimki Forest Heats Up', *Radio Free Europe Radio Liberty*, 6 May 2011, available at: www.rferl.org/content/russia_khimki_forest_environment/24093349.html, accessed 10 October 2011. On the law and the authorities' response to the protestors see Evans (2012).
34 For more on this see: 'Protesting workers in northwest Russia paid wage arrears', *RIA Novosti*, 4 June 2009, available at: http://en.ria.ru/business/20090604/155170638.html, access 7 November 2011.
35 Under Medvedev libel had been decriminalized in Autumn 2011. However, on his

return tp the presidency, Putin put it back on the statute books in August 2012 ('Federal'nyj zakon Rossijskoj Federacii ot 28 iyulya 2012 g. N 141-FZ "O vnesenii izmenenij v Ugolovnyj kodeks Rossijskoj Federacii i otdel'nye zakonodatel'nye akty Rossijskoj Federacii"', *Rossiiskaya gazeta*, 1 August 2012, available at: www.rg.ru/2012/08/01/kleveta-dok.html, accessed 17 February 2013.
36 'Russia to Create Internet Blacklist', *RIA Novosti*, 7 June 2012, available at: http://en.ria.ru/society/20120607/173902256.html, accessed 7 February 2013.
37 See Ponomareva 2013.
38 Russia: Veto Law to Restrict Online Freedom, 24 April 2014, Human Rights Watch, available at: www.hrw.org/news/2014/04/24/russia-veto-law-restrict-online-freedom, accessed 5 May 2014; 'Putin says Internet is a CIA project', 25 April 2014, *Aljazeera*, available: www.aljazeera.com/news/europe/2014/04/putin-says-internet-cia-project-201442563249711810.html, accessed 5 May 2014.
39 Media Forum of Independent Local and Regional Media, 24 April 2014, Official Website of the President of the Russian Federation, available at: http://eng.kremlin.ru/news/7075, accessed 5 May 2014.
40 Pussy Riot are a punk band that were arrested in February 2012 for their performance in the Cathedral of Christ the Saviour, in Moscow, which appeared to satirize both the Russian Orthodox Church and the figure of Putin. Their subsequent arrest and sentencing received widespread coverage in both Europe and the US, with widespread criticism of the lengthy verdict handed down to two members of the group.
41 'Kremlin Dismisses West's Pussy Riot Criticism', *RIA Novosti*, 22 August, 2012, available at: http://en.ria.ru/world/20120822/175372405.html, accessed 13 November 2012.
42 'Pussy Riot would be sentenced to longer terms in the West', *Pravda*, 23 August 2012, available at: http://english.pravda.ru/russia/politics/23–08–2012/121962-pussy_riot_west-0/, accessed 13 November 2012.
43 'Kremlin strengthens grip on Russian media', *EurActiv*, 14 March 2014, available at: www.euractiv.com/global-europe/kremlin-strengthens-grip-russian-news-534145, accessed 7 April 2014.
44 'Russian news agency RIA Novosti closed down', *BBC News*, 9 December 2013, available at: www.bbc.com/news/world-europe-25299116, accessed 10 April 2014.
45 Address to the Federal Assembly, Official Website of the President of the Russian Federation, 12 December 2012, available at: http://eng.kremlin.ru/transcripts/4739, accessed 7 April 2014.
46 'Beginning of Meeting with Security Council On National Security Strategy of the Russian Federation Through to 2020 and Measures Necessary to Implement It', Official Website of the President of the Russian Federation, 24 March 2009, available at: http://archive.kremlin.ru/eng/speeches/2009/03/24/2056_type82913_214288.shtml, accessed 11 March 2012.
47 For more detailed account of the Russia-Georgia conflict see Allison (2008); King (2008); Cornell and Starr (2009).
48 'Russia's 2008 war with Georgia prevented NATO growth – Medvedev', *RIA Novosti*, 12 November 2011, available at: http://en.ria.ru/russia/20111121/168901195.html, accessed 13 May 2012.
49 www.ln.mid.ru/bdomp/brp_4.nsf/e78a48070f128a7b43256999005bcbb3/af772ecc95d5c804c325768c0037b88d!OpenDocument
50 'EU-Russia Partnership for Modernisation', European Union, available at: http://eeas.europa.eu/delegations/russia/eu_russia/tech_financial_cooperation/partnership_modernisation_facility/index_en.htm.
51 'FSB Chief: US Steps Up Geopolitical Pressure on Russia', *RIA Novosti*, 14 February 2013, available at: http://en.ria.ru/russia/20130214/179471294.html, accessed 7 April 2013.
52 Putin has repeatedly highlighted the West's use of double standards vis-à-vis the

question of non-proliferation. Russia continued to support the denuclearization of the Korean Peninsula and the Six party talks, while with regard to Iran, Putin continued with Russia's previous position by suggesting that Iran should be allowed civilian use and uranium enrichment, but its programme should be placed under IAEA safeguards, and continuing to argue that Russia seeks a peaceful resolution to the crisis. As noted by Putin in 2012,

> the West has shown too much willingness to 'punish' certain countries. At any minor development it reaches for sanctions if not armed force. Let me remind you that we are not in the 19th century or even the 20th century now.
>
> (Putin 2012b)

53 General Staff chief Col. Gen. Valery Gerasimov stated, on 14 February 2013, that he expected increased military instability in the future due to resource wars over energy, living space and markets ('Russian Military Chief Predicts Resource Wars Soon', *RIA Novosti*, 14 February 2013, available at: http://en.ria.ru/world/20130214/179470414/Russian-Military-Chief-Predicts-Resource-Wars-Soon.html, accessed 7 April 2013).
54 Sergey Lavrov speech at the 20th Jubilee Meeting of the Council on Foreign and Defense Policy, 1 December 2012, Moscow, published in 'Russia in the 21st-Century World of Power', *Russia in Global Affairs*, 27 December 2012, available at: http://eng.globalaffairs.ru/number/Russia-in-the-21st-Century-World-of-Power-1580, accessed 15 February 2013.
55 Indeed, following the adoption of the Magnitsky Act in the US – the Russian authorities seemed to delay the signing in of the new Russian Foreign Policy concept in order to toughen the position against domestic interference ('Rossiya ishchet slova pozhestche: Kontseptsiya vneshnei politiki RF mozhet byt's popravlena', *Kommersant*, 24 January 2013, available at: http://kommersant.ru/doc/2111063, accessed 18 May 2013).
56 'Russia: Foreign policy priorities formulated', *Voice of Russia*, 14 December 2012, available at: http://voiceofrussia.com/2012_12_14/Russia-Foreign-policy-priorities-formulated/, accessed 18 November 2013.
57 Indeed following this crisis, forecasts for Russian economic indicators had been significantly revised in view of the crisis and the Western sanctions against Russia. For more information see: Mereminskaya (2014).
58 'Ukraine crisis: Russia steps up Ukraine rhetoric', *BBC News*, 25 February 2014, available at: www.bbc.com/news/world-europe-26327211, accessed 20 March 2014.
59 'Russia Accuses US of Meddling in Ukraine's Domestic Affairs', *RIA Novosti*, 18 February 2014, available at: http://en.ria.ru/world/20140218/187630180/Russia-Accuses-US-of-Meddling-in-Ukraines-Domestic-Affairs.html, accessed 10 March 2014.
60 'Statement by the Russian Ministry of Foreign Affairs regarding the aggravation of the situation in the South-Eastern regions of Ukraine', Ministry of Foreign Affairs, 13 April 2014, available at: www.mid.ru/brp_4.nsf/0/25A25347E9AB1FEC44257CBB005AFF4E, accessed 19 April 2014.
61 'Russia accuses CIA of being involved in Ukraine': *RIA Novosti*, 14 April 2014, available at: http://en.ria.ru/russia/20140414/189216143/Russia-Seeks-US-Explanation-for-CIA-Directors-Visit-to-Ukraine-.html, accessed 22 April 2014.
62 'Russia NATO Reaches New Low in Anti-Russian Rhetoric – Russian Foreign Ministry', *RIA Novosti*, 17 April 2014, available at: http://en.ria.ru/russia/20140417/189251038/NATO-Reaches-New-Low-in-Anti-Russian-Rhetoric–Russian-Foreign.htm, accessed 23 April 2014.
63 'Sovbez OON: kak noch'iyu mir osuzhdal agressiyu RF ha vostoke Ukrainu', *Liga.net*, 14 April 2014, available at: http://m.liga.net/news/politics/181937-sovbez_oon_kak_nochu_mir_osujdal_agressiu_rf_na_vostoke_ukrainy.htm, accessed 23 April 2014.

64 For an alternative reading of Germany's position vis-à-vis Russia see Mischke and Umland (2014).
65 'Pozdravlyayu putina novyy – sotz opros v Rossii shokiruet', *UAInfo*, 8 April 2014, available at: http://uainfo.org/yandex/305245-pozdravlyayu-putina-novyy-socopros-v-rossii-shokiruet.html, accessed 13 May 2014.
66 'Putin's popularity at its peak, society rallies around patriotism – spokesperson', *ITAR-TASS*, 20 April 2014, available at: http://en.itar-tass.com/russia/728796, accessed 10 May 2014.

10 Russia's policy towards the North Caucasus and Chechnya

As outlined in Chapter 8, the intertwined desecuritization processes of normalization and localization reached a formal conclusion with the decree from the Russian National Antiterrorist Committee (NAC) on 16 April 2009 that officially ended the counterterrorism operation in Chechnya. Almost immediately, however, a temporary and partial emergency situation was re-declared for some parts of Chechnya, allowing for continued operations in these areas.[1] Nonetheless, within official discourse, the 2009 decree marked the final act in both the desecuritization and rehabilitation of Chechnya into the Russian Federation. In announcing the decree, the Russia's National Antiterrorist Committee outlined that the decision to formally end the counterterrorist operation was intended 'to create conditions to further normalise the situation in the region, to restore and develop its economic and social infrastructure'. By October 2009, all command was transferred to regional FSB control. And, at the same time, Medvedev announced that all Russian forces would be withdrawn from Chechnya by 2011 (Marten 2010). Yet, insecurity and violence in other parts of the North Caucasus continued throughout the Medvedev presidency and into Putin's third term, and indeed by the time of Putin's return to the presidency there was even an increase in security incidents in Chechnya itself. Thus, the issue of insecurity in the North Caucasus remained a prominent issue within the Russian internal security agenda.

During the Medvedev presidency, mirroring the wider state development discourse of modernization, official discourse focused on what were said to be the systemic and structural problems underlying the insecurity in the North Caucasus. At the same time, counterterrorist operations in the North Caucasus continued, and an administrative change saw the creation of the North Caucasus Federal District. Indeed, in spite of the modernization rhetoric, there was little alteration in the approach taken to Chechnya and the North Caucasus during the last years of Putin's second term. In turn, the Kadyrov regime in Chechnya further strengthened its increasingly authoritarian control over counterterrorist operations in the republic, and indeed made moves to act beyond its republican borders. Yet, in spite of this independent activity, the relationship between the federal and Kadyrov regimes remained tight, and rather than Kadyrov being seen as a challenge to federal control and vice versa, they presented each other as mutually reinforcing their official discourses.

The return of Putin led to few changes in policy, but did see the North Caucasus slide further down the list of priorities within the regime's political project. Whereas on coming to power in 2000, Putin positioned Chechnya, and later the North Caucasus, as important parts of his national project, by 2012, the region was increasingly distanced from his regime's new patriotic project. Indeed, aside from the symbolic importance of the Sochi Olympics in demonstrating the reassertion of federal control over the region and the creation of a Ministry for North Caucasus Affairs in 2014, the nationalist nature of official discourse, in conjunction with the wider public debate on state expenditure on the region, saw the place of the North Caucasus, and the prioritization of the insecurity there, within the regime's political project become increasingly uncertain.

This chapter will first outline the new discourse on modernizing the North Caucasus outlined by Medvedev, before examining the policy of the Kadyrov regime and the role of the North Caucasus in Russian foreign policy during this period. Second, it examines how the return of Putin to the presidency in 2012 impacted policy on the North Caucasus, considering the symbolic significance of the 2014 Sochi Olympics and the various intersections between the North Caucasus and foreign policy since 2012.

Medvedev: modernization alongside counterinsurgency

Although it marked the official end of the federal counterterrorist operation in Chechnya, 2009 was a bad year for security in the wider North Caucasus. Aldigirei Magomedtagirov, the Interior Minister of Dagestan, was assassinated, and a terrorist attack in Ingushetia almost succeeded in killing the Ingush President, Yunus-Bek Yevkurov, while there were 50 per cent more terrorist related crimes than in 2008 (Mukhin 2010), and several high-profile clerics were assassinated, including Ismail Bostanov, the deputy mufti of the Karachai-Cherkess republic, on 20 September. As noted by Markedonov, these events caused the Russian leadership to change its discourse about the causes of the ongoing instability in the region from focusing primarily on external factors to highlighting intra-regional structural and systemic problems (Markedonov 2010). In a June 2009 speech to an expanded format of the National Security Council on the situation in the North Caucasus, Medvedev outlined that 'the situation is partially influenced by certain outside factors such as extremism brought from abroad, by some freaks who come to our country for the sole purpose of causing damage to it'. He, rather than focusing on the external influence of extremists, suggested that the insecurity and violence in the North Caucasus was in large part the result of systemic problems within the region, highlighting the impact of 'low living standards, high unemployment and massive, horrifyingly widespread corruption', as well as the 'systemically crippled regional governance and extraordinary inefficiency of local authorities'. Concluding that these systemic failings and conditions 'results in loss of confidence in and respect toward state power institutions'.[2] In this way, the need to address insecurity in the North Caucasus was enclosed within the wider official discourse of this period on tackling the systemic and structural weaknesses and shortcoming of Russia's economy, rule-of-law and governance via the modernization drive. Hence, alongside ongoing counterinsurgency operations, a renewed emphasis on tackling insecurity in the North Caucasus via modernization became a central feature of official discourse on the North Caucasus.

This modernization programme included a series of measures to counteract the escalating violence in the North Caucasus, based on a three-pronged approach: leadership reshuffles, federal restructuring and socio-economic development schemes, and tackling the endemic corruption in the region.[3] The Presidents of Ingushetia and Dagestan were replaced by Moscow in 2008, and 2010 and 2012 respectively. In 2010, a 15-year economic and development plan for the North Caucasus Federal District was announced. The 'Strategy for the Socio-economic Development of the North Caucasus Federal District until 2025'[4] was aimed at revitalizing the local economies of the North Caucasus republics and reducing societal dislocation, with plans to create 400,000 new jobs, increase average monthly income by 1.5 times, regional GDP by 1.7 times, and bring down unemployment to 5 per cent (as compared with the prevailing 17 per cent). The strategy was focused on developing tourism as a source of income for the region, by building five new resorts – Lagonaki, Arkhyz, Elbrus-Besengi, Mamison and Matlas, improving the investment climate and social infrastructure, with a planned investment of $80.9 billion over 13 years.[5] However, it did not address any of the political or religious issues that serve as root causes for violence and insurgency in the region (Markedonov 2010). Furthermore, given the limitations of the modernization drive in Russia itself, its effectiveness in the political and security climate was unsurprisingly restricted. As Malashenko noted: how can the prevailing system in the North Caucasus, based on corruption or clan politics, be changed, if these systems and processes remain prevalent in the rest of Russia (Malashenko 2009a).

Alongside the modernization strategy for the North Caucasus, a new approach to the counterinsurgency effort was developed. In 2010, the North Caucasus was officially separated from the larger Southern Federal District to form the North Caucasus Federal District. Reflecting the centrality of Medvedev's modernization discourse in the official discourse at this time, Alexander Khloponin, a technocrat with extensive business experience, rather than a representative of the power ministries, was appointed in January 2010 as its head. At the same time, in October 2010, the North Caucasus Federal Military district was widened to become the Southern Federal Military district, with the aim of strengthening Russia's counterterrorist campaign. With these changes in the counterinsurgency strategy, commentators began to suggest that the role of the federal forces operating in the North Caucasus was closer to fighting a 'war', than conducting operations against extremism (Mukhin 2011). In 2011, the Russian authorities claimed to uncover 199 foreign spies, with the FSB credited with preventing 94 'crimes of a terrorist nature', including eight terrorist attacks in that same year.[6]

In spite of these new initiatives and attempts at modernization, the federal approach to the North Caucasus can be characterized as remaining more or less the same as during the second half of the 2000s, emphasizing the need for better economic conditions, muting issues of poor political governance, and relying upon counterterrorist operations (Fuller 2011). However, the attempts to isolate the insecurity in the North Caucasus from the rest of Russia were not very successful, as throughout 2009–2012 (until the Caucasus Emirate's moratorium on targeting civilians in 2012) extremist groups from the North Caucasus continued to conduct regular terrorist attacks in major Russian cities. Indeed, the everyday violence was increasingly spreading beyond the North Caucasus, with ethnic clashes between ethnic Russians and North Caucasians in areas adjacent to the region. For example, between December 2011 and January 2012 in Nevinnomyssk, Stavropol Kray, police made mass arrests to prevent clashes between ethnic Russians and those from North Caucasus.[7]

Politics of Chechnya and the North Caucasus: ongoing Ramzanification, a model for the North Caucasus? and a Russian success story

From 2009 onwards, in line with the decree marking the official end of federal counterterrorist operations, the main securitizing actor in Chechnya became the Kadyrov regime. Indeed, the 'Ramzanification' of Chechnya continued in a manner similar to the previous period, including the violent targeting of potential rivals to Kadyrov's ruling authority. This entailed a policy of targeting the families of insurgents, and a practice of deeming that entire families have 'collective responsibility' for instability caused by a single family-member.[8] In this respect, the Kadyrov regime was able to function as the primary securitizing actor within Chechnya, adopting its own policy approaches not seen elsewhere in Russia. Furthermore, following the 2009 decree, the Kadyrov regime increasingly displayed a tendency to act beyond the limits of its republican borders, targeting what they deemed as 'security threats' within the territory of other North Caucasian republics. Hence, Kadyrov not only operated as the main securitizing actor in Chechnya, beyond federal oversight in this respect, but he also enacted securitization practices in other republican jurisdictions of the North Caucasus.

Yet, in spite of the increasingly localized, independent and autocratic nature of the Kadyrov regime's power, its strong link with the federal regime was maintained, and has been subsequently continued into the early years of the third Putin presidency. This prolongation of the close-knit federal-Chechnya relationship occurred, in spite of many commentators suggestion that the model of desecuritization/normalization set up in conjunction with the Kadyrov regime during Putin's second term was overly dependent on Kadyrov's personal relationship with Putin and the federal centre in general. Furthermore, the form and strength of this relationship has been much commented upon by analysts, with Malashenko suggesting that 'Ramzan [Kadyrov] is not a Caucasian politician; he is a Russian politician "of Caucasian ethnicity"' (Malashenko 2009a), and Furman arguing that there is 'semi-feudal relationship' between Kadyrov and the federal centre (Furman 2009, p. 5).

The extension of spatial reach of the Kadyrov regime's operations beyond its republican borders, as noted previously, was linked with another continuing trend within its discourse from the previous period, which presented Chechnya as a Russian, and Putin regime, success story, and saw Kadyrov boasting that Chechnya's economic situation is better than anywhere else in Russia.[9] However, the role played by the increasingly independent and powerful Kadyrov regime within the rest of the North Caucasus became a controversial issue during the Medvedev presidency, as it was touted as a possible model to be emulated in the rest of the region, with Kadyrov attempting to assert this position as the representative voice for the whole region.[10] Following the assassination attempt on the Ingush President, Yunus-bek Yevkurov, on 22 June 2009, the Kadyrov regime tried to position itself as the leading regional securitizing actor, by trying to claim a role for itself in shaping the direction and implementation of regional counterterrorist operations across the rest of the North Caucasus.[11] Some suggestions were also made that Kadyrov's model of governance and security could be supplanted onto, and rolled out into, the rest of the region to counteract the ongoing insurgency. Both of these ideas were met with resistance from other regional leaders. Indeed, a growing rivalry between Chechen and Ingush regimes developed, including in relation to their undemarcated border (Muradov *et al.* 2012).

Furthermore, this rivalry, between Chechnya and the other regional leaders in the North Caucasus, was also defined by opposing models of governance put forward or supported by the federal centre for the region. As outlined by Malashenko, during this period two alternate models of political and security governance can be seen as having emerged in the North Caucasus: one, the softer model centred on dialogue with society, put forward by Yevkurov in Ingushetia, and another, harder and more authoritarian, put forward by Kadyrov in Chechnya (Malashenko 2009b). Indeed, Kadyrov has repeatedly berated Yevkurov for taking 'too soft' an approach to internal security (Bobrova 2012). And, in spite of the modernization rhetoric of official discourse, it is the Kadyrov model for which the Russian authorities have shown a preference at least when it came to Chechen affairs.

Chechnya and the North Caucasus in foreign policy

Alongside the federal official discourse supporting the Kadyrov regime against its critics, both domestic and international, the Kadyrov regime continued to lend its support to the federal regime, both in relation to Chechnya, but also more broadly. A vivid example was the rhetorical and practical support provided to the Russian authorities during the Russia-Georgia conflict in August 2008. Aside from the involvement of Chechen military operatives, such as the Vostok Battalion, in Russian military operations (Closson 2008), the Chechen leadership also publicly endorsed Russia's policy.[12] Such support was also offered to Russia's policy towards the Middle East. In addition, the Kadyrov regime continued to criticize the West for not recognizing the changes it had brought about in Chechnya, as well as for its policy towards Russia in general. For example, following the terrorist attack at Domodedovo airport in 2011 and subsequent criticism from the West of Russia's policy in the North Caucasus, Kadyrov stated that '[t[hey [the West] are not interested in the Chechen republic. Their attitude to the Caucasus is dictated by their global interest. The West is interested in ruining the sovereign state of Russia'.[13]

While the federal regime continued to see insecurity in the North Caucasus as a primary challenge to internal stability, there were continuing ramifications for regional and international security during Medvedev's presidency. Geopolitically, instability in the North Caucasus contributed negatively to conflict transformation and stabilization efforts in the wider Caucasus region. First, the 'Caucasus Emirate' group continued to proclaim that its rebels and operatives function not only within Russia's borders, but also further afield, including in Azerbaijan. Second, the North Caucasus has emerged as an additional fault line within Russian-Georgian relations. Moscow criticized the establishment by Georgia of a visa-free regime on its border with the Russian North Caucasus in October 2010 and a speech by Georgian President, Mikheil Saakashvili, to the United Nations General Assembly in September 2010, in which he outlined his vision of a 'unified Caucasus' (Nodia 2010). Despite its attempts to curtail the negative regional and international impact of the North Caucasus, Medvedev's regime was unsuccessful in doing so in practice.

The return of Putin – fatigue or lack of ideas

The return of Putin to the presidency in 2012 resulted in few changes within federal policy towards Chechnya and the North Caucasus. Indeed, Putin's policy priorities for the North Caucasus Federal District, as set out in September 2013 at a Security Council meeting, reiterated many of the themes and concerns outlined by Medvedev in 2009, and even those of his second term. At this meeting, Putin called for 'faster social and economic growth', efforts to 'raise the level of security in the region', a 'fight against corruption', and raised concerns about 'the accusations spread by some foreign media and reports of international organisations on supposed mass violations of people's rights in the North Caucasus'.[14] Meanwhile, Chechnya continued to be presented as the success story within the North Caucasus, as noted both by Kadyrov and the Chairman of the Accounts Chamber of Russia Sergei Stepashin in September 2013,[15] and, evidenced by the federally approved Kadyrov regime initiative to set up a special economic zone between Chechnya, Karachayevo-Cherkessia and Stavropol Krai.

Alongside these familiar discourses, as noted by Laub (2014), there was, however, a shift away from favouring the appointment of more conciliatory-minded governors in the North Caucasus, as seen under Medvedev. For example, Magomedsalam Magomedov was replaced with Ramazan Abdulatipov in Dagestan in January 2013, whilst the Dagestani rehabilitation commission was closed, and an increase in mass arrests and a more prominent securitization of

Salafis (Laub 2014). At the same time, however, many continued to advocate a less militarized approach to North Caucasus, based on preventative measures, such as dialogue between different religious and ethnic groups, rather than exclusively on the use of force. And experts continued to blame the instability and violence on the poor socio-economic conditions, high unemployment and the absence of transparent rule-of-law (Mukhin 2012a).

It was not only federal policy that followed the same pattern as under Medvedev, the insecurity and persistence of violence on the ground in the North Caucasus also continued in a manner similar. Indeed, in spite of a reduction in the numbers of casualties from insurgent and counterinsurgent activity in the region, from 1,710 in 2010, to 986 in 2013 (Laub 2014),[16] violence remained part of everyday life in parts of the North Caucasus. Assassinations of high-profile figures continued to occur sporadically, such as the killing of the Dagestani cleric, Sheikh Said Afandi al-Chirkawi, in August 2012. There was, however, a partial relocation of the main hot-spot for conflict from Ingushetia to Dagestan (Mukhin 2012b), and an increase in instability and terrorist activity in Chechnya. The ongoing low-level insecurity in the North Caucasus, and the operation of insurgent and extremist groups there, also continued to sporadically spill over into terrorist actions beyond the North Caucasus, forcing the Russian authorities and public to recognize that the insecurity and violence was ongoing in North Caucasus. The most high-profile of these, following the end of the Caucasus Emirate's moratorium on targeting civilians (announced by Umarov in July 2013), was the *terakts* in Volgograd in December 2013 that targeted a train station and a trolleybus, resulting in the deaths of 34 people. Thus, in spite of the federal authorities attempt to keep the North Caucasus coherently within the Russian political landscape by suggesting that it was a normal region like any other, the distinctive situation in parts of the North Caucasus, as insecure and violent spaces, continued to emerge at times of *terakts*.

The reproduction of previous official discourses about Chechnya and the North Caucasus reflected a sense that the federal regime had run out of ideas about how to bring lasting stability to the North Caucasus. Indeed, to some extent, this uncertainty paralleled the lack of direction within the regime's wider political project during the initial period of Putin's third term. As Petrov highlights, the situation in the North Caucasus appeared to reach an impasse, with the federal regime lacking a coherent discourse on how to account for this and what to do to remedy the situation. He suggested that it is,

> not so much connected with any specific fatal mistakes that the Kremlin might have committed recently. It is rather a cumulative effect of numerous small mistakes made in past or inaction when action was needed, as well as the lack of a distinct strategy.
>
> (Petrov (2013a)

In this context, a wider reconsideration of the insecurity in, and the place of, the North Caucasus within Russian official discourse emerged. Whereas, during the 2000s, official discourse about Chechnya and the North Caucasus was shaped by the federal policy towards the region and the assertion of the region's importance to Russia's development – first, in the form of asserting the imperative need to prevent separatist elements operating there, and subsequently, as a sidelined policy that asserted the need to develop the region – by the 2010s, as Markedonov outlines, it began to be driven by the question of the way in which the rest of Russia perceived and related to the North Caucasus (Markedonov 2013). Such a perspective emerged within the context of the wider shift in public debate, and then official discourse, towards nationalism. Russian right-wing nationalist groups, such as the Russian Civil Union, the Russian Public Movement, the Russian Platform and the New Force Party, sought to introduce an ethnic Russian nationalist perspective into the debate on how Russia should approach the North Caucasus and put forward slogans such as 'Stop Feeding the Caucasus'.[17] Indeed, even well-known nationalist opposition figures such as Alexei Navalny, picked up on this sentiment during his campaigns, attracting significant national attention and support.

Hence, whereas for most of the 2000s, it was the Putin regime that had almost exclusive control over the terms of the public discourse about the North Caucasus, with the rise of the nationalist protest movement, this began to change. As a result, increasing calls from within Russian society were heard for a greater decentralization, whereby the North Caucasus would function in an increasingly detached manner from the rest of Russia (Petrov 2013b). This included suggestions that rather than pursuing a wide-ranging modernization of the North Caucasus, advocated by Medvedev in 2009, a less comprehensive approach should be taken, with a reduction in the amount of the federal budget devoted to modernizing and developing the region. While, others argued that the North Caucasus should be allowed to leave the Russian Federation. This viewpoint stands in direct contrast to the position taken by the Putin regime on coming to power in 2000, in which ensuring Russian sovereign control over Chechnya was considered as vital to Russian national and security interests. However, as Petrov writes, 'the very idea to separate the Caucasus from Russia which seemed exotic a while ago, gets increasingly more supporters, not as much in the Caucasus as in the rest of the country' (Petrov 2013a).

Against this context, parallel discourses that, on the one hand, sought to present the North Caucasus region as an integral and 'normal' part of the Russian Federation, and, on the other, as a distinct and different, became central to the regime's political strategy for the region. Upon returning to the presidency in 2012, Putin continued the previous strategy of regularly reshuffling the leading political figures in the North Caucasus republics with the greatest security problems. To this end, although Putin restored the direct-election for governors of Russia's 85 federal subjects, an amendment was included, that allowed for each federal subject to reject this change and retain the arrangement whereby Moscow appoints its governor, with the suggestion that this was done with the North Caucasus in mind (de Carbonnel 2013). Following Kabardino-Balkaria's parliamentary decision to reject direct elections for its governor the day after this amendment was adopted, Adalbi Shkhagoshev, a Duma deputy and member of United Russia, outlined this arrangement was

> an adequate solution for the situation in the North Caucasus—to wait for a little while and foil any radical forces' attempts to take advantage of the situation in the North Caucasus and influence the situation, especially through elections.
>
> (Dzutsev 2014)

In practice, as of April 2014, five of the seven republics of the North Caucasus had opted for their governor to be directly appointed by the federal authorities, with some analysts arguing that 'Moscow's unofficial policy in the North Caucasus is to preclude the region's residents from electing their leaders' (Dzutsev 2014).

Thus, with this new arrangement, the federal regime was acknowledging that despite its normalization discourse, local circumstances in the region remained distinct from the rest of Russia. Furthermore, it also seemed to indicate that the Putin regime was set on undoing many of the changes to centre-periphery relations it had initially introduced in the early 2000s. Indeed, the Putin regime's policy towards the North Caucasus from 2012 onwards, and the designation of the region, along with Crimea and the Far East, as special areas of interest that necessitated the creation of specific federal ministries, highlighted that the 2000s project of establishing equilibration in federal-subject relations was now being reversed.

Furthermore, in contrast to the 2000s, the adoption of a political project centred on Russian nationalism and patriotism would seem to have altered the perspective from which the North Caucasus is considered by the regime, even if the violence on the ground has begun to partially decline. Whilst in the past, as noted in the previous chapter, Putin's patriotism was more closely linked to statism, rather than nationalism, by 2012–2013 it had begun to take on aspects of an ethnic-nationalist ideology, even if this was not spelled out explicitly. At same time, officially the regime's political project was premised on an all-inclusive Russian identity, as seen by the establishment of the Presidential Council for Inter-Ethnic Relations (which held its first session on 24 August 2012) and the adoption of the State National Policy Strategy up until 2025 (endorsed on 19 December 2012). However, by 2013, the line between patriotism and ethnic nationalism had narrowed, with official discourse increasingly appealing to Russian history and the notion of kinship with, and responsibility to, Russian compatriots abroad, casting doubt on the robustness of this inclusive conception of the Russian state.

Indeed, the Ukraine crisis and Russia's annexation of Crimea in March 2014 served to heighten Russian patriotism, and further brought into focus the question of what it means to be 'Russian' and a Russian compatriot, opening the door to questions about how integrated and represented non-Russian ethnic groups, such as those found in the North Caucasus, are within such a state project. As noted by Markedonov, whilst the situation in the North Caucasus and its place within Putin's Russia is currently overshadowed by the accession of Crimea into Russia and the Ukraine Crisis in general, with the upsurge in ethnic Russian patriotism and usage of historical images in official discourse, it remains uncertain how the Putin regime will seek to manage the ongoing insecurity within the North Caucasus in this altered context, and how the North Caucasus will be presented as fitting into the regime's new patriotic and increasingly nationalist project for Russia (Markedonov 2014).

Sochi 2014 Olympics: a failed attempt to normalize the North Caucasus

The relationship between the North Caucasus and Russia within official discourse also came into focus around the hosting of the Winter Olympics in Sochi in February 2014. Furthermore, this event represented a direct interjection between Russia's domestic political and security context and policies, its foreign policy and its discourse around its place in the world. Indeed, the Sochi Olympics mega-project was deeply embedded within the regime's state identity discourse from the announcement that Russia had won the right to host them in 2007. This centred on the regime's discourse about it having rehabilitated Russia from its decline and weakness of the late 1990s to become strong and capable again by the end of Putin's second term, with the hosting of Olympics in Sochi said to be not only a symbol of this domestically, but also from the international community.

As well as being presented as an emblem of Russia's great power capability and a source of patriotic pride within official discourse, it was, as noted by Petersson, also proclaimed to be a significant step 'in rehabilitating southern Russia and turning it, as the phrase goes, into a "normal" part of the Russian Federation' (Petersson 2014). In this way, such discourse can be seen as a continuation and extension of the official discourse on Chechnya that was evident from the second half of Putin's second term onwards, to cover the wider North Caucasus, and as a symbol of the successes of the Russian state in re-imposing its sovereign rights and security over the region. As Petersson suggests,

> holding a successful Games in Sochi, near the foothills of the Caucasus Mountains in what was the unruliest of borderlands, would add to the triumph, since it would demonstrate that the center at last has firm control everywhere in the Federation
>
> (Petersson 2014).

Similarly to the normalization of Chechnya during the 2000s, the role of the Sochi Olympics in normalizing the North Caucasus was centred on simultaneous principles of securitization and desecuritization, tightly interlinked around the discourses and practices of the Putin's wider political project. Hence, the regime sought to control and securitize the local context, while, at the same time, discussing issues of development and modernization. A central theme of the justification for state expenditure on the Olympics project was that, in line with the wider focus on modernization, it would serve to develop Sochi and the area around it, establishing the region as a foreign tourist destination and boosting its economic potential (Müller 2011, also see Müller 2014 and Orttung and Zhemukhov 2014). It was argued that the Sochi Olympics was not only going to be an event for the Russian public and the global community to enjoy, but also an infrastructural mega-project to benefit the region in the long-term (Arnold and Foxall 2012). By situating this project in relation to historical memories of Sochi as a major tourist destination for Soviet holidaymakers, official discourse not only connected the Olympic mega-project to a historical image in which the country was a great power, but it also served to tap into the sense of patriotism, mixed with romanticism for past Soviet glories that the regime's discourse increasingly drew upon.

In parallel with the discourse about the Sochi Olympics playing a key role in developing and normalizing the North Caucasus, the various problems and concerns about the construction of the infrastructure for the games (such as rampant corruption in and around the project and concerns over the treatment of migrant laborers coming into the region to work on the construction of the project), criticism of its impact on the local population (including that the building-project violated sacred areas of the Circassian community, bringing questions over Moscow's mistreatment of indigenous rights and the actions of the troops of Tsar Nicholas I's in 1864 to national attention, resulting in a major revitalization of the Circassian nationalist movement around their criticism of the hosting of the Olympics at the site in Sochi)[18] and fears about the targeting of the Olympic Games by extremist groups were incorporated in various strands of securitization discourses, which sought to ensure the event went ahead without disruption or negative publicity.

Hence, the regime sought to tightly control developments on the ground, seeking to separate-off and control the area in and around Sochi. This included geopolitically repositioning Kransnodar Krai, the region in which Sochi is located by refolding it within the the Southern Federal District in 2010, and administratively separating and distinguishing it from the North Caucasus (Zhemukhov 2014).

As 2014 approached, it became clear that, in spite of the federal authorities hopes to the contrary, insecurity, violence and extremist groups continued to beset the North Caucasus, leading to concerns about possible terrorist attacks disrupting the games. Indeed, Doku Umarov, the head of the Caucasus Emirate, openly threatened to target the games,[19] and large-scale *terakts* in Volgograd in November 2013 illustrated the continued commitment of insurgent groups to conduct terrorist attacks against civilians in Russia. In this context, many questioned the capacity of Russia's security apparatus to ensure security during the games (Zhemukhov and Orttung 2014b, also see Sánchez Nieto 2011). In response, a heavily-armed security and police force of 70,000 troops was deployed in and around Sochi, in both the lead up to, and during, the Olympic

Games, and the event passed without a major *terakt*. Indeed, in spite of some negative international headlines about the facilities and the regime's policies on other issues, Putin was able to claim that the event was a success, and to suggest that it demonstrated Russia's ability to successfully host such a mega-event and assert its status as an important international actor.

Connecting the insecurity in the North Caucasus to a global jihad

Beyond the Sochi Olympics, the continued insecurity in the North Caucasus re-emerged within an international context every so often, particularly at times when domestic North Caucasus dynamics interconnected with events abroad. This was seen most prominently in relation to the Boston Marathon bombing in April 2013 by the Tsarnaev brothers, US citizens with Chechen family roots who were said to have been in contact with insurgent groups in the North Caucasus. The Putin regime sought to present this act as vindicating their previous assertions about the 'global' nature of the terrorist threat in the North Caucasus.[20] At the same time, official discourse around this incident underlined the wider ongoing tensions and distrust in Russia's relations with the West, with the regime frequently noting the US's unwillingness to fully share their information and sources or to take on board Russia's warnings when it came to terrorist activities both in the US and elsewhere.[21]

The regime also sought to relate what it considered an ongoing 'global jihad' to the insecurity within the North Caucasus, most notably in terms of the civil war in Syria, and in particular the international focus on the issue of 'foreign fighters', whereby citizens from other countries travelled to Syria to join the Islamist groups fighting the Assad regime. Among these, there was a high number of fighters coming from Russia,[22] said to range somewhere between 400–500 fighters in December 2013.[23] Mirroring wider international concerns, the regime outlined its fear that those Russian citizens going to fight in Syria would return to Russia to continue fighting for the jihadist cause, against the Putin regime, in Russia and the North Caucasus specifically.[24] Indeed, one of the key arguments made by the Putin regime in support of the Assad regime, or at least in objection to a possible Western intervention in Syria, has been that a functioning regime in Syria is a better source of defence against the spread of jihad and foreign fighters (Hahn 2013b). And, to a certain extent, this argument found common ground with Western states during 2013–2014.

Conclusion

According to the policy trajectory set out by the Putin regime in the early 2000s, the desecuritization and normalization of Chechnya, and the North Caucasus, should have been completed by 2010. And, to this effect, a number of key milestones during the Medvedev and early years of the third Putin presidency were supposed to represent the culmination, and act as symbols, of this process, most notably the formal end of the federal counterterrorist operation in Chechnya in

2009, and Sochi's hosting of the 2014 Winter Olympics. Furthermore, these milestones were complemented by federal programmes, in line with the wider national focus on modernization, of infrastructural projects and on economic development in the region. At the same time, various small-scale securitization discourses continued, with occasional new ones emerging, primarily when the dynamics of insecurity in the North Caucasus intersected with other security priorities and discourses. This included major *terakts* conducted by groups from the North Caucasus in other Russian cities, and in terms of Russia's foreign policy stance on Syria, and in relation to the international attention on the issue of foreign fighters.

As detailed in previous chapters, during the latter years of Putin's second term, the federal authorities seemed to be actively attempting to silence the issue of insecurity in the North Caucasus. By contrast, under Medvedev and then in the early years of Putin's third term, official discourse was more forthcoming in recognizing the geographical expansion, and the ongoing nature, of security problems in the North Caucasus. Yet, in spite of this greater recognition of the scale of the insecurity and need for federal investment, the political importance attributed to addressing it declined. Whereas, at the end of the 1990s, the conflict and violence in Chechnya associated with radical Islamist and separatist groups – which then later spread to the wider region of the North Caucasus – was seen as a fundamental challenge to Russian domestic security, by 2010s, the seemingly permanent and significant levels of conflict and violence in broadly the same geographical space was no longer considered by the regime or official discourse to be an 'existential' concern, or even as a first-order issue. To the contrary, as suggested by Malashenko, instability in the North Caucasus 'has become normal for Russia. War has become normal. The abnormal is now normal. We have grown accustomed to it; we are indifferent. We think it's happening far away, in the Caucasus. Russian people don't want to hear or think about the Caucasus anymore' (Tsvetkova 2012).

Therefore, counter-intuitively to the official discourse of the 2000s that suggested that it would be with improvement of the situation on the ground in Chechnya and the North Caucasus that the region would be desecuritized and normalized, a form of normalization emerged as a result of fatigue, a lack of ideas, and reprioritizations in the regime's larger state project. This saw the ongoing low-level insecurity in the North Caucasus increasingly acknowledged as a 'normal' situation, and the importance of the North Caucasus within state identity discourse downgraded. Indeed, whilst previously the regime held a hegemonic position on situating the issue of insecurity in the North Caucasus within the national political and security agenda, during the 2010s, Russian nationalist groups sought to put forward an alternative discourse on the North Caucasus, questioning whether it should be considered a priority for state expenditure and even suggesting that the rest of Russia should be separated from the region. This ethnic Russian nationalist discourse changed the context in which the regime considered the North Caucasus. While the regime's patriotic discourse on the 2014 Ukraine/Crimea crisis indicated that it was seeking to take back control of the increasingly nationalist context of public discourse in Russia and away from nationalist opposition figures, this discourse also flirted with ethnic Russian nationalism more than the inclusive multi-ethnic patriotism of the 2000s. Against this background, the place of non-ethnic Russian populations, such as the North Caucasus, has become uncertain. Furthermore, in recent years the regime has, to a certain extent, begun to consider the insecurity in the North Caucasus as separate and detached from their political project for the rest of Russia. Against this background, by 2014, it was not clear whether and how the North Caucasus was positioned in the regime's increasingly patriotic official discourse.

Notes

1 'Russia warns may have individual security ops in Chechnya', Interfax, 19 April 2009, taken from: Johnson's Russia List, #3 – JRL 2009–72, available at: www.cdi.org/russia/johnson/2009–72–3.cfm, accessed 30 August 2010.
2 'Speech at Expanded Format Security Council Meeting', Presidential website, 9 June 2009, available at: http://archive.kremlin.ru/eng/speeches/2009/06/09/1904_type-82912type82913_217581.shtml, accessed 22 March 2014.
3 On the discussion about corruption in the region by Medvedev see Samarina (2010), on corruption see Muradov (2011).
4 http://government.ru/media/2010/10/4/35578/file/1485.doc.
5 'Russia to lavish $80 Bln on North Caucasus by 2025', RIA Novosti, 15 December 2012, available at: http://en.rian.ru/business/20121213/178135137.html, accessed 12 May 2014.
6 'Russia Busted 200 Spies Last Year – Medvedev', RIA Novosti, 7 February 2012, available at: http://en.rian.ru/russia/20120207/171195509.html, accessed 20 February 2013.
7 'Stavropol'skie natsionalisti trebuyut osobogo rezhima', 28 January 2013, Kommersant, available at: www.kommersant.ru/doc/2114620, accessed 20 May 2014.
8 'Opasnei Umarova: v Chechne unitchozheny bratiya Gakaevy', ITAR-TASS, 25 January 2013, available at: www.itar-tass.com/c188/631506.html, accessed 20 March 2014.
9 'Ekonomika Chechni priznana samoy effektivnoy v Rossii, coobschil Kadyrov Putinu', ITAR-TASS, 5 February 2013, available at: www.itar-tass.com/c12/640827.html, accessed 10 March 2014.
10 'No More "Mr. Nice Guy"', Caucasus Report, Radio Free Europe Radio Liberty, 18 May 2009, available at: www.rferl.org/content/No_More_Mr_Nice_Guy/1734191.html, accessed 4 May 2010.
11 'Kadyrov pledges "cruel revenge"', BBC News, 24 June 2009, available at http://news.bbc.co.uk/2/hi/europe/8117416.stm, accessed 5 July 2010. Also see Bobrova (2009).
12 'Ramzan Kadyrov: v sluchae resheniya rukovodstva Rossii my gotovy vmeshat'sya v Yuznoi Osetii', Regnum.ru, 8 August 2008, available at: www.regnum.ru/news/1038315.html#ixzz10YG75WWF, accessed 17 June 2010.
13 'The US should leave the Caucasus alone – Chechen leader', Russia Today, 27 January 2011, available at: http://rt.com/news/kadyrov-chechen-negative-image/, accessed 19 March 2014.
14 Security Council meeting, Presidential website, 9 September 2013, available at: http://eng.state.kremlin.ru/face/5961, accessed 10 April 2014.
15 'V Groznom proshlo soveschanye rukovoditeley Stchetnykh palyat bole 60 subyektov

Rossii', Chechen Presidential Website, 24 June 2013, www.chechnya.gov.ru/page.php?r=126&id=13292, accessed 10 May 2014.
16 For more information on numbers of casualties in 2013 see 'Infographics. Statistics of victims in Northern Caucasus of 2013 under the data of the Caucasian Knot', *Kakaz-Uzel*, 27 January 2014, available at: http://eng.kavkaz-uzel.ru/articles/27109/, accessed 11 May 2014.
17 'Nationalists demand Moscow "stop feeding the Caucasus"', *Russia Today*, 29 September 2011, available at: http://rt.com/politics/moscow-stop-feeding-caucasus-651/, accessed 10 April 2014.
18 For more on the Circassian nationalist movement see Zhemukhov (2012).
19 'Caucasus Emirate Leader Calls On Insurgents To Thwart Sochi Winter Olympics', Radio Free Europe Radio Liberty, 3 July 2013, available at: www.rferl.org/content/sochi-olympics-terrorism-umarov/25035408.html, accessed 16 May 2014.
20 'Direct Line with Vladimir Putin', Presidential website, 25 April 2013, available at: http://eng.kremlin.ru/transcripts/5328, accessed 14 May 2014.
21 Ibid.
22 Critically, not all of the Chechens fighting in Syria were Russian citizens, nor were they always coming directly from the North Caucasus. Many of them are habitually resided elsewhere, particularly in the Middle East, due to diasporic links dating back to the nineteenth century, but also in Europe as refugees fleeing from the two Chechen conflicts. A number have also travelled from the Pankisi Gorge, a region in Georgia bordering with the North Caucasus. Many of the returnee foreign fighters will therefore be going back to Europe, Georgia or the Middle East rather than to Russia.
23 'Up to 11,000 foreign fighters in Syria; steep rise among Western Europeans', The International Centre for the Study of Radicalisation, 17 December 2013, available at: http://icsr.info/2013/12/icsr-insight-11000-foreign-fighters-syria-steep-rise-among-western-europeans/, accessed 15 May 2014.
24 'Rossiya gotovit spetsnaz k protivostoyaniyu boevikam iz Sirii', MIGnews.com, 6 December 2013, available at: www.mignews.com/news/society/world/051213_152234_59587.html, accessed 14 May 2014.

11 Conclusion

This book has traced the Putin regime's official discourse on state identity, its security priorities and its policy towards Chechnya/North Caucasus since Putin came to power in 2000. In some respects, the situation in which the regime finds itself in the middle of its fourth term in power, and third with Putin as president, resembles that which it found when it first came to power nearly a decade and a half ago, with Russia again struggling to define and position itself in relation to an uncertain domestic environment and changing global landscape. However, its response to these situations has been markedly different to that of the 2000s. At the start of Putin's first term as president, the regime suggested that Russia was suffering from several domestic structural crises which threatened to see it decline into a 'weak' state, and, hence, that addressing these internal issues was the main objective with positive relations with the outside world considered as beneficial to this goal. By contrast, in Putin's third term as president, the regime now argued that Russia is once again a 'strong' state, but that an unholy alliance between domestic 'anti-regime', and thus 'anti-Russian', groups and Western powers was seeking to undermine the regime from within. In response, it adopted an aggressive and confrontational conservative-nationalist and anti-Western discourse as a way of solidifying an increasingly disgruntled and shaky domestic order. This found a high-profile manifestation in the regime's decision to annex the Crimea in early 2014 and the lingering threat of further Russian military actions in eastern Ukraine, suggesting that the regime had set this agenda not only domestically but also on the international stage. Indeed, the move to annex the Crimea caught the vast majority of policy practitioners and analysts off guard, highlighting not just the continued significance of understanding Russia as a security actor, but also the difficulty and complexity in so doing.

So, if the Putin regime as a security actor took very different perspectives and decisions between 2000 and 2014, it begs the question: how do we account for this? This book has set out to answer this, by tracing the evolution of, and the interplay between, the various elements that go into forming and shaping Russian security policy and its nature as a security actor. Hence, it has sought to investigate the changing relationship between the regime's state identity discourses and its definition, prioritization and enactment of it security agenda, between macro national discourses and individual issue areas, and between the internal and external security context. It is argued that by tracing how these aspects of the Russian political and security context interact, and how this interaction evolves, it is possible to develop a nuanced understanding of Russia as a security actor. This concluding chapter will thus detail both the main findings from its application of this approach to investigating Russia as a security actor since 2000, and outline the advantages of taking such a perspective to analysing Russia, or indeed any other state, as a security actor.

To this end, it begins by outlining the main changes and turning points within the Putin regime's construction of Russian state identity since 2000, detailing the key security priorities and considerations that have driven Russia's security agenda during this period, and highlighting how the two have been constructed in relation to one another. This interrelationship is then considered in relation to the regime's specific policy discourse and practices towards Chechnya and the North Caucasus, assessing both how the relationship between national and security agendas played out in this issue area, and how the discourse and practices on Chechnya and the North Caucasus were not only shaped by, but also shaped, the nexus of these wider national and security agendas. Second, the chapter will consider what implications can be drawn from this multifaceted and longitudinal approach to analysing Russian security policy, which treats domestic and foreign security policy as inherently interconnected and traces the evolution and changes within security discourse over time respectively, for understanding Russia as a security actor. Third, the theoretical insights that can be taken from this study are discussed. It is suggested that a more interpretivist, contextually-situated and longitudinal perspective is needed both to provide a more nuanced reading of the notions of 'weak' and 'strong' states within the existing IR literature, and in the study of security in non-Western contexts.

The evolution of Russia as a security actor 2000–2014

The changing national agenda within Putin's Russia: from weak to strong, to weak and strong

During the first two terms of the Putin presidency, the regime's national agenda underwent a substantial evolution. The aim of making Russia strong again served as a discourse hook around which the Putin regime sought to hang its programme for national development during the 2000s. On taking office for his first full-term as president, Putin identified the weak grip of federal state structures over certain policy areas and regional jurisdictions, the fragility and chaotic nature of the economy and the threat from violent secessionist groups to Russian territorial integrity as the key problems facing Russia at the turn of the twenty-first century. The regime thus spent most of Putin's first term attempting to alleviate these major domestic instabilities and weaknesses, including the conducting of military operations in Chechnya with aim of bringing this restive republic back under the control of the federal centre, and by doing so, end the lingering concern about its cessation from the Russian Federation. During this period, official discourse positioned Russia as at an important juncture, whereby it could slide further towards becoming a 'weak' state, or take the necessary steps – those identified by the regime – to address its weakness and begin the process of rebuilding Russia as a strong state.

By 2004, aided by the buoyant oil prices, the Putin regime had begun to assert that its plan of action for redressing the major ills facing Russia had been successful, whereby the federal centre had managed to reassert state control over the whole country, resolve secessionist security concerns (including Chechnya) and was in the process of rebuilding the economy. Official discourse, therefore, depicted Russia as in a period of transition, in which it was rebuilding itself domestically on the path to becoming strong once more. Yet, alongside the reconstruction of Russia's domestic sphere outlined above, the mid-2000s also witnessed the start of an unprecedented and concerted effort by the regime to systematically and persistently deepen and widen its power over, and reach within, the fabric of political, economic and social life in Russia. So much so, that by 2008, the regime had transformed the Russian state into something akin to a 'network state' (Kononenko and Moshes 2011) or a 'dual state' (Sakwa 2011), whereby governance was based on a two-track system: a formal constitutional state and an informal 'behind the scenes' regime politics centred around the figure of Putin.

With the regime taking an increasingly strong grip over all matters within Russia, in conjunction with a period of sustained economic growth delivering noticeable improvements in economic well-being for many, by the second half of Putin's second term as president, official discourse began to herald Russia's successful transition from the chaos, insecurity and ultimately what was said to be weakness of the late 1990s, through a period of rebuilding of Russia in which its main internal challenges has been addressed, to a context in which Russia had regained the status of a strong state. This fact was illustrated by its more assertive foreign policy stance in relation to the West, a discourse asserting Russia's credentials as a 'great power' within the international system, and the emergence of a sense of pride in the new Russia and its power.

This sense of elation was, however, rather short lived. The period since 2008 has been marked by three major counterpoints to Putin's first two terms as president: the impact of the 2008/2009 global financial and economic crisis, the failed modernization agenda of the Medvedev presidency, and the return to power of Vladimir Putin in 2012 and the subsequent attempt to redefine what constitutes Putin's Russia within a markedly different domestic and global context.

The 2008/2009 global financial crisis had significant negative repercussions for Russia's economic fortunes and the model underwriting the development of the Putin regime during 2000s. Its impact and after-effects swept away many of the economic gains made in the 2000s, challenging domestic stability and the representation of Russia as being a great power once again. Despite its rhetoric, Medvedev's modernization project was unsuccessful in rectifying this slide, with this downward economic trend culminating in the popular protests against the regime during the 2011/2012 electoral cycle. The latent impact of 2008/2009 global financial crisis seemed to undermine the informal social model underwriting the regime's approach during 2000s, not only in economic terms but also in altering the terms of the 'informal contract' between the regime and the population within which the populace waived political and social freedoms in return for economic growth and increasing prosperity. Within this context, official discourse still considered Russia as a strong state, but one which had to address a number of significant structural, and primarily technical, problems, namely modernizing and diversifying its economy and tackling endemic corruption,

The renewed sense of uncertainty and lack of direction that emerged under Medvedev was not immediately remedied by the return of Putin to the presidency in 2012. Indeed, rather than representing a return of a strong leader to provide a new sense of direction, as many had forecast, Putin's return has seen the regime scrambling to find a suitable ideology or political agenda capable of ensuring the continuation of the status quo. Thus far, the national priorities outlined by the third Putin presidency have increasingly resembled a narrow focus on ensuring the survival and maintenance of the regime, and latterly on the promotion of patriotism and traditional Russian values, an agenda previously reserved for the fringes of Russia's social and political spectrum. Within this official discourse, Russia is seen as under threat from actors both within and beyond, and who are often said to be acting in concert, that are intent on both undermining the traditional values underpinning Russia and its strength, and seeing Russia return to a state of weakness. By 2014, the regime seemed to be consolidating a new patriotic programme and vision for Russia, in which it was positioned as standing up to such actors, both at home and abroad, and as working to preserve the uniqueness of Russia, and its status as a 'great power'. At home, claiming to be a bastion of traditional values, securitizing those actors seen as standing against a patriotic Russia and moving to limit the extent of influence that foreign actors have over Russian domestic affairs. And abroad, taking a strong stance against what the regime saw as the 'illegal' removal of the Yanukovych in Ukraine, and stressing Russia's patriotic duty to protect the interests of 'Russian compatriots' abroad in relation to its annexation of Crimea and support for anti-Kiev groups in eastern Ukraine. Illustrative of the continual changes within its political programme and discourse on state identity since coming to power, the Putin regime of 2014 can be seen as outlining a vision for Russia that is in part centred on undoing and reversing many of the original policy choices and themes of its first years in power.

An evolution in security priorities: from strengthening the state to regime security

Alongside the radical overhaul of national priorities during the 2000s outlined previously, the Russian security agenda also underwent a dramatic shift, particularly within the domestic sphere. In the early 2000s, domestic structural collapse, secessionism and failing economy were all securitized as the biggest threats to Russia's internal security, in relation to the fear that Russia was becoming a 'weak' state, and that decisive action needed to be taken to rebuild Russia as a 'strong' state. The primary threat to Russia's security and future was therefore Russia itself, and hence redressing domestic weakness, instabilities and threats was prioritized over foreign policy. At the same time, this weakened Russia was seen as partly due to it being a victim of both the impacts of globalization and the proliferation of 'new' transnational security threats, primarily international terrorism. Combining these emphasizes the redressing of the weakness of the state from within and the new globalized and transnational threat of international terrorism. The main issue on the security agenda was bringing the restive Chechen republic firmly back under Moscow's control, and thus removing the prime threat of secessionism within the Federation. In external affairs, the return of Russia to the status of a 'great power' once it had addressed its domestic weakness was set as a mid-term goal, and to this end, Putin called for international cooperation on addressing the challenge on international terrorism.

By the mid-2000s, Russia was transitioning to a new stage of development in its state identity discourse, but not one in which domestic insecurities had been eliminated. On the contrary, as the Putin regime increasingly came to adopt an authoritarian position in the aftermath of the colour revolutions, particularly the 'Orange revolution' in Ukraine in 2004, with which regime security came to the fore, and was seen as a form of national security within Russia's security agenda. At the same time, as a state security actor, Russia was being progressively presented as a 'strong' or at least 'stronger' state, with many of the weaknesses identified in 2000 systematically said to have been addressed during Putin's second term. This was crystallized in the opening paragraph of the 2009 National Security Strategy, which outlined that Russia had overcome the major 'systemic political and socio-economic crisis of the end of the 20th century'. This combination of discourses thus began to equate the security of the state with the maintenance, strength and extent of control of the regime. Indeed, a key difference between the 2000 and 2009 National Security Strategy documents, as noted by Giles, was in their perspective on individual rights. While previously the maintenance of individual rights was deemed a primary concern, now they were intrinsically linked with and guaranteed by state and societal security, rather than functioning as a priority above or primary to state security. In this way, any attempt to change or undermine Russia's political order, its sovereignty or state power came to be securitized as a major threat to wider national security.

By the late-2000s, the focus on regime security retained a prime position within the security agenda, but a change in the ordering of threats to the regime was evident. Reflecting a shifting domestic and external environment and Medvedev's modernization agenda, economic security began to overshadow international terrorism as the key security priority on the security agenda. The impact of the global financial crisis saw economic security together with a focus on need for technological development and ensuring energy security situated alongside fears about the emergence of conflicts over resources as key future security concerns. Furthermore, in the wake of the 2008 Russian-Georgia conflict and more recently the 2014 Ukraine crisis, an emphasis on strengthening Russia's border security across its Far East and the Arctic and emerged, together with an increasingly concern about state management of information security, with the colour revolutions in other post-Soviet state and the protests against the regime in 2011/2012 seen as the product of insecure information spaces.

Thus, the shifting prioritization within the domestic security agenda has largely mirrored changes within the wider national priorities. As such, the Putin regime's initial security focus at the start of the 2000s, in line with the concern about Russia's domestic structural weakness, revolved around preventing the country from succumbing to the centrifugal forces, by among other things addressing secessionism. Over the course of 2000s, however, with concerns about state weakness giving way to a preoccupation with strengthening the regime's security, the domestic agenda has been dominated by targeting foreign and domestic enemies that were said to be trying to undermine the existing order from within.

By contrast to the domestic security agenda, Russia's foreign security agenda has remained fairly consistent in terms of its basic principles and concerns since 2000, as demonstrated in the similarity of the official Foreign Policy Concepts (2000, 2008, 2013), National Security Strategies (2000, 2009) and military doctrines (2000, 2010) which set out Russia's foreign security agenda. Whilst it was suggested that large-scale conflict was now an unlikely scenario, NATO has continued to be presented as a threat since 2000 due to its build-up of forces and troops, the deployment of strategic missile defence systems and what was said to be the attempts of certain NATO members to destabilize Russia from within. As set out in its 2010 Military Doctrine, Russia continued to reserve the right to use nuclear forces in retaliation to the weapons of mass destruction or nuclear weapons strike against Russia, as well the possibility of using its forces outside its territory in order to protect Russia's interest and that of its citizens, and to ensure international peace and security. One of the most changeable elements to Russia's foreign security policy since 2000 has been its zigzagging relationship with the West, which has shifted through a spirit of potential cooperation and rapprochement in the early 2000, to a downward spiral throughout the mid-2000s, a partial 'reset' in the late 2000s, followed by a further downturn particularly since Putin's return to the presidency in 2012, and most notably in relation to the 2014 Ukraine crisis.

Since coming to power in 2000, the Putin regime has repeatedly struggled in its attempts to manage Russia's diminished international role, while, at the same time, attempting to retain its position as a 'great power'. Russian officials have continually argued that their voice should be heard on key issues in international security, such as the 'war on terror' of the mid-2000s, the crises in Afghanistan (2001–2014) and Iraq (2003), nuclear proliferation particularly over Iran, questions about humanitarian interventions regarding Libya (2011) and Syria (2011–2014), and in terms of what Russia considers its region, most notably in term of the 2008 Russia-Georgia conflict and the 2013/2014 Ukraine crisis.

Conclusion

However, on all these issues and over the course of this period, the regime has increasingly had to face the prospect that it may be overshadowed or excluded from the centre-stage of world affairs, due to Russia's decline relative to the West and also 'rising powers' such as China. Yet, this has not made Russia's foreign and security position any more pliant to foreign or external influences, as demonstrated by its bellicose position towards the Ukrainian crisis and the incorporation of Crimea into Russia in March 2014.

Indeed, the Ukraine crisis in 2013–2014 demonstrated that despite its domestic structural weaknesses and limited future economic prospects, the current regime is seeking to promote a more assertive position internationally. Indeed, playing hard-ball on the international, and even more so on the regional, stage, serves as a method by which the regime promotes Russia as a power that needs to be taken into account in international and regional security affairs. Russian official discourse surrounding the 2014 Ukraine crisis has laid bare the extent to which nationalist and patriotic fervour is now central to the 2010s-Putin regime, both domestically and in its foreign security agenda. This is at odds with the early Putin approach, in which aggressive patriotism played a much lesser role in Russia's foreign policy. Yet, the regime's discourse during the Ukrainian crisis, however, reinforces the original thesis of this book that domestic and foreign security concerns are tightly interrelated sides of the same policy agenda. Indeed, as noted by Lukyanov (2012b), in Putin's address to the Federal Assembly in December 2012: 'the external and the internal were inseparably intertwined; one fed the other, creating a turbulent "swirl" '. Thus, mitigating external risks in order to ensure domestic stability, development and prosperity domestically is critically important to the regime's security policy. Yet, despite the assertive stances in foreign security policy taken by the Putin regime in recent years, seemingly aimed at protecting domestic stability, there seems little chance that these moves will reverse Russia's decline. With ongoing domestic problem and long-standing fractious relations with its major foreign partners, such as the US and the EU, and uncertainty surrounding its future relations with the other major world players, particularly China, Russia's role and position in the world remains in the balance.

In summary, Russia's security agenda since 2000 can be found nested within the disjointed and often contradictory sets of national priorities. Throughout this period, domestic security considerations have remained tightly interlinked not only with the overall security agenda, but also wider political priorities. Fears about terrorism, the role played by external, and particularly Western, actors in both Russia and the international system, wider regional and economic insecurity, regime security and Russia's role and place in the world have all been prevalent in both internal and external security policy. Indeed, this overlap between internal and external security agendas is symptomatic of the regime's movement towards a broader security agenda within which any actor or activity seen as threat to the regime has been included and in the process of which the domestic and foreign contexts have been regularly blurred and have been often claimed to be interdependent.

Official discourse on Chechnya and the North Caucasus: state-breaker to state-maker?

This book has argued that in analysing Russia's security policy on a specific issue, it is necessary to take into account not only the discourse and practices towards this issue area, but also its interplay with the wider security sphere and agenda in which it is embedded. Equally, in accounting for Russia as a generalized security actor, it is also important to take into account how specific issue areas and the policy towards them impact and shape wider national and security agendas. Furthermore, it has been suggested that in seeking to examine this relationship between an individual policy area and the wider security agenda, it is beneficial to take a longitudinal perspective that captures the way in which shifting and divergent policy strands develop over time. In this way, this book's study of official Russian discourse and policy on Chechnya/North Caucasus has shown how this policy and discourse was shaped by macro-state identity and security discourses, and likewise how it shaped these wider policy priorities. In addition, it has highlighted how this interplay, and its impacts on policy in this single issue area and macro-state and security discourses, has changed and evolved since 2000.

In the preceding chapters, it has been outlined that the Putin regime's policy towards and construction of discourses in relation to Chechnya and the North Caucasus have been, to greater and lesser extents across this period, filtered through its wider national priorities. In the early 2000s, the main conceptual prism through which the regime articulated Russian state identity and its position as a security actor was that of fear about an imminent national collapse and the need to eliminate all perceived sources of domestic insecurity, of which terrorism and Chechnya was a key concern. Yet, only half a decade later, with the macro discourse on state identity having changed from positioning Russia as a 'weak' state to that of a 'strong' one, the continued low-scale terrorist activity in Chechnya, alongside a significant intensification and increase in regularity in large-scale terrorist acts and insecurity within the republics neighbouring Chechnya, was no longer presented by the regime as an existential threat to Russia. It was rather said to be a problem that could be solved through administrative means alone. Hence, these problems were recast with a different significance by the regime, regardless of the fact that arguably little had changed on the ground, or rather that the geographical locus of the insecurity shifted to the wider North Caucasus. Indeed, by the time of Putin's third term as president, the continued insecurity in combination with a sense that the regime had run out of ideas about how to address it, saw the North Caucasus increasingly treated as distinct part of Russia. In spite of the regime's stated aim of reintegrating, first, Chechnya and, then, the North Caucasus as 'normal' parts of the federation, by 2014 it was becoming increasingly 'normal' for it to approach the region as a permanently insecure and distinct space to their political programme for the rest of the country. This was not, however, presented as a threat or challenge to this political programme, as it had been in the early 2000s.

At the same time, the proclaimed success of federal policy, and consequently, the gradual desecuritization of the Chechen issue, also played an important role within the change in official discourse on state identity and security priorities, The, at least partial, mitigation of the Chechen threat as articulated between 1999 and 2001, enabled the recasting of Russia as a 'strong' or at least 'stronger' state, in contrast to the 'weak' or 'weaker' state that official discourse depicted in 2000. This mutual transformation of discourses were facilitated by a shift in prioritization of security concerns, with Chechnya replaced as the number one concern by the West and regime security during the mid-2000s. This reordering saw developments on the ground in Chechnya and the wider North Caucasus relegated to a less prescient position in its security agenda than previously, with attention focused on this new prime concern. When the ongoing insecurity in the Chechnya and the North Caucasus was discussed, it was with a different tone and significance, one which no longer placed such events as an integral and immediate danger requiring swift action. This change in significance within both national and Chechnya-specific priorities accounts for the way in which the emergence of Ramzan Kadyrov as an independent Chechen leader with significant influence and power over the republic was not treated as an existential threat, as the rise of similar regimes had been in the past, most notably the Ichkerian administration under Maskadov. By contrast, the strong leadership of Kadyrov was said to be a sign of Russia's strength and progress, and not a threat to the influence and control of Moscow over far-flung regions.

On the basis of this tracing of the ongoing shifts in the interrelationship between wider national and security discourses and that of this specific issue area, this book has shown that the Putin regime's policies and discourses on Chechnya, as well as the North Caucasus, was shaped by, and also played a role in shaping, its generalized security discourse and prioritization to a much greater extent than is often acknowledged in the current literature.

Analysing Russia as a security actor: the internal-external security nexus and a longitudinal approach

As outlined in the opening chapters, this book – in contrast to many accounts of Russia as a security actor – takes the perspective that considerations of domestic security should be given equal, if not greater, weight to external ones, in seeking to account for Russia as a security actor. Although Russia's discourse on international affairs often involves proclaimations about 'great power' status and high-profile disagreements and confrontations between Russia and the West make headlines around the world, a careful analysis of the Putin regime's security agenda reveals that Russia can be considered as much of a domestically-orientated, as a foreign-orientated, actor in security affairs.

Even with domestic security concerns about Chechnya and terrorism somewhat fading from view within the regime's security discourses in recent years, they have, for the most part, been replaced by other domestically-focused issues, namely an emphasis on regime security, and a fear that independent groups operating within the domestic space in league with Western actors are seeking to undermine the existing political order. At the same time, there have in recent years been major dalliances in foreign security affairs, such as the regime's emphasis on vetoing Western-sponsored UN resolutions to endorse intervention in Syria that have made headlines both inside and outside of Russia and which have been at top of the Ministry of Foreign Affairs' agenda. However, these in turn are often read through the domestic security lenses. And, against the background of the ousting of the Yanukovych regime in Ukraine by popular protest in 2014, which set a dangerous precedent from the perspective of the Putin regime in light of the ongoing activities of a protest movement within Russia, this emphasis on internal security concerns, or rather regime security concerns, is likely to be further enhanced, if their reaction to the Orange revolution in 2004 is anything to go by.

So, while much of the popular attention may be taken up by the perception that Putin is seeking to challenge Western actors in international affairs, many of the factors underlying such discourses stem from the domestic, rather than the foreign, security context. Furthermore, changes within domestic security discourses have shaped the overall tone of wider national and security priorities as much as developments within the external sphere. Notably, the regime's successful articulation of the desecuritization of Chechnya as an existential threat in the internal sphere was influential in their wider re-articulation of security priorities from focusing on existential threats to security 'risks', and from state security to regime security.

Aside from arguing that domestic security concerns play a key part alongside foreign ones in shaping the Putin regime's discourse on national priorities, its wider security agenda and its individual policies since coming to power in 2000, this book also suggests that the two security realms – internal and external – are often directly interlinked and interrelated. Indeed, while there has been a significant shift and evolution in Russia's security policy and discourse since 2000, a tight interconnection between internal and external security contexts has remained a constant throughout this period.

A prominent case-in-point is Russia's relationship with the West on security, and other matters, which has ebbed and flowed between friends and foes, often in direct conjunction with how confident the Putin regime has been in asserting stability and security in domestic and foreign affairs. Until the return of Putin to the presidency in 2012, which to some extent has served as a significant shift in tone within the relationship, a pattern in the regime's approach to is relationship with the West was evident. During periods in which Russia was domestically insecure, notably the early 2000s and around the 2008 global financial crisis, tended to correlate with the regime taking a more favourable view on developing better relations with the West. While the relationship has soured during periods in which the regime was proclaiming more confidently that the domestic context was secure and stable, and thus positioning Russia as a 'strong' state within the international system. In other words, during the 2000s there was an inverse relationship between the regime's articulation of Russia as a 'strong' domestic security actor and its external relationship with the West. Taking this into account, this book posits that in order to garner a more nuanced reading of the most prescient drivers and factors within Russian security discourse and practice in external affairs, it is necessary to consider their relationship to domestic security discourses and priorities.

As well as highlighting the false dichotomy between internal and external security and macro and individual discourses and policies, this study has sought to highlight the significance and value of situating Russia's security agenda within a contextually-sensitive and longitudinal analysis. It is, thus, argued that the nature of a security actor cannot be assumed to be fixed, static and inherent. As the previous chapters have shown, Russia's official security agenda and individual security policies have significantly changed since Putin came to power in 2000. Hence, rather than presenting Russia or the Putin regime as a more or less fixed entity, a longitudinal approach reveals that the nature of Russia as a security actor has evolved in a much more dynamic manner than is usually suggested.

Indeed, the regime's security discourse and prioritizations during Putin's third term as president are in many ways a radical departure from those of the 2000s. The focus on anti-Western discourse and the painting of the US and Europe as a threat both domestically and internationally is in stark contrast to the approach the regime took in the early 2000s, during which time, as noted previously, they responded to domestic uncertainty and insecurity by seeking to build more cooperative relations with the West. This would seem to suggest that the current domestic context of insecurity facing the regime should be considered as much greater than the previous period, or rather that the regime seems less able to formulate a coherent response to it, for it combines not only structural and economic weaknesses, but also entails a much more volatile and unpredictable leader in the figure of Putin. Until recently, most commentators depicted Putin as an astute leader able to navigate the choppy waters of foreign and security policy with significant coherence and skill. However, in his third term of president, many have questioned these previous assumptions in light of changes within the domestic and international contexts in which the regime is operating. Furthermore, his turn towards a strongly patriotic, and in many respects more traditionalist, political project stands in contrast to several elements of his political vision of the 2000s, such as opening Russia up to the global economy, a statist and all-inclusive concept of patriotism, and an emphasis on reintegrating the North Caucasus as a 'normal' region within the Russian Federation. And, hence, interpreting the Putin regime's response to the current situation, based solely on previous examples of their actions in the 2000s, neglects important changes in the context shaping this response.

Such changes in context should not be neglected in analysing Russia as a security actor, whereby the problems, events or circumstances facing the regime may appear outwardly to be similar to previous cases and periods, but as both the internal context of the regime, and its contextual place with regard to the Russian domestic space and wider international space is constantly evolving, their conceptualization, representation and response to these problems, events or circumstances will most likely be different. Therefore, it is important to trace the evolution of a security actor and the context in which it operates, in order to situate it within the specific temporal context in which it acts rather than uncritically drawing implications for previous cases that will exclude the contextual nuances shaping their discourse and behaviour in this particular case.

Implications for IR theory and critical security studies

As well offering a number of insights about how we can understand and characterize Russia – and the Putin regime – as a security actor, this book also seeks to make a contribution to the literature on International Relations (IR) and Critical Security Studies, respectively. Proceeding from its post-positivist and context-centred perspective, and drawing on the empirical insights outlined previously, it is argued, first, that a more constructivist perspective on notions of 'strong' and 'weak' states provides a more nuanced reading of how these concepts impact on the nature of state security actors. And second, how a wider consideration of the discourses that contextualize an actor's security policy can strengthen the 'securitization' framework by enabling a more fluid understanding of the relationship between securitization and desecuritization discourses and a more contextually-informed understanding of 'normal' politics in non-Western contexts, how security discourse relate to wider political discourses and how the significance of notions of securitization, desecuritization and normal politics can change within a context over time. In this way, this book hopes to contribute to the emerging agenda of applying theories and concepts from Critical Security Studies to non-Western contexts, and provide some insights into how non-Western powers, such as Russia, can better be analysed as security actors.

Theories of strong and weak states

As detailed in both the introduction and theoretical framework chapter, the concepts of 'weak' and 'strong' states have often been employed within the IR and security studies literature as an objectively-identifiable binary framework for assessing and categorizing states (see for e.g. Ayoob 1995; Desch 1996; Rotberg 2003), whereby states with limited control over their domestic affairs are deemed to be 'weak', while those with coherent and stable domestic political contexts are viewed as 'strong'. However, as argued in Chapter 2, from a post-positivist perspective such an approach overlooks the discursive impact of labelling a state as 'strong' and 'weak', including within a state actor's own discourse, has on shaping how states construct themselves as security actors, define their security priorities and enact their policies. In the process of tracing Russia's official state identity and security discourses since 2000, including how it has at various times constructed itself as 'weak' and 'strong', this book has highlighted three modifications that should be made to how the literature treats the notions of 'strong' and 'weak' states.

First, it is suggested that rather than seeing these notions as objective labels that are imposed onto a state by an analyst, they should be seen as discourses that can in certain circumstances be developed by the state actor's themselves. This study has traced the way in which the Putin regime went from presenting Russia as a 'weak' state to promoting itself as a 'strong' and more powerful actor in the mid-late 2000s. Hence, in the case of Russia during the 2000s, the concepts of 'weak' and 'strong' states became a key referent frame for the Putin regime's articulation of Russian state identity, which in turn shaped its definition of its security agenda – from concentrating on domestic challenges to its existence and status a 'strong state' during the early 2000s in which state identity was positioned as being that of a 'weak' state, to a shift towards a more assertive foreign policy and an emphasis on regime security from the mid-2000s onwards, as state identity was rearticulated to position itself as a 'strong' state – and the nature of specific practices, rather than functioning as framework for objectively determining Russia's actual status as a strong or weak state.

Second, the prevailing ideas in the literature associated with the categorization of states as 'strong' and 'weak' assumes an objective quality to this classification, but in practise these labels function as discourses that do not need to rest on such a definitive judgement of a given reality. Hence, the Putin regime was able to identify itself as a 'strong' state within its official discourse with notable success, even though it continued to face significant internal security challenges, some of which it had previously argued was the reason why Russia was becoming a 'weak' state. This depiction and identification of Russia as a 'strong' state, while internal security issue remained unresolved, directly contradicts the binary model of classification within much of the literature. This model is based on objective criterion for differentiating between 'weak' and 'strong' states, which see the absence of significant internal challenges to the authority of the regime and the fundamentals of the nation-state as the criteria for identifying a state as 'strong'. According to this criterion, with the regime's sovereign control over parts of the North Caucasus still in doubt due to ongoing insurgencies, Russia in the mid-2000s should have been categorized as a 'weak' and not a 'strong' state. That the Putin regime was able to represent Russia as a 'strong' state with significant acceptance and resonance within and beyond Russia illustrates the constructed nature of the notions of 'strong' and 'weak' states. Indeed, the significance of these notions lies not in the classification of states according to a set of universal objective criteria, but in how they are articulated and utilized by state actors, and the significance and impact this has on their wider national and security agendas.

Taking this into account, a third modification to existing usage of the concepts of 'strong/weak' states, is to take them as social constructs, and investigate and trace the discourses and practices related to them and their impact within a particular context. It has been shown that the regime's rearticulation of Russia as a 'strong' state in the mid-2000s had significant consequences for its policy and discourse on domestic insecurities, and in particular Chechnya and the wider North Caucasus. It entailed a refocusing away from the instability in this region

Conclusion 201

and towards the West as the main threat to the regime, in spite of the fact that terrorist, insurgent and generalized violent activity in the region led to significant, which previously was seen as top priority, continued. In the new construction of Russia as a 'strong' state, these issues were silenced, as the regime's attention was devoted elsewhere, most recently on the crisis in Ukraine and Russia's annexation of Crimea.

In light of the focus on 'rising powers' and changing the global order that has emerged in recent years, notions and concepts of 'strong/weak' states are likely to be drawn on to analyse these actors and processes, with questions being asked about whether 'rising powers' have successfully transitioned from 'weak' and peripheral states, to 'strong' and influential ones. In so doing, attention should be given to investigating the way in which notions such as 'weak/strong' states, 'great' or 'rising' powers and 'emerging' powers are constructed within these actor's discourse on their state identity and security agenda, and with what effect on their policy and behaviour as security actors, rather than using these notions as objective criteria against which these states are then judged.

Implications from the Russian-Chechen case study for (de)securitization studies

As set out in Chapter 2 and then operationalized during the subsequent empirical chapters, this book has drawn on a modified version of the Copenhagen School's securitization framework. In utilizing this framework to examine Russia's securitization and then desecuritization of Chechnya since 2000, this study has reached several conclusions that of relevance to the ongoing debate about the development of (de)securitization theory. These insights relate to two main respects of securitization theory: first, the nature of, and interrelationship between, desecuritization and securitization processes; and second, how best to investigate and capture the divergent and multifaceted nature of (de)securitizations processes in empirical analysis.

Desecuritization and securitization processes: the nature of the interrelationship

In contrast to the way in the original framework is laid out, the case of Russia's securitization, and then desecuritization, of Chechnya since 2000 suggests that rather than seeing them as mutually contradictory and exclusive, processes and discourses of securitization and desecuritization processes can in fact be deployed simultaneously. Indeed, as outlined in previous chapters, the Putin regime utilized discourses and practices that simultaneously securitized and desecuritized Chechnya to the end of rearticulating Chechnya as a normal republic in the Russian Federation, or in Copenhagen School terminology 'normal politics' in Putin's Russia. This centred, on the one hand, on continuing to securitize those groups deemed to be a threat, whilst, on the other, trying to re-establish political structures and normal life in Chechnya. This suggests that dual securitizations/desecuritizations can be used in order to deal with, pacify or normalize a particular issue or geographical area – particularly once the goals of an initial securitization process have been achieved.

This insight about the nature of such dual securitization/desecuritization approaches echoes an increasingly noted phenomenon in terms of desecuritization: the use of national development and economic policies discourses as a form of desecuritization. Other scholars have noted such occurrences in China's attempts to deal with instability and frontier security in its Western region provinces (Cui and Li 2011), and within the growing interlinkages between security policies and development programmes, particularly in the case of international humanitarian assistance in relation to new wars in Africa, the Balkans, Central Asia (Duffield 2001, cited in MacKenzie 2009, p. 243). Furthermore, this two-pronged approach that combines both security measures and development/state-building strategies, to some extent, resembles the counterinsurgency strategies deployed by the Western-led coalitions in Afghanistan and Iraq (see Betz and Cormack 2009; Dixon 2009; Lopez 2007; Metz 2003). Similarly, to the Russian-Chechen case, these Western-led operations were simultaneously focused on dealing with security threats on the ground by targeting those identified as the insurgents, whilst bringing in development and state-building programmes aimed at alleviating poor living conditions and restoring political life to the area concerned. Indeed, in all these cases, this two-pronged approach was presented as the most effective and efficient way of dealing with the diverse challenges in these difficult terrains. The diversity of these cases also illustrates that this security/development nexus is not only the preserve of the international community or Western actors, but is also being exercised by non-Western actors. Whilst their success on the ground in restoring normal life to these difficult contexts is debatable (Slim 2004), the use by the Putin regime of simultaneous securitization (targeting of insurgents) and desecuritization (state-building programmes) discourses and practices in relation to Chechnya in the mid-2000s can, nonetheless, be seen as part of a larger trend in 'doing' security/peacebuilding/development during recent years.

At the same time, another way in which to account for the dual securitization/desecuritization process followed by the Putin regime is to consider it as an intermediary stage between a full securitization and a full desecuritization, akin to Oelsner's (2005) suggestion that desecuritization processes develop in two stages – first, centred on peace stabilization, and then moving towards peace consolidation (Oelsner 2005). In the Russian-Chechen case, the deployment of both security and stabilization methods during the mid-2000s appears to correspond to the first stage in this two-step process. However, this conceptualization is more problematic for accounting for a 'second' stage of desecuritization in the case of Russia and Chechnya. Since the mid-to-late 2000s, the federal Russian authorities have attempted to redefine their relationship with their former Chechen antagonists, as part of the second phase of normalization of Chechnya. However, as detailed in previous chapters, this has centred less on peace consolidation, and more on the decentralization and delegation of security functions from federal to local republican authorities. Thus, the second stage of desecuritization is based on implicit and subtle changes to governance structures, particularly in relation to 'who' is in charge of 'doing' or 'speaking' security in Chechnya, rather than moves to end all security measures/policies on the ground. If 'peace consolidation' is meant to represent the end of security measures, then in light of the ongoing security operations on the ground in Chechnya carried out by the Chechen authorities themselves, it is unlikely that Chechnya itself will reach the full stage of reconciliation any time soon. Hence, the case of the Putin regime's attempts to desecuritize Chechnya highlights the importance that context plays in determining the nature of, and the path taken by, desecuritizations. Therefore, this study suggests that it is imperative to trace the evolution of such desecuritization discourses and practices, situating their role and significance within the context in which they operate, rather than assuming a universal and static sequence of steps through which a desecuritization process must proceed.

Desecuritization in non-Western contexts: what is normal politics?

Following this logic that (de)securitizations need to be considered in relation to the context in which they operate, the complexity and specificity of the Russian authorities desecuritization of Chechnya detailed in this book, supports Wilkinson's (2007) assertion that one must be careful when applying (de)securitization theories to non-Western contexts, in order to avoid falling into the trap of universalizing Western-centric assumptions about what constitutes normal politics (see also Vuori 2008). Within the Copenhagen model of securitization, a conceptual difference is identified between 'normal' politics and 'securitized' or 'exceptional' politics in which an actor may assert the need for extraordinary measures not sanctioned in 'normal' politics to meet this heightened state of security, with a successful and completed securitization moving an issue from 'normal' to 'exceptional' politics, and a successful and completed desecuritization seeing an issue returned from 'exceptional' to 'normal' politics. However, as noted by Acharya, this difference between 'normal' politics and 'exceptional' politics has little relevance in some contexts. He argues that,

> one cannot claim securitization and politicization to be two neatly separate or distinct outcomes. Securitization is essentially a political act. But the nature of politics can differ from country to country, hence securitization is highly context dependent, the degree of which depends not just on the issue area, but also on the political system of securitizing states, and their leadership.
> (Acharya 2006, p. 250)

Furthermore, the question raised by investigating desecuritization processes in some non-Western contexts, such as Russia, is the extent to which one can talk about a desecuritization as 'taking place', or even the possibility that such a desecuritization can occur within political/security contexts that are inherently highly securitized at the outset of a particular (de)securitization process. In investigating contexts that differ significantly from the 'Western' liberal-democratic model and culture of politics, it is necessary to move away from what McDonald calls 'the close relationship between democratic deliberation and desecuritization' (McDonald 2011, p. 283) within the classical model of (de)securitization. And, instead, concentrate in allowing the local context to come through in the analysis by adopting a more inductive analytical approach.

Thus, rather than trying to objectively deduce whether or not an issue has been desecuritized, or in other words, has it been returned to the sphere of 'normal' open politics, a more appropriate approach is to consider if it has been returned to the 'normal' politics of the context in which it was enacted. In this study, the desecuritization of Chechnya entailed the republic being returned to what constituted 'normal' Russian politics during Putin's second term. The desecuritization of Chechnya involved the emergence of the authoritarian Kadyrov regime in Chechnya and its represseive security practices. If viewed from the perspective of a Western European context, such a desecuritization actually be interpreted as indistinguishable from continued 'securitized' politics, discourses and practices, but which, within the wider political context of Russia and the North Caucasus during the second half of 2000s, represented something akin to – albeit a extreme version of – 'normalized' politics.

Desecuritization with a wider political context: divergent and multifaceted processes

Taking the previous observations into account, the dual approach of securitization and desecuritization towards Chechnya, followed by the Russian authorities, can be seen as a series of different strategies that intended to bring the Chechen issue back into the fold of what they conceived of as 'normal' politics in Putin's Russia. Indeed, the multiple forms that a desecuritization may take has become a discussion point within the securitization literature. In a recent article, Hansen suggested that a process of desecuritizaiton may take four different forms: One, change through stabilization, whereby 'an issue is cast in terms other than security, but where the larger conflict still looms'. Two, replacement, whereby 'an issue is removed from the securitised, while another securitisation takes its place'. Three, rearticulation, whereby 'an issue is moved from the securitised to the politicised due to a resolution of the threats and dangers'. Four, silencing, whereby an issue is depoliticized and 'marginalises potentially insecure subjects' (Hansen 2012, p. 529). In the case of the Putin regime's desecuritization of Chechnya, most of the four sets/types of desecuritization processes outlined by Hansen (2012) were in evidence.

While some aspects of the regime's policy of normalization centred on rearticulating Chechnya from representing an existential threat to being considered as a normal issue like any other in Russian politics, other strands sought to silence the Chechen question altogether, particularly during the early stages of this normalization drive (early-to-mid 2000s) when federal control over the area was not yet completely assured. At the same time, there was also a process of altering Chechnya's role and position within the Russian security agenda, from being the epicentre of insecurity and the prime threat to Russian security to gradually being replaced by newer issues coming onto the agenda. This involved a slow securitization of the whole region of the North Caucasus, while simultaneously arguing that Chechnya no longer posed an existential threat. This securitization of the wider North Caucasus was built upon many of the discursive constructs that had been initially used to articulate the existential threat that Chechnya represented to the Russian Federation between 1999 and 2001. As the regime gradually desecuritized and deprioritized the Chechen issue within wider state and national security discourse, a form of a détente between Russia and Chechnya emerged, whereby the threat from Chechnya appeared to be fading from national attention only to re-emerge once more and be asserted as a prime threat at times of major terrorist incidents, most notably those in Beslan (2004) and Dubrovka (2002), before being sidelined again thereafter.

In addition to these four forms of desecuritization, akin to Hansen's (2012) suggestions, another important process in the case of Russian discourse on Chechnya from the mid-2000s onwards was that of historicization, whereby the threat from Chechnya was rearticulated as a 'past' threat that Russia should never return to. As argued in chapters 8 and 10 historicization of this problem area into Russia's recent history became an important theme in Putin's attempts to normalize the region within the official Russian discourse. Taking this into account, this study suggests that in analysing desecuritization process, it is important to consider whether a discourse of historicization plays a role in this desecuritizing move.

As illustrated in previous paragraphs, Russia's attempts to deal with the Chechen issue once the initial 'securitization' was said to be complete, did not function as a single form or instance of desecuritization as is implied by the original Copenhagen model, but rather operated through the deployment of a policy of normalization that operated across many different modalities at the same time. Within such a context, it is difficult ascertain whether or not a particular issue has been successfully and completely desecuritized or not. As outlined in previous chapters, the role played by Chechnya within Russian politics and its security agenda continues to be a complex, opaque and uncertain one. And, as such, it is difficult to say definitely whether Chechnya has been fully desecuritized as an issue within Putin's Russia. This is a reflection of the fact, and borne out by the case of Russia and Chechnya, that in practice assessing the extent and success of any desecuritization may well depend on which particular aspect of the (de)securitized issue one is talking about and what criteria are being applied. In the case of Chechnya, the answer varies not only depending on which particular strand of Russia's policy is examined, but is also dependent on whether or not we are talking about Chechnya representing an existential threat to Russia's security, or a more localized security threat, for example in Chechnya itself or in the North Caucasus region more broadly. It also depends on whether or not the discussion is centred on the domestic or international level.

Hence, as others have already suggested, securitization is not defined by speech acts or static processes, but by 'incremental processes and representations' (McDonald 2008, p. 564). Neither securitization, nor desecuritization, emerge overnight or as a one-off process. As shown in the case of Russian and Chechnya, there can be a series of securitizations and desecuritizations, creating situations in which different aspects of an issue may be securitized, desecuritized or even resecuritized at different times (McDonald 2011). Therefore, when discussing the nature of (de)securitization processes, it might be more appropriate to talk about different degrees of desecuritization or desecuritization processes in relation to different issue areas or levels of analysis, rather than considering an outright process of desecuritization.

Furthermore, the empirical investigation of the Putin regime's securitization and subsequent desecuritization of Chechnya also highlights that it is not only instances of securitization that can play an important function in the realm of symbolic politics, or national identity, but so too can desecuritizations (Balzacq 2008). Indeed, perhaps somewhat unexpectedly, the more advanced the process of desecuritizing Chechnya became during the second half of the 2000s the more it acquired, or more accurately reacquired, some of its previous status as a symbolically powerful issue within wider Russian politics. In some instances, for example, it came to be used in the Russian official political discourse as a symbol of Russia rebuilding itself and its success in overcoming its earlier weaknesses. This suggests that in much the same way as in securitization processes, processes of desecuritizations can have wider implications for identity and symbolic politics.

The full cycle of (de)securitization processes

Taking all of the points raised into account, this book posits that no single instance of (de)securitization can be seen or understood in isolation, because all discourses, including the proclamation of the need to move an issue 'out' of security politics and frame it as one of 'normal' politics, are embedded within a wider context and understandings of political and security discourses and practices. Contextualizing (de)securitization processes within their particular settings and wider political and security agendas (Balzacq 2005; McDonald 2008; Cuita 2009; Stritzel 2011; Guzzini 2011) is hence crucial, in order to be able to fully ascertain the nature of these diverse processes within their particular milieu. In carrying out its analysis, this book has therefore focused not only on the way in which the Russian authorities constructed and carried out the normalization policy towards Chechnya, but it also sought to take into account the wider sets of relations, policy clusters, levels and roles that came to be associated with the issue of Chechnya.

In light of this, it is argued that in order to grasp the dynamic and evolutionary nature of (de)securitization processes, it is important to shift from investigating (de)securitizations as one-off instances of (de)securitization towards a greater use of longitudinal analyses capture (for another example of longitudinal approaches to the study of security discourses/practices see Hansen's study of the Western discourses during the Bosnian war, 2006). Indeed, without this shift, a contradiction remains between the theoretical suggestion that (de)securitizations develop not only as a result of one-off speech acts, but also incrementally across a longer period of time, and the methodological reality whereby most of the current studies of (de)securitization tend to focus on narrow time periods that provide only a snapshot of how (de)securitizations processes emerge and develop. By contrast, longitudinal approaches enable an analyst to pick out the nuances of the multifaceted and incremental nature of processes of desecuritization, which the use of narrow temporal and historical periods are unable to replicate.

Bibliography

Abdelal, J., Herrera, Y. M., Johnston, A. I. and McDermott, R. (2006) 'Identity as a Variable', *Perspectives on Politics*, 4, 4, pp. 695–712.
Abrahamsen, R. (2005) 'Blair's Africa: the politics of securitization and fear', *Alternatives: Global, Local and Political*, 30, pp. 50–80.
Acharya, A. (2006) 'Securitization in Asia: functional and normative implications', in Caballero Anthony, M., Emmers, R. and Acharya, A. *Non-traditional security in Asia: dilemmas in securitization* (Aldershot and Burlington: Ashgate), pp. 247–250.
Acharya, A. and Buzan, B. (eds) (2010) *Non-Western International Relations Theory: Persepctives on and beyond Asia* (London: Routledge).
Adler, E. (1997) 'Seizing the Middle Ground. Constructivism in World Politics', *European Journal of International Relations*, 3, 3, pp. 319–363.
Adler, E. (2002) 'Constructivism and International Relations', in Carlsnaes, W., Rise, T. and Simmons, B. A. (eds) (2002), *Handbook of International Relations* (London: Sage Publication), pp. 95–118.
Agathangelou, A. M. and Ling, L. H. M. (2009) *Transforming world politics: from empire to multiple worlds* (New York: Routledge).
Aksenyonok, A. (2008) 'Paradigm Change in Russian Foreign Policy', Russia *in Global Affairs*, 4 October–December, available at: http://eng.globalaffairs.ru/number/n_11887, accessed 17 July 2009.
Alekseeva, A. (2003) 'The ongoing hostilities meant that 'neither referendum, nor elections can give real results', NEWSru.com, 13 January, available at: www.newsru.com/russia/11jan2003/ref_pr_print.html, accessed 4 June 2010.
Alexseev, M. (2011) 'Rubles Against the Insurgency: Paradoxes from the North Caucasus continues', *PONARS Eurasia Policy Memo*, No. 157, May, available at: www.ponarseurasia.org/sites/default/files/policy-memos-pdf/pepm_157.pdf, accessed 20 June 2012.
Allison, R. (2008) 'Russia resurgent? Moscow's campaign to "coerce Georgia to peace"', *International Affairs*, 84, 6, pp. 1145–1171.
Anonymous (2003) 'What life is like in Chechnya under the Russian occupation—the realities of today's Chechnya', *Central Asian Survey*, 22, 4, pp. 459–464.
Antonenko, O. (2001) 'Putin's Gamble', *IISS Survival*, Winter, pp. 49–60.
Antonenko O. and Giegerich B. (2009) 'Rebooting NATO–Russia Relations', *Survival*, 51, 2.
Aradau, C. (2004) 'Security and the Democratic Scene: Desecuritization and Emancipation', *Journal of International Relations and Development*, 7, 4, pp. 388–413.
Aradau, C. and Van Munster, R. (2007) 'Governing Terrorism Through Risk: Taking

Precautions, (Un)Knowing the Future', *European Journal of International Relations*, 13, 1, pp. 89–116.

Aras, B. and Polat, R. K. (2008) 'From Conflict to Cooperation: Desecuritization of Turkey's Relations with Syria and Iran', *Security Dialogue*, 39, 5, pp. 495–515.

Arbatov, A. G. (2000) 'The Transformation of Russian Military Doctrine: Lessons Learned from Kosovo and Chechnya', Occasional paper no. 2, George C Marshall Centre.

Are, D. (2008) 'A Green International in the North Caucasus mountains', *Prague Watchdog*, 27 October, available at: www.watchdog.cz/?show=000000-000005-000004-000 169&lang=1, accessed 20 June 2010.

Aris, S. (2009) 'The Shanghai Cooperation Organisation: "Tackling the Three Evils". A Regional Response to Non-traditional Security Challenges or an Anti-Western Bloc?', *Europe-Asia Studies*, 61, 3, pp. 457–482.

Aris, S. (2011) *Eurasian Regionalism: Shanghai Cooperation Organisation* (Basingstoke: Palgrave Macmillan).

Arnold, R. and Foxall, A. (2012) 'Lord of the (Five) Rings Issues at the 2014 Sochi Winter Olympic Games: Guest Editors' Introduction', *Problems of Post-Communism*, 61, 1.

Ashizawa, K. (2008) 'When Identity Matters: State Identity, Regional Institution-Building, and Japanese Foreign Policy', *International Studies Review*, 10, 3, pp. 571–598.

Åslund, A. (2004) 'Russia's Economic Transformation under Putin', *Eurasian Geography and Economics*, 45, 6, pp. 397–420.

Atkinson, M. C. and Coleman, W. D. (1989) 'Strong States and Weak States', *British Journal of Political Science* 19, 1, pp. 46–67.

Åtland, K. (2008) 'Mikhail Gorbachev, the Murmansk Initiative, and the Desecuritization of Interstate Relations in the Arctic', *Cooperation and Conflict*, 43, 3, pp. 289–311.

Averre, D. (2005) 'Russia and the European Union: Convergence or Divergence?', *European Security*, 14, 2, pp. 175–202.

Averre, D. L. (2007) '"Sovereign democracy" and Russia's relations with the European Union', *Demokratizatsiya*, 15, 2, pp. 173–190.

Averre, D. (2009) 'Competing Rationalities: Russia, the EU and the 'Shared Neighbourhood', *Europe–Asia Studies*, 61, 10, pp. 1689–1713.

Ayoob, M. (1995) *The Third World security predicament state making, regional conflict, and the international system* (London: Lynne Rienner Publishers).

Babakin, A. (2002) 'Armeiskii spetsnaz na vykhod', *Rossiiskaya gazeta*, 31 October.

Babchenko, A. (2007) *One soldier's war* (Grove Press).

Bacon, E. and Renz, B. with Cooper, J. (2006) *Securitising Russia: the domestic politics of Putin* (Manchester: Manchester University Press).

Baev, P. (2004) 'Instrumentalizing Counterterrorism for Regime Consolidation in Putin's Russia', *Studies in Conflict & Terrorism*, 27, 4, pp. 337–352.

Baev, P. (2004) 'Putin's War in Chechnya: Who steers the course?' *PONARS Policy Memo* 345, available at: http://csis.org/files/media/csis/pubs/pm_0345.pdf, accessed 6 June 2010.

Baiev, K. (2004) *The Oath: A Surgeon Under Fire* (Walker & Company).

Balzacq, T. (2005) 'The Three Faces of Securitization: Political Agency, Audience and Context', *European Journal of International Relations*, 11, 2, pp. 171–201.

Balzacq, T. (2008) 'The Policy Tools of Securitization: Information Exchange, EU Foreign and Interior Policies', *Journal of Common Market Studies*, 46, 1, pp. 75–100.

Balzacq, T. (2011) 'A theory of securitization: Origins, core assumptions, and variants', in Balzacq (ed.) (2011) *Securitization Theory: How Security Problems Emerge and Dissolve* (London: Routledge), pp. 1–30.

Balzacq, T. (ed.) (2011) *Securitization Theory: How Security Problems Emerge and Dissolve* (London: Routledge).

Balzer, H. (2003) 'Managed Pluralism: Vladimir Putin's Emerging Regime', *Post-Soviet Affairs*, 19, 3, pp. 189–227.

Banner, F. (2009) ' "Beauty Will Save the World": Beauty Discourse and the Imposition of Gender Hierarchies in the Post-War Chechen Republic', *Studies in Ethnicity and Nationalism*, 9, 1, pp. 25–48.

Barakhova, A. (2004) 'Sovet Federatsii vklyuchilsya v predvybornuyu kampaniyu', *Kommersant*, 144, 8 September.

Baranov, V. (2003) 'Interview with the Commander of the United Group of Forces in North Caucasus Region, Colonel General Valery Baranov', Ministry of the Interior of the Russian Federation, 27 November, available at: www.mvd.ru/press/interview/1725, accessed 1 September 2010.

Bardeleben, J. (ed.) (2005) *Soft or Hard Borders? Managing the Divide in an Enlarged Europe* (Ashgate: Aldershot).

Barkawi, T. and Laffey, M. (2006) 'The Postcolonial Moment in Security Studies', *Review of International Studies*, 32, 2, pp. 329–352.

Beck, U. (2002) 'The Terrorist Threat: World Risk Society Revisited', *Theory, Culture and Society*, 19, 4, pp. 39–55.

Behnke, A. (2006) 'No Way Out: Desecuritization, Emancipation and the Eternal Return of the Political – A Reply to Aradau', *Journal of International Relations and Development*, 9, 1, pp. 62–69.

Belaeff, V. (2009) 'Russia Profile Weekly Experts Panel: 2009 – Russia's Year in Review', *Russia Profile*, 31 December, available at: http://russiaprofile.org/experts_panel/a1262277858.html, accessed 12 February 2011.

Bell, C. (2006) 'Biopolitical Governance in Canada'sNational Security Policy', *Security Dialogue*, 37, 2, pp. 147–165.

Bennett, V. (1998) *Crying wolf: the return of war to Chechnya* (London: Picador/Macmillan).

Bennett, V. (2007) 'From Russia with secrets', *Time Online*, 13 May available at: www.timesonline.co.uk/article/0,,18389-1610952,00.html, accessed 14 September 2009.

Bessmertnykh, A. (2003) 'The Iraq War and Its Implications', *International Affairs*, 4, 49, pp. 24–36.

Betz, D. and Cormack, A. (2009) 'Iraq, Afghanistan and British Strategy', *ORBIS*, 53, 2, pp. 319–336.

Bevir, M. and Rhodes, R. (2004) 'Interpretation as Method, Explanation and Critique: A Reply', *The British Journal of Politics and International Relations*, 6, 2.

Bigg, C. (2008) 'Chechnya: Is Kadyrov Maintaining Hold On Power?', Radio Free Europe Radio Liberty, 27 April available at: www.rferl.org/content/article/1109638.html, accessed 4 August 2009.

Bigo, D. (2002) 'Security and immigration: towards a critique of governmentality of unease', *Alternatives*, 27, 1, pp. 63–92.

Bilgin, P. (2007) 'Making Turkey's Transformation Possible: Claiming "Security-speak" – not Desecuritization!', *Southeast European and Black Sea Studies*, 7, 4, pp. 555–571.

Bilgin, P. (2008). 'Thinking Past "Western IR" ', *Third World Quarterly*, 29, 1, pp. 5–23.

Bilgin, P. (2010) ' "Western-centrism" of Security Studies: "Blind Spot" or Constitutive Practice?', *Security Dialogue*, 41, 6, pp. 615–622.

Blandy, C. W. (2003) 'Chechnya, Normalization', *Conflict Studies Research Centre, Caucasus Series*, 40.

Blandy, C. W. (2007) 'North Caucasus Advent of Mountain brigades', *Caucasus Series Advanced Research and Assessment Group*, Defence Academy of the United Kingdom, November, available at: www.da.mod.uk/colleges/arag/document-listings/caucasus/07(35)CWB.pdf, accessed 13 June 2010.

Blum, D. W. (ed.) (2008) *Russia and globalization: identity, security, and society in an era of change* (Washington DC: Woodrow Wilson Center Press).

Bobrova, O. (2009) 'Aushev is not a phantom', *Novaya gazeta*, 29 June, p. 7.

Bobrova, O. (2012) 'Let words remain words', *Novaya gazeta*, 6 August, p. 5.

Bogomolov, Y. (2004) 'Beslannyi put' za svobodu i nezavisimost' mirolyubivoi Ichkerii', *Rossiiskaya gazeta*, 16 September.

Boikov, R. (2001) 'Zhizn' v Chechne vozrozdaetsya', *Krasnaya zvezda*, 15 September.

Booth, K. (ed.) (2005) *Critical Security Studies and World Politics* (Boulder, Colorado: Lynne Rienner Publishers).

Borisov, B. (1999) 'Rosinformtsentr soobshchaet', *Krasnaya zvezda*, 233, 2 November.

Borisov, T. (2002) 'Zakaevu "svetit" vosem' let', *Rossiiskaya gazeta*, 31 October.

Borob'ev, A. (1999) 'Bezrabotitsa – rezerv dlya naemnikov', *Rossiiskaya gazeta*, 11 September.

Bosworth, K. (2002) 'The Effect of 11 September on Russia-NATO Relations', *Perspectives on European Politics and Society*, 3, 3, pp. 361–388.

Brian, J. (ed.) (1992) *The Insecurity Dilemma: National Security of Third World States* (London: Lynne Rienner Publishers).

Browning, C. and McDonald, M. (2011) 'The Future of Critical Security Studies: Ethics and the Politics of Security', *European Journal of International Relations*, 19, 2, pp. 235–255.

Brubaker, R. and Cooper, F. (2000) 'Beyond "identity"', *Theory and Society*, 29, 1, pp. 1–47.

Bryman, A. (2001) *Social research methods* (Oxford: Oxford University Press).

Burch, K. (2002) 'Towards a Constructivist Comparative Politics', in Green, D. (ed.) (2002) *Constructivism and Comparative politics* (Armonk, NY: ME Sharpe), pp. 60–87.

Burchill, S. et al. (2nd ed.) (2001) *Theories of International Relations* (New York: Palgrave Macmillan).

Buzan, B. (1991) *People, states and fear: an agenda for international security studies in the post-cold war era* (Boulder, Colorado: Lynne Rienner).

Buzan, B. (2006) 'Will the "global war on terrorism" be the new Cold War?', *International Affairs*, 82, 6, pp. 1101–1118

Buzan, B. and Wæver, O. (1997) 'Slippery? Contradictory? Sociologically Untenable? The Copenhagen School Replies', *Review of International Studies*, 23, 2, pp. 241–250.

Buzan, B. and Wæver, O. (eds) (1998) *Security: a new framework for analysis* (Boulder, Colorado: Lynne Rienner Publishers).

Buzan, B. and Wæver, O. (2003) *Regions and powers: the structure of international security* (Cambridge: Cambridge University Press).

Buzan, B. and Hansen, L. (2009) *The evolution of international security studies* (Cambridge: Cambridge University Press).

Buzan, B., Jones, C. and Little, R. (1993) *Neorealism to Structural Realism* (New York: Columbia University Press).

Buzan, B., Wæver, O and de Wilde, J. (eds) (1998) *Security: a new framework for analysis* (Boulder, Colorado: Lynne Rienner Publishers).

Caballero Anthony, M., Emmers, R. and Acharya, A. (eds) (2006) *Non-traditional security in Asia: dilemmas in securitization* (Aldershot and Burlington: Ashgate).

Campbell, D. (1998) *Writing security: United States foreign policy and the politics of identity* (Minnesota: University of Minnesota Press).

Carlsnaes, W., Rise, T. and Simmons, B. A. (eds) (2002) *Handbook of International Relations* (London: Sage Publication).

Charap, S. (2004) 'The Petersburg Experience: Putin's Political Career and Russian Foreign Policy', *Problems of Post-Communism*, 51, 1, pp. 55–62.

Checkel, J. T. (1998) 'The constructivist turn in international relations theory', *World Politics*, 50, 2, pp. 324–348.

Checkel, J. T. (1999) 'Norms, Institutions, and National Identity in Contemporary Europe', *International Studies Quarterly*, 43, pp. 83–114.

Checkel, J. T. (2004) 'Social constructivisms in global and European politics: a review essay', *Review of International Studies*, 30, 2, pp. 229–244.

Cherkassov, A. (2003) 'Voina v Chechne i mir v Rossii. Nekotorie vliyaniya vooruzhennogo konflikta v Chechne na vnutrennyuyu politiku Rossiiskoi Federatsii – I chto s etim delati'?', *Memorial*, 8 November, available at: www.memo.ru/hr/hotpoints/caucas1/index.htm, accessed 30 August 2010.

Cheterian, V. (2008) *War and peace in the Caucasus: ethnic conflict and the new geopolitics* (New York: Columbia University Press).

Choltaev, Z. and Pohl, M. (2004) 'Between Budennovsk and Beslan', *Focal*, 44, Winter.

Cimbala, S. (2009) 'Forward to Where? U.S.-Russian Strategic Nuclear Force Reductions', *The Journal of Slavic Military Studies*, 22, 1, pp. 68–86.

CIS Member Countries (2004) 'Statement by CIS Member Countries on the State of Affairs in the OSCE', 3 July, available at: http://archive.kremlin.ru/eng/text/docs/2004/07/74223.shtml, accessed 20 August 2014.

Ciuta, F. (2009) 'Security and the problem of context: A hermeneutical critique of securitization theory', *Review of International Studies*, 35, 2.

Closs Stephens, A. and Vaughan-Williams, N. (eds) (2009) *Terrorism and the Politics of Response* (London: Routledge).

Closson, S. (2008) 'The North Caucasus after the Georgia-Russia Conflict', *Russian Analytical Digest*, 51, 4 December.

Clover, C. (2013) 'Putin decree targets elites foreign assets', *Financial Times*, 2 April, available at: www.ft.com/intl/cms/s/0/d763aaa2-9bb1-11e2-a820-00144feabdc0.html#axzz30qXe5Tkj, accessed 10 April 2014.

Clunan, A. L. (2009) *The social construction of Russia's resurgence: aspirations, identity, and security interests* (Baltimore: Johns Hopkins University Press).

Coalson, R. (2014) 'The World through the Eyes of Russian State Television', Radio Free Europe Radio Liberty, 4 April, available at: www.rferl.org/content/russia-through-eyes-of-television/25321677.html, accessed 17 April 2014.

Cockburn, P. (2002) 'Rossiya rasplachivaetsya za svoyu lozh' o vygrannoi voine', *Novaya gazeta*, 28 October.

Cornell, S. (2003) 'War against Terrorism and the Conflict in Chechnya: A Case for Distinction', *Fletcher Forum World Affairs*, 167, available at: http://heinonline.org.ezproxye.bham.ac.uk/HOL/Page?handle=hein.journals/forwa27&div=39&g_sent=1&collection=journals, accessed 20 July 2010.

Cornell, S. and Starr, F. (eds) (2009) *The Guns of August 2008: Russia's War in Georgia* (Armonk, NY: ME Sharpe).

Coskun, B. B. (2008) 'Analysing Desecuritisations: Problems and Prospects in Israeli-Palestinian Reconciliation', *Global Change, Peace & Security*, 20, 3.

Cui, S. and Li, J. (2011) '(De)securitizing frontier security in China: Beyond the positive and negative debate', *Cooperation and Conflict*, 46, 2, pp. 144–165.

Cuita, F. (2009) 'Security and the Problem of Context: A Hermeneutical Critique of Securitization Theory', *Review of International Studies*, 35, pp. 301–326.

Dannreuther, R. (2007) *International security the contemporary agenda* (Cambridge, Polity Press).

Dannreuther, R. (2010) 'Islamic radicalisation in Russia: an assessment', *International Affairs*, 86, 1, pp. 109–125.

Dannreuther, R. and March, L. (2008) 'Chechnya: Has Moscow Won?' *Survival*, 50, 4, pp. 97–112.

de Carbonnel, A. (2013) 'Putin signs law to allow him to pick Russian governors', *Reuters*, 2 April, available at: www.reuters.com/article/2013/04/02/us-russia-elections-idUSBRE9310GR20130402, accessed 15 May 2014.

de Haas, M. (2004) *Russian security and air power 1992–2002* (London: Cass).

de Haas, M. (2010) *Russia's foreign security policy in the 21st century: Putin, Medvedev and beyond* (Abingdon: Routledge).

de Waal, T. (2003) 'A journalist reflects on the two wars in Chechnya', *Central Asian Survey*, 22, 4, pp. 465–468.

Dejevsky, M. (2004) 'Russian media condemns siege 'cover-up', *The Independent*, 7 September, available at: www.independent.co.uk/news/world/europe/russian-media-condemns-siege-coverup-551611.html, accessed 12 July 2013.

Dellecker, A. and Gomart, T. (2011) *Russian energy security and foreign policy* (Abingdon and New York: Routledge).

Delyagin, M. (2012) 'How the revised Strategy-2020 could destroy the Russian economy', Valdai Discussion Club, 30 March, available at: http://valdaiclub.com/economy/40600.html, accessed 30 August 2012.

Demchenko, A. (1999) 'Aktual'naya tema. Patriotizm – ponyatie svyatoe', *Krasnaya zvezda*, 11 November.

Demos Center (2007) *Militsiia mezhdu Rossiei i Chechnei. Veterany konflikta v rossi-iskom obshchestve* (Moskva).

den Dekker, G. (2010) 'A new START to begin with: recent developments in US-Russian strategic nuclear arms reductions', *Security and Human Rights*, 21, 2, pp. 81–92.

Desch, M. C. (1996) 'War and strong states, peace and weak states?', *International Organization*, 50, pp. 237–268.

Dessler, D. and Owen, J. (2005) 'Constructivism and the problem of explanation: a review article', *Perspectives on Politics*, 3, 3, pp. 597–610.

Diener, E. and Crandall, R. (1978) *Ethics in Social and Behavioral Research* (Chicago: University of Chicago Press).

Dillon, M. and Reid, J. (2001) 'Global Liberal Governance: Biopolitics, Security and War', *Millennium: Journal of International Studies*, 30, pp. 41–66.

Dixon, P. (2009) '"Hearts and Minds"? British Counter-Insurgency from Malaya to Iraq', *Journal of Strategic Studies*, 32, 3, pp. 353–381.

Dobriansky, P. J. (2000) 'Russian foreign policy: promise or peril?', *The Washington Quarterly*, 23, 1, pp. 135–145.

Dolnik, A. and Pilch, R. (2003) 'The Moscow Theater Hostage Crisis: The Perpetrators, their Tactics, and the Russian Response', *International Negotiation*, 8, 3, pp. 577–611.

Doty, R. L. (2007) 'States of Exception on the Mexico–US Border: Security, "Decisions" and of Unease', *Alternatives*, 27, pp. 63–92.

Draganova, D. (2005) 'Peace or Perpetual War in Chechnya?', *Peace Review*, 17, 2, pp. 315–322.

Duffield, M. R. (2001) *Global Governance and the New Wars: The Merging of Development and Security* (London: Zed Books).

Duncan, P. J. S. (2005) 'Contemporary Russian Identity between East and West', *The Historical Journal*, 48, 1, pp. 277–294.

Dunlop, J. B. (1998) *Russia confronts Chechnya* (Cambridge: Cambridge University Press).

Dunlop, J. (2000) 'Russia Under Putin Reintegrating "Post-Soviet Space"', *Journal of Democracy*, 11, 3, pp. 39–47.

Dunlop, J. B. and Menon, R. (2006) 'Chaos in the North Caucasus and Russia's future', *Survival: Global Politics and Strategy*, 48, 2, pp. 97–114.

Dyson, S. B. (2001) 'Drawing policy implications from the "Operational Code" of a "new" political actor: Russian President Vladimir Putin', *Policy Sciences*, 34, 3–4, pp. 329–346.

Dzutsev, V. (2014) 'Kabardino-Balkaria Joins Russian Regions Not Allowed to Elect Governors', *Eurasia Daily Monitor*, 11, 67, *Jamestown Foundation*, available at: www.jamestown.org/regions/thecaucasus/single/?tx_ttnews[pointer]=2&tx_ttnews[tt_news]=42200&tx_ttnews[backPid]=54&cHash=78c2e8f79a7c47aebe3ff0454fc35bf4#.U3aDFyhR2nl, accessed 16 May 2014.

Eisenstadt, S. N. and Giesen, B. (1995) 'The construction of collective identity', *European Journal of Sociology*, 36, pp. 72–102.

Ekspert (2006) 'Surkov, Rossiya i demoktratiya', *Ekspert*, 519, 25, 3 July, available at: www.expert.ru/printissues/expert/2006/25/news_surkov_rossiya_i_demokratiya/, accessed 5 June 2010.

Elbe, S. (2006) 'Should HIV/AIDS be Securitized? The Ethical Dilemmas of Linking HIV/AIDS and Security', *International Studies Quarterly*, 50, 1, pp. 119–144.

Epstein, C. (2007) 'Guilty Bodies, Productive Bodies, Destructive Bodies: Crossing the Biometric Borders', *International Political Sociology*, 1, 2, pp. 149–164.

Eriksson, J. and Rhinard, M. (2009) 'Internal–External Security Nexus: Notes on an Emerging Research Agenda', *Cooperation and Conflict*, 44, 3, pp. 243–267.

Evans, A. B. (2005) 'A Russian civil society', in White, S., Gitelman, Z. and Sakwa, R. (eds) *Developments in Russian Politics 6* (New York: Palgrave), pp. 96–113.

Evans, A. B. (2012) 'Protests and civil society in Russia: The struggle for the Khimki Forest', *Communist and Post-Communist Studies*, 45, 3–4, pp. 233–242.

Ezzy, D. (1998) 'Theorizing Narrative Identity: Symbolic Interactionism and Hermeneutics', *The Sociological Quarterly*, 39, 2, pp. 239–252.

Farrell, T. (2002) 'Constructivist Security Studies: Portrait of a Research Programme', *International Studies Review*, 4, 1, pp. 49–72.

Fawkes, B. (ed.) (1998) *Russia and Chechnya: the Permanent Crisis* (Basingstoke: Macmillan).

Fawn, R. (2002) 'Encouraging the Incorrigible? Russia's Relations with the West over Chechnya', *Journal of Communist Studies and Transition Politics*, 18, 1, pp. 3–20.

Fearon, J. and Wendt, A. (2002) 'Rationalism versus Constructivism: a skeptical view', in Carlsnaes, W., Rise, T. and Simmons, B. A., pp. 52–72.

Federal Agency for Print and Mass Communication (2008) 'Socio-economic development of the Chechen Republic 2008–2011', *Russian Federal Agency for Print and Mass Communication*, available at: www.fapmc.ru/activities/chechenrepublic/, accessed 4 June 2010.

Federal Security Service (2008) 'Prezident Rossii poruchil glave FSB derzhat' pod lichnym kontrolem situatsiyu na Severnom Kavkaze', *Federal Security Service*, 11 August, available at: www.fsb.ru/fsb/comment/remark/single.htm!id%3D10434756%40fsbComment.html, accessed 4 June 2010.

Felgenhauer, P. (2002) 'The Russian army in Chechnya', *Central Asian Survey*, 21, 2, pp. 157–166.

Felgenhauer, P. (2013) 'Aggressive Nationalism and Anti-Americanism Are the Kremlin's New Ideological Pillars', *Eurasia Daily Monitor*, 10, 28, available at: www.jamestown.org/single/?no_cache=1&tx_ttnews[tt_news]=40456&tx_ttnews[backPid]=620%29#.U0_fRfuLW5c, accessed 17 April 2013.

Felshtinsky, Y. and Litvinenko, A. (2007) *Blowing up Russia: Terror from within* (London: Gibson Square Books).

Fierke, K. M. (2007) *Critical approaches to international security* (Cambridge: Polity).

Fierke, K. M. and Jørgensen, K. E. (2001) *Constructing international relations: the next generation* (Armonk, N.Y.: M.E. Sharpe).

Filippov, Yu (2004), 'Kadyrov's legacy put to the test', *RIANovosti*, 12 May 2004, available at: http://en.rian.ru/onlinenews/20040512/39915969.html, accessed 20 September 2010.

Finnemore, A. and Sikkink, K. (2001) 'Taking stock: The Constructivist Research Programme in International Relations and Comparative Politics', *Annual Review of Political Science*, 4, pp. 391–416.

Floyd, R. (2007) 'Towards a Consequentialist Evaluation of Security: Bringing Together the Copenhagen School of Security Studies and the Welsh School of Security Studies', *Review of International Studies*, 33, 2, pp. 327–350.

Forsberg, T. and Herd, G. (2005) 'The EU, Human Rights, and the Russo–Chechen Conflict', *Political Science Quarterly*, 120, 3, pp. 455–478.

Fortescue, S. (2006) *Russia's Oil Barons and Metal Magnates: Oligarchs and the State in Transition* (London: Palgrave Macmillan).

Frederking, B. (2003) 'Constructing Post-Cold War Collective Security', *American Political Science Review*, 97, 3, pp. 363–378.

Fredholm, M. (2000) 'The prospects for genocide in Chechnya and extremist retaliation against the West', *Central Asian Survey*, 19, 3, pp. 315–328.

Freire, M. R. and Kanet, R. E. (eds) (2012) *Russia and its near neighbours identity, interests and foreign policy* (Basingstoke, UK; New York: Palgrave Macmillan).

Frolov, V. (2014) 'Crimea Helped Putin Hijack the Nationalists', *The Moscow Times*, 13 April, available at: www.themoscowtimes.com/opinion/article/crimea-helped-putin-hijack-the nationalists/497956.html, accessed 13 May 2014.

Fuller, L. (2006) 'Chechnya: Shamil Basayev's Life Of War And Terror', Radio Free Europe Radio Liberty, 10 July, available at: www.rferl.org/content/article/1069740.html, accessed 20 May 2009.

Fuller, L. (2008), 'What Direction For Chechnya?', Radio Free Europe Radio Liberty, 8 July.

Fuller, L. (2009) 'Ramzan Kadyrov's Evolving Political Credo', Radio Free Europe Radio Liberty, 10 August, available at www.rferl.org/articleprintview/1796442.html, accessed 10 June 2010.

Fuller, L. (2011) 'It May Be Too Late For A New North Caucasus Policy', Radio Free

Europe Radio Liberty, 27 January, available at: www.rferl.org/content/commentary_new_north_caucasus_policy_too_late/2289607.html, accessed 17 May 2013.

Funke, O. (2005) 'Russian environmental security issues: competing frameworks for the future', *International Journal of Environmental Technology and Management*, 5, 2–3, pp. 246–275.

Furman, D. (2009) 'The feudal limits of the vertical chain of command', *Nezavisimaya gazeta*, 9 September, p. 5.

Gaddy, C. G. and Ickes, B. W. (2010) 'Russia after the Global Financial Crisis', *Eurasian Geography and Economics*, 51, 3, pp. 281–311.

Galeotti, M. (2010) 'The Security Apparatus: Putin's praetorians', in Galeotti, M. (ed.) *The Politics of Security in Modern Russia* (London: Ashgate).

Galeotti, M. (ed.) (2010) *The Politics of Security in Modern Russia* (London: Ashgate).

Gall, C. and de Waal, T. (1998) *Chechnya: calamity in the Caucasus* (Basingstoke: Pan Books).

Gammer, M. (2005) 'Between Mecca and Moscow: Islam, Politics and Political Islam in Chechnya and Daghestan', *Middle Eastern Studies*, 41, 6, pp. 833–848.

Garin, B. (1999) 'Gde gotovyat boevikov dlya voiny. Milliarder terrorist ben Laden sekretno pobyval v Chechne', *Interfaks AIF*, 2 September, accessed through East-View database.

George, A. L. and Bennett, A. (2004) *Case studies and theory development in the social sciences* (Cambridge, MA: MIT Press).

Gerber, T. P. and Mendelson, S. E. (2008) 'Casualty Sensitivity in a Post-Soviet Context: Russian Views of the Second Chechen War, 2001–2004', *Political Science Quarterly*, 123, 1, pp. 39–68.

Gerber, T. P. and Mendelson, S. E. (2009) 'Security Through Sociology: The North Caucasus and the Global Counterinsurgency Paradigm', *Studies in Conflict & Terrorism*, 32, 9, pp. 831–851.

Giles, K. (2009), Russia's National Security Strategy to 2020 (Rome: NATO Defense College), available at: http://www.conflictstudies.org.uk/files/RusNatSecStrategyto2020.pdf, accessed 20 June 2014.

Gilligan, E. (2009) Terror in Chechnya: Russia and the Tragedy of Civilians in War (Princeton: Princeton University Press).

Glenn, J. (1997) 'The Interregnum: The South's Insecurity Dilemma', *Nations and Nationalism*, 3, 1, pp. 45–64.

Gol'ts, A. (1999), 'Protivostoyanie', *Itogi*, 42, 19 October.

Goldthau, A. (2008) 'Rhetoric versus reality: Russian threats to European energy supply', *Energy Policy*, 36, 2, pp. 686–692.

Golovin, P. (1999) 'Vremya "Ch"', *Itogi*, 40, 5 October.

Gomart, T. (2008) EU-Russia Relations: toward a Way Out of Depression (Paris: IFRI, CSIS).

Goode, J. P. and Laruelle, M. (2014) 'Putin, Crimea and the legitimacy trap', Open Democracy, 13 March, available at: www.opendemocracy.net/od-russia/j-paul-goode-and-marlene-laruelle/putin-crimea-and-legitimacy-trap-nationalism, accessed 16 April 2014.

Gorodetsky, G. (ed.) (2003) *Russia between East and West: Russian foreign policy on the threshold of the twenty-first century* (London and Portland, OR: Frank Cass).

Government of the Russian Federation, 'Zayavlenie Pravitel'stva Rossiiskoi Federatsii o situatsii v Chechenskoi Respublike i merakh po ee uregulirovaniyu', *Rossiiskaya gazeta*, 23 October 1999.

Green, D. (ed.) (2002) *Constructivism and Comparative politics* (Armonk, NY: ME Sharpe).

Greenhill, B. (2008) 'Recognition and Collective Identity Formation in International Politics', *European Journal of International Relations*, 14, 2, pp. 343–368.

Gromov, A. (2006) 'Ideologicheskii fasad vlasti', *Ekspert*, 503, 9, 6 March, available at: www.expert.ru/printissues/expert/2006/09/ideologicheskiy_fasad_vlasti/, accessed 6 June 2010.

Gronskaya, N. and Makarychev, A. (2014) 'The 2014 Sochi Olympics and "Sovereign Power" A Political Linguistic Perspective', *Problems of Post-Communism*, 61, 1.

Grozny-Inform.ru (2009) 'Reis na svyashchennuyu Mekku pervyi i samyi blagoslovennyi', Grozny-Inform.ru, 16 November, available at: www.grozny-inform.ru/main.mhtml?Part=15&PubID=15287, accessed 17 June 2010.

Guzzini, S. (2011) 'Securitization as a causal mechanism', *Security Dialogue*, 42, 4–5, pp. 329–341.

Hadfield, A. (2008) 'EU-Russia Energy Relations: Aggregation and Aggravation', *Journal of Contemporary European Studies*, 16, 2, pp. 239–241.

Hahn, G. (2003) 'The Impact of Putin's Federative Reforms on Democratization in Russia', *Post-Soviet Affairs*, 19, 2, pp. 114–153.

Hahn, G. M. (2012) 'Russia at Year's End – Stuck In Gear But Poised for Change?', *Russia: Other Points of View*, 2 December, available at: www.russiaotherpointsofview.com/2012/12/russia-at-years-end-stuck-in-gear-but-poised-for-change.html, accessed 27 July 2013.

Hahn, G. M. (2013a) 'Putin's Political Perestroika: Constructing A System, Obstructing The Street', *Russia: Other Points of View*, 1 February, available at: www.russiaotherpointsofview.com/2013/02/putins-political-perestroika-constructing-a-system-obstructing-the-street.html, accessed 27 July 2013.

Hahn, G. M. (2013b) 'Chechen Extremists Force Putin's Syria Stance', *The Moscow Times*, 27 September, available at: www.themoscowtimes.com/opinion/article/chechen-extremists-force-putins-syria-stance/486706.html, accessed 15 May 2014.

Hale, H. and Taagepera, R. (2002) 'Russia consolidation or collapse', *Europe-Asia Studies*, 54, 7, pp. 1101–1126.

Hale, H. E. (2004) 'Origins of United Russia and the Putin Presidency: The Role of Contingency in Party-System Development', *Demokratizatsiya*, Spring, pp. 169–194.

Hale, H. E. (2006) *Why Not Parties in Russia? Democracy, Federalism and the State* (Cambridge: Cambridge University Press).

Hallenberg, J. and Karlsson, H. (ed.) (2006) *Changing transatlantic security relations: do the U.S., the EU and Russia form a new strategic triangle?* (London: Routledge).

Hansen, L. (2006) *Security as practice: discourse analysis and the Bosnian war* (London and New York: Routledge).

Hansen, L. (2012) 'Reconstructing desecuritisation: the normative-political in the Copenhagen School and directions for how to apply it', *Review of International Studies*, 38, 3, pp. 525–554.

Hanson, P. (2003) 'The Russian Economic Recovery: Do Four Years of Growth Tell Us that the Fundamentals have Changed?', *Europe-Asia Studies*, 55, 3, pp. 365–382.

Haukkala, H. (2009) 'Lost in Translation? Why the EU has Failed to Influence Russia's Development', *Europe–Asia Studies*, 61, 10, pp. 1757–1777.

Havel, V., Glucksmann, A., Prince Hassan bin Talal, de Klerk, F.W., Robinson, M., Sasakawa, Y., Schwarzenberg, K., Soros, G. and Tutu, D. (2006) 'End the Silence Over Chechnya', 1 March, *The Nation*, available at: http://www.nationmultimedia.com/2006/03/01/opinion/opinion_20001745.php, accessed: 20 August 2014.

Hedenskog, J., Konnander, V., Nygren, B., Oldberg, I. and Pursiainen, C. (eds) (2005) *Russia as a Great Power: dimensions of security under Putin* (Abingdon: Routledge).

Herd, G. (2000) 'The "counter-terrorist operation" in Chechnya: "Information warfare" aspects', *The Journal of Slavic Military Studies*, 13, 4, pp. 57–83.

Herd, G. P. (2002) 'The Russo-Chechen information warfare and 9/11: Al-Qaeda through the South Caucasus looking glass?', *European Security*, 11, 4, pp. 110–130.

Herd, G. (2010) 'Security Strategy: Sovereign Democracy and Great Power Aspirations' in Galeotti, M. (ed.) *The Politics of Security in Modern Russia* (Aldershot: Gower Publishing Company), pp. 7–29.

Herspring, D. R. (2003) 'Introduction' in Herspring, D. R. (ed.) (2003), pp. 1–13.

Herspring, D. R. (ed.) (2003) *Putin's Russia: past imperfect, future uncertain* (Lanham, MD and Oxford: Rowman and Littlefield Publishers).

Herszenhorn, D. M. and Kramer, A. E. (2013) 'Another Reset With Russia in Obama's Second Term', *New York Times*, 1 February.

Hertog, K. (2005) 'Assessing a self-fulfilling prophecy: the seeds of Islamic radicalisation in Chechnya', *Religion, State and Society*, 33, 3, pp. 239–252.

Hill, Ronald (2008) 'Introduction: Perspectives on Putin', *The Journal of Communist Studies and Transition Politics*, 24, 4, pp. 473–479.

Hobson, J. (2007) 'Is Critical Theory Always For the White West and For Western Imperialism? Beyond Westphalian, Towards a Post-Racist International Relations', *Review of International Studies* 33, pp. 91–116.

Hobson, J. (2012) *The Eurocentric Conception of World Politics: Western International Theory, 1760–2010* (Cambridge: Cambridge University Press).

Holland, M. (2004) 'Chechnya's Internally Displaced and the Role of Russia's Non-Governmental Organizations', *Journal of Refugee Studies*, 17, 3, pp. 334–346.

Honneland, G. (1998) 'Identity Formation in the Barents Euro-Arctic Region', *Cooperation and Conflict*, 33, 3, pp. 277–297.

Hopf, T. (2002) *Social Construction of International Politics. Identities and Foreign Policies, Moscow 1955 and 1999* (Ithaca: Cornell University Press).

Hopf, T. (2005) 'Identity, Legitimacy, and the Use of Military Force: Russia's Great Power Identities and Military Intervention in Abkhazia', *Review of International Studies*, 31, S1 pp. 225–243.

Horowitz, M. (2002) 'Research Report on the Use of Identity Concept in International Relation', Weatherhead Center for International Relations and the Harvard Identity Project, available at: www.wcfia.harvard.edu/misc/initiative/identity/publications/horowitz1.pdf, accessed 2 February 2012.

Howarth, D. (2000) 'Introducing discourse theory and political analysis' in Howarth, D., Norval, A. J. and Stavrakakis, Y. (eds) (2000), pp. 1–23.

Howarth, D., Norval A. J and Stavrakakis Y. (2000) *Discourse theory and political analysis* (Manchester: Manchester University Press).

Hughes, J. (2001) 'Managing Secession Potential in the Russian Federation', *Regional & Federal Studies*, 11, 3, pp. 36–68.

Hughes, J. (2008) *Chechnya: from Nationalism to Jihad* (Philadelphia: University of Pennsylvania Press).

Human Rights Watch (2002) 'Russia, Chechnya, Swept Under: Torture, Forced Disappearances, and Extra Judicial Killings during Sweep Operations in Chechnya', *Human Rights Watch*, 14, 2.

Huysmans, J. (1995) 'Migrants as a Security Problem: Dangers of "Securitizing" Societal

Issues', in Miles, R. and Thraenhart, D. (eds) *Migration and European Integration: The Dynamics of Inclusion and Exclusion* (London: Pinter), pp. 53–72.

Huysmans, J. (1998) 'The Question of the Limit: Desecuritisation and the Aesthetics of Horror in Political Realism', *Millennium: Journal of International Studies*, 27, 3, pp. 569–589.

Huysmans, J. (2000) 'The European Union and the Securitization of Migration', *Journal of Common Market Studies*, 38, 5, pp. 751–777.

Huysmans, J. (2006) *The Politics of Insecurity: Security, Migration and Asylum in the EU* (London: Routledge).

Hyde, M. (2001) 'Putin's federal reforms and their implications for presidential power in Russia', *Europe–Asia Studies*, 53, 5, pp. 719–743.

Interfax (2004) 'Za poslednie 4 goda okolo 7 tysiyach boevikov reshili pokonchit' so svoim kriminal'nym proshlym i vernut'sya k mirnoi zhizni. Ob etom v pererive zasedanuya glav sub'ektov. YUFO v Kislovodske zayavil president', in *Statements and Commentaries, Memorial*, 17 December, www.memo.ru/hr/hotpoints/caucas1/index.htm, accessed 10 June 2010.

Interfax (2008a) 'Illegal armed groups still operating in Chechnya – commander', Interfax, 20 May, posted on Johnson's Russia List, available at: www.cdi.org/russia/johnson/2008-99-19.cfm, accessed 30 June 2010.

Interfax (2008b) 'Russian president's envoy tours Chechnya', Interfax, 29 May, taken from Johnson's Russia List, #21 – JRL 2008–106, available at: www.cdi.org/russia/johnson/2008-106-21.cfm, accessed 14 April 2010.

Interfax (2008c), 'Russian Defence Ministry denies shoot-out incident in Chechnya was serious', Interfax, 16 April, taken from Johnson's Russia List, #24 – JRL 2008–78, available at: www.cdi.org/russia/johnson/2008-78-24.cfm, accessed 4 March 2010.

Ishchenko, S. (2001) 'Antiterror, vozmesdie. Ministr Oboroni RF Sergei Ivanov otchechaet na vorposi', *Trud*, 27 September.

ITAR-TASS (2008a) 'Serviceman and local resident killed in Chechnya', *Itar Tass Daily*, 29 June, available at: http://dlib.eastview.com.ezproxyd.bham.ac.uk/browse/doc/18545355, accessed 20 August 2010.

ITAR-TASS (2008b) 'Chechen people resolve many problems in 2007 – Kadyrov', *ITAR-TASS Daily*, 29 January, available at: http://dlib.eastview.com/browse/doc/13344935, accessed 14 April 2010.

ITAR-TASS (2008c) 'Chechnya seeks to attract more foreign investments in 2008', *ITAR-TASS Daily*, 4 February, available at: http://dlib.eastview.com/browse/doc/13377341, accessed 5 July 2010.

ITAR-TASS (2008d) 'Jordanian – Chechen treaty on healthcare, education restoration to be fruitful', *ITAR-TASS Daily*, 29 February, available at: http://dlib.eastview.com/browse/doc/13524359, accessed 5 June 2010.

ITAR-TASS (2008e) 'Terrorist activity in North Caucasus eases – General Kulikov', *ITAR-TASS Daily*, 20 February, available at: http://dlib.eastview.com/browse/doc/13462804, accessed 17 June 2010.

Ivanov, I. (1999) 'Speech to the French Senate on 27 October 1999', *Diplomaticheskii vestnik*, 11, November.

Ivanov, I. (2000) 'Speech at the 106th meeting of the Committee of Ministers of the Council of Europe, on the issue of "The Russian input into the Council of Europe and the recommendations from PACE (1456) about the situation in the Chechen Republic"', 11 May 2000.

Ivanov, I. (2002) 'Round the World with Igor Ivanov', *Rossiiskaya gazeta*, 30 December.

Ivanov, I. (2003a) 'Transcript of Russian Minister of Foreign Affairs Igor Ivanov Interview with TVTs Television Company', 25 January, available at: www.ln.mid.ru/Brp_4. nsf/arh/1D1C016B1F8D675943256CBC0053750A?OpenDocument, accessed 10 September 2010.

Ivanov, I. (2003b) 'Interview in "The Times" on 28 November 2003', cited in *Statements and Commentaries, Memorial*, available at: www.memo.ru/hr/hotpoints/caucas1/rubr/3/l200312.htm, accessed 10 June 2010.

Ivanov, I. (2005) 'Interview of the Head of Security Council Igor Ivanov, for the Magazine 'Strategiya Rossii', 4 May 2005, Russian Security Council, available at: www.scrf.gov.ru/news/98.html, accessed 12 September 2010.

Ivanov I. (2007) 'Vystuplenie Sekretarya Soveta Bezopasnosti Rossiiskoi Federatsii I.S. Ivanova na Assamblee Soveta po vneshnei i oboronnoi politike', Russian Security Council, 17 March, available at: www.scrf.gov.ru/news/177.html, accessed 3 June 2010.

Ivanov, S. (2003a) 'Keynote speech by Sergey Ivanov, Minister of Defense of the Russian Federation, at the 39th Munich Conference on Security Policy', Press service, Ministry for Foreign Affairs of the Russian Federation, 8 February, available at: www.mid.ru/Brp_4.nsf/arh/C361362CB0E593A0C3256EC9001D196C?OpenDocument, accessed 23 August 2010.

Ivanov, S. (2003b) 'Na territorii Chechni deistvuyt okolo 1300 aktivnyikh boevikov' Newsru.com, 16 July, available at: www.newsru.com/russia/16jul2003/boeviki_print.html, accessed 23 August 2010.

Jackson, R. (2005) *Writing the War on Terrorism: Language, Politics, and Counter-Terrorism* (Manchester: Manchester University Press).

Jersild, A. (2004) 'The Chechen wars in historical perspective: New work on contemporary Russian–Chechen Relations', *Slavic Review*, 63, pp. 367–377.

Johnson, J. (2012), 'Mission Impossible: Modernization in Russia after the Global Financial Crisis', *PONARS Eurasia Policy Memo*, 196, June.

Jones, B. G. (ed.) (2006) *Decolonising International Relations* (Lanham, MD: Rowman and Littlefield).

Jordan, W. (2014) 'Russia sanctions: public support weaker in France and Germany', YouGov, 1 April, available at: http://yougov.co.uk/news/2014/04/01/russia-sanctions-public-support-france-and-germany, accessed 13 May 2014.

Jutila, M. (2006) 'Desecuritizing Minority Rights: Against Determinism', *Security Dialogue*, 37, 2, pp. 167–185.

Kaczmarski, M. (2010) 'Foreign policy at the service of modernization: old wine in a new wineskin', *OSW Commentary*, 38, 31 Aug, available at: www.osw.waw.pl/sites/default/files/Commentary_39.pdf, accessed 7 March 2012.

Kadyrov, R. (2006a) 'Ramzan Kadyrov: Kontakti Chechenskoi Respubliki s drugimi rossiiskimi regionami razvivayutsya planomerno I prinosyat vzaimnuyu vygodu', Official Website of President Ramzan Kadyrov, 22 September, available at: www.ramzan-kadyrov.ru/smi.php?releases&smi_id=18, accessed 4 June 2010.

Kadyrov, R. (2006b) 'Zayavlenie Predsedatelya Pravitel'stva Chechenskoi Respubliki, sekretarya regional'nogo otdeleniya "Edinoi Rossii" Ramzana Kadyrova', Official Website of President Kadyrov, 4 September, available at: www.ramzan-kadyrov.ru/press.php?releases&press_id=391, accessed 5 June 2010.

Kadyrov, R. (2007) 'Poslanie Prezidenta Chechenskoi Respubliki Ramzana Akhmatovicha Kadyrova narodu i Parlamentu Chechenskoi Respubliki', Official Website of President Ramzan Kadyrov, 9 July, available at: www.ramzan-kadyrov.ru/press.php?releases&press_id=1032&month=07&year=2007, accessed 4 June 2010.

Kadyrov, R. (2008a) 'Interv'yu Prezidenta Chechenskoi Respubliki R.A. Kadyrov telekanaly "Russia Today"', Official Website of President Ramzan Kadyrov, 28 January, available at: www.ramzan-kadyrov.ru/smi.php?releases&smi_id=52&month=01&year=2008, accessed 19 June 2010.

Kadyrov, R. (2008b) 'Predstaviteli islamskikh stran poblagodarili Ramzana Kadyrova za islamskii tsentr i mechet', Official Website of President Ramzan Kadyrov, 17 October, available at: www.ramzan-kadyrov.ru/press.php?releases&press_id=1783&month=10&year=2008, accessed 10 July 2010.

Kadyrov, R. (2008c) 'Segodnya v Groznom sostoyalos' torzhestvennoe otkrytie mecheti im. Akhmata Kadyrova "Serdtse Chechni"', Official Website of President Ramzan Kadyrov, 17 October, available at: www.ramzan-kadyrov.ru/press.php?releases&press_id=1782&month=10&year=2008, accessed 6 July 2010.

Kadyrov, R. (2010) Official Website of President Kadyrov, available at: www.ramzan-kadyrov.ru/position.php, accessed 15 June 2010.

Kaftan, L. (2004) 'Zamestitel' glavi administratsii Prezidenta RF Vladislav Surkov: Putin ukreplyaet gosudarstvo, a ne sebya', *Komsomol'skaya pravda*, 28 September.

Kalland, T. (2004) 'The EU-Russia Relationship: What is missing?', *SIPRI Policy Brief*, available at: http://oikosneteurope.sharepointhosting.ch/archives/Annual%20Conferences/Annual%20Conference%202004%20in%20Moscow/SIPRI%20on%20EU-Russian%20Relationship.pdf, accessed 7 March 2010.

Kamynin, M. (Spokesman of Ministry for Foreign Affairs of the Russian Federation) (2007) 'Interview with RIA Novosti on the Upcoming OSCE Ministerial Council Meeting in Madrid', 27 November, Ministry for Foreign Affairs of the Russian Federation, available at: www.mid.ru/brp_4.nsf/e78a48070f128a7b43256999005bcbb3/abea360a8970ac2fc32573a300219f37?OpenDocument, accessed 10 June 2010.

Kamynin, M. (Spokesman of Ministry for Foreign Affairs of the Russian Federation) (2007) 'Interview with RIA Novosti on the Upcoming Russia-NATO Council Meeting', Ministry for Foreign Affairs of the Russian Federation, 6 December, available at: www.mid.ru/brp_4.nsf/e78a48070f128a7b43256999005bcbb3/d8913d1dfe5358e7c32573aa00235f77?OpenDocument, accessed 5 June 2010.

Kanet, R. E. (ed.) (2005) *The new security environment: the impact on Russia, Central and Eastern Europe* (Aldershot: Ashgate).

Kanet, R. E. (2007) *Russia: Re-Emerging Great Power* (Houndmills: Palgrave Macmillan).

Karaganov, S. (2003) 'Russia, Europe, and New Challenges', *Russia in Global Affairs*, March.

Karaganov, S. (2012) 'Keeping the Powder Dry: Why Russia Should Build Up Its Military Might Even in a Favorable Foreign Environment', *Russia in Global Affairs*, 27 December, available at: http://eng.globalaffairs.ru/number/Keeping-the-Powder-Dry-15810, accessed 18 February 2013.

Karaganov, S. and Bordachev, T. (2009) *Towards a new Euro-Atlantic Security Architecture* (Valdia Discussion Club Report).

Karev, S. (2000) 'Sergei Karev, Speech of the representative of the Russian Federation at the VI Committee of the 55th session of UN General Assembly', 13 November 2000, available at: www.un.org.ezproxyd.bham.ac.uk/News/Press/docs/2000/20001113.gal3167.doc.html, accessed 19 February 2009.

Kassianova, A. (2001) 'Russia: Still Open to the West? Evolution of the State Identity in the Foreign Policy and Security Discourse', *Europe-Asia Studies*, 53, 6, pp. 971–972.

Katz, M. (2008) 'The Emerging Saudi-Russian Partnership', *Mideast monitor*, 3, 1.

Katzenstein P. J. (ed.) (1996) *The culture of national security norms and identity in world politics* (New York: Columbia University Press).

Katzenstein, P. J. (2005) *A world of regions: Asia and Europe in the American imperium*, (Ithaca, NY: Cornell University Press).

Kaveshnikov, N. (2010) 'The issue of energy security in relations between Russia and the European Union', *European Security*, 19, 4, pp. 585–605.

Kavkazkii, uzel (1999) 'Bezopasnost' s garantiei', *Rossiiskaya gazeta*, 5 November.

Kelly, L. and Gutterman, S. (2012) 'Russian rally tests opposition power, Putin tactics', Reuters, 11 June, available at: www.reuters.com/article/2012/06/11/us-russia-protests-idUSBRE85A18M20120611, accessed 7 March 2012.

Kelstrup, M. and Williams, M. C. (eds) (2000) *International Relations Theory and the Politics of European Integration* (London: Routledge).

Kennedy-Pipe, C. and Welch, S. (2005) 'Russia and the United States After 9/11', *Terrorism and Political Violence*, 17, 1, pp. 279–291.

Kerr, D. (2009) 'Dilemmas of the 'Middle Continent': Russian Strategy for Eastern Eurasia', *International Spectator*, 44, 2, pp. 75–94.

King, C. (2008) 'The Five-Way War: Managing Moscow After the Georgia Crisis', *Foreign Affairs* 87, 6, pp.2–11.

Kipp, J. W. (2003) 'Putin and Russia's wars in Chechnya', Herspring, D. R. (ed.) (2003) *Putin's Russia: past imperfect, future uncertain* (Lanham, MD and Oxford: Rowman & Littlefield), pp. 177–200.

Knezys, S. and Sedlickas, R. (1999) *The war in Chechnya* (College Station, TX: A&M University Press).

Knyaz'kov, S. (1999) 'Dokhodnyi promysel', *Krasnaya zvezda*, 218, 12 October.

Kobrinskaya, I. (2005) 'The CIS in Russian Foreign Policy: Causes and Effects', in H. Smith (ed.), *Russia and its foreign policy* (Helsinki: Kikimora), pp. 77–92.

Koesel, K. J. and Bunce, V. J. (2012) 'Putin, Popular Protests, and Political Trajectories in Russia: A Comparative Perspective', *Post-Soviet Affairs* 28, 4, pp. 403–423.

Kolossov, V. and Toal, G. (2007) 'An Empire's Fraying Edge? The North Caucasus Instability in Contemporary Russian Geopolitical Culture', *Eurasian Geography and Economics*, 48, 2, pp. 202–225.

Koltsova, O. (2006) *News media and power in Russia* (London and New York: Routledge).

Kononenko, V. and Moshes, A. (eds) (2011) *Russia as a network state: what works in Russia when state institutions do not?* (Basingstoke: Palgrave Macmillan).

Korinman, M. and Laughlin, J. (eds) (2008) *Russia: A New Cold War?* (London and Portland: Vallentine Mitchell Academic).

Korotchenko, I. (1999) 'Ser'eznye orgmeropriyatiya na Lubyanke', *Nezavisimaya gazeta*, 161, 1 September.

Kosals, L. (2010) 'Police in Russia: Reform or Business Restructuring?', *Russian Analytical Digest*, 84, pp. 2–6.

Kozhevnikova, G. (2008) 'Winter 2007–2008: An Epidemic of Murders against the Backdrop of Elections', *Reports and Analyse, SOVA Centre*, 23 March, available at: http://www.sova-center.ru/en/xenophobia/reports-analyses/2008/03/d12920/, accessed, 15 April 2014.

Kozlovsky, B. and Lukin, P. (2012) 'From Activity to Effectiveness', *Russia in Global Affairs*, 7 October, available at: http://eng.globalaffairs.ru/number/From-Activity-to-Effectiveness-15684, accessed 18 March 2013.

Kozyrev, V. (2014) 'Russia–Vietnam Strategic Partnership: The Return of the Brotherhood in Arms?', *Russian Analytical Digest*, 145.

Kozyreva, A. (1999) 'My pereshagnuli strashnyi porog, schitaet predsedatel' Komiteta Gosudarstvennoi Dumy general Roman Popkovich', *Rossiiskaya gazeta*, 8 September.

Kozyreva, A. (2000) 'Postav' minu – poluchish' 100 dollarov', *Rossiiskaya gazeta*, 185, 26 September.

Krahmann, E. (2003) 'Conceptualizing security governance', *Cooperation and Conflict*, 38, 1, pp. 5–26.

Kramer, M. (2004–2005) 'The Perils of Counterinsurgency: Russia's War in Chechnya', *International Security*, 29, 3, pp. 5–62.

Kramer, M. (2005) 'Guerrilla Warfare, Counterinsurgency and Terrorism in the North Caucasus: The Military Dimension of the Russian – Chechen Conflict', *Europe-Asia Studies*, 57, 2, pp. 209–290.

Krasnaya zvezda (1999) 'Ni odin terrorist ne uidet ot vozmezdinya besedu vel', *Krasnaya zvezda*, 28 October.

Krasnaya zvezda (1999) 'Obsuzhdaem proekt voennoi doktriny. S uchetom vozmozhnostei strany', *Krasnaya zvezda*, 19 October.

Krastev, I. (2005) 'Russia's post-orange empire', Open Democracy, 20 October, available at: www.opendemocracy.net/content/articles/PDF/2947.pdf, accessed 5 June 2006.

Krastev, I. (2006) '"Sovereign democracy", Russian-style', Open Democracy, 16 November, available at: www.opendemocracy.net/globalizationinstitutions_government/sovereign_democracy_4104.jsp, 6 June 2007.

Kratochvíl, P. (2004) 'The balance of threat considered: construction of threat in contemporary Russia', Paper presented at the Fifth Pan-European Conference Netherlands, The Hague, 9–11 September.

Kravtsova, Y. (2014) 'Russia's Top Diplomatic School in Turmoil Over Crimea Annexation', *The Moscow Times*, April 8.

Kremlin (1999) Presidential Decree of the Russian Federation N1255c on 23 September 1999, 'On measures for increasing the effectiveness of the counter-terrorist operation on the territory of the North Caucasus region of Russian Federation'.

Kremlin (2006) 'Transcript of Meeting with the Government Cabinet', 13 February, available at: http://archive.kremlin.ru/appears/2006/02/13/1647_type63378type63381_101589.shtml, accessed 4 April 2010.

Kremlin (2007) 'Stenograficheskii otchet o vstreche c chlenami Soveta Obshchestvennoi palaty Rossii', 16 May, available at: http://archive.kremlin.ru/appears/2007/05/16/2214_type63376type63381_129310.shtml, accessed 10 July 2010.

Kuchins, A. C. and Zevelev, I. A. (2012) 'Russian Foreign Policy: Continuity in Change', *The Washington Quarterly*, 35, 1, pp. 147–161.

Kuchins, A. C., Malarkey, M. and Markedonov, S. (2011) 'The North Caucasus Russia's volatile frontier', *Center for Strategic and International Studies*, available at: http://csis.org/files/publication/110321_Kuchins_NorthCaucasus_WEB.pdf, accessed 10 April 2013.

Kupchan, C. (2012) *No One's World: The West, the Rising Rest, and the Coming Global Turn* (Oxford: Oxford University Press).

Kuus, M. (2002) 'European Integration in Identity Narratives in Estonia: A Quest for Security', *Journal of Peace Research*, 39, 1, pp. 91–108.

Lahille, E. (2008) 'Russia's comeback to the arms market: a strategic choice, Atoms for Peace', *International Journal*, 2, 2, pp. 188–202.

Lapidus, G. W. (2002) 'Putin's War on Terrorism: Lessons from Chechnya', *Post-Soviet Affairs*, 18, 1, pp. 41–48.

Lapskii, V. (1999) 'Boevikam pomogaet zagranitsa', *Rossiiskaya gazeta*, 7 September.

Latynina, Y. (2004) 'Broadening the Chechen Peace Process', *Moscow Times*, 30 June, taken from Johnson's Russia List, #8 – JRL 8275, available at: www.cdi.org/russia/johnson/8275-8.cfm, accessed 10 May 2010.

Laub, Z. (2014) 'Instability in Russia's North Caucasus Region', *Council on Foreign Relations*, 6 February, available at: www.cfr.org/russian-federation/instability-russias-north-caucasus-region/p9021#p7, accessed 14 May 2014.

Lavenex, S. (2005) 'Politics of Exclusion and Inclusion in the Wider Europe', in Bardeleben (2005), pp. 123–144.

Lavrov, S. (2004) 'Transcript of Remarks and Replies to Media Questions by Minister of Foreign Affairs at Press Conference Following Talks with Minister of Foreign Affairs of Israel Silvan Shalom', 6 September, available at: www.ln.mid.ru/brp_4.nsf/e78a480 70f128a7b43256999005bcbb3/73e5093ffa04ae25c3256f090054c960?OpenDocument, accessed 18 June 2005.

Lavrov, S. (2005a) 'Main points of the Address by the Foreign Minister of the Russian Federation at Stanford University', 20 September, available at: www.mid.ru/Brp_4.nsf/arh/8CD3437CC7575184C3257086002DB677?OpenDocument, accessed 20 September 2010.

Lavrov, S. (2005b) 'Democracy, International Governance, and the Future World Order', *Russia in Global Affairs*, 1, January–March, available at: http://eng.globalaffairs.ru/number/n_4422, accessed 20 September 2010.

Lavrov, S. (2006a) 'Transcript of Remarks and Replies to Media Questions by Russian Foreign Affairs Minister Sergey Lavrov at the Press Conference on the Results of the Activities of Russian Diplomacy in 2006, Moscow, 20 December 2006', Ministry for Foreign Affairs of the Russian Federation, available at: www.mid.ru/brp_4.nsf/e78a48070f128a7b43256999005bcbb3/b8ee0eabc0e37ab4c325724b00579bdd?OpenDocument, accessed 3 June 2010.

Lavrov, S. (2006b) 'Transcript of Remarks and Replies to Media Questions by Russian Minister of Foreign Affairs Sergey Lavrov Following Meeting with Luxembourg Deputy Prime Minister and Minister of Foreign Affairs Jean Asselborn, Moscow, July 12, 2006', Press Service, Ministry for Foreign Affairs of the Russian Federation, 12 July, available at: www.mid.ru/Brp_4.nsf/arh/476185F64BD9031EC32571A9005AF0B4?OpenDocument, accessed 1 June 2010.

Lavrov, S. (2007a) 'The Foreign Policy of Russia: A New Phase', *Ekspert*, 17 December, cited by Press Service, Ministry for Foreign Affairs of the Russian Federation, available at: www.mid.ru/brp_4.nsf/e78a48070f128a7b43256999005bcbb3/969279ee85a9b046c32573b60048c175?OpenDocument, accessed 20 December 2009.

Lavrov, S. (2007b) Interview with the *Vremya Novostei*, 26 December, cited by Press Service, Ministry for Foreign Affairs of the Russian Federation, available at: www.mid.ru/brp_4.nsf/e78a48070f128a7b43256999005bcbb3/dc07853785fc201ec32573bd005e7190?OpenDocument, accessed 3 June 2010.

Lavrov, S. (2007c) 'The Present and the Future of Global Politics', *Russia in Global Affairs*, 2, April–June, available at: http://eng.globalaffairs.ru/number/n_8554, accessed 10 December 2010.

Leahy, K. (2009) Implication of the Yevkurov Attack: Does a new regional role beckon for Ramzan Kadyrov', *Central Asia Caucasus Analyst*, 7 January, available at: www.cacianalyst.org/?q=node/5138, accessed 17 May 2010.

Legvold, R. (2001) 'Russia's Unformed Foreign Policy', *Foreign Affairs*, 80, 5, pp. 62–75.

Legvold, R. (2009) 'The Russia File How to Move Toward a Strategic Partnership', *Foreign Affairs*, 88, 4.

Lemaître, R. (2006) 'The Rollback of Democracy in Russia after Beslan', *Review of Central and East European Law*, 31, 4, pp. 369–411.

Levesque, R. (2008) 'Russia and the Muslim World: The Chechnya Factor and Beyond', *Russian Analytical Digest*, 44.

Lieven, A. (1998) *Chechnya: Tombstone of Russian Power* (New Haven: Yale University Press).

Lieven, A. (2002) 'The Secret Policeman's Ball: the United States, Russia and the international order after 11 September', *International Affairs*, 78, 2, pp. 245–259.

Lintonen, R. (2004) 'Understanding EU Crisis Decision-making: The Case of Chechnya and the Finnish Presidency', *Journal of Contingencies and Crisis Management*, 12, 1, pp. 29–38.

Lipman, M. (2005) 'Constrained or Irrelevant: The Media in Putin's Russia', *Current History*, October, pp. 319–324.

Lipman, M. (2006a) 'Fear of the West in Russia', *Washington Post*, 2 May.

Lipman, M. (2006b) 'Putin's "Sovereign Democracy"', *Washington Post*, 15 July.

Litovkin, V. (2007) 'General Gareyev: Russia changing its military doctrine', interview with General Gareyev, in *RIA Novosti*, 17 January, available at: http://en.rian.ru/analysis/20070117/59247629.html, accessed 3 June 2010; Part 2 18 January 2007, available at: http://en.rian.ru/analysis/20070118/59307373.html, accessed 3 June 2010.

Lo, B. (2003) *Vladimir Putin and the evolution of Russian foreign policy* (Oxford: Blackwell).

Lohman, D. (2000) 'The international community fails to monitor Chechnya abuses', *Helsinki Monitor*, 11, 3.

Lomagin, N. A. (2007) 'Forming a New Security Identity under Vladimir Putin', in Kanet, R. E. (2007).

Lopez, A. (2007) 'Engaging or withdrawing, winning or losing? The contradictions of counterinsurgency policy in Afghanistan and Iraq', *Third World Quarterly*, 28, 2, pp. 245–260.

Lucas, E. (2008) *The New Cold War: how the Kremlin menaces both Russia and the West* (London: Bloomsbury).

Lukov, V. (Russian Ambassador to Belgium) (2005) '"Whom Does Chechnya Support?", "Tijd" Belgian Newspaper', cited by Press Department, Ministry for Foreign Affairs of the Russian Federation, 19 January, available at: www.ln.mid.ru/Brp_4.nsf/arh/46346AD8DF78B2D7C3256F9500372D37?OpenDocument, accessed 3 June 2010.

Lukyanov, F. (2005a) 'Passions Over Sovereignty', *Russia in Global Affairs*, 4, October–December.

Lukyanov, F. (2005b) 'Debates About Values, Russia', *Russia in Global Affairs*, 3.

Lukyanov, F. (2012a) cited in 'Talking point: the logic of Russian foreign policy. Marie Mendras and Fyodor Lukyanov join oDRussia editor Oliver Carroll for a debate in Paris', *Russia in Global Affairs*, 13 December, available at: http://eng.globalaffairs.ru/event/Talking-point-the-logic-of-Russian-foreign-policy-Marie-Mendras-and-Fyodor-Lukyanov-join-oDRussia-ed, accessed 13 April 2013.

Lukyanov, F. (2012b) 'Russian president Vladimir Putin reveals his moral vision in address to Federal Assembly', *The Telegraph*, 18 December, available at: www.telegraph.co.uk/sponsored/rbth/politics/9753829/vladimir-putin-federal-assembly-address.html, accessed 7 March 2013.

Lunze, K. (2009) 'Health and human rights: no miracle in post-conflict Chechnya', *The Lancet*, 374, 28 November.

Lupovici, A. (2009) 'Constructivist Methods: A Plea and Manifesto for Pluralism', *Review of International Studies*, 3, 1, pp. 195–218.

Lyall, J. (2009) 'Does Indiscriminate Violence Incite Insurgent Attacks?' *Journal of Conflict Resolution*, 53, 3, pp. 331–362.

Lynch, A. (2001) 'The Realism of Russia's Foreign Policy', *Europe-Asia Studies*, 53, 1, pp. 7–31.

Lynch, D. (2004) 'Russia's Strategic Partnership with Europe', *The Washington Quarterly*, 27, 2, pp. 99–118.

Lynch. D. (2005) '"The enemy is at the gate": Russia after Beslan', *International Affairs*, 81, 1, pp. 141–161.

MacKenzie, M. (2009) 'Securitization and Desecuritization: Female Soldiers and the Reconstruction of Women in Post-Conflict Sierra Leone', *Security Studies*, 18, 2, pp. 241–261.

MacKinnon, M. (2007) *The new cold war: revolutions, rigged elections and pipeline politics in the former Soviet Union* (Toronto: Random House Canada).

Makarkin, A. (2012) cited in 'Russia's Protests: Government Tactics Got Tougher with Time', *RIA Novosti*, 10 December, available at: http://en.ria.ru/analysis/20121210/178056253.html, accessed 13 April 2013.

Makarychev, A. S. (2009) 'Russia and its "New Security Architecture" in Europe: a Critical Examination of the Concept', *CEPS Working Document*, 310, February, available at: http://new.ceps.eu/files/book/1790.pdf, accessed 20 July 2010.

Maksakov, I. (1999a) 'K novoi voine v Chechne pochti vse gotovo, armiya v otlichie ot politikov uzhe nastroena na lyuboe razvitie sobytii', *Nezavisimaya gazeta*, 1777, 23 September.

Maksakov, I. (1999b) 'Plan rossiiskikh voennykh "Upolovinit" Chechnyu', *Nezavisimaya gazeta*, 181, 29 September.

Malashenko, A. (2007) 'The two faces of Chechnya', *Carnegie Policy Brief*, 9, 3.

Malashenko, A. (2009a) 'A rollback is in full swing in the Russian Caucasus, and it's not even clear what century it's going back to', *The New Times*, 6 July, pp. 16–17.

Malashenko, A. (2009b) 'Losing the Caucasus', *Carnegie Moscow Briefing*, 11, 3.

Malinova, O. (2012) 'A Workable Past', *Russia in Global Affairs*, 27 December, available at: http://eng.globalaffairs.ru/number/A-Workable-Past-15815, accessed 3 July 2013.

Mankoff, J. (2012) *Russian foreign policy the return of great power politics* (Lanham, MD: Rowman & Littlefield).

Marcussen, M., Risse, T., Engelmann-Martin, D., Knopf, H. J. and Roscher, K. (1999) 'Constructing Europe? The evolution of French, British and German nation state identities', *Journal of European Public Policy*, 6, 4, pp. 614–633.

Markedonov, S. (2008) 'Similar, But Different, Radical Islam is the universal challenge in Chechnya, Ingushetia and Dagestan', Johnson's Russia list, taken from *Russia Profile*, 22 July, available at: http://www.russialist.org/archives/2008-137-19.php, accessed 10 May 2014.

Markedonov, S. (2010) 'A strategy for North Caucasus: don't mention politics or religion!', 1 November, Open Democracy, available at: www.opendemocracy.net/od-russia/sergei-markedonov/strategy-for-north-caucasus-don%E2%80%99t-mention-politics-or-religion, accessed 15 May 2014.

Markedonov, S. (2013) 'The North Caucasus: The Value and Costs for Russia', *Russia in*

Global Affairs, 27 December, available at: http://eng.globalaffairs.ru/number/The-North-Caucasus-The-Value-and-Costs-for-Russia-16287, accessed 12 April 2014.

Markedonov, S. (2014) 'Sevenyi Kavkaz bez Umarova', *Politcom.ru*, 9 April 2014, available at: www.politcom.ru/17436.html, accessed 15 May 2014.

Marten, K. (2010) 'Russia, Chechnya and the Sovereign Kadyrov', PONARS Memo, N.116, available at: www.ponarseurasia.org/sites/default/files/policy-memos-pdf/pepm_116.pdf, accessed 15 May 2014.

Mason, J. and Kelly, L. (2014) 'U.S., EU to work together on tougher Russia sanctions', Reuters, 26 March, available at: www.reuters.com/article/2014/03/26/us-ukraine-crisis-idUSBREA2P0VB20140326, accessed 17 April 2014.

Mathers, J. G. (2012) 'Nuclear Weapons in Russian Foreign Policy: Patterns in Presidential Discourse 2000 2010', *Europe-Asia Studies*, 64, 3, pp. 495–519.

Matveeva, A. (2007) 'Chechnya: Dynamics of War and Peace', *Problems of Post-Communism*, 54, 3, pp. 3–17.

Matyushkin, G. (Russian Deputy Justice Minister) (2009) 'Speech of G. Matyushkin at the meeting of PACE Committee on Legal Affairs and Human Rights remedies for Human Rights violations in North Caucasus', 11 September, available at: www.londonmet.ac.uk/londonmet/fms/MRSite/Research/HRSJ/EHRAC/Matyushkin%20speech%20execution%20of%20judgments%2011_9_09.pdf, accessed 4 June 2010.

Mauer, V. and Kussmann, N. (2005) 'Interview with Vladislav Surkov, "The West does not have to love us"', *Der Spiegel*, 20 June.

McDonald, M. (2008) 'Securitization and the Construction of Security', *European Journal of International Relations*, 14, 4, pp. 563–587.

McDonald, M. (2011) 'Deliberation and Resecuritization: Australia, Asylum-Seekers and the Normative Limits of the Copenhagen School', *Australian Journal of Political Science*, 46, 2, pp. 281–229.

McFaul, M. (2000) 'Russia Under Putin One Step Forward, Two Steps Back', *Journal of Democracy*, 11, 3, pp. 19–33.

McFaul, M. (2007) 'New Russia, New Threat: Working with the West Is No Longer the Goal as the Kremlin Flexes Its Muscle and Rethinks Its Role in the World', *Los Angeles Times*, 2 September.

McFaul, M. and Stoner-Weiss, K. (2008) 'Myth of the Authoritarian Model – How Putin's Crackdown Holds Russia Back', *Foreign Affairs*, 87, 1, pp. 68–84.

Medvedev, D. (2008) 'Interview with "Figaro"', *RIA Novosti*, 13 November, available at: http://en.rian.ru/analysis/20081113/118289835.html, accessed 5 August 2010.

Medvedev, D. (2009) 'Rossiya, vpered! Stat'ya Dmitriya Medvedeva', Official Website of the President of the Russian Federation, 10 September, available at http://kremlin.ru/transcripts/5413, accessed 28 September 2011.

Medvedev, D. (2011) 'Address to the Federal Assembly', Official Website of the President of the Russian Federation, 22 December, available at: http://eng.kremlin.ru/news/3268, accessed 15 March 2012.

Meier, A. (2005) *Chechnya: to the heart of a conflict* (Norton).

Memorial (2003) 'Uslovnoe pravosodie – o situatsii s rassledovaniem prestuplenii protiv grazhdanskikh lits, sovershennykh predstavitelyami federal'nykh sil na territorii Chechenskoi respubliki v khode voennykh deistvii 1999–2003', *Memorial*, 2 June, available at: www.memo.ru/hr/hotpoints/caucas1/index.htm, accessed 10 June 2010.

Memorial (2006) '"Counterterrorism Operation" by the Russian Federation in the North Caucasus throughout 1999–2006', *Memorial*, available at: www.memo.ru/hr/hotpoints/N-Caucas/dkeng.htm, accessed 14 April 2007.

Memorial (2009) 'Russia: Prosecute Rights Violations in North Caucasus: European Court Has Issued 104 Rulings Against Moscow Over Killings, Other Attacks', *Memorial*, 4 June, available at: www.memo.ru/2009/06/05/0506092.htm, accessed 5 July 2010.

Mendelson, S. (2000) 'The Putin path: civil liberties and human rights in retreat', *Problems of Post-Communism*, 47, 5, pp. 3–12.

Mendelson, S. (2002) 'Russians' Rights Imperiled: Has Anybody Noticed?', *International Security*, 26, 4, pp. 39–69.

Mendras, M. (2012) *Russian Politics: The Paradox of a Weak State* (London: C. Hurst & Co Publishers).

Mereminskaya, E. (2014) 'Stsenarri krizisa: Minekonomrazitiya napisalo <<shokovyi>> stsenarii razvitiya ekonomiki', *Gazeta.Ru*, 9 April, available at: www.gazeta.ru/business/2014/04/08/5985645.shtml, accessed 17 April 2014.

Mereu, F. (2001) 'Russia: Media Say Attacks Were Not Only Against US', Radio Free Europe, Radio Liberty, 12 September available at: www.rferl.org/features/2001/09/12092001125639.asp, accessed 5 April 2007.

Metz, S. (2003) 'Insurgency and counterinsurgency in Iraq', *The Washington Quarterly* 27, 1, pp. 25–36.

Miles, R. and Thraenhart, D. (eds) (1995) *Migration and European Integration: The Dynamics of Inclusion and Exclusion* (London: Pinter), pp. 53–72.

Milliken, J. (2001) *The social construction of the Korean war: conflict and its possibilities* (New York: Manchester University Press).

Ministry for Foreign Affairs of the Russian Federation (1999) 'Osnovnye napravleniya vneshnei politili Rossii na sovremennom etape. Vystuplenie stats-sekretarya – zamestitelya ministra inostrannykh del Rossii V.D Sredina v akademii gosudarstvennoi sluzhby pri prezidente rossiiskoi federatsii, 28 sentyabrya', *Diplomaticheskii vestnik*, 10, October.

Ministry for Foreign Affairs of the Russian Federation (2000) 'Kontseptsiya vneshnei politiki Rossiiskoi Federatsii', *Diplomaticheskii vestnik*, 8.

Ministry for Foreign Affairs of the Russian Federation (2000) 'Kontseptsiya natsional'noi bezopasnosti Rossiiskoi Federatsii', *Diplomaticheskii vestnik*, 2.

Ministry for Foreign Affairs of the Russian Federation (2000) 'Situation in the Chechen Republic', News Bulletin from the Ministry for Foreign Affairs of the Russian Federation, 29 August, available at: www.ln.mid.ru/Ns-rkonfl.nsf/8850205d7c032570432569e000362cb1/803ad74f4d8e893d43256ce10046b895?OpenDocument, accessed 5 April 2010.

Ministry for Foreign Affairs of the Russian Federation (2000) 'Statement from the Ministry of Foreign Affairs', 7 April, *Diplomaticheskii Vestnik*, May, available at: www.ln.mid.ru/dip_vest.nsf/99b2ddc4f717c733c32567370042ee43/e9c96e639cff38b1c32568ef0027c966?OpenDocument, accessed 5 January 2009.

Ministry for Foreign Affairs of the Russian Federation (2002) 'Regarding the Showing on Czech Public TV Channels of a Film in Support of Chechen Terrorists', Press Release, Ministry for Foreign Affairs of the Russian Federation, 6 November available at: www.mid.ru/brp_4.nsf/e78a48070f128a7b43256999005bcbb3/b2417df92e6e2c4343256c6a0028e072?OpenDocument, accessed 12 June 2010.

Ministry for Foreign Affairs of the Russian Federation (2002) 'Russian Foreign Ministry Spokesman Mikhail Kamynin's Interview with Interfax News Agency on Various Aspects of Cooperation of Russia with Foreign Countries and International Organisations in Struggle Against Terrorism', Ministry for Foreign Affairs of the Russian

Federation, available at: www.ln.mid.ru/Brp_4.nsf/arh/C4F8E3C6B8D77BFFC325707B002550A7?OpenDocument, accessed 5 June 2010.

Ministry for Foreign Affairs of the Russian Federation (2003) 'Interview with First Deputy Foreign Minister of Russia Vyacheslav Trubnikov to ITAR-TASS News Agency', 15 January, available at: www.ln.mid.ru/Brp_4.nsf/arh/8498405114D9D09C43256CB0002E6BA8?OpenDocument, accessed 20 September 2010.

Ministry for Foreign Affairs of the Russian Federation (2003) 'Concerning the Holding of a Republican Referendum in Chechnya', Press release, Ministry for Foreign Affairs of the Russian Federation, available at: www.mid.ru/Brp_4.nsf/arh/116684CEB052E226C3256EC9001CD30D?OpenDocument, accessed 10 June 2010.

Ministry for Foreign Affairs of the Russian Federation (2004) 'Interview with the Deputy Foreign Minister Aleksandr Safonov on the issue of the fight against international terrorism', Press release, Ministry for Foreign Affairs of the Russian Federation, 21 January, available at: www.mid.ru/ns-rkonfl.nsf/ac72b85191b0db0643256adc002905c1/30e74d191e2478f9c3256e76004781a7?OpenDocument, accessed 26 January 2008.

Ministry for Foreign Affairs of the Russian Federation (2005) 'Information and Press Department Commentary Regarding the Elimination of Aslan Maskhadov', 11 March, available at: www.ln.mid.ru/Brp_4.nsf/arh/F88E779A93731B3FC3256FC40055765E?, accessed 3 June 2010.

Ministry for Foreign Affairs of the Russian Federation (2005) 'Russian Foreign Ministry Spokesman Mikhail Kamynin's Interview with Interfax News Agency on Various Aspects of Cooperation of Russia with Foreign Countries and International Organisations in Struggle Against Terrorism', 12 September, available at: www.ln.mid.ru/Brp_4.nsf/arh/C4F8E3C6B8D77BFFC325707B002550A7?OpenDocument, accessed 13 July 2010.

Ministry for Foreign Affairs of the Russian Federation (2006) 'A major press conference given by President Vladimir Putin for the Russian and foreign media has taken place at the Kremlin, Moscow, January 31, 2006', Ministry for Foreign Affairs of the Russian Federation, available at: www.mid.ru/Brp_4.nsf/arh/784A0038F85FDA38C325710A002B086F?OpenDocument, accessed 15 June 2010.

Ministry for Foreign Affairs of the Russian Federation (2006) 'Russia's Activities at the UN: Results of 2006', Ministry for Foreign Affairs of the Russian Federation, available at www.mid.ru/brp_4.nsf/e78a48070f128a7b43256999005bcbb3/281ee0e34a13b1a8c325726f0047c561?OpenDocument, accessed 4 June 2010.

Ministry for Foreign Affairs of the Russian Federation (2006) 'Foreign Journalists' Trip to the Chechen Republic', Press Release, Ministry for Foreign Affairs of the Russian Federation, 28 February, available at:www.mid.ru/Brp_4.nsf/arh/841DDFECB4FB29D1C3257123005D14C0?OpenDocument, accessed 5 September 2010.

Ministry for Foreign Affairs of the Russian Federation (2007) 'Statement by the Russian Ministry of Foreign Affairs on Russian-British Relations', Ministry for Foreign Affairs of the Russian Federation, 16 July, available at: www.ln.mid.ru/brp_4.nsf/e78a48070f128a7b43256999005bcbb3/77832e42834f1149c325731b00272191?OpenDocument, accessed 5 July 2010.

Ministry for Foreign Affairs of the Russian Federation (2008) 'Talks between Vladimir Putin and Silvio Berlusconi continued after a working breakfast at Villa Certosa, Sardinia, April 18, 2008', Press Service, Ministry for Foreign Affairs of the Russian Federation, 19 April, available at: www.mid.ru/Brp_4.nsf/arh/EA4328F5B48B03D0C32574320024A071?OpenDocument, accessed 1 July 2010.

Ministry for Foreign Affairs of the Russian Federation (2008) 'Russian Foreign Policy

Bibliography

Concept', 12 July, available at: www.mid.ru/ns-osndoc.nsf/1e5f0de28fe77fdcc32575d900298676/869c9d2b87ad8014c32575d9002b1c38?OpenDocument, accessed 3 May 2009.

Ministry of Economic Development and Trade (2005) 'Itogi Deyatel'stva Ministerstva Economicheskogo Razvitiya i Torgovli Rossiiskoi Federatsii v 2004 godu i Zadachi Ministerstva na 2005 god' Rasshirennoe Zasedanie Kollegii', 29 March, available at: www.economy.gov.ru, accessed 10 December 2008.

Ministry of the Interior of the Russian Federation (1999) 'Ministr inostrannykh del RF Igor Ivanov: "V odnu diplomatiyu nel'zya voiti dvazhdy"', *Vek*, (VEK-No. 044), 12 November.

Ministry of Interior of the Russian Federation (2002) 'Iz vystupleniya Ministra vnutrinikh del Rossii Borisa Gryzlova na rasshirennom zasedanii Kollegii MVD RF', Press release, Ministry of the Interior of the Russian Federation, available at: www.mvd.ru/press/interview/15/381/, accessed 3 June 2010.

Ministry of Interior of the Russian Federation (2004) 'Interv'yu I. O. Ministra vnutrinikh del Chechenskoi Respubliki Ruslana Shakhaevicha Alkhanova po itogam operativno-sluzhebnoi deyatel'nosti v 2004 godu', Press release, Ministry of the Interior of the Russian Federation, 28 July, available at: www.mvd.ru/press/interview/2825/, accessed 2 August 2010.

Ministry of Interior of the Russian Federation (2005) 'Interv'yu zamestitelya Ministra vnutrennikh del Rossii general-polkovnika militsii Arkadiya Edeleva razete "Shchit i mech"', Press release, Ministry of the Interior of the Russian Federation, 6 October, available at: www.mvd.ru/press/interview/3708/, accessed 2 September 2010.

Ministry of the Interior of the Russian Federation (2005) 'Interv'yu Ministra vnutrynnikh del Rossii general-polkovnika Rashida Nurgalieva "Rossiiskoi gazete"', Press release, Ministry of the Interior of the Russian Federation, 29 September, available at: twww.mvd.ru/press/interview/3690/, accessed 17 June 2010.

Ministry of the Interior of the Russian Federation (2007) 'Chechenskaya Respublika nakanune vyborov', Ministry of the Interior of the Russian Federation, 13 November, available at:www.mvd.ru/news/13215/, accessed 3 September 2010.

Ministry of the Interior of the Russian Federation (2007) 'Interv'yu zamestitelya Ministra vnutrennikh del Rossiiskoi Federatsii general-polkovnika militsii Akradiya Edeleva "Rossiiskoi gazete"', Ministry of the Interior of the Russian Federation, 2 February, available at: www.mvd.ru/news/10468/, accessed 7 June 2010.

Ministry of the Interior of the Russian Federation (2007) 'Segodnya v Chechenskoi Respublike otkryt memorial'nyi pamyatnik', Ministry of the Interior of the Russian Federation, 11 October, available at: www.mvd.ru/news/12711, accessed 30 July 2010.

Ministry of the Interior of the Russian Federation (2008) 'Vosem' let vremennoi operativnoi gruppirovke organov i podrazdelenii MVD Rossii', Ministry of the Interior of the Russian Federation, 22 April, available at: www.mvd.ru/news/15621/, accessed 4 September 2010.

Ministry of the Interior of the Russian Federation (2008) 'Chechnya derzhit kurs na ekonomicheskogo razvitie', Ministry of the Interior of the Russian Federation, 25 March, available at: www.mvd.ru/news/15015/, accessed 20 June 2010.

Ministry of the Interior of the Russian Federation (2008) 'Segodnya v zasedanii MVD po Chechenskoi Respublike sostoyalos' Koordinatsionnoe soveshchanie MVD Rossii po voprosu "Ob uchastii organov vnutrinnykh del Chechenskoi Respubliki po obespechenii realizatsii prioretetnykh natsional'nykh proektov i federal'nykh tselevykh programm, raspredelenii kompensatsionniykh vyplat za utrachennoe i razrushennoe zhil'e', Ministry of the Interior of the Russian Federation, 31 July, available at: www.mvd.ru/news/18090/, accessed 3 June 2010.

Mischke, J. and Umland, A. (2014) 'Germany's New Ostpolitik An Old Foreign Policy Doctrine Gets a Makeover', *Foreign Affairs*, 9 April, available at: www.foreignaffairs.com/articles/141115/jakob-mischke-and-andreas-umland/germanys-new-ostpolitik?cid=soc-facebook-in-snapshots-germanys_new_ostpolitik-041114, accessed 20 April 2014.

Mishra, A. (2007) *Security in new Russia* (Delhi).

Mitzen, J. (2006) 'Ontological security in world politics: State identity and the security dilemma', *European Journal of International Relations*, 12, 3, pp. 341–370.

Mohsin Hashim, S. (2005) 'Putin's Etatization project and limits to democratic reforms in Russia', *Communist and Post-Communist Studies*, 38, 1, pp. 25–48.

Monaghan, A. (2008) '"An enemy at the gates" or "from victory to victory"? Russian foreign policy', *International Affairs*, 84, 4, pp. 717–733.

Monaghan, A. (2012) 'The vertikal: power and authority in Russia', *International Affairs*, 88, pp. 1–16.

Moore, C. (2006) 'Reading the hermeneutics of violence: The literary turn and Chechnya', *Global Society*, 20, 2, pp. 179–198.

Moore, C. (2007) 'Inter-Generational Change and the Integration of Regional Groups in the Chechen Resistance', *Central Asia Caucasus Analyst*, 9, 9, pp. 9–11.

Moore, C. (2006) 'Reading the hermeneutics of violence: The literary turn and Chechnya', *Global Society*, 20, 2, pp. 179–198.

Moore, C. (2007) 'Inter-Generational Change and the Integration of Regional Groups in the Chechen Resistance', *Central Asia Caucasus Analyst*, 9, 9, pp. 9–11.

Moore, C. (2008) 'Russia's post-colonial war(s)?', *Europe-Asia Studies*, 60, 5, pp. 851–861.

Moore, C. and Tumelty, P. (2008) 'Foreign Fighters and the Case of Chechnya: A Critical Assessment', *Studies in Conflict and Terrorism*, 31, 5, pp. 5–53.

Moore, C. and Tumelty, P. (2009) 'Unholy Alliances in Chechnya: From Communism and Nationalism to Islamism and Salafism', *The Journal of Communist Studies and Transition Politics*, 25, 1, pp. 73–94.

Moore, C. and Wills, D. (2008) 'Securitising the Caucasus: From Political Violence to Place Branding in Chechnya', *Place Branding and Public Diplomacy*, 4, 3, pp. 252–262.

Moore, K. (2003) 'Russia: How Western Attitudes Toward Wars Have Shifted (Part 3)', Radio Free Europe, Radio Liberty, 3 October, available at: http://www.rferl.org/content/article/1104549.html, accessed: 19 August 2014.

Morozov, V. (2002) 'Resisting Entropy, Discarding Human Rights Romantic Realism and Securitization of Identity in Russia', *Cooperation and Conflict*, 37, 4, pp. 409–430.

Morozov, V. (2008) 'Sovereignty and democracy in contemporary Russia: a modern subject faces the post-modern world', *Journal of International Relations and Development*, 11, pp. 152–180.

Moshe, G. (ed.) (2007) *Ethno-Nationalism, Islam and the State in the Caucasus: Post-Soviet Disorder* (Abingdon: Routledge).

Moshes, A. (2012) 'Russia's European policy under Medvedev: how sustainable is a new compromise?', *International Affairs*, 88, 1, pp. 17–30.

Mukhin, V. (2010) 'The magic of anti-terrorist initiatives' *Nezavisimaya gazeta*, 19 January, p. 3.

Mukhin, V. (2011) 'This is not a fight against extremism, it's a war', *Nezavisimaya gazeta*, 1 August.

Mukhin, V. (2012a) 'Dagestan looking more like a Gaza strip', *Nezavisimaya gazeta*, 6 July, p. 2.
Mukhin, V. (2012b) 'The third Chechen war', *Nezavisimaya gazeta*, 10 October, p. 3.
Müller, M. (2011) 'State Dirigisme in Megaprojects: Governing the 2014 Winter Olympics in Sochi', *Environment and Planning A*, 43, 9, pp. 2091–2108.
Müller, M. (2014) 'Introduction: Winter Olympics Sochi 2014: what is at stake?', *East European Politics*.
Muradov, M. (2006) 'Vladimir Putin Leaves Chechnya to Ramzan Kadyrov', *Kommersant*, 10 August, available at: www.kommersant.com/page.asp?idr=527&id=696515, accessed 4 March 2008.
Muradov, M. (2011) 'Vladimir Putin finds a way of dealing with militants', *Kommersant*, 24 August.
Muradov, M., Larintseva, A. and Ivanov, M. (2012) 'Aleksandr Khloponin draws the line between his subordinates', *Kommersant*, 8 September, p. 1.
Murray, D. and Brown, D. (eds) (2012) *Multipolarity in the 21st Century: A New World Order* (London: Routledge).
Neal, A. W. (2009) 'Securitization and Risk at the EU Border: The Origins of FRONTEX', *Journal of Common Market Studies*, 47, 2, pp. 333–356.
Neumann, I. (1999) *Uses of the other: "The East" in European identity formation* (Minneapolis: University of Minnesota Press).
Neumann, I. (2005) 'Russia as a Great Power' in Hedenskog, J. *et al.* (eds) (2005), pp. 13–28.
Neumann, I. (2008) 'Russia as a Great Power, 1815–2007', *Journal of International Relations and Development*, 11, pp. 128–151.
Newsru.com (2001) 'Rossiiskii ombudsmen prizval musul'man Rossii pomoch' ureguli-rovat' situatsiyu v Chechne', Newsru.com, 30 July, available at: www.newsru.com/arch/religy/30jul2001/invocation.html, accessed 30 June 2008.
Newsru.com (2002) 'Bush: problema Chechni – vnutrenee delo Rossii', NewsRu.com, 21 November, available at: www.newsru.com/world/21nov2002/bush_print.html, accessed 3 May 2010.
Newsru.com (2002) 'V svyazi s teraktom v Groznom militsiya v Moskve i oblasti perevedena na usilennyi rezhim sluzhby', NewsRu.com, 27 December, available at: www.newsru.com/russia/27dec2002/force_print.htmlNEWSru.com, accessed 10 September 2010.
Newsru.com (2002) 'Vpervie posle teraktov 11 sentyabrya SShA kritikuyut deistviya Rossii v Chechne', 11 January, available at: www.newsru.com/world/11jan2002/usa_chech_print.html, accessed 2 May 2010.
Newsru.com (2003) 'Rossiiskie pogranichniki provodyat na granitse Gruzii i Chechni operatsiyu "Eshelon-2003"', NewsRu.com, 15 June, available at: www.newsru.com/russia/15jun2003/esh_print.html, accessed 20 August 2010.
Newsru.com (2003) 'Na territorii Chechni deistvuet okolo 1300 aktivnikh boevikov', 16 July, available at: www.newsru.com/russia/16jul2003/boeviki_print.html, accessed 13 June 2010.
Newsru.com (2008) 'Putin utverdil Kontseptsiyu sotsial'no-ekonomicheskogo razvitiya Rossii do 2020 goda', NewsRu.com, 25 November, available at: http://txt.newsru.com/finance/25nov2008/conception.html, accessed 16 April 2009.
Newsru.com (2009) 'Za neispolnenie reshenii Strasburgskogo suda Rossiyu mogut vremenno vygnat' iz Soveta Evropy', Newsru.com, 2 March, available at: http://txt.newsru.com/russia/02mar2009/eurosud_kovler.html, accessed 18 July 2010.

Nezavisimaya gazeta (2001) 'Rossiya dolzhna ychest' oshibki Ameriki. V Chechne neobkhodimo politicheskoe uregulirovanie', *Nezavisimaya gazeta*, 13 September.

Nicholson, M. (2001) 'Putin's Russia: slowing the pendulum without stopping the clock', *International Affairs*, 77, 4, pp. 867–884.

Nivat, A. (2005) 'The Black Widows: Chechen Women Join the Fight for Independence—and Allah', *Studies in Conflict and Terrorism*, 28, 5, pp. 413–419.

Nizamutdinov, A. (2003) 'Il'yasov, v Chechne net voiny', *RIA Novosti*, 15 May, available at: www.rian.ru/politics/20030515/379747.html, accessed 6 June 2010.

Navalny, A. A. (2014) 'How to Punish Putin', *New York Times*, 19 March.

Nodia, G. (2010) 'What Is Georgia's Strategy In The North Caucasus?', Radio Free Europe Radio Liberty, 3 November, available at: www.rferl.org/content/What_Is_Georgias_Strategy_In_The_North_Caucasus/2208382.html, accessed 10 May 2014.

Novoprudsky, S. (2004) 'Znak pobedy, V Rossii nastupilo drugoe istoricheskoe vremya', *Vremya Novostei*, 6 September.

Nygren, B. (2005) 'Russia's Relations with Ukraine and Belarus', in Kanet, R. E. (2005), pp. 149–164.

Nygren, B. (2007a) 'Putin's Attempts to Subjugate Georgia: From Sabre-Rattling to the Power of the Purse', in Kanet, R. E. (2007), pp. 107–123.

Nygren, B. (2007b). *The Rebuilding of Greater Russia: Putin's Foreign Policy toward the CIS Countries* (Abingdon: Routledge).

O'Loughlin, J., Holland, J. E. and Witmer, F. (2011) 'The Changing Geography of Violence in Russia's North Caucasus, 1999–2011: Regional Trends and Local Dynamics in Dagestan, Ingushetia, and KabardinoBalkaria', *Eurasian Geography and Economics*, 52, 5, pp. 596–630.

O'Loughlin, J., Tuathail, G. and Kolossov, V. (2004) 'A 'Risky Westward Turn'? Putin's 9–11 Script and Ordinary Russians', *Europe-Asia Studies*, 56, 1, pp. 3–34.

Oates, S. (2006) 'Framing fear: Findings from a study of election news and terrorist threat in Russia', *Europe-Asia Studies*, 58, 2, pp. 281–290.

Oates, S., Lee Kaid, L. and Berry, M. (2009) *Terrorism, elections, and democracy political campaigns in the United States, Great Britain, and Russia* (New York: Palgrave Macmillan).

Oelsner, A. (2005) '(De)Securitisation Theory and Regional Peace: Some Theoretical Reflections and a Case Study on the Way to Stable Peace', *EUI Working Paper*, RSCAS no. 2.

O'Flynn, K. (2012) 'Big-name writers lead protest rally of 10,000', *The Moscow Times*, May 14.

Okara, A. (2007) 'Sovereign Democracy: A new Russian idea or a PR project?', *Russia in Global Affairs*.

Ordzhonikidze, S. (2001) 'Statement by Sergei Ordzhonikidze, Deputy Foreign Minister of the Russian Federation and head of the Russian delegation, in the course of a high-level dialogue within the 56 session of the United Nations General Assembly on the theme "Responding to globalization: facilitating the integration of developing countries into the world economy in the 21 century"', Ministry for Foreign Affairs of the Russian Federation, 20 September 2001, available at: www.mid.ru/brp_4.nsf/e78a48070f128a7b43256999005bcbb3/93c846d40ba8489543256ad4003ccd26?OpenDocument, accessed 14 February 2007.

Ortmann, S. (2008) 'Diffusion as discourse of danger: Russian self-representations and the framing of the Tulip Revolution', *Central Asian Survey*, 27, 3–4, pp. 363–378.

Ortmann, S. (2008) *Re-imagining Westphalia: identity in IR and the construction of the Russian State* (London School of Economics and Political Science. PhD Thesis).

Orttung, R. W. and Zhemukhov, S. (2014) 'The 2014 Sochi Olympic mega-project and Russia's political economy', *East European Politics*.

Overland, I. (2011) 'Modernization after Medvedev?', *Russian Analytical Digest*, 105, pp. 2–4.

Pain, E. (2000) 'The Second Chechen War: The Information Component', *Military Review*, July–August.

Pain, E. (2005) 'The Chechen War in the Context of Contemporary Russian Politics', in Sakwa, R. (ed.) *Chechnya: from past to future* (London: Anthem Press), pp. 67–78.

Pallin, C. V. (2009) *A failed exercise in defence decision making* (Abingdon: Routledge).

Panchenkov, V. (2008) 'Situatsiya pod kontrolom', *Rossiiskaya gazeta*, 10 January.

Paramonov, V., Strokov, A. and Stolpovski, O. (2009) *Russia in Central Asia: policy, security, and economics* (Brown, NY: Nova Science Pub).

Parfitt, T. (2007) 'The battle for the soul of Chechnya', *The Guardian*, 22 November.

Patrushev, N. (1999) 'Iz perepiski glavnogo redaktora', *Moskovskii komsomolets*, 25 September.

Pchelov, O. (2008) 'Mir Prishel na Kavkaz', *Krasnaya zvezda*, 47, 21 March.

Penketh, A. (2007) 'Putin urged to restore peace in Chechnya', *The Independent*, 7 May.

Peoples, C. and Vaughan-Williams, N. (2010) *Critical Security Studies: An Introduction* (Abingdon: Routledge).

Petersson, B. (2014) 'Still Embodying the Myth? Russia's Recognition as a Great Power and the Sochi Winter Games', *Problems of Post-Communism*, 61, 1, January–February 2014, pp. 30–40.

Petrov, N. (2013a) 'Russia Minus Caucasus', *Carnegie Endowment for Peace*, 16 July, available at: http://carnegie.ru/eurasiaoutlook/?fa=52409, accessed 14 March 2014.

Petrov, N. (2013b) 'Failed North Caucasus Policy', *The Moscow Times*, 22 July, available at: www.themoscowtimes.com/opinion/article/failed-north-caucasus-policy/483441.html, accessed 14 March 2014.

Petrov, N. and McFaul, M. (2005) 'The Essence of Putin's Managed Democracy', Russian and Eurasian Programme at the Carnegie Endowment for International Peace, 18 October, available at www.carnegieendowment.org/events/index.cfm?fa=eventDetail&id=819, accessed 6 June 2008.

Petrov, N., Lipman, M. and Hale, H. E. (2010) 'Overmanaged Democracy in Russia: Governance Implications of Hybrid Regimes', Russian and Eurasian Programme at the Carnegie Endowment for International Peace, available at: http://carnegieendowment.org/2010/02/25/overmanaged-democracy-in-russia-governance-implicationsof-hybrid-regimes/27c, accessed 10 November 2012.

Pettenger, M. E. (2007) *The social construction of climate change: power, knowledge, norms, discourses* (Burlington: Ashgate).

Pilipchuk, A. (2003) 'Nasha glavnaya zadacha, zakonnym putem neytralizovat' bandgruppy' Strana.ru, 25 December, cited in Statements and Commentaries, *Memorial*, www.memo.ru/hr/hotpoints/caucas1/rubr/3/l200312.htm, accessed 15 April 2007.

Pirchner, H. (2005) *Reviving greater Russia?: The future of Russia's borders with Belarus, Georgia, Kazakhstan, Moldova and Ukraine* (Washington, DC: American Foreign Policy Council).

Polikovsky, A. (2001) 'Interv'yu v nomer general', *Novaya gazeta*, 20 September.

Polit.ru (1999) 'Ministr po delam natsional'nostei schitaet neobkhodimoi skoreishuyu vstrechu Putina i Maskhadov', *Polit.ru*, 18 September, available at: www.polit.ru/news/1999/09/18/536951.html, accessed 18 February 2008.

Politkovskaya, A. (2003) *A small corner of hell: dispatches from Chechnya* (Chicago: University of Chicago Press).

Ponomareva, Y. (2013) 'Russia sinks to 148th place on Press Freedom Index', *Russia Beyond the Headlines*, 4 February, available at: http://rbth.com/society/2013/02/04/russia_sinks_to_148th_place_on_press_freedom_index_22479.html, accessed 7 June 2013.

Popescu, N. (2006) 'Russia's Soft Power Ambitions', *CEPS Policy Briefs*, 112.

Póti, L. (2008) 'Evolving Russian Foreign and Security Policy: Interpreting the Putin doctrine', *Acta Slavica Iaponica (Acta Slavica Iaponica)*, 25.

Pouliot, V. (2004) 'The Essence of Constructivism', *Journal of International Relations and Development*, 7, 3, pp. 319–336.

Pouliot, V. (2007) ' "Sobjectivism": Toward a Constructivist Methodology', *International Studies Quarterly*, 51, pp. 359–384.

Pouliot, V. (2010) *International security in practice the politics of NATO-Russia diplomacy* (Cambridge: Cambridge University Press).

Pravda, A. (2003) 'Putin's foreign policy after 11 September: radical or revolutionary?', in Gorodetsky (ed.) (2003), pp. 39–57.

Pravda, A. (ed.) (2005) *Leading Russia, Putin in Perspective, Essays in honour of Archie Brown* (Oxford: Oxford University Press).

Pretorius, J. (2008) 'The Security Imaginary: Explaining Military Isomorphism', *Security Dialogue*, 39, pp. 99–120.

Proedrou, F. (2007) 'The EU-Russia Energy Approach under the Prism of Interdependence', *European Security*, 16, 3–4, pp. 329–355.

Pruganov, S. (Colonel) (1999) 'Chechnya stala golovom mezhdunarodnogo terrorizma', *Krasnaya zvezda*, 225, 21 October.

Putin, V. (2002d) 'Vystuplenie na vstreche s predstavitelyami chechenskoi obshchestvenosti', 10 November, available at: www.kremlin.ru/text/appears/2002/11/29549.shtml, accessed 22 June 2005.

Putin, V. (1999a) 'Russia at the turn of the millennium', 29 December, available at www.pravitelstvo.gov.ru, accessed 25 May 2005.

Putin, V. (1999b) 'Chechnya yavlyaetsya rossiiskoi territoriei, i dislotsirovat'sya nashi voiska gde ugodno', *SPB Vedomosti*, 1 October.

Putin, V. (1999c) 'Interview with the German Journal "Focus" ', *Diplomaticheskii vestnik*, 1999, 11.

Putin, V. (2000a) 'Annual Address to the Federal Assembly', 8 July 2000, available at: www.kremlin.ru/appears/2000/07/08/0000_type63372type63374type82634_28782.shtml, accessed 1 December 2008.

Putin, V. (2000b) 'Interview with the French Newspaper', *Le Figaro*, 26 October 2000, available at http://archive.kremlin.ru/eng/speeches/2000/10/26/0000_type82916_134301.shtml, accessed 2 December 2008.

Putin, V. (2000c) 'Interview with the French television channel TF1, France 3, radio station RFI and television channel ORT', 23 October, available at: http://archive.kremlin.ru/appears/2000/10/23/0000_type63379_28955.shtml, accessed 2 December 2008.

Putin, V. (2000d) 'Interview with the ORT TV channel', 15 January, available at: http://archive.kremlin.ru/eng/speeches/2000/01/15/0000_type82912type82916_122607.shtml, accessed 15 November 2008.

Putin, V. (2000e) 'Opening statement at the Enlarged meeting of the Russian Ministry of Interior Board', 21 January, available at: www.kremlin.ru/text/appears/2000/01/28807.shtml, accessed 26 June 2009.

Putin, V. (2000f) 'Statement Concerning Violation of Human Rights in the Course of the Counterterrorist Operation in the North Caucasus, 13 April, available at: http://archive.kremlin.ru/eng/speeches/2000/04/13/0000_type82912_122397.shtml, accessed 12 March 2008.

Putin, V. (2001a) 'Interview with the Finnish Newspaper "Helsingen sanomat"', 1 September, available at http://archive.kremlin.ru/eng/speeches/2001/09/01/0002_type82916_162305.shtml, accessed 12 April 2008.

Putin, V. (2001b) 'Interview with the German Magazine "Focus"', 19 September, available at: http://archive.kremlin.ru/eng/speeches/2001/09/19/0001_type82916_136377.shtml, accessed 17 February 2008.

Putin, V. (2001c) 'Interview with the German Newspaper "Bild"', 18 September, available at http://archive.kremlin.ru/eng/speeches/2001/09/18/0001_type82916_136376.shtml, accessed 20 April 2008.

Putin, V. (2001d) 'Zayavlenie Prezidenta Rossii', 24 September, available at: http://archive.kremlin.ru/appears/2001/09/24/0002_type63374type82634_28639.shtml, accessed 20 December 2008.

Putin, V. (2001e) 'Speech at CIS Heads of Government Council Meeting', 28 September, available at: http://archive.kremlin.ru/eng/speeches/2001/09/28/0001_type82912type82914_138536.shtml, accessed 20 May 2009.

Putin, V. (2002a) 'Address to the Federal Assembly', 18 April, available at: http://archive.kremlin.ru/appears/2002/04/18/0001_type63372type63374type82634_28876.shtml, accessed 20 September 2010.

Putin, V. (2002b) 'Introductory Remarks at a Security Council Meeting on the situation in Chechen Republic', 27 February, available at: http://archive.kremlin.ru/appears/2002/02/27/0000_type63374type63378_28817.shtml, accessed 10 August 2010.

Putin, V. (2002c) 'Vstupitel'noe slovo na soveshchanii po voprosam sotsial'no-ekonomicheskogo razvitiya Yuzhnogo Federal'nogo okruga', 16 May, available at: http://archive.kremlin.ru/appears/2002/05/16/0003_type63374type63378_28906.shtml, accessed 20 September 2010.

Putin, V. (2003) 'Address to the Chechen Nation', 16 March, available at: http://archive.kremlin.ru/appears/2003/03/16/0803_type63374type82634_40680.shtml, accessed 15 September 2010.

Putin, V. (2004a) 'Annual Address at the Federal Assembly', 26 May, available at: http://archive.kremlin.ru/appears/2004/05/26/0003_type63372type63374type82634_71501.shtml, accessed 10 September 2010.

Putin, V. (2004b) 'Excerpt from a Press Conference at the End of a Visit to the Kamchatka Region', 24 June, available at: http://archive.kremlin.ru/eng/speeches/2004/06/24/2129_type82915_73435.shtml, accessed 10 September 2010.

Putin, V. (2004c) 'Press Conference', 23 December, Ministry for Foreign Affairs of the Russian Federation, available at: www.ln.mid.ru/Brp_4.nsf/arh/4FB0F1F9C0D53683C3256F740024DEC4?OpenDocument, accessed 12 September 2010.

Putin, V. (2004d) 'Speech at the World Congress of Media Agencies', 24 September, available at: http://president.kremlin.ru/eng/speeches/2004/09/24/1700_type82913_77199.shtml, accessed 10 June 2010.

Putin, V. (2004e) 'Address to the Nation', 4 September, available at: http://president.kremlin.ru/eng/speeches/2004/09/04/1958_type82912_76332.shtml, accessed 16 June 2005.

Putin, V. (2004f) 'Po vertikali' (Speech at the Enlarged Government meeting with the Government and Heads of the Regions), 13 September, reported in *Rossiiskaya gazeta*, 14 September 2004.

Putin, V. (2004g) 'Speech at a Meeting with the Cabinet Members', 11 May, available at: http://archive.kremlin.ru/appears/2004/05/11/1702_type63374type63378type63381_64304.shtml, accessed 20 September 2010.

Putin, V. (2005a) 'Meeting with Aimani Kadyrova and Ramzan Kadyrov', 21 August, available at: www.kremlin.ru/eng/text/speeches/2005/08/21/1425_type84779_92700.shtml, accessed 20 June 2010.

Putin, V. (2005b) 'Speech at the Meeting with the Cabinet Members, the Heads of the Federal Assembly, and State Council Members', 5 September, available at http://archive.kremlin.ru/appears/2005/09/05/1531_type63374type63378type82634_93296.shtml, accessed 20 September 2010.

Putin, V. (2005c) 'The opening of the Meeting with the Leadership of the Republic of Chechnya', 21 December, available at: http://archive.kremlin.ru/appears/2005/12/21/1949_type63374type63378type82634_99215.shtml, accessed 30 June 2010.

Putin, V. (2005d) 'Interview with Television Channel Nederland 1 and Newspaper NRC Handelsblad', 31 October, available at: http://archive.kremlin.ru/appears/2005/10/31/1836_type63379_96446.shtml, accessed 10 September 2010.

Putin, V. (2005e) 'Opening Remarks at Meeting with the Leadership of the Republic of Chechnya', 21 December, available at: http://archive.kremlin.ru/appears/2005/12/21/2204_type63378_99273.shtml, accessed 30 June 2010.

Putin, V. (2006a) 'Annual Address to the Federal Assembly', 10 May, available at: http://archive.kremlin.ru/eng/speeches/2006/05/10/1823_type70029type82912_105566.shtml, accessed 10 June 2010.

Putin, V. (2006b) 'Interview with TF-1 Television Channel (France)', 12 July, available at: http://archive.kremlin.ru/appears/2006/07/12/1133_type63379_108509.shtml, accessed 30 July 2010.

Putin, V. (2006c) 'Nachalo vstrechi s liderami musul'manskikh organisatsii Rossii', Presidential website, 10 January, available at: http://archive.kremlin.ru/appears/2006/01/10/1920_type63376_100096.shtml, accessed 7 June 2010.

Putin, V. (2006d) 'Speech at a Meeting of the Board of the Federal Security Service (FSB)', 7 February 2006, available at: http://archive.kremlin.ru/eng/speeches/2006/02/07/1946_type82912type82913_101157.shtml, accessed 20 June 2010.

Putin, V. (2006e) 'Transcript of the Press Conference for the Russian and Foreign Media', 31 January 2006, available at: http://archive.kremlin.ru/eng/speeches/2006/01/31/0953_type82915type82917_100901.shtml, accessed 1 June 2010.

Putin, V. (2006f) 'Vystuplenie na Rossiisko-Kitaiskom ekonomicheskom forume', Presidential website, 22 March, available at: http://archive.kremlin.ru/appears/2006/03/22/1123_type63376type63377type82634_103471.shtml, accessed 5 July 2009.

Putin, V. (2007a) 'Address to the Federal Assembly', 26 April 2007, available at: http://archive.kremlin.ru/appears/2007/04/26/1156_type63372type63374type82634_125339.shtml, accessed 2 June 2010.

Putin, V. (2007b) 'Interv'yu mezharabskomu sputnikovomu telekanalu "Al Jazeera"', Presidential website, 10 February, available at: http://archive.kremlin.ru/appears/2007/02/10/2042_type63379_118108.shtml, accessed 15 July 2010.

Putin, V. (2007c) 'Nachalo vstrechi s general'nom sekretarem Soveta natsional'noi bezopasnosti Saudovskoi Aravii printsem Bandarom ibn Sultanom', Presidential website, 2 August, available at: http://archive.kremlin.ru/appears/2007/08/02/1541_type63377_139461.shtml, accessed 5 June 2010.

Putin, V. (2007d) 'Speech and the Following Discussion at the Munich Conference on Security Policy', 10 February, available at: http://archive.kremlin.ru/eng/speeches/2007/

02/10/0138_type82912type82914type82917type84779_118123.shtml, accessed 3 June 2010.

Putin, V. (2012a) 'Address to the Federal Assembly', Official Website of the President of the Russian Federation, 12 December, available at: http://eng.kremlin.ru/news/4739, accessed 29 June 2013.

Putin, V. (2012b) 'Rossiya i menyayushchiisya mir: Stat'ya Vladimira Putina v <<Moskovskikh novostyakh>>', *Moskovskie Novosti,* 27 February, available at: www.mn.ru/politics/20120227/312306749.html, accessed 7 March 2013.

Putin, V. (2012c) 'Vladimir Putin: byt' sil'nymi: garantii natsional'noi bezopasnosti dlya Rossii', *Rossiskaya Gazeta,* 20 February, available at: http://pda.rg.ru/2012/02/20/putin-armiya.html, accessed 7 March 2013.

Putin, V. 'Russia at the turn of the millennium', 29 December 1999, reported in *Rossiiskaya gazeta,* 30 December 1999.

Radio Free Europe/Radio Liberty (2007) 'If You're A Leader, People Should Fear You', Radio Free Europe/Radio Liberty, 27 February, available at: www.rferl.org/content/article/1074952.html, accessed 10 June 2010.

Radio Free Europe/Radio Liberty (2009) 'Chechen Leader Denies Blame For Killings, Accuses West Of Violence', Radio Free Europe Radio Liberty, 9 August, available at: www.rferl.org/articleprintview/1795686.html, accessed 5 June 2010.

Radnitz, S. (2006) 'Look who's talking! Islamic discourse in the Chechen wars', *Nationalities Papers,* 34, 2, pp. 237–256.

Reddaway, P. (2009) 'Two-Part Czar', *The National Interest* (May/June).

Reddaway, P. and Orttung, R. (2005) *The dynamics of Russian politics: Putin's reform of federal-regional relations* (Lanham: Rowman & Littlefield).

Regnum.ru (2008) 'Ramzan Kadyrov: v sluchae resheniya rukovodstva Rossii my gotovy vmeshat'sya v Yuznoi Ossetii', Regnum.ru, 8 August, available at: www.regnum.ru/news/1038315.html#ixzz10YG75WWF, accessed 17 June 2010.

Remington, T. (2009) 'Putin, Parliament, and Presidential Exploitation of the Terrorist Threat', *Journal of Legislative Studies,* 15, 2–3, pp. 219–238.

Renz, B. (2006) 'Putin's militocracy? An alternative interpretation of Siloviki in contemporary Russian politics', *Europe-Asia Studies,* 58, 6, pp. 903–924.

Reus-Smith, C. (2001) 'Constructivism' in Burchill, S. *et al.* (2001).

RIA Novosti (2002) 'Bolee dvukh tysyach chechenskikh boevikov vernulis' k mirnoi zhizni s 2000 goda', 14 November, available at: www.rian.ru/society/20021114/263567.html, accessed 10 August 2010.

RIA Novosti (2004) 'Alkanov negates possibility of talks with Maskhadov and Basayev', 11 October, available at: http://en.rian.ru/onlinenews/20041011/39770985.html, accessed 20 August 2013.

RIA Novosti (2005) 'Putin calls for more resolute struggle with manifestations of extremism among young people', *RIA Novisti,* 25 January, cited by Johnson's Russia List, #20 – JRL 9033, available at: www.cdi.org/russia/Johnson/9033-20.cfm, accessed 4 June 2010.

RIA Novosti (2006a) 'Chechnya PM tells Europeans of republic's bright prospects', *RIA Novosti,* 2 June, available at: http://en.rian.ru/russia/20060602/48973932.html, accessed 30 June 2010.

RIA Novosti (2006b) 'Wrap: Russia's terrorist no. 1 Basayev killed in south Russia operation', *RIA Novosti,* 19 July, available at: http://en.rian.ru/russia/20060710/51142822.html, accessed 10 June 2010.

RIA Novosti (2007a) 'Chechen president insists Putin should stay for third term', *RIA*

Novosti, 12 July, available at: www.cdi.org/russia/johnson/2007-153-10.cfm, accessed 4 July 2010.

RIA Novosti (2007b) 'PACE urges international probe into Politkovskaya murder', *RIA Novosti*, 5 October, available at: http://en.rian.ru/society/20071005/82677496.html, accessed 14 July 2010.

RIA Novosti (2007c) 'Russia says Litvinenko visited Chechnya to kill for Berezovsky-1', *RIA Novosti*, 1 June, available at: http://en.rian.ru/russia/20070601/66514612.html, accessed 10 July 2010.

RIA Novosti (2007d) 'Russia demands explanation over Zakayev's visit to Strasbourg', World, *RIA Novosti*, 29 June 2007, available at: http://en.rian.ru/world/20070629/68062369.html, accessed 6 July 2010.

RIA Novosti (2007e) 'Time for Europe to close "Chechen issue" – speaker', *RIA Novosti*, 30 March, available at: www.ramzan-kadyrov.ru/smi.php?releases&smi_id=52&month=01&year=2008, accessed 18 June 2010.

RIA Novosti (2007f) 'UN scaling down North Caucasus projects', *RIA Novosti*, 22 November, available at: http://en.rian.ru/russia/20071122/89078873.html, accessed 6 July 2010.

RIA Novosti (2007g) 'United Russia wins over 99% of vote in Chechnya – preliminary data', *RIA Novosti*, 3 December, available at: http://en.rian.ru/russia/20071203/90609389.html, accessed 17 August 2010.

RIA Novosti (2008) 'Pravitel'stvo RF rassmotrit kontseptsiyu razvitiya strany do 2020', *RIA Novosti*, 1 January, available: www.rian.ru/economy/20081001/151746239.html, accessed 16 May 2009.

RIA Novosti (2008a) 'Foreign NGOs support terrorism in Russia – senior senator', *RIA Novosti*, 8 April, cited in Johnson's Russia List, #24 – JRL 2008–72, available at: www.cdi.org/russia/johnson/2008-72-24.cfm, accessed 10 August 2010.

RIA Novosti (2008b) 'Law enforcers killed 72 militants in Chechnya in 2007', *RIA Novosti*, 16 January, available at: http://en.rian.ru/russia/20080116/97117813.html, accessed 30 June 2010.

RIA Novosti (2008c) 'Moscow accuses Stockholm of political hypocrisy', *RIA Novosti*, 4 July, available at: http://en.rian.ru/russia/20080704/113103264.html, accessed 6 June 2010.

RIA Novosti (2009) 'Former leaders of Chechnya admit their ideology was wrong', *RIA Novosti*, 30 May, taken from Johnson's Russia List, #18 – JRL 2009–101, available at: www.cdi.org/russia/johnson/2009-101-18.cfm, accessed 4 August 2010.

Rich, P. B. (2009) 'Russia as a Great Power', *Small Wars & Insurgencies*, 20, 2, pp. 276–299.

Richardson, P. (2014) 'Russia's Turn to Asia: China, Japan, and the APEC 2012 Legacy', *Russian Analytical Digest*, 145.

Ringmar, E. (2008) *Identity, interest and action: a cultural explanation of Sweden's intervention in the Thirty Years War* (New York: Cambridge University Press).

Ritchie, J. and Lewis, J. (2003) *Qualitative research practice: A guide for social science students and researchers* (London, Thousand Oaks, New Delhi: Sage Publications).

Robinson, N. (2012) 'Institutional factors and Russian political parties: the changing needs of regime consolidation in a neo-patrimonial system', *East European Politics*, 28, 3, pp. 298–309.

Roe, P. (2006) 'Reconstructing Identities or Managing Minorities? Desecuritizing Minority Rights: A Response to Jutila', *Security Dialogue*, 37, 3, pp. 425–438.

Ross, C. (ed.) (2004) *Russian politics under Putin* (Manchester: Manchester University Press).

Rossiiskaya gazeta (1999a) 'Kol'tso bezopasnosti szhimaetsya', *Rossiiskaya gazeta*, 213, 27 October.
Rossiiskaya gazeta (1999b) 'Poseesh veter – pozhnesh' buryu', *Rossiiskaya gazeta*, 18 November 1999.
Rotberg, R. I. (2003) *State failure and state weakness in a time of terror* (Cambridge, MA: Washington DC, World Peace Foundation, Brookings Institution Press).
Rozhnov, K. (2010) 'Russia counts the cost of drought and wildfires', BBC, 26 August, available at: www.bbc.co.uk/news/business-11084236, accessed 9 March 2012.
Ruggie, J. G. (1998) 'What Makes the World Hang Together? Neo-utilitarianism and the Social Constructivist Challenge', *International Organization*, 52, pp. 855–886.
Rumelili, B. (2004) 'Constructing Identity and Relating to Difference: Understanding the EU's Mode of Differentiation', *Review of International Studies*, 30, 1, pp. 27–47.
Rushailo, V. (1999) 'Bandity budut unichtozheny', *Rossiiskaya gazeta*, 189, 25 September.
Rushailo, V. (2002) 'Konstitutsiyu Chechni nado prinimat' na referendume', Newsru. com, 2 June, available at: www.newsru.com/russia/02jun2002/rush_print.html, accessed 17 August 2010.
Russell, J. (2002) 'Mujahedeen, Mafia, Madmen: Russian Perceptions of Chechens During the Wars in Chechnya, 1994–96 and 1999–2001', *Journal of Communist Studies and Transition Politics*, 18, 1, pp. 73–96.
Russell, J. (2005) 'Terrorists, bandits, spooks and thieves: Russian demonisation of the Chechens before and since 9/11', *Third World Quarterly*, 26, 1, pp. 101–116.
Russell, J. (2006) 'Obstacles to peace in Chechnya: What scope for international involvement?', *Europe-Asia Studies*, 58, 6, pp. 941–964.
Russell, J. (2007) *Chechnya—Russia's 'War on Terror'* (Abingdon: Routledge).
Russell, J. (2008) 'Ramzan Kadyrov: The Indigenous Key to Success in Putin's Chechenization Strategy?', *Nationalities Papers*, 36, 4, pp. 659–687.
Russian Government (1999) 'Zayavlenie Pravitel'stva Rossiiskoi Federatsii o situatsii v Chechenskoi Respublike i merakh po uregulirovaniyu', *Rossiiskaia gazeta*, 23 October.
Rywkin, M. (2003) 'Russia and the Near Abroad Under Putin', *American Foreign Policy Interests: The Journal of the National Committee on American Foreign Policy*, 25, 1, pp.3–12
Ryzhkov, V. (2004) 'Vlast' kak plokhoi bokser, propuskaet vse udary, kotorye prikhodyatsya ne stol'ko po nei, skol'ko po ostal'nym grazhdanam Rossii', *Nezavisimaya gazeta*, 6 September.
Sabaratnam, M. (2011) 'IR in Dialogue ... but Can We Change the Subjects? A Typology of Decolonising Strategies for the Study of World Politics', *Millennium: Journal of International Studies*, 39, 3, pp. 781–803.
Sagramoso, D. (2007) 'Violence and conflict in the Russian North Caucasus', *International Affairs*, 83, 4, pp. 681–705.
Sakwa, R. (2004) 'Regime Change From Yeltsin to Putin: Normality, Normalcy or Normalisation?' in Ross, C. (ed.) (2004), pp. 17–38.
Sakwa, R. (ed.) (2005) *Chechnya: from past to future* (London: Anthem Press).
Sakwa, R. (2005) 'The 2003–2004 Russian Elections and Prospects for Democracy', *Europe-Asia Studies*, 57, 3.
Sakwa, R. (2008a) *Putin: Russia's choice* (2nd ed.) (New York, Oxon: Routledge).
Sakwa, R (2008b) '"New Cold War" or twenty years' crisis? Russia and international politics', *International Affairs*, 84, 2, pp. 241–267.
Sakwa, R. (2009) *The quality of freedom: Khodorkovsky, Putin, and the Yukos affair* (Oxford and New York: Oxford University Press).

Sakwa, R. (2011) *The Crisis of Russian Democracy: The Dual State, Factionalism and the Medvedev Succession* (Cambridge: Cambridge University Press).

Sakwa, R. (2012) 'Putin Redux: Continuity and change', Valdai Discussion Club, 19 September, available at: http://valdaiclub.com/politics/49000.html, accessed 15 July 2013.

Salter, M. B. (2006) 'The Global visa Regime and the Political Technologies of the International Self: Borders, Bodies, Biopolitics', *Alternatives*, 31, 2, pp. 167–189.

Salter, M. B. (2008) 'Securitization and Desecuritization: Dramaturgical Analysis and the Canadian Aviation Transport Security Authority', *Journal of International Relations and Development*, 11, 4, pp. 321–349.

Samarina, A. (2010) 'Dmitry Medvedev: these are our courts', *Nezavisimaya gazeta*, 20 May.

Sánchez Nieto, W. A. (2011) 'The Olympic Challenge: Russia's Strategy for the Establishment of Security in the North Caucasus before 2014', *The Journal of Slavic Military Studies*, 24, 4, pp. 582–604.

Sasse, G. (2005) 'Securitization or Securing Rights? Exploring the Conceptual Foundations of Policies towards Migrants and Minorities in Europe', *Journal of Common Market Studies*, 43, 4, pp. 673–693.

Security Council of the Russian Federation (2005a) 'Interview of the Head of Security Council Igor Ivanov, for the Magazine "Strategiya Rossii"', 4 May, available at: www.scrf.gov.ru/news/98.html, accessed 12 September 2010.

Security Council of the Russian Federation (2005b) 'Statement from the Secretary of the Security Council at the All-Russian Conference "Problems of strengthening national and societal security. The role of civil society actors"', 1 December, available at: www.scrf.gov.ru/news/63.html, accessed 19 September 2010.

Security Council of the Russian Federation (2005c), 'Interv'yu Sekretarya Bezopasnosti Rossiiskoi Federatsii I.S. Ivanova zhurnalu "Strategiya Rossii"', *News and Information, Security Council,* 4 May, available at: www.scrf.gov.ru/news/98.html, accessed 10 September 2010.

Security Council of the Russian Federation (2005d), 'Interv'yu Zamestitelya Sekretarya Bezopasnosti Rossiiskoi Federatsii N Spasskogo "Rossiiskoi gazete" "Mi zalozhniki svoego proshlogo"', *News and Information, Russian Security Council*, 5 October 2005, available at: www.scrf.gov.ru/news/70.html, accessed 13 September 2010.

Sedik, D., Sotnikov, S. and Wiesmann, D. (2003) *Food security in the Russian Federation* (Rome: Food and Agriculture Organisation of the United Nations).

Seierstad, A. (2008) *The Angel of Grozny: Orphans of a Forgotten War* (London: Virago Press).

Selezneva, L. (2002) 'Post-Soviet Russian foreign policy: between doctrine and pragmatism', *European Security*, 11, 4, pp. 10–28.

Semenyuk, M. (1999) 'Kto stoit za potokom bezhentsev iz Chechni?', *Rossiiskaya gazeta*, 1 October.

Seth, S. (2011) 'Postcolonial Theory and the Critique of International Relations', *Millennium*, 40, 1, pp. 167–183.

Sevriukova, E. (2007) 'Moskva prishla v Groznyi', *Rossiiskaya gazeta*, 28 December.

Shani, G. (2008) 'Toward a Post-Western IR: The *Umma, Khalsa Panth*, and Critical International Relations Theory', *International Studies Review*, 10, pp. 722–734.

Sharlet, R. (2001) 'Putin and the politics of law in Russia', *Post-Soviet Affairs*, 17, 3, pp. 195–234.

Sharov, A. (2002) 'Potomki proklyanut terroristov', *Rossiiskaya gazeta*, 26 October.

Shevtsova, L. (2004) 'The limits of bureaucratic authoritarianism', *Journal of Democracy*, 15, 3, pp. 67–77.

Shevtsova, L. (2012a) 'Russia under Putin: Titanic looking for its iceberg?', *Communist and Post-Communist Studies*, 45, 3–4, pp. 209–216.

Shevtsova, L. (2012b) 'Putinism Under Siege: Implosion, Atrophy, or Revolution?', *Journal of Democracy*, 23, 3, pp. 19–32.

Shilliam, R. (2010) *International Relations and Non-Western Thoughts: Imperialism, Colonialism and Investigations of Global Modernity* (London: Routledge).

Shkalov D. V., Lozovanov, D. A., Filippov, S. G. (2002) 'Osoboe mnenie gruppi chlenov obshchestva "Memorial"', at the International Conference on 'Za prekrashchenie voini I ustanovlenie mira v Chechenskoi Respublike', 9–10 November, available at: www.memo.ru/hr/hotpoints/caucas1/index.htm, accessed 10 June 2010.

Shlapentokh, D. (2008) 'The Rise of the Chechen Emirate?', *Middle East Quarterly*, Summer.

Shlapentokh, D. (2010) 'The Rise of the Russian Khalifat: The View from the Jihadist Side', *Iran and the Caucasus*, 14, 1, pp. 117–142.

Shlykov, V. (2004) 'The Anti-Oligarchy Campaign and its Implications for Russia's Security', *The Journal of Slavic Military Studies*, 17, 1, pp. 111–128.

Shoumikhin, A. (2002) 'Evolving Russian Perspectives on Missile Defense: The Emerging Accommodation', *Comparative Strategy*, 21, 4, pp. 311–336.

Simes, D. K. (2007) 'Losing Russia, the cost of renewed confrontation', *Foreign Affairs*, November-December, pp. 36–52.

Simmons, B. A. and Martin, L. A. (2002) 'International organisations and institutions', in Carlsnaes, W., Risse, T. and Simmons, B. A., (eds) (2002), pp. 192–211.

Simons, G. (2010) *Mass media and modern warfare: reporting on the Russian war on terrorism* (Farnham, Burlington, VT: Ashgate).

Sjostedt, R. (2008), 'Exploring the construction of threats: The securitization of HIV/AIDS in Russia', *Security Dialogue*, 39, 1, pp. 7–30.

Slider, D. (2008) 'Putin's "Southern Strategy": Dmitriy Kozak and the. Dilemmas of Recentralization', *Journal of Post Soviet Affairs*, 24, 2, pp. 177–197.

Slim, H. (2004) 'With or against? Humanitarian agencies and coalition counter-insurgency', *Refugee Survey Quarterly*, 23, 4, pp. 34–47.

Smith, H. (2005) (ed.) *Russia and its foreign policy* (Helsinki: Kikimora).

Smith, K. C. (2008) *Russia and European energy security: divide and dominate* (Washington DC: Center for Strategic and International Studies).

Smith, S. (2005) 'The contested concept of security', in Booth, K. (ed.) (2005), pp. 27–61.

Snetkov, A. (2007) 'The image of the terrorist threat in the official Russian press: the Moscow theatre crisis (2002) and the Beslan hostage crisis (2004)', *Europe–Asia Studies*, 59, 8, pp. 1349–1365.

Sokirianskaia, E. (2002) 'Families and clans in Ingushetia and Chechnya. A fieldwork report', *Central Asian Survey*, 24, 4, pp. 469–489.

Soldatov, A. and Borogan, I. (2010) *The new nobility: the restoration of Russia's security state and the enduring legacy of the KGB* (New York: PublicAffairs).

Soldatenko, B. (1999a) 'Utverzhdaya vlast' zakona', *Krasnaya zvezda*, 21 October.

Soldatenko, B. (1999b) 'Ni odin terrorist ne uidet ot vozmezdiya', *Krasnaya zvezda*, 230, 28 October.

Souleimanov, E. (2007) *An endless war: the Russian-Chechen conflict in perspective* (Frankfurt am Main: Peter Lang Publishing Group).

Souleimanov, E. and Ditrych, O. (2008) 'The Internationalisation of the Russian-Chechen Conflict: Myths and Reality', *Europe-Asia Studies*, 60, 7, pp. 1199–1222.

Spasskiy, N. (2011) 'The Island of Russia', *Russia in Global Affairs*, 22 June, available at: http://eng.globalaffairs.ru/number/The-Island-of-Russia-15237, accessed 17 July 2013.

Speckhard, A. and Ahkmedova, K. 'The Making of a Martyr: Chechen Suicide Terrorism', *Studies in Conflict and Terrorism*, 29, 5, pp. 429–492.

Stent, A. (2008) 'Restoration and Revolution in Putin's Foreign Policy', *Europe-Asia Studies*, 60, 6, pp. 1089–1106.

Stepanchenko, N. (1999) 'Sudiby nezhdannyi povorot', *Rossiiskaya gazeta*, 23 October.

Stritzel, H. (2007) 'Towards a Theory of Securitization: Copenhagen and Beyond', *European Journal of International Relations*, 13, 3, pp. 357–383.

Stritzel, H. (2011) 'Security as Translation: Threats, Discourse, and the Politics of Localisation', *Review of International Studies*, 37, 5, pp. 2491–2251.

Stuvøy, K. (2010) 'Human Security Research Practices: Conceptualizing Security for Women's Crisis Centres in Russia', *Security Dialogue*, 41, 3, pp. 279–299.

Sukhov, I. (2008) 'The Power Vertical and the Nation's Self-Consciousness', *Russia in Global Affairs*, 2.

Sumsky, V. and Kanaev, E. (2014) 'Russia's Progress in Southeast Asia: Modest but Steady', *Russian Analytical Digest* 145.

Taureck, R. (2006), 'Securitization theory and securitization studies', *Journal of International Relations and Development*, 9, pp. 53–61.

Taylor, B. (2003) 'Putin's State Building Project Issues for the Second Term', *PONARS Policy Memo* 323.

Taylor, B. (2007) 'Putin's "Historic Mission": State-Building and the Power Ministries in the North Caucasus', *Problems of Post-Communism*, 54, 6, pp. 3–16.

Thomas, T. (2005) 'Russian Tactical Lessons Learned Fighting Chechen Separatists', *The Journal of Slavic Military Studies*, 18, 4, pp. 731–766.

Tickner, A. and Wæver, O. (eds) (2009) *International Relations Scholarship around the World* (London: Routledge).

Timmins, G. (2004) 'Coping with the new Neighbours: The evolution of European Union policy towards Russia', *Perspectives on European Politics and Society*, 5, 2, pp. 357–374.

Tishkov, V. (2004) *Chechnya: Life in a War-Torn Society* (Berkeley and Los Angeles, CA and London: University of California Press).

Tompson, W. (2005) 'Putting Yukos in Perspective', *Post-Soviet Affairs*, 21, 2.

Torbakov, I. (2003). 'Russia Seeks to Use Energy Abundance to Increase Political Leverage', *Eurasia Insight*, 19 November.

Torbakov, I. (2005) 'Russia And The War On Terror: Not A Trusted U.S Ally', *Terrorism Monitor*, 2, 1, 5 May.

Torshin, A., quoted in *RIA Novosti*, 8 April, cited in 'Foreign NGOs support terrorism in Russia – senior senator' in Johnson's Russia List, #24 – JRL 2008–72, available at: www.cdi.org/russia/johnson/2008-72-24.cfm, accessed 1 May 2009.

Treisman, D. (2002) 'Russia Renewed?', *Foreign Affairs*, November/December, pp. 58–72.

Trenin, D. (2002) *The end of Eurasia: Russia on the border between geopolitics and globalization* (Washington and Moscow: Carnegie Endownment).

Trenin, D. (2004) 'Russia and global security norms', *The Washington Quarterly*, 27, 2, pp. 63–78.

Trenin, D. (2004) 'Russia and the West: what you see is what you get', *The World Today*, 60, 4, pp. 13–15.

Trenin, D. (2007) 'Russia Redefines Itself and Its Relations with the West', *The Washington Quarterly*, 30, 2, pp. 95–106.

Trenin, D. V. and Malashenko, A. V. with Lieven, A. (2004) *Russia's Restless Frontier: The Chechnya Factor in Post-Soviet Russia* (Washington DC: Carnegie Endowment for International Peace).

Trenin, D., Kuchins, A. C. and Gomart, T. (2008) *Toward a new Euro-Atlantic "hard" security agenda: prospects for trilateral U.S.-EU-Russia cooperation* (Washington DC: Center for Strategic and International Studies).

Trenin, D. (2009) 'Russia Reborn Reimagining Moscow's Foreign Policy', *Foreign Affairs*, 64, 88, 6.

Trenin, D. (2013) 'Vladimir Putin's Fourth Vector', *Russia in Global Affairs*, 30 June, available at: http://eng.globalaffairs.ru/number/Vladimir-Putins-Fourth-Vector—16048, accessed 4 January 2014.

Tsvetkova, R. (2012), 'In terms of mentality, culture and worldview, the Caucasus is drifting away from Russia', *Nezavisimaya gazeta*, 18 September, p. 1.

Tsygankov, A. P. (2005) 'Vladimir Putin's Vision of Russia as a Normal Great Power', *Post-Soviet Affairs*, 21, 2, pp. 132–158.

Tsygankov, A. P. (2007) 'Finding a Civilisational Idea: "West," Eurasia," and "Euro-East" in Russia's Foreign Policy', *Geopolitics*, 12, 3, pp. 375–399.

Tsygankov, A. P. (2013) *Russia's foreign policy change and continuity in national identity* (Lanham: Rowman & Littlefield Publishers).

Tsypkin, M. (2009) 'Russian politics, policy-making and American missile defence', *International Affairs*, 85, 4, pp. 781–799.

UN Security Council Resolution 1333, available at: www.un.org/News/Press/docs/2000/20001219.sc6979.doc.html, accessed 20 November 2008.

Ustyuzhanin, V. (1999) 'Putin predlagaet "lechit'" Chechnyu karantinom', *Komsomol'skaya pravda*, 170, 15 September.

Van Munster, R. (2007) 'Review Essay: Security on a Shoestring: A Hitchhiker's Guide to Critical Schools of Security in Europe', *Cooperation and Conflict*, 42, 2, pp. 235–243.

Vendil, C. (2009) *Russian military reform: a failed exercise in defence decision making* (New York: Routledge).

Vendina, O. I. et al. (2007) 'The Wars in Chechnya and Their Effects on Neighbouring Regions', *Eurasian Geography and Economics*, 48, 2, pp. 178–201.

Verkhovsky, A. and Kozhevnikova, G. (2005) 'Three Years of Combating Extremism', SOVA Center, 8 December, available at: www.sova-center.ru/en/xenophobia/reports-analyses/2005/12/d6638/, accessed 10 June 2009.

Volkhonsky, B. (2002) 'Sammit Rossia – ES pereekhal', *Kommersant*, 29 October.

Vorob'ev, V. (2002) 'Terrorism nagleet', *Rossiiskaya gazeta*, 29 October.

Vuori, J. A. (2008) 'Illocutionary Logic and Strands of Securitization: Applying the Theory of Securitization to the Study of Non-Democratic Political Orders', *European Journal of International Relations*, 14, 1, pp. 65–99.

Vuori, J. A. (2010) 'A Timely Prophet? The Doomsday Clock as a Visualization of Securitization Moves with a Global Referent Object', *Security Dialogue*, 41, 3, pp. 255–277.

Wæver, O. (1995) 'Securitization and Desecuritization', in Lipschutz, R. D. (ed.), *On Security* (New York: Columbia University Press).

Wæver, O. (1999) 'Securitizing Sectors? Reply to Eriksson', *Cooperation and Conflict*, 34, 3.

Wæver, O. (2000) 'The EU as a Security Actor: Reflections From a Pessimistic Construc-

tivist on Post-Sovereign Security Orders', in Kelstrup, M. and Williams, M. C. (eds) (2000), pp. 250–294.
Wæver, O. (2011) 'Politics, security, theory', *Security Dialogue*, 42, 4–5, pp. 465–480.
Walker, E. W. (2005) 'Islam, Territory, and Contested Space in Post-Soviet Russia', *Eurasian Geography and Economics*, 46, 4, pp. 247–271.
Waltz, K. (1979) *Theory of International Politics* (New York: McGraw Hill).
Ware, R. (1995) *Russia and the Chechens* (London: House of Commons Library).
Wegren, S. K. (ed.) (2003) *Russia's Policy Challenges: Security, Stability and Development*, (Armonk, NY: M.E. Sharpe).
Wegren, S. K. (2011) 'Food Security and Russia's 2010 Drought' *Eurasian Geography and Economics*, 52, 1.
Welton, G. (2011) 'The impact of Russia's 2010 grain export ban' (Oxford: Oxfam).
Wendt, A. (1992) 'Anarchy Is What States Make of It: The Social Construction of Power Politics', *International Organization*, 46, pp. 335–370.
Wendt, A. (2003) 'Why a World State is Inevitable', *European Journal of International Relations December*, 9, 4, pp. 491–542.
White, S. and McAllister, I. (2003) 'Putin and his Supporters', *Europe-Asia Studies*, 55, 3, pp. 383–399.
White, S., Gitelman, Z. and Sakwa, R. (eds) (2005) *Developments in Russian Politics 6* (New York: Palgrave).
Whitefield, S. (2005) 'Putin's popularity and its implications for democracy in Russia', in Pravda, A. (ed.) (2005) *Leading Russia, Putin in Perspective, Essays in honour of Archie Brown* (Oxford: Oxford University Press), pp. 139–159.
Whitmore, B. (2011) 'Exit "The Tandem," Enter "The Team"', Radio Free Europe Radio Liberty, June 7.
Wilhelmsen, J. (2005) 'Between a Rock and a Hard Place: The Islamisation of the Chechen Separatist Movement', *Europe-Asia Studies*, 57, 1, pp. 35–59.
Wilkinson C. (2007) 'The Copenhagen School on Tour in Kyrgyzstan: Is Securitization Theory Useable Outside Europe?' *Security Dialogue*, 38, 1, pp. 5–25.
Williams, B. J. (2004) 'From "Secessionist Rebels" to "Al-Qaeda Shock Brigades": Assessing Russia's Efforts to Extend the Post-September 11th War on Terror to Chechnya', *Comparative Studies of South Asia, Africa and the Middle East*, 24, 1.
Williams, M. C. and Neumann, I. (2000) 'From Alliance to Security Community: NATO, Russia, and the Power of Identity', *Millennium: Journal of International Studies*, 29, 2, pp. 357–388.
Wodak, R. (2001) "The discourse-historical approach", in Wodak, R. and Meyer, M. (eds) *Methods of Critical Discourse Analysis* (London: Sage).
Wood, T. (2007) *Chechnya, the case for independence* (London: Verso).
Wood, J. (2009) *Russia, the asymmetric threat to the United States: a potent mixture of energy and missiles* (Santa Barbara: Praeger Security International).
Yamshanov, B. (2004) Nam ob'yavili voinu bez fronta, *Rossiiskaya gazeta*, 2 September.
Yasterzhembski S. (2001) 'Pyat' bukv, napisannykh krov'yu. Segodnya – 10 let nezavisimosti Chechni', *Izvestiia*, 6 September.
Yemelianova, G. Y. (2002) *Russia and Islam: a historical survey* (Basingstoke and New York: Palgrave).
Yerkel, Y. (2010) 'Identity in International Relations: Turkey's Proactive Middle Eastern Policy since 2002', *Alternative Perspectives*, June 12, available at: http://yerkel.wordpress.com/2010/06/12/identity-in-international-relations-turkey%E2%80%99s-proactive-middle-eastern-policy-since-2002/, accessed 17 April 2011.

Zakaev, A. (2008) Speech at the conference: 'Chechnya After The War', held at the School of Oriental and African Studies London, 27 November, programme available at: http://www.soas.ac.uk/cccac/events/27nov2008-conference-chechnya-after-the-war.html.

Zakaria, F. (2011) *The Post-American World, Release 2.0* (London: W. W. Norton & Company).

Zakatnova, A. (2004) S kem my voiyuem, *Rossiiskaya gazeta*, 3 September.

Zakharov, M. (2010) 'St Petersburg's tower vertical defeated. For now...', Open Democracy, 15 December, available at: www.opendemocracy.net/od-russia/mikhail-zakharov/st-petersburgs-tower-vertical-defeated-for-now, accessed 7 November 2011.

Zehfuss, M. (2001) 'Constructivism and Identity: A Dangerous Liaison', *European Journal of International Relations*, 7, pp. 315–348.

Zelkina, A. (2007) 'The Lone Wolf and the Bear: Three Centuries of Chechen Defiance of Russian Rule' Review of Moshe Gammer, *Journal of Islamic Studies*, 18, 2, pp. 267–268.

Zhemukhov, S. (2012) 'The birth of modern Circassian nationalism', *Nationalities Papers: The Journal of Nationalism and Ethnicity*, 40, 4, pp. 503–524.

Zhemukhov, S. (2014) 'Migrant Workers and the Sochi Olympics', *Russian Analytical Digest*, 9 February.

Zhemukhov, S. and Orttung, R. W. (2014b) 'Munich Syndrome Russian Security in the 2014 Sochi Olympics', *Problems of Post-Communism*, 61, 1, pp. 13–29.

Zubov, V. (2005) 'Interview with First Deputy Secretary of the Duma Committee on banks, financial and credit markets', *Radio Svoboda*, 3 January, available at: http://archive.svoboda.org/programs/ftf/2005/ftf.010305.asp, accessed 18 September 2010.

Zurn, M. (2010) 'The View of Old and New Powers on the Legitimacy of International Institutions', *Politics*, 30, 1.

Index

Acharya, A. 203
Afghanistan 41, 56
Al Qaeda 56
Aliev, Mukhu 51
Alkhanov, Alu 81
Annual Addresses to the Federal Assembly 69
Anti-Ballistic Missile Treaty 42
Arab Spring 159–60
Arbatov, A. G. 52
Are, D. 118
arms control 41–2
Ashizawa, K. 16, 17
Atkinson, M. C. 21
Ayoob, Mohammed 21

Bacon, E. 48
Baev, P. 46
Basayev, Shamil 116
Berezovky, Boris 68
Bevir, M. 7, 18
'Big Government and the Politburo 2.0' (Minchenko Consulting Group) 147
Bin Laden, Osama 49, 56
black boxing 4–5, 5–6
blogs 153
Borisov, B. 81
Boucher, Richard 91
Bryman, A. 9
Bunce, V. J. 143
Buzan, B. 6, 15–16, 21, 24, 39

case study plus method 7–8
'Caucasus Emirate' group 122, 178, 179, 183
Caucasus Front 116–17, 122
Chechnya 1–2, 7, 8, 33, 43–4, 202; (de)securitization studies, implications from the Russian-Chechen case study for 201; changes in official discourse 184–6, 195–6; changing role in the Russian domestic agenda 84–8; characterization as a failed region 47–8; compensation payments to Chechens 126; counterterrorist securitization strategies 82–3; creating a common front between Russia and the West 56–8; criticism of Russian authorities from within Russia 83, 84; decentralization and the emergence of a federal-local alliance 117–20, 128; desecuritization at a local level 114–20; desecuritization, divergent and multifaceted processes of 204–6; desecuritization policies 80–4; desecuritization/securitization, dual policies of 79, 80, 94–5, 201–3; deterioration of local security 48–9; domestic, political and security agenda role 120–4; economic and infrastructure rebuilding 81–2; emergence of a double identity 50, 54, 60n5; in foreign policy 177–8; formal ending of counterterrorist operation 2009 173; as a global threat 54–8; growing influence of international Islamic terrorists 49; as a growing international player 126–7; historicization of threat image 120–1; image and role as a regional player in North Caucasus 124; as an image of Russian policy success 125, 128; information security 85–6, 193; and international terrorism 54–6; invasion of Dagestan 51;

248 *Index*

Chechnya *continued*
  Kadyrov's personal relationship with Putin 176; large scale development programmes 115; military operations 8, 52–3, 56–7, 82–3; modernization and counterinsurgency under Medvedev 174–8; negative role in Russia's security construction 86–7; non-military operations to rebuild Chechnya 53–4; 'normal' politics 115–16, 119; normalization policy 59, 79–97, 203; peace consolidation 203; perceived causes of increasing insecurity 48–9; political normalization 80–1; proposed measures to deal with the existential threat of Chechnya 51–2; Putin's third term as President 178–84; 'Ramzanification' of Chechnya 176–7; removal of federal troops 117; role in the external security agenda 88–93, 124–7; securitization to desecuritization 26, 27; securitization of 46–61; security risks 116–17; 'Socio-economic development of the Chechen Republic 2008–2011' 115; as a symbol of Russia's failure and weakness 19, 46, 79; as a threat to domestic security 38–9, 46; Western criticism of Russian policies 79, 91, 94, 125–6
Checkel, J. T. 7
China 18, 42, 94–5, 159, 202
civil society 71–2
Coalson, R. 164
Coleman, W. D. 21
Collective Security Treaty Organization (CSTO) 57, 89
colour revolutions 65, 66, 71–2, 73, 75, 106–7, 111, 154, 159, 192
Commission for Modernization and Technological Development of Russia's Economy 140–1
Committee of Soldiers Mothers of Russia 83
Commonwealth of Independent States (CIS) 34, 38, 91
Communist Party 68
compensation payments 126
'Concept of Long-term Socio-economic Development of the Russian Federation to 2020' 102
Cooperative Airspace Initiative 89
Copenhagen School of Security (CS) 20, 24–5, 26, 50, 51, 53, 80, 114, 201, 203
corruption 141, 142

Coskun, B. B. 25, 26
Council of Europe 56, 58, 126, 158, 165
Counter Terrorism Law 2006 108
Crimea 148–9, 154, 162–6, 181–2, 188
critical security studies 5–7; desecuritization in non-Western contexts: normal politics 203–4; desecuritization processes 204–7; implications from the Russian-Chechen case study for (de)securitization studies 201; interrelationship between desecuritization and securitization processes 201–3
Cuita, F. 24

Dagestan 51, 52–3, 178–9
Dannreuther, R. 89
de Wilde, J. 15–16, 24
decentralization 117–20, 128, 180, 186
Delyagin, M. 142
deoffshorizatsiya 155
derzhavnost concept 39
Desch, M. C. 21, 22–3
desecuritization 6–7; Chechnya 80–4, 114–20; dual policies of securitization/descuritization 79, 80, 94–5, 201–3; full cycle of desecuritization processes 206–7; implications from the Russian-Chechen case study for (de)securitization studies 201; interrelationship between desecuritization and securitization processes 201–3; movement of an issue from securitized to 'normal' politics 24, 25, 26, 203–4; non-Western contexts 24–7, 203–4
Dessler, D. 8
Directorate for Social Projects 146
discourse analysis 7–11, 19; case study plus method 7–8; confirmability 10; fieldwork 9; historicization of meanings 8; intertextuality 10; interviews 9–10; time periods 11; triangulation 8
discursive disappearance 19
Dvorkovich, Arkadii 148

Echelon-2003 83
economic security 151, 192–3
Edelev, Arkady 121, 124
elections and electoral reforms 67–8; Chechnya 88; protest movement and the 2011–2012 electoral cycle 142–4; Putin's third term 146
Eurasian Union 162

Euromaidan 163, 164
European Court of Human Rights 126
European Union (EU): condemnation of Chechen military operations 56–7, 58; internal security concerns 23; Medvedev's relations with 157–8; Russian policy towards 92
Evans, A. B. 72

fascism 164
Federal Security Service 160
Fierke, K. M. 19
'Fighters are helped from abroad' (Lapskii) 49
financial crisis 2008–2009 139, 140, 190–1
food security 151
Foreign Agents NGO Law 153
foreign policy and relations 5, 40, 42, 69–71; anti-Western discourse 72–3, 75, 92–3, 109–10, 153–4, 160–1, 164, 165, 197–8; co-dependency of Russia and the West 165; Foreign Policy Concept 38, 40, 109, 193; growing tensions due to divergent visions for the war on terror 90–1; under Medvedev 156, 157–9; network diplomacy principle 158–9; 'new' Cold War 101, 105; non-Western views of 17–18; North Caucasus and Chechnya 177–8; Putin's third term 160–2; relations with EU 92; relations with Middle East 89–90, 125, 133n53; Russia-Ukraine crisis 2013–2014 162–6; Russian regional relations 89; Western criticism of Russian policies in Chechnya 79, 91, 94, 125–6
FSB 48
Furman, Dmitry 110, 176

Gaddy, C. G. 139
Galeotti, M. 37, 156
Gareyev, Makhmut 106
Georgia 156–7, 159, 178
Gerber, T. P. 123
Giles, K. 192
'Go Russia' (article, Medvedev) 140, 157
Gref, German 67
Gronskaya, N. 148
Grozny 115
Gusinsky, Vladimir 68
GUUAM 34

Hahn, G. M. 146, 147
Hansen, L. 7–8, 9, 25, 204, 205

Helsinki Group 83
Herd, G. 37, 103
Hill, Ronald 33
historicization 8, 102, 120–1
Hopf, T. 10, 15, 17
human rights 58, 87, 91, 126, 153

Ickes, B. W. 139
Ilyasov, Stanislav 82
India 18
information security 85–6, 193
'International Peace-making Forum: Islam – religion of peace' 127
international relations (IR) theory 4, 199–207; desecuritization in non-Western contexts 203–4; processes of desecuritization 204–6; full cycle of desecuritization processes 206–7; implications from the Russian-Chechen case study for (de)securitization studies 201; interrelationship between desecuritization and securitization processes 201–3; theories of 'strong' and 'weak' states 199–201
internet 85, 90, 143, 152, 153, 154
Iraq 71, 75, 89–90
Islam 122, 159; influence of international terrorists 49; promotion of official forms of Islam 123–4; Russian-Muslim relations 50; Salafi form of 54
Ivanov, Igor 41, 55, 71, 75, 108
Ivanov, Sergei 80, 82–3

Kadyrov, Akhmat 53–4, 81, 83, 84, 114, 116, 118
Kadyrov, Ramzan and Kadyrov regime 81, 118–20, 120, 124, 126–7, 130n22, 173, 196; foreign policy and relations 177–8; personal relationship with Putin 176; 'Ramzanification' of Chechnya 176–7
Kalland, T. 92
Karaganov, Sergei 70
Katz, M. 89–90
Katzenstein, P. J. 15
Kavkaz Center 85, 90
Khloponin, Alexander 175
Khordorkovsky, Mikhail 68
Koesel, K. J. 143
Kolossov, V. 83
Kosovo 52
Kovler, Anatoly 126
Kozak, Dmitry 87, 123
Kuchins, A. C. 92, 160
Kulikov, Anatoly 118

250   *Index*

Lapskii, Vladimir 49
Latynina, Y. 83
Laub, Z. 178
Lavrov, Sergei 68, 71, 77–8n15, 86, 104, 110, 161
Lebanon 125
legitimacy 163, 164
Legvold, R. 158
Libya 159–60
Lieven, A. 57
Lo, B. 69–70
Lukyanov, F. 71, 145, 150, 161, 194
Lupovici, A. 27
Lynch, D. 36, 92

Magnitsky list 154
Magnitsky, Sergei 150–1
Makarkin, A. 144
Makarychev, A. S. 148
Malashenko, A. 119, 175, 176, 177, 185
Malinova, O. 146
managed democracy 67
managed pluralism 67
Manilov, Valerii 56
'March of the Million' 143–4
Markedonov, S. 174, 180, 182
Maskhadov, President 48, 53, 82, 91–2, 116
Mathers, J. G. 41–2
McAllister, I. 35
McDonald, M. 204
media 68, 74, 77–8n15, 85–6, 152, 154
Medvedev, Dmitry 145, 163, 166, 167, 173, 174; changeover from Putin to Medvedev 2008 137–42; domestic security 150; foreign policy and relations 156, 157–9; 'Go Russia' (article) 140, 157; less securitized domestic context 150–2; modernization programme 140–2, 190–1; protest movement and the 2011–2012 electoral cycle 142–4
Memorial 83, 150
Mendelson, S. 85, 87, 123
Mikhailov, Vyacheslav 49
Military Doctrine 2010 193
military operations 8, 52–3, 56–7, 82–3, 156–7, 159
Millennium Manifesto (Putin) 35, 35–6, 39, 69
Minchenko Consulting Group 147
Ministry of the Interior 115
Mironov, Valery 142
Monaghan, A. 139
Moore, C. 120

Morozov, V. 92, 101
Moscow apartment bombings 48, 51
Moslem, Ziyad Sabsabi 127
multipolarity 34, 42

Nashi 104
National Anti-terrorist Committee (NAC) 108, 109, 122, 173
national identity *see* state identity
National Security Concept 36, 37, 38, 42
National Security Strategy 156, 192, 193
nationalism 164–5, 180, 181, 194
NATO 34, 52, 57, 71, 89, 157, 158, 159, 160, 165, 193; NATO-centrism 40; NATO-Russia Council (NRC) 70, 89
Navalny, Alexei 148, 152, 154, 180
Nazran 73
network diplomacy principle 158–9, 189–91
NGOs 83, 87, 109; Foreign Agents NGO Law 153
non-military operations 53–4
normal politics 24, 26, 114, 115–16, 119, 127–8, 199, 203–4
normalization: of Chechnya 59, 79–97; Chechnya's changing role in the Russian domestic agenda 84–8; counterterrorist securitization strategies 82–3; criticism of Russian authorities from within Russia 83, 84; economic and infrastructure rebuilding 81–2; information security 85–6, 193; loss of Chechen status in Russian political agenda 85; negative role of Chechnya in Russia's security construction 86–7; political normalization 80–1; role of Chechnya in Russia's external security agenda 88–93; Western criticism of Russian policies in Chechnya 91, 94
North Caucasus 2, 86–7, 94, 116–17; 'Caucasus Emirate' group 178, 179, 183; changes in official discourse 184–6, 195–6; domestic insecurity and global jihad 184; direct appointment of governors by federal authorities 180–1; discourse on perceptions of the rest of Russia 180; in foreign policy 177–8; regional image of Chechnya 124; increasing support for decentralization 180, 186; insurgency and counterinsurgency 121–4, 128; modernization and counterinsurgency under Medvedev 174–8; North Caucasus Federal District 173, 175, 178; poor economic situation 123; promotion

of official forms of Islam 123–4; Putin's third term as President 178–84; 'Ramzanification' of Chechnya 176–7; renewed emphasis on tackling insecurity 174–5; Sochi Winter Olympics 2014, as a failed attempt to normalize North Caucasus 182–4; 'Stop Feeding the Caucasus' campaign 148, 180; 'Strategy for the Socio-economic Development of the North Caucasus Federal District until 2025' 175
nuclear deterrence 41–2

obraz vraga (image of the threat) 74, 101, 106–7
Oelsner, A. 202
Okara, A. 67, 103
oligarchs 33, 67, 68, 74
Organization for Security and Co-operation in Europe (OSCE) 38, 56, 91
Organization of the Islamic Conference (OIC) 90, 125
Ortmann, S. 8–9, 16
'Other Russia, The' 108
Overland, I. 138
Owen, J. 8

Pain, E. 52–3
Parliamentary Assembly of the Council of Europe (PACE) 126
patriotism 104, 111, 146, 147–8, 149, 155, 166–7, 174, 181–2, 191, 194
Patrushev, Nikolai 48
Patten, Chris 56–7
peace consolidation 203
Peskov, Dmitri 153
Petersson, B. 102, 182
Petrov, N. 103–4, 179, 180
political elites 15–16, 147
political parties 67–8
post-positivism: accounts of the internal-external nexus 4–5; approaches to security 14; case study plus method 7–8; confirmability of discourse analysis 10; fieldwork 9; historicization of meanings 8; importance of context 17; intertextuality 10; interviews 9–10; methods, sources and data analysis 7–11; time periods 11; triangulation 8
Presidential Council for Inter-Ethnic Relations 181
Press Freedom Index 152
Primakov, Yevgeny 34, 42

privatization 141
Proliferation Security Initiative 89
protest movements 142–4, 151–2, 163–4
Protocol on the Convention for the Protection of Human Rights and Fundamental Freedoms (Council of Europe) 158
Pussy Riot 154
Putin, Vladimir and Putin regime 87, 190–1; on actors trying derail new found Russian strength (quote) 106; on annexation of the Crimea (quote) 149; approach to Chechnya and North Caucasus during third term 178–84; change in priority from strengthening the state to regime security 191–5, 197; changeover from Putin to Medvedev 2008 137–42; changing themes in Putin's Annual Addresses to the Federal Assembly 69; comparison of official discourse during first and third terms 188; control over political arena 67–8, 76; crackdown on oligarchs and independent media 68; creating a common front between Russia and the West 56–8; on deterioration of local security in Chechnya 48–9; discourse on Putin as a leader 198; draws contract between his regime and Yeltsin period (quote) 102; expectations for Russia's future 37, 43–4; increasingly authoritarian nature of 68, 87–8, 92, 103–4, 192; late 1990s crisis and rise of Putin 32–5; linking of Chechnya with 9/11 events 57; and mass media and security 85; Millennium Manifesto 31, 35–6, 39, 69; on money from abroad and external intervention (quote) 107; on national identity (quote) 146; on normalization policies in Chechnya (quote) 80, 81; paranoid image of a strong Russia in official discourse 111; as a 'people's choice' 35; on political developments in rebuilt Chechnya (quote) 115–16; political divisions in the regime's elite 147; post-Beslan speech (quote) 93; pro-Western stance 41, 43; promotion of discourse from 'managed democracy' to 'sovereign democracy' 103; Putin project 35–7; re-elected as President 2012 143; realization of Russia's weakened state in 1999 31–2, 36–7; reassertion of Russia's position in the post-Soviet space 42, 161–2;

252 *Index*

Putin, Vladimir and Putin regime *continued*
  on rebuilding of Chechnya (quote) 115;
  on relations with Lebanon (quote) 125;
  relations with US 41–2; retention of
  themes from Medvedev's presidency
  145–6; Sochi Winter Olympics 2014
  148, 182–4; strong grip on Russian
  official discourse 8–9; on terrorist
  attacks in Nazran (quote) 73; third term
  as President 144–9; third term as
  President, foreign policy and relations
  160–2; third term as President,
  resecuritization 152–5; third term as
  President, reversal of original policy
  choices 191; understanding of the threat
  of international terrorism 55; view of
  Chechnya as an integral part of Russia
  50; on war on terrorism (quote) 87–8;
  Western academic community's
  comments on 32–3; *see also* security

rebuilding of Russia 79; changing security
  agenda 72–6; colour revolutions 71–2;
  crackdown on oligarchs and independent
  media 68; development from a weak
  state to a power rebuilding itself 66–9;
  domestic security concerns 73–4, 76;
  economic reforms 67–8; electoral and
  political party reform 67–8; external
  security concerns 74–5; federal reforms
  67; foreign policy, relations with the
  West and the impact on the domestic
  sphere 69–71; increasingly authoritarian
  nature of Putin regime 68; lack of
  Western recognition of the success of
  rebuilding 70–1, 75; perception of the
  West as a threat 72–3, 75; Putin
  regime's control over the political arena
  67–8, 76; civil society 71–2; state
  building 67
Renz, B. 48
Rhodes, R. 7, 18
RIA Novosti 154
Rich, P. B. 67
Rossiiskaya gazeta 49, 51, 82
Rotberg, R. I. 21
Russia 167, 193; changeover from Putin to
  Medvedev 2008 137–42; consideration
  of domestic and foreign security policy
  as separate 1–2; creation of a common
  front with the West 56–8; economic
  situation 1990s 33–4; effects of
  2008–2009 financial crisis 139, 140,
  190–1; external relations with
  post-Soviet states 3, 34; 'great power'
  status 1, 2, 5, 18, 22, 36, 40, 41, 42,
  101–13, 167, 193–4; Medvedev's
  modernization programme 140–2;
  international standing 1990s 34;
  'new' Cold War 101, 105, 126; new
  image as a strong state 102–5; paranoid
  image of a strong Russia in official
  discourse 111; problematic relations
  with individual neighbours 34–5;
  promotion of discourse from 'managed
  democracy' to 'sovereign democracy'
  103; protest movement and the
  2011–2012 electoral cycle 142–4; role
  in 'war on terror' 57; 'strong' and
  'weak' state interpretations 20–2, 31–2,
  36–7, 102–5, 189–91, 192, 196,
  199–201; weak status in 1999 31–2,
  36–7; *see also* rebuilding of Russia;
  security
Russia-Georgia war August 2008 156–7,
  159
Russia-NATO Council 70
Russia Today 154
Russia-Ukraine crisis 2013–2014 162–6,
  181–2, 194; accusations that the West
  orchestrated the crisis 165;
  co-dependency of Russia and the West
  165; discourse on disorder created by
  removal of Yanukovych 164; image of
  protest movement in official discourse
  164–5
Russian Audit Chamber 142
Russian-Chinese Business Communities'
  Economic Forum 125
Russian-Chinese Strategic Partnership
  Agreement 42
Russian Foreign Policy Concept 2000 40
Rywkin, M. 41

Sadulaev, Shaykh Abdul Khalim 116–17
Sakwa, R. 42, 68, 110, 147
Saudi Arabia 89–90
securitization model 6, 24–5, 26, 39, 50,
  51, 53, 80, 114, 201, 203; *see also*
  Chechnya; desecuritization
security 3, 5, 36, 42; analysis in a non-
  Western context 14–28; analysis of
  Russia as a security actor 196–9; anti-
  Western discourse 72–3, 75, 92–3,
  109–10, 153–4, 160–1, 197–8; black
  boxing 4–5, 5–6; blurring of 'normal'
  and 'security' politics 26–7; change in
  priority from strengthening the state to

regime security 191–5, 197; changes in discourse on national identity and the impact on security priorities 106; changing security agenda during the rebuilding of Russia 72–6; Chechnya's role in the domestic, political and security agenda 120–4; Chechnya's role in the external security agenda 124–7; concern about links between state and non-state actors 73–4; constructivist approach 14–15; context and the non-Western experience 17–18; critical security studies 5–7, 199–207; desecuritization, discourses and practices in a non-Western context 24–7; domestic security concerns 38–9, 43, 73–4, 76, 107–9, 150, 192–3, 194; dominant themes of strength, stability and achievement 105–6; economic and food security 151; economic security 151, 192–3; events, effects of 19; evolution of Russia as a security actor 2000–2014 189–96; external-internal divide in analysing security policy 3–4, 22–3, 196–9; external security concerns 39–42, 74–5, 109–11, 193–4; human security agenda 38; and identities 5, 15–17; information security 85–6, 193; internal-external nexus 4–5; key concepts and analytical tools 20–7; less securitized domestic context under Medvedev 150–2; movement of an issue from securitized to 'normal' politics 24, 25, 26; National Security Concept 36, 37, 38, 42; National Security Strategy 156, 192, 193; evolution across time 19; notions of self and other 107, 110; paranoid image of a strong Russia in official discourse 111; policies against opposition movements 108, 111; post-positivist approaches to 14; Putin regime's proposals for dealing with internal securities 39; Putin's third term, resecuritization 152–5; reconceptualization of security threats 108–9; rejection of Western values 107–8; role of security policy in wider state policy 18–19; Russia's security agenda 37–42, 105–11; security policy, a comprehensive and multifaceted analysis of 18–20; security risks in rebuilt Chechnya 116–17; fear and the colour revolutions 106–7; 'strong' and 'weak' state interpretations 20–2, 31–2, 36–7, 102–5, 189–91, 192, 196, 199–201; *vrag* (enemy), notion of 107; *see also* desecuritization

Security: A new framework for analysis (Butan et al) 6, 24
Shanghai Cooperation Organization (SCO) 42, 57, 89, 159
Shevtsova, L. 144
Shlapentokh, D. 33–4, 35
Skhkhhagoshev, Adalbi 181
Skolkovo project 141
Slider, D. 119
Smith, H. 36
Sochi Winter Olympics 2014 148, 182–4
social constructivism 22, 28n4, 199
social media 153
'Socio-economic development of the Chechen Republic 2008–2011' 115
sovereignty 38, 43–4, 57–8, 71; 'sovereign democracy' 103
START II treaty 42, 158
state building 67
state identity 28n2, 36, 146, 166, 182, 196; all-inclusive identity 181; changes in discourse on national identity and the impact on security priorities 106; changing construction of state identity in Putin's Russia 189–91; citizens' perception of 16; context and the non-Western experience 17–18; interrelationship with security discourses 2; promotion of discourse from 'managed democracy' to 'sovereign democracy' 103; and security 5, 15–17; 'strong' and 'weak' state interpretations 20–2, 31–2, 36–7, 102–5, 189–91, 192, 196, 199–201
State National Policy Strategy 181
'Strategy for the Socio-economic Development of the North Caucasus Federal District until 2025' 175
Stritzel, H. 27
Sukhov, I. 122, 124
Surkov, Vladislav 73–4, 103, 118
Syria 160–1, 184, 197

Taliban 56
Taylor, B. 67
Tchaika, Yuri 88
terakty 83, 84, 85, 86, 151, 179, 183–4
terrorism 23, 39, 40, 57, 72, 122; 9/11 terrorist attacks on US 41, 55, 57, 59; assassinations in North Caucasus 174, 179; attacks in Nazran 2004 73;

terrorism *continued*
  attacks on Moscow metro 83, 151; Beslan crisis 2004 82, 85, 86, 89, 90, 93; Boston Marathon bombing 184; Chechnya and international terrorism 54–6; Counter Terrorism Law 2006 108; counterterrorist securitization strategies in Chechnya 82–3; Dubrovka Theatre siege 2002 82, 83, 84, 86; influence of international Islamic terrorists 49; insurgency and counterinsurgency in North Caucasus 121–4, 128, 176, 183–4; Moscow apartment bombings 1999 48, 51; National Anti-terrorist Committee (NAC) 108, 109, 122; war on terror 54, 57, 59, 87–8, 89, 90–1
Toal, G. 83
Torshin, Aleksandr 109
traitor (website) 155
Treaty on Conventional Armed Forces 110
Trenin, D. 75, 105, 152, 156
trial by jury 117
Trubnikov, Vyacheslav 70, 90

Ukraine 1, 35, 65, 66, 75, 148–9, 154–5; Russia-Ukraine crisis 2013–2014 162–6, 181–2, 194
Umarov, Doku 122, 183
UN Security Council 40; Resolution 1267 56; Resolution 1333 56
UN Security Council Counter Terrorism Committee 57, 89
unilateralism 90, 110
Union of Right Forces 68
United Nations (UN) 38, 89
United Russia 68, 143, 144

United States (US) 40; acceptance of Russian role in 'war on terror' 57; Boston Marathon bombing 184; condemnation of Chechen military operations 56; invasion of Iraq 71, 89–90; relations with Russia 41–2, 158
Ushakov, Yuri 92

Vendina, O. I. 83
Vershbow, Aleksandr 92, 93
vrag (enemy), notion of 107

Wæver, O. 6, 15–16, 21, 24, 39
Wahhabism 54, 56
weapons of mass destruction 89, 158, 193
websites 85, 90, 143, 152, 153, 154, 155
White, S. 35
Wilkinson, C. 203
Williams, B. J. 57
Wills, D. 120
World Chechen Congress 2002 90
World Congress of News Agencies 85
World Trade Organization (WTO) 71

Yabloko 68
Yanukovych, Viktor 144, 162, 164
Yastrzhembskii, Sergei 48
Yeltsin, Boris 32, 33, 102
Yerkel, Y. 16
Yevkurov, Yunus-bek 177
youth movements 104

Zelkina, A. 50
Zevelev, I. A. 160
Zubov, Andrei 154
Zubov, Valerii 73